Deatl

Representation

Parallax  Re-visions of Culture
and Society

*Stephen G. Nichols, Gerald Prince, and*
*Wendy Steiner, Series Editors*

# Death and Representation

Edited by Sarah Webster Goodwin
and Elisabeth Bronfen

The Johns Hopkins University Press
Baltimore and London

For Steve   S. W. G.

For Teresa and Michael   E. B.

The Johns Hopkins University Press
2715 North Charles Street
Baltimore, Maryland 21218-4319
The Johns Hopkins Press Ltd., London

Library of Congress Cataloging-in-Publication Data

Death and representation / edited by Sarah Webster Goodwin and
    Elisabeth Bronfen.
        p.   cm. — (Parallax)
    Chiefly a collection of essays originally presented at a
colloquium held Nov. 1988 at the Harvard Center for Literary and
Cultural Studies.
    Includes bibliographical references and index.
    Contents: Touching death / Ernst van Alphen — A valediction
for bidding mourning : death and the narratee in Brontë's Villette /
Garrett Stewart — Lacan, the death drive, and the dream of the
burning child / — [etc.].
    ISBN 0-8018-4624-2. — ISBN 0-8018-4627-7 (pbk.)
    1. Death in literature—Congresses.   2. Mimesis in literature—
Congresses.   3. Women in literature—Congresses.   4. Literature—
History and criticism—Congresses.   I. Goodwin, Sarah McKim
Webster, 1953–   .   II. Bronfen, Elisabeth.   III. Series: Parallax
(Baltimore, Md.)
PN56.D4D43   1993
809'.93354—dc20                                               93-15169

A catalog record for this book is available from the British Library.

# Contents

# Preface

In November 1988 there took place at the Harvard Center for Literary and Cultural Studies a colloquium that many of us will not soon forget. Conceived by Margaret Alexiou, Margaret Higonnet, and Elisabeth Bronfen but organized principally by Alexiou, the colloquium brought together scholars from several disciplines to present and discuss work in progress on death. The planning allowed for a small audience and provided ample time for discussion. Several of the chapters in this volume resulted from that colloquium. More important, the book's conception came out of it: like the colloquium itself, this work has been an intensely collaborative effort; the essays give only an idea of the many conversations and mutually supported revisions that have helped bring it forth.

One of the most deeply moving moments of the colloquium came during the evening lecture and slide presentation given by Sandra Bertman, a psychologist who counsels the terminally ill. After a day of papers on mourning rituals and testamentary documents in distant cultures and periods, Bertman's talk brought the subject home. Her topic was the use of art in therapy for the dying; gradually we became aware that this was in fact our topic too. During her talk she often quoted her patients. One of them had said, "There is a wall between us and the living." That patient, knowing her own death was imminent, felt herself already cut off from life. This is a wall erected by all concerned—needed, perhaps, by all—one of those necessary fictions we live by. And yet it is a wall that fascinates us, draws us toward itself—that had in some sense brought us together in the colloquium.

We would like to extend our particular thanks to Margaret Alexiou for her hard work in organizing that extraordinary event. Our thanks also go to those who took part in it, formally and informally, among them Barbara Johnson and Marjorie Garber, who hosted it, and Svetlana Boym, Loring M. Danforth, Bridget Murnaghan, Gregory Nagy, Fred Paxton, Charles Stewart, and Emily Vermeule. The colloquium itself emerged as the result of a year-long informal seminar among a small group of scholars from different disciplines who shared their research on death, their time, and not a little life-sustaining food and drink. Again, Margaret Alexiou deserves special thanks here. Thanks go also to Mark Toher for his useful and expert suggestions in response to the book's introduction. Finally, we thank Eric Halpern and Alice Bennett for their editorial help in preparing this book.

We also gratefully acknowledge grants from the Mellon Foundation and the American Council of Learned Societies. Skidmore College, thanks to Dean of the Faculty Phyllis Roth, has been unstintingly generous in financial support of what turned out to be an expensive transatlantic editorial process.

Elisabeth Bronfen's chapter, "Risky Resemblances: On Repetition, Mourning, and Representation," was originally published as a portion of her book *Over Her Dead Body: Death, Femininity and the Aesthetic* (Manchester: Manchester UP; New York: Routledge, 1992). It is used here by permission.

A longer version of Regina Janes's chapter, "Beheadings," was originally published in *Representations* 35 (Summer 1991): 21–52. It is used here by permission.

Sander Gilman's chapter, " 'Who Kills Whores?' 'I Do, Says Jack,' " is a revised version of a portion of his book *Sexuality: An Illustrated History*, copyright © 1991 by John Wiley and Sons. Reprinted by permission of John Wiley and Sons, Inc.

# Death and

# Representation

■

# Introduction

## *Elisabeth Bronfen and Sarah Webster Goodwin*

Scholars who study the relation between death and culture can claim no special authority concerning death itself, nor perhaps even any special courage. Still, death is not a topic like any other. For one thing, it is genuinely of universal interest. Every discipline is pertinent, every scholar has a body of reflections to draw on, every reader has experiences to bring to bear on the scholarship of death. Perhaps because of death's unique power, it feels more perilous, more damagingly sentimental, to write about it with anything but careful distance. But then, in turn, the distancing risks falsification, as though one were to assert that in analyzing cultural artifacts and theorizing about their relation to death we were achieving some commensurate power of our own.

In a sense we are. Not power over death, of course—to any significant extent—but nevertheless an important kind of power. As human beings we are uniquely able to reflect on our death. Although the Western philosophical tradition represents such reflection as a solitary activity, perhaps the very definition of self-fashioning solitude, in fact much of what we call culture comes together around the collective response to death. We suggest that this book is one such response, joining its several voices of reflection to those of other scholars currently studying and writing on the ways cultures represent death.

Death figures abundantly in theoretical and esthetic discourse—it is, as Schopenhauer puts it, "the muse of philosophy." At the same time, culture often makes it a forbidden subject, an embarrassment one would like to silence, allowing it to emerge only in ritually determined moments or in

3

circumstances of communal violence. Death is thus necessarily constructed by a culture; it grounds the many ways a culture stabilizes and represents itself, and yet it always does so as a signifier with an incessantly receding, ungraspable signified, always pointing to other signifiers, other means of representing what finally is just absent. Representations of death thus often serve as metatropes for the process of representation itself: its necessity, its excess, its failure, and its uses for the polis.

Perhaps the most obvious thing about death is that it is always only represented. There is no knowing death, no experiencing it and then returning to write about it, no intrinsic grounds for authority in the discourse surrounding it. As Kenneth Burke has written, no one can "write of death from an immediate experience of it, the imaging of death necessarily involves images not directly belonging to it. . . . [It lies] beyond the realm of such images as the living body knows" (369). Indeed, it is as antagonist that we most clearly figure death: it stands as a challenge to all our systems of meaning, order, governance, and civilization. Any given cultural construct—from religion and poetry to psychoanalysis and medical technology—may be construed as a response to the disordering force of death. Culture itself would then be an attempt both to represent death and to contain it, to make it comprehensible and thereby to diffuse some of its power.[1]

It seems impossible to doubt either the effectiveness or the hopelessness of this enterprise. What may be possible is to move beyond it, to make a rather different claim both for the meaning of death and for its function in relation to culture. In the reflections underlying much of the work in this book, death repeatedly emerges as referring to more than one state, as the site of paradoxes. To abandon the binary conception of death and culture—the conception that sees them as struggling against each other—is to make oneself available to the complexity, and to the historical specificity, of the ways death has been represented. As a group, these essays show that the tidy binary opposition between a representing order and a represented chaos is unsound: politically, psychologically, aesthetically.

The importance of death to any theory of representation is clearest if we remember that the term *representation* comes to current critical usage from essentially two sources: politics and psychoanalysis. It is not always evident how its two meanings relate to each other. The common denominator, of course, is power, and the body politic defends itself against a powerful enemy common to the physical body. Nor is the difference in any simple sense one of scale; social organization, with all its necessary reliance on representative bodies, ostensibly exists to defend people against both mass *and* individual death, as the history of medicine makes clear. Representations of death necessarily engage questions about power: its locus, its authenticity, its sources, and how it is passed on. The very mobility and instability of power help undermine the simplistic binaries of life and death. Not surprisingly, it is Michel Foucault who has provided us with an exemplary dialectical reading of death and political representation in his chapter "Right of Death and Power over Life" in *The History of Sexuality*. For Foucault, death is at once the locus and the instrument of power: that is, an independent power inheres in death itself, but other forms of power rely on death to disclose and enforce themselves. Death—not in the abstract, but people dying and the processes by which they die—may signify by turns a monarch's sovereignty, a people's own power, and the primacy of biology over culture. There is probably no more universal signpost of urgency and magnitude than body counts. Governments know that to manipulate public reaction to violent events they must maintain control over information about deaths. People want to know: How many died? How did they die? Who has the power over these deaths? This last question, to return to Foucault, essentially asks, What do these deaths signify, what do they represent? What power can I/we exercise over them?

This volume of essays emerges at a moment, then, when critical inquiry has been revising the ways we understand death. Interest in death has mushroomed in virtually all academic disciplines during the past two or three decades, and most recently there has been a surge of theoretically sophisticated work done on death in literary contexts.[2] Studies in cultural anthropology have sharpened the available theoretical tools.[3] At the same time, since Philippe Ariès published his monumental volume *L'homme devant la mort* in 1976, there has been a perhaps unprecedented sense of work to be done: Ariès, along with McManners, Vovelle, and others, has historicized, and thereby destabilized, our sense of death's meanings, yet without convincing us that he is right on all counts.[4] To begin with, there is Ariès's title itself: What about woman before death? Or is woman, as Hélène Cixous has argued, inevitably aligned with death in the binary pairing? The question leads us to interrogate the assumptions lying behind the pair: *L'homme devant la mort* ("Man before death"—the English title is *The Hour of Our Death*) aligns too easily, and dangerously, with man/life before woman/death. We immediately suspect the binary opposition may be loaded with other explosives, and we question the vision based on it. Part of historicizing death, we are beginning to see, will entail looking at the history of gender as it appears in the shifting ways death has been perceived.

Just as the theoretical lines drawn between binary oppositions have been coming under fire, so the actual—living and breathing—boundary between life and death has become a matter of urgent debate, for both ends of the life cycle. The definition of when a human life begins is by no means clear, and it shows no signs of being settled in the near future. That boundary's very indeterminacy has led to one of the most heated political debates of recent times: the argument over the ethics of abortion. Similarly, medical technology has made it more difficult, rather than easier, to determine when a human life ends.[5] Again, the instability of that boundary today simply mirrors, in greater detail and complexity, a traditional problem. There is a reason folk literature and popular culture often depict people being buried alive and coming back to consciousness, just as myths have had various ways of construing the journey to death in spatial, reversible terms. The possibility of misreading the body as corpse is a nightmare fantasy, but it is also a practical difficulty with widespread ramifications. The literature of the revenant, which Ariès so richly explores, recurs with almost infinite variation and subtlety.[6]

Thus we can figure the relation between death and representation as one that involves not just abstract terms but also real bodies. That is to say, death is not simply a general term, but also a very particular one, represented in and through the dead. Many of the cultural systems concerned with death are in fact constructed to give a voice to the silenced dead. The question might be asked, Who or what represents the corpse? In this question's linguistic ambiguities lie many of the theoretical difficulties we are concerned with here. On the one hand, it can mean, How do we represent the point at which a body becomes a corpse? What is the truth-value of the technological response(s) to this question? And even here we might well ask who "we" are who are doing the representing, to what audience, for what purpose. How is a corpse represented differently for the purposes of law, of mourning, of the news media, of aestheticization in a symbol?

Our original question—who or what represents the corpse—might be construed as a legal one. Does the testamentary will represent the corpse? What kind of voice does the body have in the text, the linguistic traces, it leaves behind? Does the signature represent the corpse? If so, then it surely also represents a good deal more: the corpse come back to life, so to speak, as a powerful social force. (Anyone who has seen the effects of a complex will on a surviving family will understand the brunt of the phrase "social force." George Eliot found the apt title for the section of *Middlemarch* in which Casaubon's will exerts its effects on his widow: "The Dead Hand.") A more gruesome but nevertheless pertinent question, especially given the thematics of fragmentation that the subject of death occasions, is How much of the body is needed to represent the corpse—legally, technically, emotionally? How does the representation of the corpse in a grave, in an urn, in scattered ashes, or on a cross differ in each case? What kind of "voice," authority, presence, or repose does each marker give the dead? And what kind of metaphor does it provide the survivors who must use the body's traces to provide closure for themselves? For cultures that have located many of their most central meanings in a crucified body, the question assumes the greatest possible proportions. To give a voice to the corpse, to represent the body, is in a sense to return it to life: the voice represents not so much the dead as the once living, juxtaposed with the needs of the yet living.

In the aesthetic arena, the question of who or what represents the corpse also has multiple meanings—always, we suspect, grounded in the power of fascination. As Aristotle reminds us, "Though the objects themselves may be painful to see, we delight to view the most realistic representations of them in art, the forms for example of the lowest animals and of dead bodies" (227). In classical dramaturgy, death must occur offstage: the corpse is pointedly not to be represented. Yet it is difficult to imagine a literary corpse more poignant than that of Hippolyte in Racine's *Phèdre,* when Théramène describes the mangled body dragged through the dirt by horses. The death is not staged, but it is amply represented in the poetry of Racine's verses it gives rise to—enabling it, in turn, to represent a vaster body of violence.[7] More literal corpses abound in European painting. Some are sentimentalized to the point that we suspect what is represented is not a corpse at all but a pose, a congealed configuration of cultural meanings; others—for example the many nineteenth-century Ophelias—are transparent as depictions of live models figuring a conception of femininity that draws on death's connotations without, for all that, its "real" corpses.

Not only are the simplistic oppositions death/life and death/culture problematic, but so is the equally basic question of what it is to *represent* death. Representation presupposes an original presence, and in the case of death that is clearly paradoxical. In any representation of death, it is strikingly an absence that is at stake, so that the presentation is itself at a remove from what is figured. This is not just to claim that any representation of death in fact targets something else—the terms in which it chooses to make itself known—though no doubt some would argue just that. Any representational discourse implies the muteness, absence, nonbeing—in short, the death—of the object it seeks to designate. Death, as the real process of division, can perhaps best be expressed through figures of liminality, figures that expressly signify allegorically and thus speak the nonsignifiable "Other" through negation or displacement. As Jacques Derrida argues, "All graphemes are of a testamentary essence. And the original absence of the subject of writing is also the absence of the thing or the referent" (69). The text is substituted for the body, the material object of its reference: "The letter killeth."[8] At the same time, this fatal distancing between letter and referent involves more than a multiple death of the textualized object, which is abolished and called into being in one and the same representational gesture. Equally at stake is the subject's own authority. One component of the representational act may be, paradoxically, a *loss* of power, what Francis Baker has called "a suicidal denaturing of the subject which the decorporalized discourse defines" (106). While the author creates a text in order to make meanings through it and to control it, it in turn possesses—controls—the writer. Thus the text inaugurates the presence of the subject at the same time that it effects an erasure of that presence.[9]

One practical example will illustrate the dialectical movement we are describing as it works itself out on the level of social interaction in culture. Orlando Patterson, in his book *Slavery and Social Death,* argues persuasively that the most coherent definition of slavery is as social death. Not only does slavery represent a substitute for death (captivity rather than killing in war, for example, or the commutation of the death sentence), but, Patterson argues, it bears all the marks of life-in-death: the slave is alienated from his birthright, family, ancestors, and descendants; he also loses all access to such cultural meanings as honor and power. Patterson refers to the "liminal state of social death" as "institutionalized marginality" (46). It will be asserted, and rightly, that social death is not the same as physical death. The difference is all. And yet social death as a particular position has much in common with other kinds of figurative death, those in which the "texts" are not the living bodies of slaves. To translate Patterson's model into textual terms, the slave's owner or "author" creates this text largely to control it; power is at issue. In turn, the "text"/slave possesses the master, whose meanings both derive from and depend on the liminal subject he controls. Patterson moves outward from this Hegelian point to generalize about slavery's meanings in culture: "The marginal person, while a threat to the moral and social order, was often also essential for its survival. In cultural terms the very anomaly of the slave emphasized what was most important and stable" (46). Like a death figure or revenant, the slave can cross the boundaries "between life and death, community and chaos, the sacred and the secular . . . [with] supernatural impunity" (51). His very existence draws the lines.[10]

We might apply this argument equally well to the ways political systems inaugurate their power by using ritual representations of death. A recourse to death often serves as antidote to a crisis in belief, as confirmation of moral and social values. This may work to some extent because so much of Western culture finds legitimacy and value in material being: as Elaine Scarry has argued, "When some central idea or ideology or cultural construct has ceased to elicit a population's belief—either because it is manifestly fictitious or because it has for some reason been divested of ordinary forms of substantiation—the sheer material factualness of the human body will be borrowed to lend that cultural construct the aura of a 'realness' and 'certainty' " (14). Thus, for example, when antiabortion forces campaign against women's choice of abortion, they proliferate images of dead fetuses, the ultimate authority. Not even numbers can compete with the impact of that image, representing the dead to whom they claim to give a voice.

The dead body's peculiar power became superlatively clear when anti-Semitic demonstrators desecrated the Jewish cemetery in Carpentras, France, in June 1990. The press interpreted the violation as a unique moment in French postwar history because for the first time the phantom of French anti-Semitism appeared unmistakably and publicly. The response of the populace was also unique. For the first time since the liberation of France, a head of state, François Mitterrand, marched with 100,000 demonstrators in the streets of Paris. Yet what caused the greatest stir was that the aggressors, besides defacing thirty-four gravestones, had opened the grave of an eighty-one-year-old man, buried for just two weeks, and pierced his corpse with an umbrella. Precisely because it involved the cultural taboo of disturbing a dead body, this violence was seen as being worse than the usual anti-Semitic assaults, including the bombing of synagogues and restaurants. As Serge Klarsfeld argued in the *Frankfurter Allgemeine Zeitung,* the incident shows that "to injure the dead is to declare total war, total hatred." The act was seen as an unparalleled atrocity because it not only profaned a dead body but also used the profanation as an icon of collective hatred and power.

Ironically, then, the corpse may have more authority than any other political body. The more corpses, the more authority. The Holocaust is given at most only brief treatment in this book. But the violence of the Holocaust everywhere underwrites the work here, not least in the cultural configurations and events marking the personal histories of the editorial partnership that has brought the volume together. The experience of death that the Holocaust represents has had the authority to call more into question than any other event in the twentieth century. If we choose to be reticent on the subject here, it is simply because it is at once too vast and too familiar for us to begin to do justice to it. One has repeatedly, in the face of such a subject, the sense of nothing more to say.[11] Nevertheless, it is precisely the scale and the familiarity of death in the Holocaust that have shaped our sense of the reverberating meanings—and challenges to meaning—of death, both mass and individual.

## Sign, Psyche, Text

We have clustered the essays in order to set up resonances among them, so that their affinities of concern will emerge. Nevertheless, it will be clear that the divisions between the groups are heuristic fictions. The book opens with a section on the nexus of problems we have called "Reading Death: Sign, Psyche, Text." This section brings together essays studying representations of death as texts, foregrounding their textuality while at the same time insisting on the seriousness of the referent. To speak of *reading* death is already to have shifted the referent, since we read texts, representations of the real. Hence the importance of psychoanalysis, whose assumptions are pervasive if not everywhere explicit: death is the major agon of the psyche, the major subject of the text. No consideration of psychic representation can afford to ignore or deny the centrality of death to the psyche's self-constructs, just as no semiotics can suppress the positioning of the sign in reference to the nonsemiotic, the perpetually resistant reality that death represents.

What Freud called *Vorstellung,* a placing forward, as though to bring onstage or project onto a screen, in English is translated as *representation,* a word with rather different, though complementary, connotations. Like *Vorstellung,* representation has a rich theatrical history and brings to the psychoanalytic vocabulary for the mind a dramatic metaphor—indeed a phantasmagoric one.[12] What *Vorstellung* lacks is the baggage of political meanings that representation has accrued during the development of democratic governments. It offers instead a kind of *Verknüpfung,* a metaphoric attachment, between the concrete reality of *Stelle* (place) and the mind (as *sich etwas vorstellen* is to imagine something). The verb *vorstellen* is as comfortable with furniture as it is with ideas, so that there is something uneasily solid about the Freudian symptomatic *Vorstellung.* The essays in this section reflect something of the dual nature of *Vorstellung:* they alternate in their concern between an emphasis on the real image—the representation asking for interpretation, the symptom inscribed on the body, even the corpse—and a focus (one's language returns resolutely to the visual) on the process of representation itself, as psychoanalysis describes it. Collectively they ask, How does the psyche represent death? What forms does that representation take? How does the process take place? What are the purposes and meanings of such representations?

Psychoanalysis locates death in several registers of the psyche. For one, the human body's fatality—decay, decomposition—demonstrates the way death gains presence in life in the realm of the real. In a different form, death is also articulated in the pure destructive force of the unconscious, which needs to be constrained if any social or personal existence is to be upheld, and in whose interest social laws are transgressed in moments of ecstasy and violence. At the same time, culture, in order to support the interests of the group, must protect itself against the violence of real, natural materiality as well as against destructive impulses originating from its individual members. Freud therefore also locates an aspect of the death drive at the heart of guilt, in the subject's relation to cultural norms and laws. The superego functions as an agency that authorizes each individual to subject himself or herself to the interdictions of the community's laws. Yet—in one of Freud's many paradoxical turns during his elaboration of this theory—when the superego imposes too thoroughly on the ego's self-preservation, the result can be a "pure culture of the death drive" ("The Ego and the Id," *SE* 19: 52). Still, even without any violent curtailment's taking place, an individual's insertion in any cultural network implies a relationship with death. As Moustafa Safouan suggests, "What is properly 'inanimate' are the name and image from which the subject could never strip its 'reality' and outside of which reality is simply inconceivable" (93). Thus if the body is animate, and therefore a living metonymy for death, the cultural codes that govern it signify death in the opposite way, by being inanimate: already deathlike.

On two scores, death is also always implicated in the subject's narcissistically informed desire for pleasure. The subject's imaginary desire is most eloquently expressed in fantasies of wholeness and security, to be found in union with the beloved, a relationship modeled on the infant-mother dyad. Yet this sense of integral being also recalls the prenatal stasis of the womb and thus contrasts radically with the change, tension, discontinuity, and difference that constitute life. Thus romantic fantasies will often merge love and death, as in the *Liebestod* theme, in the necrophilia so prominent in nineteenth-century culture, and in the depiction of eroticism as "a little death."[13] Freud thus identifies some aspects of erotic love with the death drive. At the same time, as Jacques Lacan has enlarged upon Freud, all self-constructions are illusions, based on an originary void—the experience of birth as loss—and are thus informed by another kind of death, namely that very lack they are meant to occult.[14] The death drive, then, refers both to a desire for the inanimate state before life and to that force that produces division, that fragments, castrates, and separates unities. Death, the seeming opposite of life, emerges as its ground, its vanishing point, *and* its sustaining force.

Because Freud's discussion links the presence of death to aspects of repetition—to the compulsion to repeat, to the uncanniness of the double that repeats its model, but with a crucial difference—critics have recently tried to theorize the connection to notions of representation thus opened.[15] Maurice Blanchot posits an analogy between corpse and image: both the corpse and a representation are "uncanny" in that they suspend stable categories of reference and position in time and space. The cadaverous presence is such that it simultaneously occupies two places, the here and the nowhere. Neither of this world nor entirely absent from it, the cadaver thus mediates between these two incompatible positions. Uncanniness emerges because the corpse, resembling itself, is in a sense its own double. It has no relation to the world it appears in except that of an image. Thus the chiasmic relation: the corpse as uncanny image/the image uncannily as corpse.[16]

Sarah Kofman, elaborating on Blanchot, suggests that the analogy between a representation and a corpse resides in the former's seeming status of revenant. What makes art effective, she argues, is its self-reflexive moment. That moment emerges because, in its contingency on loss, art exemplifies a surplus meaning. Substituting for an absent object, art represents something it both is and is not. At the same time the aesthetic form both is and is not eternal. Both a representation and a corpse have no clear position even as they elicit a desire for stability. Based on a relation of resemblance and doubling, a representation functions like a revenant and thus, says Kofman, always has death as one of its signifieds.

The opening essay of part 1, by Ernst van Alphen, uses the work of the Dutch writer and artist Armando to develop a theoretical vocabulary for describing representations of death in which death is conceived as unspeakable, unique, and therefore unrepresentable. Armando's work is concerned with the particular violence of World War II, and van Alphen argues that the artist proceeds not by establishing a relation of similarity to those suffering its horrors, but by constructing a nonmetaphorical language based on contiguity and silences. The result is both a better understanding of Armando's historicity and a model for representing death as sublime and unspeakable.

Garrett Stewart's piece, "A Valediction For Bidding Mourning: Death and the Narratee in Brontë's *Villette*," again considers death in the context of narrative. Stewart argues that Charlotte Brontë's rhetoric inscribes the reader even as it inscribes life and death. As he puts it, in *Villette,* death comes to the narratee. What this means for Stewart, to reduce his complex argument, is that like the novel's protagonist, the reader must "pass through—and so overcome—the domain of her own double . . . who stands for the simultaneous neutralization of both death and life," and who also refuses to die. As Stewart points out, the novel leaves crucially open, and thus calls into question, both the life/death opposition and the reader's place.

In a rather different kind of investigation, Ellie Ragland discusses death and representation in terms of Lacanian psychoanalytic theory. She argues that for Lacan, representation and the death drive are connected because language, desire, behavior, and affect are positioned around loss. Representations are fantasies of wholeness, invented to protect each human being from confronting an initial traumatic experience that installed them in the first place as split-off meanings, as re-presented. Any encounter with the real, she argues, is an encounter with the death drive, as the "more" that lies behind or disrupts stable representations. Death qua the real, then, is what representations try to screen out. The question she raises is whether interpretation, like the awakening from a dream—which itself is understood as an encounter with the real—may not be seen as an attempt to repair the inconsistencies and deny the lack there apprehended. If dreams dramatize the failure in representation, the real that Lacan equates with death, interpretation may be the way to recuperate it.

Also working from the psychoanalytic theory of the death drive, Elisabeth Bronfen's essay relates mourning and representation by suggesting that both processes involve the repetition of a lost object, a beloved or a model.[17] Elaborating on the way Freud's concept of the death drive implies two forms of repetition—a series of similar versions inscribed with difference as well as the return to an initial inanimate state—she analyzes two narrative versions of the same common literary theme, Poe's "Ligeia" and Hitchcock's *Vertigo*. Each version recounts a man's loss of his first beloved and his choosing a second one because she bears an uncanny resemblance to the dead woman. Bronfen suggests that mourning can be seen as analogous to representation, in that both gestures deny a loss they are simultaneously forced to acknowledge.

## Death and Gender

Bronfen's essay points us toward the second group of essays in its specifically gendered model of the "masculine" artist's relation to the "feminine" death represented. Death, as the limit of cultural representation, has been associated with that other enigma, the multiply coded feminine body. As the mother, "woman" is the original prenatal dwelling place; as the beloved, she draws fantasies of desire and otherness; and as Mother Earth, she is the anticipated final resting place. Freud has made this much clear: femininity and death are Western culture's two major tropes for the enigma. At the same time, our culture posits death and the feminine as what is radically other to the norm, the living or surviving masculine subject; they represent the disruption and difference that ground a narcissistic sense of self and stability in a cultural system. But the system must also eliminate them or posit them as limit in order to survive.[18]

Death and femininity appear in cultural discourses as the point of impossibility, the blind spot the representational system seeks to refuse even as it constantly addresses it. In Jacqueline Rose's words, "The system is constituted as a system or whole only as a function of what it is attempting to evade and it is within this process that the woman finds herself symbolically placed. Set up as the guarantee of the system she comes to represent two things—what the man is not, that is difference, and what he has to give up, that is excess" (219). Both difference and excess apply equally, as attributes, to our cultural understanding of death. The kinds of power attributed to death are also those associated with the woman, because they are the confounding power of the body. Just as woman *is* the body, she is also the body's caretaker, the nurse, the layer-out of the corpse. If death is a kind of return to her care, then she is also contaminated by it, so that rituals must be found first to enable her care and then to dissociate her from the corpse. Like the decaying body, the feminine is unstable, liminal, disturbing. Both mourning rituals and representations of death may seek strategies to stabilize the body, which entails removing it from the feminine and transforming it into a monument, an enduring stone. Stable object, stable meanings: the surviving subject appropriates death's power in his monuments to the dead.

A portrait may serve as just such a monument. Carol Christ, in "Painting the Dead: Portraiture and Necrophilia in Victorian Art and Poetry," argues that nineteenth-century artists frequently use the poetic rendition of a woman's portrait to reflect on the way feminine sexuality and portraiture are connected to death. In the poems she considers, femininity is destabilizing, threatening. The portrait, she argues, reveals the very anxiety it is meant to suppress: it at once resists and represents the catastrophe of death. Portraits record an ambivalent desire both to look at a forbidden sexual object and to appropriate the life of the dead, the feminine body.

There is perhaps no more forbidden woman than the prostitute, and Sarah Webster Goodwin's essay, "Romanticism and the Ghost of Prostitution," explores the traditional alignment of the prostitute with death. The prostitute, Goodwin argues, haunts romantic texts with all the force of a bad conscience. What is most deathly about the prostitute is the way she transforms the woman's body into the site of economic exchange, "killing" value. She is thus doubly haunting for the male subject: as the uncanny but forbidden and strange home to which he is drawn, and as a figure for himself, caught in a diseased market of exchange where there is no reliable transcendent value.

For the female subject, in contrast, the prostitute is the uncanny double, the body she does not know as her own, death dealing in ways she can record but not elude.

Such representations of death often try to circumscribe its powers. In "Writing as Voodoo: Sorcery, Hysteria, and Art," Regina Barreca looks at women writers who instead appropriate death's power. The voodoo curse, the curse unto death, Barreca argues, represents a resource and a metaphor for the woman writer: voodoo is "feminine," and it demonstrates the capacity of the performative word to become real, however destructively. Reading a number of narratives by women writers, Barreca notes that the practitioner of voodoo is dangerous, unstable—deathlike. In these texts she also stands in metaphorically for the woman writer, no longer enigma but agent.

If femininity intersects with death by way of enigma, then how would we characterize the intersection of death and masculinity? Margaret Higonnet addresses some aspects of this question in her essay "Women in the Forbidden Zone: War, Women, and Death." As Higonnet points out, death in war can be understood to define manhood; the young man's corpse guarantees authentic virility. Literary representations of death in war not only have subscribed to this idea, they have helped construct it, extending the hero's authenticity to the poet. In the texts about World War I by women writers that Higonnet considers, a distinct difference emerges between the poems and the fiction. The poems "construct peace as a woman's text," reinscribing old polarities. The fiction, in contrast, often blurs the boundaries between war and peace, death and life, masculinity and femininity. "Heroic" death not only is deflated, as we might expect, it is redefined as an uncanny disease that invades the social body and corrupts the collective psyche.

## History, Power, Ideology

Thus, the essays in part 2 suggest, death and femininity have formed two possible axes of negation and enigma in relation to masculine subjectivity and culture. Higonnet's chapter, with its focus on a cultural group in a historical moment, leads us into the final section. Here the essays locate death in history and define it as a social and cultural phenomenon: both threat to and instrument of power.

Just as the mind defines itself in response to an imagined Other, cultures need images of alterity and sacrifice to define their own boundaries. Communities, as René Girard has shown, identify a dangerous body that needs to be eliminated for the stability of the whole. The community's idea of itself in history cannot be disentangled from the ways it represents death. At the extreme this can be understood as referring to those it chooses to kill, literally and symbolically: scapegoats. Kings, revolutionaries, widows, prostitutes, soldiers—all help define the community with their sacrificial corpses. Both individual executions and the collective violence of war may purge and thus restabilize an unstable group. In wartime propaganda as in any other discourse, representing the enemy Other serves to master and control the disturbing alterity within.

A group may organize its meanings around other ways of representing death as well. In many instances, for example—one thinks of nineteenth-century caricatures—death has a social class: it is the proletariat, the revolutionary crowd in some contexts; the middle class, bored and boring, the marketplace, kitsch, in others.[19] Social rituals, too, are a means for representing death. Deathbed and mourning rituals help a given family or society to confirm its structures, both social and ideological. Ariès and Vovelle have seen death as inevitably encoded; they argue that death in the modern period has become strange, distanced from society, banned to the outskirts. At the same time, the alienation of death has led to a fascination with it, culminating in an ambivalent attitude toward the dead as both dangerous and powerfully healing. Death is thus both rejected as a presence in everyday life and excessively staged in public funerals and tombstone sculptures.

Ariès and Vovelle follow Edgar Morin's argument that attitudes toward death are intrinsically connected with notions of individuality and consciousness. Witnessing death affirms a sense of personal individuality in the survivors, while society resorts to rituals that imply the refusal to accept mortality.[20] As that which threatens individuality, death also becomes, in the modern period, a supreme confirmation of individuality: it enables the individual to design for himself or herself the fiction of a permanent monument, in testament, grave sculpture, or legacy. Such icons of survival, Humphreys suggests, represent the symbolic transformation of "what was a living person and is now a decaying cadaver into something permanent and stable" (267).

It may be that Ariès's periodization of attitudes locates "modernity" entirely too late. François Villon's *Testament* and Montaigne's *Essais* are surely as much monuments to individualism as Wordsworth's "Intimations" ode.[21] As McManners states, "Dying is the loneliest, and therefore the most highly individual thing we do" ("Death and the French Historians" 130); thus he concludes that the historian of death is really writing about cultural attitudes toward survival, about society affirming itself, the family expressing its coherence, the church exemplifying its beliefs, and the mourners creating beautiful and memorable monuments. Here, as before, we see death as an allegorical sign for something other than itself, simultaneously presenting the impossibility of its own presentation. It seems necessary, in the midst of the effort to historicize representations of death, to bear in mind Whaley's critique of Ariès: though it is possible to speak of the Enlightenment's attitude toward death or a Victorian way of dying, such general periodizations also seem to dissolve into an almost infinite diversity of emotions, relevant in all ages (9). Louis-Vincent Thomas's anthropological work implies that the dead body presents above all a site where a multitude of fantasies, often complex and contradictory, converge: from love to hate, fascination to repugnance. The corpse may become supreme signifier for anything from human destiny and its redemption to life's meaninglessness (52).

And yet, as Foucault has shown us, such contradictory fantasies are not independent of ideology but complexly implicated within it. Nor is ideology in any simple sense monolithic; it may consist most realistically in competing paradigms and in the fissures between them (Macherey). Here too the representation of death may be peculiarly apt to figure the gaps in a culture's articulate meanings. Since death is most often powerful—supremely so— the representation of death may covertly, or incidentally, assign power in ways that cannot be directly realized within a particular culture at a given moment in history. One of the most suggestive theorists of death in recent years is Jean Baudrillard, who has explored some of the subtle ways death may help to divide and circulate power in our culture. Baudrillard argues that social survival depends on a prohibition against death. People thus accrue power and control by manipulating and legislating death: by breaking any unity between life and death, disrupting any exchange between the two, and imposing a taboo on the dead. Power emerges precisely over this *first* boundary, and all later, secondary aspects of division—between soul and body, masculinity and femininity, good and bad—feed off this initial separation that partitions life off from death. All forms of ensuing economy— monetary, libidinal, or aesthetic—are, he argues, based on this separation.[22] Baudrillard thus offers a theoretical argument that might well be useful for more pointedly historical readings of specific representations of death.

The essays in part 3 do not generalize about death in various "periods" (themselves constructs we would want to scrutinize), nor do they propose another diachronic sweep. Instead, each closely analyzes a text or group of texts for historical insights. The essays themselves represent a wide range of what might be considered germane to historical analysis. They may take as their texts the more conventional historical sources such as contemporary accounts of events (Janes, Gilman), but they treat such accounts as texts subject like any others to analysis. Segal and Sunder Rajan focus almost exclusively on literary texts—without themselves drawing that distinct category—but they do so in order to analyze the representations of death within a historical moment.

In this section's first chapter, Charles Segal examines Euripides' *Alcestis* for its attitudes toward death and mourning, as it represents a wife and mother dying a natural death. The play presents a double fantasy: of escaping death by having someone else die in one's place, and of forcing death to yield its victim. Segal argues that the play also proclaims the necessity and inevitability of death, even as it feeds one's wishful thinking that death can be revoked and thus defeated. By virtue of a double focus on death's horror and a comic triumph over it, Euripides allows the audience a dual identification with the dying person and with the play's survivors. As this play resolves the double focus, it confirms the normality and virtue of dying at one's appointed time.

Addressing a much later time in Western history, Regina Janes's essay, "Beheadings," moves from the private arena of death in the home to the public one of executions. Janes argues that there are two distinct discourses within the category of beheadings: that of the pike and that of the guillotine. Their connotations differ widely, both because of their histories and because of their physical qualities. The guillotine, for example, has been coded feminine whereas the pike, intuitively, could not be. Janes's essay goes well beyond historical curiosity: in the ways that the guillotine technologizes and tidies violent death, we can see an important dimension of modern execution and warfare.

Sander Gilman's essay in turn suggests the ways a culture can deny death, giving it only covert and prohibited circulation. His chapter, which analyses texts surrounding the case of Jack the Ripper, argues that only another social outcast—Jack, the sexual deviant, diseased and corrupt—can destroy the equally corrupt and destructive prostitute. Contemporary documents reveal Jack to be a multiply dangerous Other: as Jew and as revolutionary. The perversion of both the Jew and the prostitute lies in their relation to capital, the inanimate body of money, as yet another aspect of death connecting them. The Jew, the prostitute, and the power of money are all tropes for carriers of sexually transmitted diseases, which may signify fatal punishment. Thus Jew and prostitute converge as the enemy within the body politic, as the force of death and destruction in the midst of late Victorian culture.

The volume's final essay, Rajeswari Sunder Rajan's "Representing Sati: Continuities and Discontinuities," moves us beyond the confines of a narrowly Western culture and history to a more global view of sati (widow suicide/death) in colonial and postcolonial discourses. Sunder Rajan traces the presence and significance of sati from precolonial to postcolonial literatures, with particular attention to the way texts frame the woman's subjectivity in the choice of suicide. The chief paradigm at work since the colonial representations of sati has been one of chivalric rescue, saving the woman/martyr from a cruel death. For the woman herself, ironicially, it is death—her husband's then her own—that defines her as a social subject.

Following part 3, Ronald Schleifer provides an afterword that is at once a response to the essays published here and a treatment in its own right of the ways Walter Benjamin creates a theoretical context for them. Suggesting that the essays illustrate the "impossibility of offering a totalizing theme or approach" to their collective subject, Schleifer finds just that impossibility at work in Benjamin's thinking. Because for Benjamin death's materiality disrupts systematic knowledge or representation, a poetics of fragmentation—or, to use his words, of constellations, allegory, image, quotation—is the issue of any attempt at a totalizing theory. Schleifer thus frames the essays' various methods and rhetorics, their "local knowledge," with Benjamin's sense that death achieves its representations only in dispersed and particular instances.

The essays in this book represent a wide range of perspectives and critical approaches. They do not all work from the same givens, nor is even "death" a self-evident category common to them all. But there are, it seems, points in common.

Perhaps paramount is death's double position as anomalous, marginal, repressed, and at the same time masterful, central, everywhere manifest. Both the collective and the individual body locate their meanings within this doubled given, in a kind of perpetual vacillation. The gesture of repression, which is also a gesture to obtain (the fiction of) mastery, is so multiply encoded, so infinitely various, that we might call it pied beauty. But uncanny beauty. Every representation of death necessarily represses what it purports to reveal. It also necessarily serves other purposes that may or may not be overtly acknowledged. Nearly every essay illustrates ways the repression of death is also an expression/repression of an ideological position. Recent historicist criticism has attended closely to the complex ways works of art may at once both represent and interrogate prevailing ideologies. We suggest that representations of death, with their structural dialectic of revealing and concealing and their inevitable configurations of power and powerlessness, are rich texts for studying the ways art answers threats to its own powers of representation. Again, although the terms here are abstract, seemingly ahistorical, we are proposing a basis for a historiography of death, one that might take into fuller account the textuality of the sources on which it bases its claims.

In the course of presenting and integrating others' theories about death, we have made a number of general observations. Some key points recur and thus stand out, though none are common to every essay here, and each raises complex issues that call for elaboration. Summary oversimplifies, and the summary of summaries simplifies even further; but with that caveat, we take up again these salient points, by way of concluding and directing the reader toward the chapters that follow:

*Every representation of death is a misrepresentation.*[23] Thus the analysis of it must show not only how it claims to represent death, but also what else it in fact represents, however suppressed: assertion of alternative power, self-referential metaphor, aggression against individuals or groups, formation of group identities and ideologies, and so forth. Whether as state or as event, death cannot be represented. Attempts at representation therefore seek to appropriate that resistant power.

*Death is the constructed Other.* That which aligns with death in any given representation is Other, dangerous, enigmatic, magnetic: culturally, globally, sexually, racially, historically, economically. To study representations of death is to study how not only individuals but also groups have defined themselves against what they are not but wish to control. As we argued earlier, this idea of death as agon is in part a cultural construct, since death and life do not by nature stand in an exclusively binary relation.

*Death is gendered.* Probably without exception, at least in Western culture, representations of death bring into play the binary tensions of gender constructs, as life/death engages permutations with masculinity/femininity and with fantasies of power.

*Death is physical.* Although death poses a metaphysical problem, it is a physical event. It is real, the referent that texts may point to but not touch. As such it is also uncanny, the return of the repressed, the excess that is beyond the text and to which the text aspires even as it aims to surpass it in potency. This is where death aligns most clearly with sexuality: with the body that is too common—commonplace—the absence of spirit and intellect and grace. Thus it is frightening and elicits a visceral response that is part repression, part bodily knowledge.

Our own attempts at analysis fall inescapably—it is no confession, simply the obvious—within the purview of that gesture of repression. That is not to say they are meaningless. Meaning has its own rules and possibilities; it does not always have to bow and scrape to the hollow-eyed puppeteer. Theories of justice, of power exercised in social contexts, must continue to account for what death represents with an urgency that the theorist of literature and the arts may not always feel. But if these essays allow themselves a certain amount of free play, again and again it is nevertheless with the sense that the real body, our own death, is at stake.

## Notes

1. This is a point developed specifically by Berger (3–28), though it comes up repeatedly in the literature on death.

2. See, for example, recent works by Regina Barreca (ed.), Jahan Ramazani, Peter Sacks, Ronald Schleifer, Richard Stamelman, and Garrett Stewart.

3. Perhaps most important here are books by Maurice Bloch and Jonathan Parry, and by Richard Huntington and Peter Metcalf.

4. Louis-Vincent Thomas and Jacques Choron arc among the other influential historians of death.

5. A parallel, and even more important, issue arises in the experience of AIDS. Not only does that syndrome make the cause of death seem ambiguous—since, we are often reminded, one does not die of AIDS, but of the diseases the body can no longer defend itself against—but the social response to AIDS patients is often to define them, in many ways, as already dead. See *October* 43 (Winter 1987), a special issue on AIDS edited by Douglas Crimp. On defining death, see also Gervais and Kübler-Ross.

6. For a fascinating study of the revenant in folklore, see Paul Barber, *Vampires, Burial and Death*. Barber shows forcefully how vampire stories illustrate the power of the corpse as a destabilizing force. He argues that actions undertaken to guard against vampires or to "kill" them are in fact efforts to ensure the finality of death and to contain its potential contagion.

7. For a more on theatrical representations of death, see Clément (*Opera*) and Loraux.

8. Or, as Richard Stamelman quotes the poet Robert Hass, "a word is elegy to what it signifies" (xi). Stamelman himself makes a similar point as the basis of his work on death and absence in modern French poetry, although he emphasizes what is gained rather than what is lost: "Representation longs for the recovery of presence. But, in truth, representation involves images and traces, never origins. Loss of the original fuels the fires of artifice. Possessing an origin, what need would there be to represent it? Dispossession makes possible the creation of images, and negatively, as embodied in absence, death, and loss, animates the quest of writing and other forms of figuration" (x).

9. As Jahan Ramazani writes in his insightful study of death in Yeats's poetry, "Every day, in every act of writing, a poet rehearses death, dying to the biographical self and assuming a 'mask' or 'phantasmagoria.' . . . For Yeats, death is both the human absence that generates the anticipatory or retrospective mourning of poetry and the absence within poetry itself" (4).

10. Patterson uses the masculine pronoun throughout, and we follow him here for the sake of clarity. He seems unaware of the many parallels between his description

of the slave's position and the symbolic place of the wife in some patriarchal cultures. For example, he describes the process in which "social death" is imposed on the slave as consisting of the following: "First, the symbolic rejection by the slave of his past and his former kinsmen; second, a change of name; third, the imposition of some visible mark of servitude; and last, the assumption of a new status in the household or economic organization of the master" (52).

For a discussion of the power and danger of liminality as a deathlike state, see also Mary Douglas.

11. Of course the literature on this subject is massive. See in particular, among recent works, Friedländer and Langer.

12. We use the word *phantasmagoric* with its history in mind. The nineteenth-century phantasmagoria was itself a representation of death, and, as Terry Castle has shown, psychoanalytic theory and the phantasmagoric magic-lantern show developed together at a time when science was redefining and ostensibly circumscribing the power of death and its demons.

13. For an elaboration of this phrase's meanings, see Georges Bataille.

14. For more on Lacan's elaboration here, see Boothby.

15. See in Freud especially *Beyond the Pleasure Principle* (*SE* 18: 7–64) and "The 'Uncanny' " (*SE* 17: 217–56).

16. For a much more detailed summary of (and commentary on) Blanchot's rich meditation in *L'espace littéraire*, see Stamelman 35–47. As Stamelman notes: "Writing is the errant movement of loss. . . . And it is perpetual repetition. Because writing is always partial and incomplete, always making and then unmaking itself, it is forced to repeat again and again the emptiness that lies at its core" (43).

17. This essay is part of a chapter from Bronfen's recent book, *Over Her Dead Body*, which traces the configuration of death, femininity, and the esthetic.

18. The essays by Elisabeth Bronfen listed in the Works Cited expand upon and elaborate, in various ways, the arguments summarized here.

19. For more on death as social figure, see Paulson, and also Goodwin, *Kitsch and Culture*.

20. Elias Canetti argues, in *Macht und Masse,* that to witness another's corpse assures survivors that they are still alive. It is an insight that can be extended beyond literal corpses to represented ones.

21. Arnold Stein broaches this argument in the discussion of Ariès that concludes *The House of Death*.

22. Baudrillard, especially chapter 5, "L'échange symbolique et la mort."

23. Mieke Bal develops this point at some length.

## Works Cited

Ariès, Philippe. *L'homme devant la mort*. Paris: Gallimard, 1976.

———. *The Hour of Our Death*. Trans. Helen Weaver. New York: Knopf/Random House, 1981.

Aristotle. *The Rhetoric and Poetics of Aristotle*. Trans. Ingram Bywater. New York: Random House, 1954.

Bal, Mieke. *Reading Rembrandt: Beyond The Word-Image Opposition*. New York: Cambridge UP, 1991.

Barber, Paul. *Vampires, Burial and Death: Folklore and Reality*. New Haven: Yale UP, 1988.

Barker, Francis. *The Tremulous Private Body: Essays on Subjection*. London: Methuen, 1984.

Barreca, Regina, ed. *Sexuality and Death in Victorian Literature*. Bloomington: Indiana UP, 1990.

Bataille, Georges. *L'érotism*. Paris: Éditions de Minuit, 1957.

Baudrillard, Jean. *L'échange symbolique et la mort*. Paris: Seuil, 1976.

Berger, Peter L. *The Sacred Canopy: Elements of a Sociological Theory of Religion*. Garden City, NY: Doubleday, 1967.

Blanchot, Maurice. "Two Versions of the Imaginary." *The Gaze of Orpheus and Other Literary Essays*. Barrytown, NY: Station Hill, 1981. 79–89.

Bloch, Maurice, and Jonathan Parry. *Death and the Regeneration of Life*. Cambridge: Cambridge UP, 1982.

Boothby, Richard. *Death and Desire: Psychoanalytic Theory in Lacan's Return to Freud*. New York: Routledge, 1991.

Bronfen, Elisabeth. "Dialogue with the Dead: The Deceased Beloved as Muse." Barreca 241–59.

———. "The Lady Vanishes: Sophie Freud and *Beyond the Pleasure Principle*." *Rereadings in the Freudian Field*. Ed. Leigh de Neef. Spec. issue of *South Atlantic Quarterly* 88.4 (1989): 961–91.

———. *Over Her Dead Body: Death, Femininity and the Aesthetic*. Manchester: Manchester UP; New York: Routledge, 1992.

———. "Die schöne Leiche: Weiblicher Tod als motivische Konstante von der Mitte des 18. Jhd. bis in die Moderne." *Weiblichkeit und Tod in der Literatur*. Ed. Renate Berger and Inge Stephan. Cologne: Berlau, 1987. 87–115.

Burke, Kenneth. "Thanatopsis for Critics: A Brief Thesaurus of Deaths and Dyings." *Essays in Criticism* 2.4 (1952): 369–75.

Canetti, Elias. *Macht und Masse*. Frankfurt am Main: Fischer, 1960.

Castle, Terry. "Phantasmagoria." *Critical Inquiry* 15.1 (1988): 26–61.

Choron, Jacques. *Death and Western Thought*. New York: Macmillan, 1963.

Cixous, Hélène. "Sorties." *New French Feminisms*. Ed. Elaine Marks and Isabelle de Courtivron. New York: Schocken, 1981. 90–98.

Clément, Catherine. *Opera, or The Undoing of Woman*. Minneapolis: U of Minnesota P, 1988.

Corbin, Alain. "Commercial Sexuality in Nineteenth-Century France: A System of Images and Regulations." *The Making of the Modern Body: Sexuality and Society in the Nineteenth Century*. Ed. Catherine Gallagher and Thomas Laqueur. Berkeley: U of California P, 1987. 209–19.

Crimp, Douglas, ed. *AIDS*. Spec. issue of *October* 43 (Winter 1987).

Derrida, Jacques. *Of Grammatology*. Trans. Gayatri Chakravorty Spivak. Baltimore: Johns Hopkins UP, 1974.

Douglas, Mary. *Purity and Pollution*. London: Routledge and Kegan Paul, 1966.

Foucault, Michel. *The History of Sexuality*. Vol. 1. Trans. Robert Hurley. New York: Pantheon, 1978.

Freud, Sigmund. *The Standard Edition of the Complete Psychological Works* (*SE*). Trans. and ed. James Strachey. 24 vols. 1953–74. London: Hogarth, 1986.

Friedländer, Saul. *Kitsch and Death*. New York: Harper and Row, 1983.

———. *Representing the Holocaust*. Cambridge: Harvard UP, 1991.

Gervais, Karen Grandstrand. *Redefining Death*. New Haven: Yale UP, 1980.

Girard, René. *Violence and the Sacred*. Trans. Patrick Gregory. Baltimore: Johns Hopkins UP, 1979.

Goodwin, Sarah Webster. *Kitsch and Culture: The Dance of Death in Nineteeth-Century Literature and Graphic Arts*. New York: Garland, 1988.

Humphreys, Sally. "Death and Time." Ed. S. Humphreys and Helen King. *Mortality and Immortality: The Anthropology and Archaeology of Death*. London: Academic, 1981. 261–83.

Huntington, Richard, and Peter Metcalf. *Celebrations of Death: The Anthropology of Mortuary Ritual*. Cambridge: Cambridge UP, 1979.

Klarsfeld, Serge. Article in *Frankfurter Allgemeine Zeitung*, 16 June 1990, no. 137.

Kofman, Sarah. *Mélancolie de l'art*. Paris: Galilée, 1985.

Kübler-Ross, Elisabeth. *On Death and Dying*. New York: Macmillan, 1969.

Langer, Lawrence L. *The Holocaust and the Literary Imagination*. New Haven: Yale UP, 1945.

Loraux, Nicole. *Façons tragiques de tuer une femme*. Paris: Hachette, 1985.

Machery, Pierre. *A Theory of Literary Production*. Trans. Geoffrey Wall. London: Routledge and Kegan Paul. 1978.

McManners, John. *Death and the Enlightenment*. Oxford: Oxford UP, 1981.

———. "Death and the French Historians." Ed. Joachim Whaley. *Mirrors of Mortality: Studies in the Social History of Death*. New York: St. Martin's, 1981.

Morin, Edgar. *L'homme et la mort*. Paris: Seuil, 1951.

Patterson, Orlando. *Slavery and Social Death*. Cambridge: Harvard UP, 1982.

Paulson, Ronald. *Representations of Revolution (1789–1820)*. New Haven: Yale UP, 1983.

Ramazani, Jahan. *Yeats and the Poetry of Death: Elegy, Self-Elegy, and the Sublime*. New Haven: Yale UP, 1990.

Rose, Jacqueline, and Juliet Mitchell, eds. *Feminine Sexuality: Jacques Lacan and the Ecole Freudienne*. New York: Norton, 1985.

Sacks, Peter. *The English Elegy*. Baltimore: Johns Hopkins UP, 1985.

Safouan, Moustafa. *Pleasure and Being: Hedonism from a Psychoanalytic Point of View*. London: Macmillan, 1983.

Scarry, Elaine. *The Body in Pain*. Oxford: Oxford UP, 1985.

Schleifer, Ronald. *Rhetoric and Death: The Language of Modernism and Postmodern Discourse Theory*. Urbana: U of Illinois P, 1990.

Stamelman, Richard. *Lost beyond Telling: Representations of Death and Absence in Modern French Poetry*. Ithaca: Cornell UP, 1990.

Stein, Arnold. *The House of Death: Messages from the English Renaissance*. Baltimore: Johns Hopkins UP, 1986.

Stewart, Garrett. *Death Sentences: Styles of Dying in British Fiction*. Cambridge: Harvard UP, 1984.

Thomas, Louis-Vincent. *Le cadavre: De la biologie à l'anthropologie*. Brussels: Edition Comlexe, 1980.

Vovelle, Michel. *La mort et l'Occident, de 1300 à nos jours*. Paris: Gallimard, 1983.

Whaley, Joachim. *Mirrors of Mortality: Studies in the Social History of Death*. New York: St. Martin's, 1981.

# Reading Death

# Sign, Psyche, Text

## I

■

# Touching Death

## *Ernst van Alphen*

> The crucial point here is the changed symbolic status of an
> event: when it erupts for the first time it is experienced as a
> contingent trauma, as an intrusion of a certain nonsymbolized
> Real; only through repetition is this event recognized in its
> symbolic necessity.
>
> Slavoj Zizek, *The Sublime Object of Ideology*

## Death versus Representation

The work of Dutch writer and visual artist Armando is about the Second
World War—in Dutch, simply "the war." This seemingly simple formulation
turns out to effectively summarize the paradox of his project. This phrase
"the war" refers not to the general concept of war but to that one particular
war that dwarfs all others: World War II. Compared with that one, previous
wars were not really wars. World War II has been so traumatic that this true
history has become the model for the very concept.

Reading "the war" as World War II entails a generic qualification of
Armando's work. His visual work belongs to history painting, his literary
work to historical literature. His work is then the representation of a specific
historical period, comparable to the novels of Walter Scott or the paintings
of Delacroix or David, which represent episodes from English or French
history. Yet this is not at all the way Armando's work is being read. Most
interpretations rightly suggest that it is not historical in any traditional sense,
because the moments or events described cannot easily be pinpointed histori-

cally or geographically. In semiotic terms, time and space are not referential. Armando's war appears to occur in an archetypal vacuum. Even if Armando's war experiences—he spent his childhood in the close vicinity of Camp Amersfoort—are the *occasion* or trigger of his work, their *meaning* is allegedly much more general and can be expressed only in generalizing terms. This apparent dilemma is the very one implied in the question of the representation of death. Therefore Armando's work on the war acutely poses and, as I will show, resolves that basic question.

For I contend, and will try to demonstrate, that this view of Armando's work as metaphorical rather than historical has far-reaching consequences. According to R. L. K. Fokkema, for example, "Nowhere in his poetry does Armando describe specific events or a specific place. His work is not at all anecdotal; rather, it is a visual examination of the abstractions of war and battle, of relationships between people. Essentially the war is for him a metaphor of *la condition humaine,* and Amersfoort as a location is a metaphor of the world."[1] Carel Blotkamp claims something similar about Armando's visual images, even using the same phrase. In the catalog for Armando's exhibition at the Fruitmarket gallery in Edinburgh (1989) he wrote: "It isn't the specific situation in which he found himself which is conveyed in his paintings and drawings, poems and prose. It is more as though war has become, for him, a metaphor for the human condition." In Western culture the notion that the value of art and literature lies in their metaphoric quality is so self-evident that Fokkema's and Blotkamp's understanding of Armando's work seems indisputable. For it is supposed to be precisely the *similarity* between the specific work and the general human condition under which the reader and viewer also suffer that enables artists to seduce the public into reading literature and art. In Armando's case, however, the implications of such a metaphorical reading are far from innocent.

The focus on similarities between the Second World War and the human condition implies a leveling out, a naturalization, of that war's horror. According to such views, everyone is equally able to understand how the victims of World War II have suffered, for all of us today, by the sheer fact of our humanity, and hence our being defined by the human condition, ultimately experience the same thing, or at least something similar.

This logical consequence of metaphorical reading is clearly unacceptable. Whether we see the war as a pathetic aggrandizement of our own suffering or as a trivializing of war's experiences, the effect is the same: the Second World War is not unique; we can make the experiences of that chunk of history speakable through our own experiences. Or conversely and even more exploitatively, we can make our own experiences speakable by making those of the Second World War the point of comparison.

In this chapter I develop an opposite reading of Armando's work and, by extension, of the problem it poses. His texts and images do not "use" World War II as a motif that enables him to make the human condition speakable. Rather, they strive to make us understand the absolute uniqueness of that war's experiences, a war that lies outside the human condition. That war is incomparable, that each new war is unique, has consequences for the way it can be represented, and this includes the nonanecdotal character of those representations. The war's uniqueness implies that those tropes aimed at demonstrating similarity between two items, such as comparison and metaphor, are by definition inadequate. For the claim to similiarity automatically renders the unique quality of the experience radically but slyly unspeakable and violently overrules it with the similarity to something else. In other words, the uniqueness must be shown by different devices. One must construct a nonmetaphorical language capable of getting in touch with the very unspeakability of death as experience,[2] of which "the war" is the most extreme, the unique as well as exemplary occurrence. Armando develops such a language.[3]

Tropes such as metaphor, but also metonymy and synecdoche, use language to shape a new language. In the terms developed by the semiotician Juri Lotman, tropes form a secondary modeling system, using the so-called primary modeling system—language—as their material. Precisely because the meaning of the Second World War is unique, the metaphorical impulse assumes that the primary system of language does not yet contain elements usable for the secondary system. Strictly speaking—if we look only at the grammar and idiom of a language—this might entail the need for metaphors. But perhaps a more encompassing view of meaning, like that of American semiotics, is better able to provide the primary modeling system with a means of expression that is not based on similarity and hence on commonality. The very distinction between primary and secondary modeling systems becomes superfluous. Rather, we need to take a closer look at modeling systems in general and at the ways meaning is produced in them.

The basic principles of semiotics show how signs can be produced on that primary level. The American philosopher Charles Sanders Peirce has distinguished three categories of signs based on the relation between sign and meaning, categories that are not limited to language: icon, index, and symbol. Since I will take these categories quite seriously and literally, let me review them. An icon is a sign that has some feature in common with the thing or concept it stands for; it is motivated by similarity. A footprint resembles the foot of which this sign is a print, so it is capable of functioning as a sign of the meaning "foot." An index is a sign motivated by contiguity, one form of which is continuity; there is juxtaposition in time or space or causality between the sign and the object it stands for. Thus there is an existential relation of contiguity between a footprint and the human or animal that left it. Footprint and creature are "in touch." The footprint *refers* to the presence of person or animal. The same relationship holds for temporally and causally connected items: smoke is an index of fire because the consequence, smoke, refers to the cause of which the smoke is a sign—fire. A symbol, finally, is an unmotivated, arbitrary sign. It becomes a sign by virtue of a convention, an implicit agreement. The traffic sign is the classic example. But most elements of verbal language are also symbols. There is no motivated relation between the word "horse" and the animal we immediately think of when we hear the word.

This distinction in categories of signs enables me to describe the language Armando develops to make the uniqueness, the incomparability, of deadly war experiences speakable without flattening them out. *His language is radically indexical.* He "encircles" the unspeakable of "the war" by speaking, or representing, what is contiguous to it, what touches it. Not the violence and destruction of death itself, but what was present when it happened is what he formulates or shapes. Just as the footprint is a silent witness to the past presence of a human being, so the signs his work consists of are indexical traces of the unspeakable and the unrepresentable.

American art historian Rosalind Krauss has argued, in two influential articles, that much of contemporary art can be understood only in terms of the principle of indexical meaning production. Her definition of the index clarifies what makes Armando's work so special: "Indexes are the marks or traces of a particular cause, and that cause is the thing to which they refer, the object they signify" (198). The intriguing effect of the index is caused by time: because of time, the past (transient and ungraspable by definition) is provided with an existential and physical presence. Krauss writes about the effectiveness of indexicality in a work by the artist Lucio Pozzi: "It fills the work with an extraordinary sense of time past. Though they are produced by a physical cause, the trace, the impression, the clue, are vestiges of that cause which is itself no longer present in the giving sign. Like traces, the works I have been describing represent the building through the paradox of being physically present but temporally remote" (217). The motifs of Armando's work are all understandable from this perspective. He shows the traces that the unbearable and unrepresentable horror has left, and he makes sure those traces are not effaced. He is engaged in a struggle against time, memory, story line, and nature, which all conspire to erase the traces.

## The Edge of the Forest

In his literary as well as his visual work, Armando has declared the landscape guilty. Paintings and drawings bear titles like *Guilty Landscape;* in his texts trees, in particular at the edge of the forest, are considered guilty (fig. 1). What can we make of such personifications of trees? Perhaps it is possible to consider a tree a metaphor of the culprit. The similarity between tree and criminal could be, for example, that both are imperturbable. Trees grow on as if nothing had happened, just as the perpetrator, untouched by the destruction he committed, the death he dealt, went on with the violence. Because of the very absurdity of declaring trees guilty, the gesture seemingly can only be metaphorical. The personification of trees would then be an indictment of people: people are accused of being as impassive as trees.

Such an interpretation becomes impossible, however, when we realize that for Armando not just any tree is guilty. He addresses his indictment to those trees that were present at the scene of violence. In an interview in 1985 he said: "They grow and keep still. Whatever happens. Quite a bit happened near those trees. Stalking and shooting, thrashing and humiliating. One could therefore say that the trees are complicit, are also guilty. But no: they're just trees. They cannot be blamed. The edge of a forest, for example. The trees in front must have seen a thing or two. Those behind them can hardly be blamed, they could never see anything. But the edge, the seam of the forest— that one has seen it. There are quite a few edges, here and there, of which I know a few things." [4] The presence of the trees at the scene of violence, the contiguity between the edge of the forest and the perpetrator, are the reason the trees are pronounced guilty. The meaning is produced not by metaphors of the imperturbable perpetrator, but by the traces of the violence used at that particular place. The trees were witnesses but do not testify. Their refusal to testify, to serve as traces of "the war," constitutes their guilt:

> Look at the images on which the enemy is busy doing his business: there they are, laughing in the background. And not just the pine and spruce-fir; the other trees as well.
>
> Shouldn't something be said about that, for once?
>
> I thought so, because some of them are still there, the trees, the edge of the forest, the timber, at the same spot where they used to stand. Don't think they have changed places; they are still there as indifferent witnesses. [5]

Figure 1. Armando, *Forest Outskirts 19-04-83*. Oil on canvas, 155 × 225 cm. Collection Lindlar. Berlin. Used by permission.

Trees are guilty not only because of their inability or unwillingness to testify, but because they efface the traces left by the violence. They overgrow the place where it happened.

> Finally the time came that the trees could tell about the old days. How admirable. How noble. But they covered a lot up, if not everything.[6]

The "covering up"—in Dutch, covering with flowers—by the trees must be taken figuratively as well as literally. By bearing flowers time and again, by growing on, the trees cover the absolute uniqueness, the absurd event that took place there; it is buried by flowers. The growth of the trees demonstrates and embodies the work of time: time produces forgetting, just as nature overgrows the place of action. In particular in *Dagboek van een dader* (*Diary of a Perpetrator*), Armando has denounced this destructive effect of nature, of time, but also of representation—on which more shortly.

> *16 August*
> This landscape has committed evil. I can surmise the armies. It is peaceful here, but unfitting. Silence sometimes comes after noise: here was pain, here fellow-men were thrashed. Time has guilt, everything grows again, but thinking

is forgotten. Betrayal! This battlefield remains my property, even if I live badly on.

*2 September*
Nature has really gotten into my black books. First she was cowardly, then she abandoned me continuously. And don't the trees eternally allow the wind to push them, without resistance to speak of? . . . And the Soil. The Soil lends a hand to the fall of the heroes. Places tolerate first, overgrow later. Oh, the spot must have been covered with growth. Yes, spots are always overgrown.[7]

The guilt of the trees consists of the invisibility of the violence and the evil that took place at their feet, an invisibility they "caused." Thereby they betray the indexical meaning of their presence.

## Postcards as Indexes

The indexical effect brought about in these fragments can also be felt in Armando's visual art. In the seventies Armando made drawings that incorporated old postcards. For example, in *The Unknown Soldier* (triptych, 1973), *Guilty Landscape* (triptych, 1973), *The Unknown Soldier* (1974) (fig. 2), and *De plek, der Ort, the Spot* (1974), he has blown up old photographs from "the war" to get a grainy effect. On the photograph or the paper he mounted it on, he has made marks with a pencil or crayon. In *Riesengebirge* (1980), *Waldsee* (1980) (fig. 3), and *Anmerkungen zur Vergangenheit* (1982) he has pasted postcards directly on cardboard and again applied traces of pencil to the postcard and the paper behind it to connect the two.

Of course the photographic images do represent "the war" iconically. There is maximum similarity between the image and the photographed object. The pencil and crayon lines demonstrate, however, that Armando is less interested in the iconic aspect of these images than in their indexical aspect. For him they are tangible objects that put him in touch with the people who have actually handled the postcards, who wrote on them, or who were present at the making of the photographs—they draw lines between him and them. There has been contiguity between the representation on the photos or postcards and the people who made these images, wrote on them, or looked at them. Armando thus sharpens views of photography to the extreme standard. Photographs are perfect icons because there is maximum similarity between the images and the objects they refer to; but they are often seen as the exemplary index. Photographs are also indexes because there has been an existential relation of touch between the light the object emits and the sensitive layer of the film the light fell on (Barthes). Arrmando, however, is interested not in this general indexical relationship but in that between the

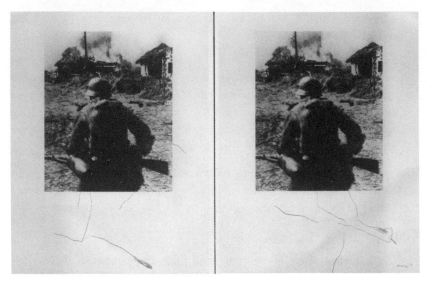

Figure 2. Armando, *Der unbekannte Soldat* (*The Unknown Soldier*), 1974. Diptych, 100 × 75 cm each. Used by permission.

postcard and its users: the people who had it in their hands. The postcard gives not an iconic image of a past long gone, but an indexical trace that instills in us the spatial presence of the trace and the distance and absence in time it refers to.

In an interview with Martijn Sanders, Armando explained his motivation for using postcards in his drawings: "These are German postcards, things history has stepped on. Leftovers. Very tangible remains of the past, with traces of people on them. At home I have a postcard of a soldier in the uniform of the First World War, with traces of pencil on it. I haven't done anything with it yet. . . . The drawings with postcards, for me, are total melancholy. . . . the people who have had such a card in their hands and who wrote on it are dead."[8] Armando cares not about the soldier represented but about the world where the postcard has circulated and to which it now refers as an index, because as a part of that world it still exists. Unlike the guilty trees, the postcards not only make the past visible, they make it present again, in an acute literalization of re-presentation.

## Isolation and Annexation as Indexical Strategies

In 1964 Armando published a programmatic text in the journal *Gard Sivik* in which he exposed the common principle of the "Zero movement" and "total poetry." This often-quoted text, titled "An International Primer," is

Figure 3. Armando, *Waldsee* (*Forest Lake*), 1982. Postcard and pencil, cardboard, 73 × 51 cm. Collection Sanders, Amsterdam. Used by permission.

still relevant to understanding his work from the Zero period, from which he distanced himself later on. But the poetic he formulates there holds as well, albeit in a less strident, more subtle, yet fundamental manner, for his work of the seventies and eighties. He sees the vocation of the artist or poet as follows: "Not to stifle Reality with moralism or interpretation (dis-art-iculate it), but to intensify it. Starting point: a consistent acceptance of Reality. Interest in a more autonomous appearance of Reality, already noticeable in journalism, TV reports, and film. Working method: isolating, annexing. Hence: authenticity. Not of the maker, but of the information. The artist, who is no longer an artist: a cool, efficient eye."[9] The method Armando recommends here, isolation and annexation, consists of practices typical of the war: those were the methods through which the Nazis tried to shape Germany. Jews, gays, and gypsies were isolated, countries were annexed. Armando's poetic does not so much deal with "the war" as it *is* war. He said something like this in an interview in 1971: "I have hated the war so much that I have come to identify with it. I have become the war."[10] Whereas Armando's early work concerns not so much the war as violent situations in general, his poetic does consist of strategies that characterize "the war"— that particular, only one. A poem from the "Karl May Cycle" demonstrates this convincingly:

> He has spit blood and lost two teeth,
> which proves
> that his club blow had not been particularly caressing.[11]

This poem is in fact *ready made* or an *objet trouvé* in the manner of Marcel Duchamp. Armando annexes one of the Karl May westerns, boys' reading— he isolates a passage and presents that passage as a poem. This strategy breaks open the story line of the original fabula, and the violence it contains is thereby foregrounded. That gesture is necessary because storylines work like time. The progression of the fabula, of the story line, leads us away from the violence inherent in it by pushing us toward the ending (Brooks). This working method of disrupting the fabula allows Armando to bring to light its overgrown violence.

The agency of time in a story line is similar to that of context in space. Armando breaks through spatial context as well. Just as he breaks the story line in the "Karl May Cycle," he breaks up the context in the "agricultural cycle." He presents passages from the instructions that come with farm machines and makes poems out of them. The text ceases to serve the practical purpose it was written for in order to be presented as autonomous. Two examples from the cycle demonstrate this:

> 5
> the machine is equipped with 4 chopping boards
> the machine has 3 wheels with air tires
> the machine also operates with 3 groups of 2 boards
> the machine requires little maintenance
> the machine's operation is very clean

> 13
> the steel teeth
> do not damage the roots of the seedlings.

weeds are killed in the germ.
with steel teeth
the effect of "clean land" must be flabbergasting.[12]

This isolation and annexation policy has a strong effect: suddenly our attention is geared toward the values these texts propagate: the perfectly functioning, oiled system. The violence presupposed by such a system has been brought traumatically to light by Nazism; and perfectly oiled that system was.

Again the effect of these poems is produced indexically. Death is nowhere named, described, or rendered visible through comparisons. Like the footprint that refers to the presence of an animal or a human being, this isolated discourse refers to cold-blooded and perfectly organized murder. Because the death of "the war" was so traumatic that it could not be spoken, all Armando can do is show its traces. Such traces of a power that was also at the foundation of "the war" can be found in language. This does not mean there is similarity between language and war, but it means one can trace "the war" in language.

Traces can also signify negatively, referring to what they are not. In *Aantekeningen over de vijand (Notes about the Enemy)* (1981) Armando wrote: "The "neckshot." Strange you have never heard of that. Neckshot: the word is telling. You really never heard of it? Never mind. Odd word, anyway, don't you think: *neckshot*. Oh yeah" (25). The following example does not quite come across in translation. The word isolated here, *boekstaven*, means "to record," "to register," but it can be broken down into the nouns *boek* (book) and *staven* (club), used by the military police to thrash people in mobs. "By all means let's 'record' it. He said: 'record.' Again such a word, do watch out" (70).[13] In these brief passages Armando isolates single words. Those come ready made too. Precisely because these words lack the context of a sentence or a narrative, because they are surrounded by silence, they enigmatically refer to a situation of violence. The silence or emptiness that surrounds the word is indispensable: that is where the violence occurs, to which the word refers by contiguity:

*June 22*
Oh, the cries of a bird!
I listen to the bird. It talks
now this, now that.
Short phrases. Silence between
the phrases is always
of equal length. . . .
The animal is strong and firm,

thus I too must my own song
sing. Good example, the bird.[14]

Although the sounds the bird produces are not important in themselves because they are not clearly distinguished—it talks now this, now that—the silences in between are precisely defined: always of equal length. It seems as if the bird sings to produce the silence in which something can be heard. The song delimits the silences; the phrases are juxtaposed to them. That is how each phrase is an index for the silence that follows or precedes it. In that silence the unspeakable can be heard; only there can "the war" be memorized and remembered, because there are no words, no images, no similarities that can sustain symbolization, nor any memory in repetition.

Isolation is an indispensable tool to produce such meaningful silences based on indexicality. The *ready made,* the principle on which so many of Armando's early texts as well as his visual works of the Zero period are based, produces its specific meanings through isolation. In Krauss's words: "The ready-made's parallel with the photograph is established by its process of production. It's about the physical transposition of an object from the continuum of reality into the fixed condition of the art-image by a moment of isolation or selection" (206). The idea of isolation "from the continuum of reality" is acutely relevant for a better understanding of the nature of Armando's work. It helps us see the failure of many attempts to deal with this work, such as Nijs's summarizing Armando's method of isolation and annexation with the term "the montage principle" (8). The way montage produces meaning is exactly the opposite of what happens in Armando's work. Montage collates arbitrary elements into a new continuum. Armando, by contrast, breaks up an existing continuum and presents loose elements of it in isolation. He refuses, precisely, to create a reassuring new whole. Those very dimensions of our reality that appear to form a continuum are broken open by means of isolation: language, nature (its growth), and time. This oeuvre contains many reflections that explain his distrust of time.

*29 July*
Time pushed again.
How can I ever stand still?
*(Diary of a Perpetrator)*

*8 August*
Today a dismal awareness:
survivors grow older.
It is ever longer ago.

Centuries. And fellowman
knows but to linger and
forget.
    *Diary of a Perpetrator*[15]

The course of time leads us away from the traumatic moment for which no expression has yet been found. Also, the continuum of time suggests coherence, and hence meaningfulness. The experience of war, however, was so traumatic exactly because all coherence was destroyed by it and no coherence enables one to understand it, to give it meaning: "Look, coherence lacks, you see? And it has to be that way: for no coherence exists" *(Notes about the Enemy)*.[16] But the paradox is that without a form of coherence, no meaning production is possible. That is why Armando looks for semiotic salvation in the index, the ground to stand on where not coherence but coexistence is possible.

## Repetition against Narrativity

Armando also keeps at bay the comfort of a narrative continuum. His texts are strikingly antinarrative: there is never a sequence of events. Even his *The Street and the Shrubs* (1988), though clearly an autobiography, is antinarrative in structure. The short chapters that compose this work do follow each other in chronological order, presenting the life history of the narrator. But each chapter repeats the same themes: heroism, the fascination with violent death. Each moment of his prewar childhood is presented as a proleptic index that announces the war, and postwar moments are presented as analeptic indexes referring back. In Armando's autobiography the principle of *repetition* predominates, whereas the idea of succession and change is fought off as a semiotic enemy. The continuum of the narrative story is turned into a record that gets stuck.

In one of those little chapters Armando reflects on the working of memory. This reflection can also be taken as an explanation of his antinarrative stance. The narrative story is then an imagined memory of a sequence of events:

> You have the past, you have the present, and then there is also the future.
>
> That makes three.
>
> But there is a fourth: the past of the memory, of the imagination. And that is a different past. It has been colored in with the index, kneaded and bent, it has been displaced and shrunk, it has been crumpled, thick here, thin there, and people think that's how it should be.
>
> There is a question here of the unswerving desire for *the idyll*. (328)[17]

Just as memory turns the past into an idyll, so the classical story manipulates events. Classical narrative consists of the following sequence: a beginning—childhood, for example—a crisis, followed by a denouement, preferably a happy ending then a return to the idyll. And because we read for the ending (see Brooks), we overlook the crisis.

The British painter Francis Bacon appears to struggle in his paintings with the same kind of problem that preoccupies Armando in his visual and literary works: How can one represent events in a nonnarrative manner?[18] In the famous interviews with David Sylvester, Bacon explains why he objects to narrativity: "In the complicated stage in which painting is now, the moment there are several figures—at any rate several figures on the same canvas—the story begins to be elaborated. And the moment the story is elaborated, the boredom sets in; the story talks louder than the paint" (22). "I think that the moment a number of figures become involved, you immediately come on to the story-telling aspect of the relationships between figures. And that immediately sets up a kind of narrative. I always hope to be able to make a great number of figures without a narrative" (63). The final sentence especially renders succinctly the crucial feature of Armando's short narratives in his later literary work. His visual works go in a different direction, however. Even if some of his paintings, lithographs, or drawings contain figurative representations (flags, trees, Prussian crosses, heads, skulls) these do not so much represent events or situations, as in Bacon, but rather represent things, objects. As far as there is narrativity, it is not the representation or illustration of an event that produces it, but rather the tension triggered by the way the pencil or paintbrush has been handled.

This effect is most clearly visible in the drawings that are obviously abstract. Armando's drawings are never composed of smooth lines along which the spectator's eye can smoothly wander. Just as he avoids story lines in his narrative, he refuses smooth compositions in his images. His drawings are collections of dots or scratches: lines are not allowed to form a continuum. He says about his drawings of the fifties: "I can't deny it: this kind of drawings emerged out of hatred. . . . It was the continuation of a process. I once said to somebody: 'Such a drawing, a human being was murdered in it.' I have done away with quite a few people that way. And that is then art. It does have to do with a kind of hysteria. You have to gear yourself up quite a bit to make such a drawing. You can't do it every hour of the day. It is not a relaxed kind of drawing, it is very cramped and done with a lot of force, but not fast."[19] The lines in the drawings are deliberately cramped (figs. 4 and 5). One can read in them the traces of an obsessed hand.

Obsession also speaks in another aspect of Armando's visual art: repeti-

Figure 4. Armando, *Drawing*, 1982. 24 × 16 1/2 cm. Used by permission.

tion. The series of painted flags, trees, and edges of woods instill a desire for repetition rather than continuity, change, or innovation. Repetition is in charge of experiencing *for the first time* the traumatic event that could not be truly experienced because there was no language available to express it. The repetitions of black flags (fig. 6) or trees do not represent "the war" but cause it and thus, paradoxically, make it possible to experience it *as event* for the first time.[20] The combination of the uniqueness in repetition and the thematic centrality of nature achieves yet another dimension when considered within the framework of the sublime.

## The Sublime as Index

The relevance of the romantic concept of the sublime to Armando's work has already been argued by others.[21] In the mid-eighteenth century early romantics became fascinated with the boundless and unrestrained forces of

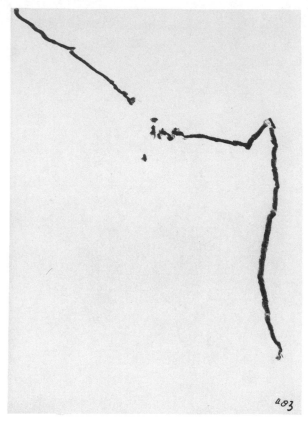

Figure 5. Armando, *Drawing*, 1983. Ver. 2, 18 × 13 cm. Helen van der Mey, London. Used by permission.

nature. Confronted with these, man[22] was only a puny little being. Man is attracted and repulsed by that nature because it can be neither controlled nor understood. That experience of ambivalence has been described by the term "the sublime." Perhaps the most famous example of this romantic sublime is in the paintings of Caspar Friedrich.[23] Friedrich shows "man" on mountain-tops, on the shore, in the forest, in all his smallness *over against* an endless, boundless, indomitable nature that exceeds all understanding. Another fa-mous example is in the paintings of J. M. W. Turner, representing great seas and cloudy skies that are usually characterized as "sublime." Turner represents the forces of nature as possessed by supernatural and inhuman forces.

Armando seems attracted by the paintings of the German romantics, in particular Friedrich's. The cover of *Diary of a Perpetrator* reproduces

Figure 6. Armando, *Fahne* (*Flags*), 1984. Paintings at the National Gallery, Berlin. Used by permission.

Friedrich's painting *Chasseur im Walde*, a meaningful choice. That appeal must not, however, be seen as an indication that Armando is trying to do the same thing they did. On the contrary; I contend that the concept of "the sublime" applies to Armando's work for an altogether different reason than holds for the German romantics. The romantics locate the sublime first of all within nature. Subsequently art must contend with nature—in other words, attempt to embody the quality of the sublime. Nature then stands for, to use the words of de Nijs, "timeless and endlessly innovating beauty" (19). According to de Nijs nature has the same meaning in Armando's work. In light of the analysis above this is hardly plausible. The role of nature is the opposite of the romantic one. Whereas there man was represented as a spectator on the border of, but still outside, sublime nature, in Armando's work nature itself is the spectator of something—something "sublime"—that has occurred in the presence of nature: the violent, evil death that war generates.

But how is it possible to call the violence of war, this evil, "sublime"? To answer this question Kant's *Critique of Judgement* provides the key. Kant makes his well-known distinction there between beauty and the sublime. These two qualities are each other's opposites. The opposition becomes meaningful when juxtaposed with the following oppositions: quality versus quantity, shaped versus shapeless, limited versus boundless. Whereas beauty calms, the sublime makes restless and excited. Beauty is an experience caused when a supersensuous Idea manifests itself harmoniously in a material form; the sublime, in contrast, is an experience caused by illimited, chaotic, and awe-inspiring phenomena like a furious sea or craggy mountains. Whereas beauty is a property of objects, the sublime must be located both in the object and in the subject: beauty is a property, whereas the sublime is an experience.

But for Kant the sublime is opposed to beauty first of all because the latter produces a pleasant feeling of well-being, whereas "the object is experienced with pleasure only when well-being is mediated by discomfort" (Kant 102). The paradox of the sublime can thus be seen as follows: In principle there is an unbridgeable gap between the empirical, phenomenologically experienced world of objects and the supersensuous Idea. No empirical object, no representation (*Vorstellung*), can adequately make present (*darstellen*) the Idea. The sublime is an object that triggers the experiencing of precisely this *impossibility*, the permanent failure of representation to render the true dimension of the Idea. It is by means of the very moments when the shortcomings of representation become clear that we get a sense, a proleptic indication, of the true dimension of the unspeakable, unrepresentable Idea. This also explains why the sublime triggers pleasure as well as discomfort. It triggers discomfort because it is a relentlessly inadequate representation of the Idea. But it triggers pleasure because that inadequacy is indexically a promise, a foreboding, of the true, incomparable greatness of the Idea. In Kant's words: "The feeling of the Sublime is therefore at once a feeling of displeasure, arising from the inadequacy of imagination in the aesthetic estimation of magnitude to attain to its estimation by reason, and a simultaneously awakened pleasure, arising from this very judgment of the inadequacy of the greatest faculty of sense being in accord with ideas of reason, so far as the effort to attain to these is for us a law" (106). Hence the sublime consists of the paradox produced by an object when, as a representation, it allows us negatively, through its failure as such, a glimpse of what cannot be represented. And this is precisely what the fragments of *Diary of a Perpetrator* (22 June) said about the song of a bird that delimits the silence between its sounds.

Kant's definition of the sublime is also the tersest characterization of Armando's imaginative commemoration of "the war." Each of the motifs that populate his works triggers experiences of the sublime. Although they explicitly fail as direct representations of "the war," that very failure provides a view of the unspeakable that is the trauma of war experience. Because it is consistently negatively indexical, his work can be sublime. It points out to us, time and again and by repetition, what it is that by definition cannot be represented because it was experienced as incomparable.

## Notes

1. "Toch beschrijft Armando nergens in zijn poëzie specifieke gebeurtenissen of een speciale plaats. Anekdotisch is zijn werk bepaald niet, eerder gaat het om een beeldend onderzoek van de abstracties oorlog en strijd, om verhoudingen tussen mensen. In wezen is de oorlog voor hem de metafoor van *la condition humaine,* en is Amersfoort als plek de metafoor van de wereld" (64).

2. The concept of experience needs some qualification here. Experience is a challenge to representation because it is utterly subjective, whereas representation is an attempt to make it intersubjectively accessible. See de Lauretis.

3. Thus, as I will demonstrate, he provides a solution to the dilemma of representing death in a way that complements that proposed by Rembrandt's paintings, as Mieke Bal argues.

4. "Ze groeien en zwijgen. Wat er ook gebeurt. Er is nogal wat gebeurd bij de bomen. Men besloop en beschoot, men ranselde en vernederde. Je zou dus kunnen zeggen dat de bomen medeplichtig zijn, zich schuldig gemaakt hebben. Maar nee: het zijn maar bomen. Die treft geen blaam. Een bosrand bijvoorbeeld. De voorste bomen moeten het een en ander gezien hebben. Die daarachter staan kun je nauwelijks iets kwalijk nemen, die hebben nooit iets kunnen zien. Maar de bosrand, de woudzoom, die heeft het gezien. Er zijn heel wat bosranden, her en der, van wie ik het een en ander weet" (*NRC-Handelsblad,* 3 May 1985).

5. "Kijk naar de afbeeldingen waarop de vijand doende is: daar staan ze op de achtergrond te lachen. En niet alleen de denne- en sparrebomen, de andere bomen ook.

Moet daar niet es iets van gezegd worden?

Ik dacht van wel, want ze staan er soms nog, de bomen, de bosrand en het geboomte, op dezelfde plek waar ze destijds ook stonden, je moet er niet aan denken dat ze verderop zijn gaan staan, ze staan er nog steeds als onverschillige getuigen" (*De straat en het struikgewas* 245–46).

6. "Eindelijk kwam de tijd dat de bomen konden vertellen over vroeger. Hoe bewonderenswaardig. Hoe edelmoedig. Maar ze verbloemden veel, zo niet alles" (*De straat en het struikgewas* 118–19).

7. "*16 augustus*
Dit landschap heeft kwaad gedaan. Ik kan de legers vermoeden. Het is hier vredig, maar opgepast. Stilte komt soms na lawaai: hier was pijn, hier ranselde de medemens. De tijd heeft schuld, alles groeit weer, maar denken wordt vergeten. Verraad! Dit slagveld blijft mijn eigendom, al leef ik nog zo erg.

*2 september*
De Natuur hceft het wel verbruid. Eerst was Zij laf, toen liet Zij mij aanhoudend in de steek. En laten de bomen zich niet eeuwig duwen door de wind, zonder noemenswaard verzet? . . . En de Bodem. De Bodem leent zich voor de val der helden. Plekken dulden eerst, begroeien later. O, de plek zal wel begroeid zijn. Ja, plekken zijn altijd begroeid."

8. "Het zijn Duitse kaarten, Voorwerpen waar de geschiedenis overheen is gegaan. Resten. Zeer tastbare resten van het verleden, met sporen van mensen erop. Ik heb thuis een kaart van een soldaat in uniform uit de eerste wereldoorlog, waar sporen van potlood opzitten. Ik heb er nog steeds niets mee gedaan. . . . De tekeningen met ansichtkaarten, die zijn voor mij de totale melancholie. . . . de mensen die zo'n kaart in handen hebben gehad en hebben beschreven zijn dood" (Sanders 12).

9. "Niet de Realiteit be-moraliseren of interpreteren (ver-kunsten), maar intensiveren. Uitgangspunt: een konsekwent aanvaarden van de Realiteit. Interesse voor een meer autonoom optreden van de Realiteit, al op te merken in de journalistiek, tv-reportages en film. Werkmethode: isoleren, annexeren. Dus: authenticiteit. Niet van de maker, maar van de informatie. De kunstenaar, die geen kunstenaar meer is: een koel zakelijk oog" (1964; reprinted in *De nieuwe stijl, 1959–1966*).

10. "Ik heb de oorlog zo gehaat dat ik me er mee ben gaan identificeren. Ik ben de oorlog zelf geworden" (Van Garrel, "Een dagje met Armando," *NRC,* 17 April 1971).

11. Hij had bloed gespuwd en twee tanden verloren,
wel een bewijs
dat zijn kolfslag niet bepaald een liefkozing geweest was."

*(Gard Sivik* 33)

12. "5
de machine is uitgerust met 4 hakborden
de machine heeft 3 luchtbandwielen
de machine werkt ook met 3 groepen van 2 borden

de machine vraagt weinig onderhoud
de machine werkt zeer schoon

13
met stalen tanden
de wortels van het gezaaide gewas worden niet beschadigd.
het onkruid wordt in de kiem gedood.
met stalen tanden

het effect 'schoon land' moet verbluffend zijn."

(1965; reprinted in *De nieuwe stijl, 1959–1966,* no. 1)

13. "Het zgn. 'nekschot.' Dat je daar nooit van gehoord hebt. Nekschot: het woord zegt het al. Heb je daar echt nooit van gehoord? Geeft niet, hoor. Gek woord

evengoed, hè: *nekschot*. Jaja" (25). "Laten we het vooral 'boekstaven.' Hij zei: 'boekstaven.' Alweer zo'n woord pas toch op" (70).

14. "*22 juni* O, het geroep van een vogel! Ik luister naar de vogel. Hij praat nu eens dit, dan weer dat. Korte gezegdes. Stilte tussen de gezegdes is steeds van lengte gelijk. . . . Het dier is sterk en wilskrachtig, zo moet ook ik een eigen lied zingen. Goed voorbeeld, de vogel" (*Dagboek van een dader*).

15. "*29 juli* / De tijd heeft weer geduwd. / Hoe kom ik ooit tot staan?" (*Dagboek van een dader*). "*8 augustus* / Heden een akelig besef: / overlevenden worden ouder. / Het is steeds langer geleden. / Wel eeuwen. En de medemens / weet slechts van talmen en / vergeten" (*Dagboek van een dader*).

16. "Kijk, de samenhang ontbreekt, begrijp je? En dat moet ook: er bestaat namelijk geen samenhang" (*Aantekeningen over de vijand* 128).

17. "Je hebt het verleden, je hebt het heden en dan is er ook nog de toekomst. Dat zijn er drie.

Maar er is nog een vierde: het verleden van de herinnering, van de verbeelding. En dat is een ander verleden. Het is met de wijsvinger ingekleurd, het is gekneed en verbogen, het is verschoven en gekrompen, het is verfomfaaid, hier dik en daar dun geworden en men denkt dat het zo hoort.

Hier is sprake van een onwrikbaar verlangen naar *de idylle*" (238).

18. For a detailed analysis of the paradoxical narrativity of Bacon's paintings, see van Alphen (1992).

19. "Ik kan er niet omheen: dit soort tekeningen is uit haat ontstaan. . . . Het was het voortzetten van een proces. Ik heb ooit eens tegen iemand gezegd: 'zo'n tekening, daar werd een mens in vermoord.' Ik heb op die manier heel wat mensen te pakken gehad. En dat is dan kunst. Het heeft wel degelijk ook met een soort hysterie te maken. Je moet jezelf ontzettend opladen om zo'n tekening te kunnen maken. Dat kun je niet elk uur van de dag. Het is geen ontspannen tekenen, het is heel verkrampt en met heel veel kracht gedaan, maar niet snel" (Sanders 9).

20. This crucial dialectic of trauma is brilliantly analyzed by Shoshana Felman and Dori Laub.

21. See Gribling and de Nijs.

22. The romantic sublime has been discussed exclusively by men and sometimes in strikingly masculine terms. My use of generic/male language in this section is therefore deliberate.

23. A seminal study of Friedrich's work is Koerner.

## Works Cited

Alphen, Ernst van. *Francis Bacon and the Loss of Self*. Cambridge: Harvard UP, 1993.

———. "The Narrative of Perception and the Perception of Narrative." *Poetics Today* 11.3 (1990): 483–510.

Armando. *Aantekeningen over de vijand*. Amsterdam: De Bezige Bij, 1980.

———. "De agrarische cyclus." *De nieuwe stijl: Werk van de Internationale*

*Avantgarde*. Amsterdam: Literaire Reuzenpocket, 1965. Rpt. in *De nieuwe stijl, 1959–1966*. Amsterdam 1989: De Bezige Bij, 1989. 33–36.

———. *Dagboek van een dader*. Leiden: Tango, 1973.

———. "Karl-May-cyclus." *Gard Sivik* 33 (1964). N.p.

———. *De straat en het struikgewas*. Amsterdam: De Bezige Bij, 1988.

Bal, Mieke. *Reading "Rembrandt" : Beyond the Word-Image Opposition*. New York: Cambridge UP, 1991.

Barthes, Roland. *Camera Lucida: Reflections on Photography*. Trans. Richard Howard. London: Jonathan Cape, 1982.

Brooks, Peter. *Reading for the Plot: Design and Intention in Narrative*. New York: Knopf, 1984.

Felman, Shoshana, and Dori Laub. *Testimony: Crises of Witnessing in Literature, Psychoanalysis, and History*. New York: Routledge, 1992.

Fokkema, R. L. K. "De dichter als nuchter romanticus." *Armando, schilder-schrijver*. Weesp: De Haan. 63–67.

Gribling, Frank. "Armando en de romantische traditie." *Armando, schilder-schrijver*. Weesp: De Haan. 49–61.

Kant, Immanuel. *Critique of Judgement*. Oxford: Oxford UP, 1964.

Koerner, Joseph Leo. *Caspar David Friedrich and the Subject of Landscape*. London: Reaktion Books, 1990.

Krauss, Rosalind. "Notes on the Index: Part 1" and "Notes on the Index: Part 2." *The Originality of the Avant-Garde and Other Modernist Myths*. Cambridge: MIT Press. 196–209 and 210–20.

Lauretis, Teresa de. *Alice Doesn't: Feminism, Semiotics, Cinema*. Bloomington: Indiana UP, 1983.

Lotman, Juri. *The Structure of the Artistic Text*. 1970. Ann Arbor: U of Michigan P, 1977.

Nijs, Pieter de. "Ik heb iets vreselijks gezien: De stoere gevoeligheid van Armando." *Bulletin* 173 (1990): 8–20.

Sanders, Martijn. "De galm van het verleden: Martijn Sanders in gesprek met Armando." *Armando: 100 tekeningen, 1952–1984*. Rotterdam: Museum Boymans van Beuningen, 1985.

Sylvester, David. *Interviews with Francis Bacon*. 1975. London: Thames and Hudson, 1985.

Zizek, Slavoj. *The Sublime Object of Ideology*. New York: Verso, 1989.

■

# A Valediction For Bidding Mourning: Death and the Narratee in Brontë's *Villette*

## *Garrett Stewart*

### I

Death marks the impossible limit of representation, while at the same time death is an inevitability of representation. This paradox is fashioned on two distinct if not discrepant models, mimetic and discursive—or narrational and textual. For one thing, for narrative agents death arrives at the very moment when there is nothing left to tell about them. For another, death as absence, the inoperable because voided referent in story, is the arguable effect of all reference. Together, then, death stands as the always inherent *end* of representation. Hence we have the two tropes of closure—death as the closing down of a plot line and the closing out of the world—that have repeatedly lent their metaphoric if not explanatory power to narratology and deconstruction, respectively. On such accounts, death recurs as a figure for plot's terminal intentions, on the one hand, and for writing's epitaphic status on the other—the text now as narrative telos, now as sheer inscription.

Concerning the Victorian period in particular, much has been said about the fetishistic interest in death pervading literary culture, as both a test of secular value and a mutated form of erotic energy, and more generally about the Victorian novel's motives for closure in relation both to death and to its obverse stasis in an equilibrating marriage.[1] In both cases, the evoked psychology and the formal logic of death are further highlighted by the fictive structure of retrospect in the first-person *Bildungsroman* so prominent in the Victorian canon—the subgenre where death as the cancellation of the protagonist's story could only be simultaneous with death as the incapacitation of discourse, and yet, short of this, where the relation of retrospect to epitaph, of memory to mourning, is continuously manifest from page to page. This relation is all the more apparent, of course, when what is chronicled by those pages not only includes an actual scene of death—the death of the Other—but locates it as a closural moment in the unfolding narrative. Moreover, the first-person treatment of a climactic third-person death may highlight the intersection of narrational with textual models in another way as well: by deploying the rhetoric of narration to cue, anticipate, or foreclose the final responses of its readers. It is in this sense, then, that death further offers itself as a touchstone for the phenomenological account of reading as well as for the narratological and deconstructive approaches—and never more openly in Victorian fiction than in Charlotte Brontë's first-person retrospect, *Villette* (1853), arguably the period's most baroque experiment in reader address and certainly its most notorious flouting of the conventional death scene.

Building on the reader apostrophes of *Jane Eyre*,[2] as before it of Thackeray's *Vanity Fair* (to whose author *Jane Eyre* was dedicated), *Villette* moves to conclusion by backing the reader into a corner at precisely the elided moment of the hero's drowning. His is a death not only left entirely to our own reactions in the absence of elegiac gestures on the part of the heroine as narrator, but left up to us as narrative event itself in the first place—ours to activate, to believe in, if we choose. As such, this closural contortion is the last of many vertiginous indignities to which the audience of Brontë's novel has been submitted en route. Even more egregiously tweaked than in Thackeray, the reader has been by turns nudged and needled, cheated, rebuked, second-guessed, and all the while coerced—until finally, it might appear, suddenly abdicated to—as if we could secure the novel's closure according to our own preferences. We seem invited by the narrator, that is, to "pause" on the verge of the hero's inevitable fatality while narrative averts its gaze, suppressing any explicit mention of the death, ceding instead to a populace of optimists. The reader is, however, more cornered here than capitulated to, I suggest, because despite the rhetoric of avoidance, we have no real choice. There is no textually sanctioned option but to recognize the death in its full inevitability, and hence to begin interpreting it not only as an unwelcome fact but as a figure for distance, loss, desire—you name it.

By exactly what phenomenological relation of reader to text, brought about by exactly what linguistic instruments of direct address, is yet another Victorian death scene, as closural trope, thus *addressed* in both senses by *Villette,* conveyed *to,* directed even without being rendered—in short, inscribed for interpretation in the very absence of narrative? This *kind* of question, *Villette* or any other single text aside, is an important one for as long as we hope not to put questions of textuality itself entirely to the side. Without monitoring prose fiction as both structuring activity and rhetorical act at once, the considerable gains of narrative theory stand little chance of being matched, at the receiving end of the textual system, by a full-scale poetics of reception. What is required is an account of textually cued response supple enough to engage, at the level of language itself, with the recent interest, for example, in the Victorian novel either as a commodity form in the marketplace of consumable properties or, more broadly, as a narrative machine for indoctrinating the Victorian readership into an ideological economy both instanced and sustained by such merchandizing of fantasy.[3] This is where the most sophisticated elaborations of narrative theory as an account of the working of story—an interception of story at precisely its point of engagement with the culture out of which it comes and to which, as text, it is returned—risk being dissolved into a leveling cultural critique that recognizes narrative everywhere, from historical pageants to dioramas to circus sideshows, but sees nowhere in detail the formal pressures, and *demands,* of its specifically literary manifestations. Quite specifically, *Villette's* strategic deployment of closural death occasions the exaggerated recognition of a third textual aspect of Victorian fiction beyond told story and the devices of its telling. Triangulated with the plotting studied by narratology and the sheer figurality of writing pursued by deconstruction, and again thrown into relief around the narrative vacuum of death, this third aspect is that of the text as circuit: not the *book* in commercial circulation (or ideological dissemination), but rather the *text* in closed rhetorical address to a reader whose responses— a case less exceptional that it might seem—are themselves textualized.

## II

Having had the grace to rescue Rochester from Bertha's flames, thus ending on a note of emotional restoration and marital union, Charlotte Brontë is urged by her father, no less, to be equally sparing with the heroine's fiancé at the end of *Villette,* urged to bring him back alive from his sea journey in order to consummate the marriage with Lucy Snowe.[4] Readers will demand it, she is assured. Having planned her story otherwise, however, and confident in its inevitability, Brontë undertakes no narrative revisions, only discursive ones. She thus complies with the plea not to make the hero drown simply by not saying so in so many words, putting it—to use a contemporary formulation—under erasure, the death as unmistakable as it is unmentioned. The effect is to leave not only M. Paul Emanuel but the reader, too, quite at sea. One of the trademarks, indeed mainstays, of Victorian fiction—the ritualized death scene—is thus turned inside out, so that plot is made a function of reader response rather than the other way around.[5] Beyond this unabashedly Victorian "anti-Victorian" sleight of hand with the sentimental investments of fiction reading, Brontë has also, as we will be exploring, stage managed the hero's death in the wings so that its inference becomes a reenactment, in extremis, of the narrative act itself: a structuring of response even in the absence of event.

From the jarring intersection of death, address, and premature closure in *Villette,* any reader is likely to be thrown back into the text with a jolt of recognition. No one can come upon the elusive play with the reader at the close, a play around which the whole (null) possibility of a happy ending turns, and not be disposed to recall the earlier and equally blatant moment when the reader's expectations are discomfited in connection with an unwritten death "scene," another textual locus of death without a delineated narrative site. Quitting her godmother's comfortable home at Bretton, Lucy Snowe is returned to "the bosom of my kindred" at the opening of the fourth chapter after a happy separation of only six months, to remain there, through unspecified tragedy (as we later barely find out), for eight years. "It will be conjectured that I was of course glad to return. . . . Well! the amiable conjecture does no harm, and may therefore be safely left uncontradicted. Far from saying nay, indeed, I will permit the reader to picture me, for the next eight years, as a bark slumbering through halcyon weather, in a harbour still as glass" (4: 94).[6] Thus begins an extended conceit ascribed to the reader's own well-wishing, a conceit spun out, attenuated, to the point of cultural cliché: "A great many women and girls are supposed to pass their lives something in that fashion; why not I with the rest?" Following immediately upon this rhetorical question, there is a more active engagement of second person in an imperative grammar of invoked narrative participation: "Picture me then idle, basking, plump, and happy, stretched on a cushioned deck, warmed with constant sunshine," and so on. Even on the terms of this protracted allegory of languor, "in that case, I must have fallen overboard, or there must have been a wreck at last," for "I too well remember a time— a long time, of cold, of danger, of contention" (4: 94).

The lulling metaphor of a torpid harborage, as if forced upon her by the reader, has been converted into the scenario of recurrent dream trauma: "To this hour, when I have the nightmare, it repeats the rush and saltiness of briny waves in my throat, and their icy pressure on my lungs" (4: 94). At "this" very hour, that is, of Lucy's retrospect years later—indeed in the very form of that retrospect as we have it before us—the nightmare of deprivation is precipitated once more in the form of the return of the repressed, memory traces successfully masked by metaphor even in this present rendition of them. Indeed, if "the nightmare" always takes this same form, of emotional turmoil and death figured as drowning, then we have all the more reason to understand the bizarre subjective status of M. Emanuel's closural death as a scene that "repeats" the originary trauma of violent breach, a watery expulsion from womblike stasis that is both birth and orphaning together, a fall into mortality. "For many days and nights . . . a heavy tempest lay on us," she nears the climactic moment of this early tragedy by recalling. "In fine, the ship was lost, the crew perished" (4: 94). When another ship is later lost at sea, "in fine" and in "Finis" (the last chapter, by that name), the hope of a husband and family sunk with it, the nightmare has come again in "this hour" of autobiographical closure.

The deflected retrospect of Lucy's eight-year ordeal, displaced as in dreamwork by figural substitution, is concluded by the memory that "I complained to no one about these troubles. Indeed, to whom could I complain?" (4: 94). This lack of community, of potentially therapeutic response, is one for which only the novelized retrospect itself, as a structure of address, finally compensates. But this happens only if we register the speaker's complaints, her muted lamentations, in defiance of the metaphoric sop (think of me this way if you like!)—or later the flat avoidance ("Here pause" so that we don't need to agree that he died!)—offered to soften these early and late passages of shipwreck and drowning. Reading right, that is, we offer the narrator, perforce, the succor of a hearing, confessional purgative.[7] Such is the tacit contractual exchange that can be played out only at the conclusion of the novel, by which point the reader has been many times invoked and jostled, hailed, dodged, enlisted, and rebuffed, at one moment even told to "cancel the whole" of a passage and rewrite it in "alternate text-hand copy" (6: 117–18). Across this web of vocative feints, evasions, and prevarications, the inscription of the reader as inscriber is a device climaxed in the "addressed" and voluntarily received death at the close, exposing as it does the deepest structure of narrative discourse as a circuitry of constituent absence and structuring summons.

## III

It is just here that two underused, almost monstrously compact essays by Julia Kristeva can be made to illuminate the connection between directed fictional discourse and the death with which such discourse must always be on strictly formal terms.[8] More comprehensively than any I know, these essays account for the rise of the novel as a *simultaneous* bracketing of exactly those paired antinomies that organize such a Victorian text as *Villette:*

life and death, narrator and narratee. As a postmedieval landmark in the transition from the culture of the symbol to the culture of the sign, from meanings full and resonant in words to meaning relative and differential, the inauguration of the novel out of the declining epic tradition is, according to Kristeva, uniquely revealing—in precisely its ideological resistance to the full operation of the sign function. The novel's differential operations house a nostalgia for the epic dispensation, monologic and absolute, which is why the novel resists the full dialogizing of the sign through gradation and ambivalence, a blurring of oppositions that holds open the possibility of synthesis. The novel is thus an artifically "bounded" text achieving closure, totality, only by subordinating the unrestrained logical implications of its own "significance," its network of signifiers, to a "meaning" wrung from them at the expense of their full interplay. To demonstrate this in its broadest terms, Kristeva begins her analysis with that most privileged of dualisms in novelistic structure, death against life. On Kristeva's showing, the novel has a unique way of handling this binarity: "Life is opposed to death in an absolute way (as is love to hate, virtue to vice, good to bad, being to nothingness)" without (in Western culture) that full complementarity that might imply "totality" (47), as for instance in Hindu religion. This is because life and death are posed against each other by a logic of "nonalternating opposition" rather than as functional equivalents in a framework of true paradigmatic alternatives. Life and death are *novelized,* one might say (gloss-ing the unexemplified density of Kristeva's assertions at this point), by being dislodged from the paradigm in order to be deployed along the syntagmatic axis, a vertical alternative between life and its negation plotted instead, horizontally, as a space of time *between.*

Concerning the life/death dualism, or any other grounding thematic oppo-sition, as it is made part of a "discursive trajectory" (47), and drawing implicitly on distinctions worked out by A. J. Greimas during the same period,[9] Kristeva suggests that the process of novelizing thematic content depends first of all on the "doubly negative movement that reduces the *difference* between two terms to a radical *disjunction* with permutation of those terms; that is, to an empty space around which they move, dying out as entities and turning into an alternating rhythm" (47). It is in this way that the novel "splits the movement of *radical negation* into two phases, disjunction and nondisjunction" (47), compromising the initial polarity by ramification. To exemplify the logic that undergirds her argument, we can say that the novel avoids the radical paradigmatic alternatives of life/death by resorting to the less mutually exclusive oppositions of life-and-death or life versus death—or, to render the poles in their minimal semic interdependence, life versus non-life. A Greimassian diagram (as in fig. 1 below) might help to clarify at this point what Kristeva seems to imply by the "split negation" required by novelistic plotting. Each half of the original dyad can be found to generate its own opposition in the disjunctive (diagonal) poles (or outright contradictions) of not-life and not-death (or not-non-life), producing in turn the less disjunctive relation between this subsidiary dyad (in what Greimas calls the axis of "subcontraries"). Beginning with the absolute antithesis of life/death would leave the novel nowhere to go. It must activate the difference as an interval, must in other words deploy narrative spacing as duration. Novelizing such a founding synchronic antithesis as life/death produces, as it were, a gray area at what Kristeva calls the "secondary level" (47) or "second stage" (48), a realm of diachronic ambiguity that generates "first of all *time:* temporality (history) is the *spacing* of this splitting negation" (47). This is a stage of admixture, transformation, *change,* all with a teleology mirrored in the potential resolution of the first-level opposition. "Rendering negation ambiguous brings about, in the same way, a finality, a theological principle (God, 'meaning')," in other words a closural logic that " 'forgets' opposition in the same way that the opposition did not 'assume' unification" (48).

Kristeva's intriguing test case for the inauguration of the novelistic enterprise is a fifteenth-century biographical fiction, a narrative couched explicitly as a letter and thus installing the "message-addressee" system coterminously with the "thematic (life-death) closure (loop)" (44). Through (*a*) the "naïveté" of its letter format and (*b*) the double foregrounding of death as literary closure, both by mentioning the hero's demise at the start and by coming round to it as already written (both cited in Latin on a tombstone and translated into French), Antoine de la Sale's Ur-novel, which can only "play itself out by rebuilding the distance between life and death" (42), elucidates the conjoint structure of the novelistic operation both as narrative and as discourse. In the process, this early narrative evinces a formal candor in the "message-addressee" construct that would later be "occluded" by the "bourgeois social text," whose impersonal omniscience, for instance, never approaches that condition of the modern "polylogue" in which "the one who writes is the same as the one who reads" (86–87). Nor of course does any Victorian novel, and yet the narratee in a text like *Villette* is prone to co-optation by the writing agency at any turn, liable indeed to some rather extreme con-scriptions. Granted that *Jane Eyre*'s famous appeal to a communal reception ("Reader, I married him") may well not escape the Victorian monological stranglehold, since the reader there is reduced essentially to a rhetorical prop, a mere signifier of the emphatic. May it not still be the case, though, that

*Villette's* incorrigible playing upon the register of reception does at least render dubiously interdependent "the one who writes" with "the one who reads," especially at the crux—the intersection and crisis—where they are both brought up short by the drawing taut of the "thematic loop" in closural death? In pressing this question to any depth, we must first turn to the narrative pressures and tensions—the oppositional force fields—that keep this loop from even more premature collapse. We must turn, in a word, to plot.

## IV

Following up to a point Jameson's application of Greimas's logic of opposition to the plotting of nineteenth-century fiction—as that logic registers the ideological coordinates by which the parameters of meaning are squared (with each other) as a closed system, a closed question—I will want eventually to suggest how the closure toward which Jameson sees all bourgeois narrative straining cannot be fully achieved, or in turn apprehended, without recourse to the discursive as well as the narrative "loop." But first a detailed examination of the narrative itself, as the plotting out (and so working out) of oppositional thematic tensions, will bring Kristeva's semiotics together with Jameson's Greimassian narratology in order to map that "schema" of opposition between life and death that will eventually, in *Villette,* be transferred onto the circuit of reception as a *reading effect.* The psychological and symbolic possibilities of such an exhaustive oppositional scheme are immediately apparent. Out of polarity, multiplicity; out of negation, propagation, both of character and incident; out of distinction, the very breakdown—in both senses, analytic and thematic—of difference. Establishing our point of departure as "polysemically" as possible[10]—in order to substitute for the mere biological definition of the seme "life" a fuller connotative range in the Brontë canon—we may call up Jane Eyre's early craving phrase, "other and more *vivid* kinds of goodness" (chap. 12), with a special stress on the etymological overtones of life as vividness. (It is, after all, on a ship named *The Vivid* that Lucy Snowe crosses in the sixth chapter from London toward that Continental destination that, though autobiographically Brussels, is here called Villette.) With living, including making a living, understood in *Villette* as a sphere of energy and emotional intensity, death is tacitly situated by opposition not just as nescience but as erotic nullification, the abrogation of ambition, of drive itself. In full negating opposition to the initial seme (S) of life as energy and momentum, a telos of fulfillment, an invigoration—whose simple, we might say passive, contrary is non-life, or in other words "death" $(-S)$—stands the contradictory term of "not-life" as an active denial or repression ($\bar{S}$), or in other words all those forces massed in the realm of "antilife" (see fig. 1). This contradiction of the first seme finds in turn its subcontrary, as well as providing simultaneously the contradiction of death (or non-life), in the negation of a negation ($-\bar{S}$), Jameson's favored, problematic, often indeterminate "fourth term": here the "not-non-life" of nonneutralized eros, or in other words desire itself, need as lack, a chief attribute of life under the aspect of longing-toward-fulfillment—in other words, a pole that contradicts death and, in the quadrilateral's own terms, is very much on the side of life. What we have sketched is therefore the exhaustive logical foundation upon which some more intuitive ratio and proportion might have been tacitly mounted, as if one were to say of the thematic structure in *Villette:* desire is to repression as life is to death.

The psychology of character that would lend weight—lend local habitation and a name—to such a proposition, such a thematic ratio, is in this mode of analysis not presumed but rather produced. Upon a grid of the kind just generated, Jameson, following Greimas, typically finds a text anthropomorphizing the positions defined by the spaces between the four poles. Between life and not-death in *Villette,* for instance, would lie the zone of energy occupied initially by the independence and vitality of Dr. John, by whom Lucy is first smitten, as well as by the intensity of Paul Emanuel later. This is exactly the locus of self-determination finally achieved by Lucy herself, who begins her plot in the adjacent bottom quadrant, trapped in a double bind between desire and denial, the realm of neither death nor life—a realm where she is "doubled" by the supposed ghostly nun who haunts her solitude (and yet who is only a young male interloper in transvestite disguise, sneaking after hours into the girls' school where Lucy has been hired as instructor). In this protracted space of blocked vivification through celibate denial (and symbolic projection), Lucy under the sign (the stigmata) of ghostly apparition borders on that right quadrant defined by the wholly negating axis between "non-life" and "not-life." It is a position not only taken up by the unnamed deaths suppressed in the narrative's early eight-year lacuna, as we have seen, but taken up by Miss Marchmont as well in the episode immediately following: Lucy's first true mentor in life looked back upon, the spinster whose lover died just before their marriage and who dies herself with only his memory on her lips.

In any move to establish a position diametrically opposed to this dead end of abject finality, Lucy Snowe must pass through—and so overcome—the domain of her own double, the figure of the ghostly nun, who stands for the simultaneous neutralization of both death and life and who, though no longer alive, refuses to die. In doing so, the heroine must occupy in transit exactly this semiotic scandal—for Kristeva, the quintessential novelistic "doubleness" or ambivalence—of the living dead. In gothic terms (terms explained away by the final revelation that spectral celibacy was only scheming desire, the young suitor de Hamal, in disguise), this melodramatic emanation of the ghostly nun encodes the idea not so much of an undead desire as of a desire not to die, a will to a life defined only negatively as the absence—the infinite deferral—of death. The "character" of the nun thus crystallizes the full novelistic "polysemy" of oppositional determination, for the composite negativity of her sexual denial and her ghostliness is materialized as reciprocal figurations of a fissured living/deadness that in turn splits—and so drives—the figuration of Lucy herself as "character."

It is Kristeva's argument that any attempted synthesis of antinomies at this stage—in Lucy's case, let us say, of lack and denial in some Victorian idealization of self-moderation, restraint, and forbearance—must reflect a reconciliation of opposites at the primary level. In the present grid, this would imply, though by no means telling us where to look for it, some improbable fusion between intensity and effacement, between the "vividly good" and the insentient, between, in short, the quick and the dead. Just as for Kristeva this ultimate resolution seeks its sanctions in the realm of theology (or transcendent "meaning"), so for Jameson it is this open-ended "complex term" that more than any other reveals the self-blinded ideological horizon of the novel. But so much of the story in *Villette* lies suspended in its closure that this complex site is especially hard to name. The stasis of the happily ever after is blocked by the inescapably conveyed but entirely unwritten death of the heroine's lover, so that no reunion scene can arrive to reunify the plot's lines of tension. Nor can this Victorian plot find resolution in that conjugal transcendence of death figured by familial (re)generation, for there are no children. These blocked syntheses therefore prevent the expected death of the heroine precisely in terms of her potential for movement from the neutral term—neither life nor death, pining but denied—toward the axis joining desire to the vividness of fulfillment.

Indeed it is the most blatant structural irony of this novel, immediately apparent from figure 1, that no sooner has Lucy Snowe extricated herself from death-in-life, to join Paul Emanuel in the realm of a passional animation that stands clearly opposed to insentience, than he is removed by fatal accident to a zone of memory (and representation) where the only vitality he has left, as remembered, can be at one only with death. In this most Victorian of structural totalities, closural death in its elegiac aspect thus provides the metaphysical counterpart to the text's earlier flirtation with the gothic and the uncanny. Even as the character functions, or actants, emerge in the

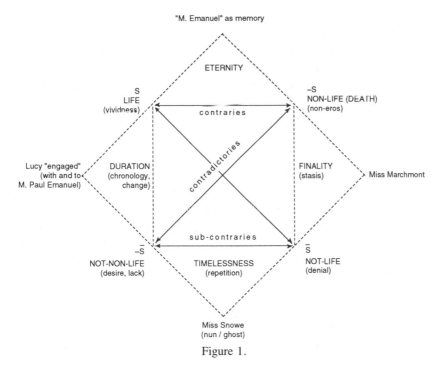

Figure 1.

counterpull of terms along the fourfold axes, so too the resulting quadrants serve at the same time to coordinate the narrative (rather than charactcrological) aspects of duration versus finality, on the one hand, and, on the other, timelessness (ghostly hauntings, traumatic returns) versus the transcendence of time into an eternity without closure. This last is a leap beyond the end-stopping of plot made possible *as text,* we are to think, only at, and on the condition of, an inscription of reading itself into the linguistic machinations of closure. Toward that closure—in its arresting dependency on "Absence" as the last (and least fully subjective) of those personifications by which the narrating "I" has conjured and projected not only an image of her "self" but of her reader reading—we now retrace the often-addressed stages of our second-person progress. That this should in fact necessitate at least a little sustained *reading* is a large part of my point.

## V

In the constitution of character through written retrospect, the activity of discourse in *Villette* (Kristeva's "compositional loop") stands in a curious—and typifying—relation to narrative. That is, the inert idioms and dead metaphors deployed in the enunciation of the self's remembered adventures become the breeding ground of personification or prosopopoeia, even apostrophe: the self's advent as the site of sheer internal figuration. Early on, for instance, Lucy recognizes that "self-reliance and exertion were forced upon me by circumstances" (4: 95). In its passive transform of such an equally idiomatic phrasing as "forced themselves upon me," the description as written barely glimpses the full psychodramatic subplot, in which Will and Exertion occupy the same ontological plane as the "me." A few pages later, again in the passive voice: "A bold thought was sent to my mind; my mind was made strong to receive it" (5: 104). Within two pages, however, this dead metaphorical play of abstractions has been galvanized into allegorical life. Ex nihilo, there appears in the plot a female character who, having "asked the waiter for a room," then "timorously called for the chambermaid" (5: 106). Unless we are reading very attentively, we may well miss the antecedent of this feminine pronoun, lodged as it is in the dead metaphor of "into the hands of" in the opening of this paragraph: "Into the hands of Commonsense I confided the matter." From there, the reification of a psychic attribute takes over in a circumscribed allegory: "Common-sense, however, was as chilled and bewildered as all my other faculties, and it was only under the spur of an inexorable necessity that she spasmodically executed her trust." She thus becomes the first of countless personifications by which various impulses, pitted against circumstance, generate subsidiary personae to do the bidding, or foil the purposes, of a central "self"—a presumed identity emerging as an abstraction in its own right, one that can be materialized only in this traced crossfire of its own displaced and delegated energies.[11] Indeed, this very process is figured at one point as the pressure behind writing itself as objectified desire; beyond providing a local image for the urge to compose a letter (to Lucy's first infatuation, Dr. John), personification is implicated here in the condition of writing per se, its need to figure the enunciating subject as embodied self: "Feeling and I turned Reason out of doors, drew against her bar and bolt, then we sat down, spread our paper, dipped in the ink an eager pen"—and wrote (23: 335). This is a composition that posits a signified (but undefined) self hovering somewhere between the signifying "I" and the simultaneously incarnate but disembodied antinomies of rationality and desire.

Then, too, writing means reading, often indeed *signifies* reading. It is no accident that the original reification of Common Sense as a momentary alter ego of the heroine, the most flamboyant personification so far in the novel, is offered, instead of a pictorial treatment of the scene, on the presumption of the reader's behest: "My reader, I know, is one who would not thank me for an elaborate reproduction of poetic first impressions" (5: 105–6). We therefore leave behind any visualizable London scene for an inward turn of the narrator's consciousness under duress, besieged by contradictory forces struggling for ascendency in the *act*. The one-way "dialogic" incorporation of a participatory reader only serves further to situate—by replaying—the inner distance of "self" from the various avatars of its faculties, or sometimes to situate the self in view of (quite literally) its own condition *tout court:* "All at once my position rose on me like a ghost. Anomalous; desolate, almost blank of hope, it stood" (5: 107). Given this characterization of the unemployed orphan's social, economic, and emotional status as "like a ghost" (the pronoun "it" registering that neutral axis in the semiotic positioning of this blocked self), followed by the dropping away of metaphor or simile altogether for the emergence of this ghostlike "position" as a free-standing phantasmal presence, it is a short distance to a reading—a collusive and all but unavoidable reading—of the narrative's later veiled presence as yet another alter ego of Lucy's complex psychic state: her immaterial cast of mind figuratively embodied in the hypothesis of a ghostly nun.

My main point about the reader's hinted complicity in these personifications is this: With the "self" (the existential rather than just narrational "I") materialized on a sliding scale of personification somewhere roughly equidistant between its personified "inner" attributes and a personified reader (otherwise an absent and abstract factor) actively invited to look in on them, this scrutiny becomes constitutive. The invoked reader is thereby stationed as the functional equivalent of these very abstractions, equally a projection of the narrator's own field of self-consciousness. If this refigures the self as its own reader, it also implies that there is no self there at all, in or as retrospect, except as *read into* (both senses) action. This is most obvious not just when the mode of apostrophe is turned upon a personification like "the coward within me" (33: 476) in an injunction like "Courage, Lucy Snowe!" (31: 450) but when the abstraction itself, say Cowardice, is directly addressed in inner and one-way dialogue. This kind of thing happens, for example, at the point where an epistemological crisis for the heroine is read, and made readable, by addressing the supposed descent of "Truth" itself: "In my infatuation, I said, 'Truth, you are a good mistress to your faithful servants!' " (39: 566). Such a feminized, reified, quasi-deified Truth is only of course the figuration of dawning perspicacity in its victory over an inner and delusive hope, as the close of this paragraph-long soliloquy makes clear, slowly losing, as it does, the form of inner apostrophe until truth is merely mentioned rather than addressed: "Truth stripped away Falsehood, and Flattery, and Expectancy, and here I stand—free!" The grammatical shifters (the locative adverb along with the overcoming of past by present tense) work to make present to itself a being that, by exiling Expectancy, the very principle of lived duration, thinks to have something left in the "here" and now.

As we near the end of the novel, the last two personifications in this vein of projected inwardness—devotion and loss figured respectively as "Constancy" and "Absence"—work together to encapsulate not only their service in reifying identity in lieu of its definition, but also, and therefore, their synecdochic relation to the work of first-person fiction as a whole. Having personified the will to write, Lucy now, in the penultimate chapter, where she is at last engaged to be married, incarnates the possibility of being read. Long ago internalizing the abstractions that assault her as the formative traces of a personality, she now becomes transparent to another besides the reader: a personification allegory *in her own person*. It is Paul Emanuel, seeing with the eyes of love, who finds Lucy legible, deciphering the insignia, explicitly in fact the "signature," of "Constancy" as it can be said to endorse Lucy's "characteristic" look. Toward this moment of decoding, Lucy's eyes lift to Paul's, and "they *were* happy now, or they would have been no interpreters of my heart" (41: 583). In this preliminary hermeneutics of the glance, what is thus legible—by immanent reading—is the translation, already the interpretation, of what is first "written" elsewhere and inwardly. But this metaphor of the body as the reader ("interpreter") rather than just mediator of feeling is now shifted outward in M. Emanuel's more normative phrenological response, whereby the inner life impresses its text directly upon the body, to be interpreted from without. In the "expression," so to speak, on Lucy's face he discovers that "signature" he most values, wondering aloud about its emotional toll: "Constancy wrote it; her pen is of iron. Was the record painful?" Lucy admits that "I can bear its inscribing force no more" (41: 583). To observe these climactic details in their metatextual interplay, we note that Constancy in life, in plot, is an "inscribed" mode of existence homologous to Memory at the level of written retrospect, a retrospect whose rehearsal of the irretrievable past comes to a climax with another bodiless visitation, that capitalized "Presence nameless" (of something like joy "divine" [41: 591]), which, hovering over Lucy's last edenic stroll with Paul Emanuel (hovering as not quite a personification, merely an abstract and indwelling spirit), dissipates with his departure from the plot on the next page.

The brutal masculine figure of "Absence" now supplants this evanescent "Presence" not only as the final gendered personification in the novel but as the summary figure in and for plot as a discursive transaction with the reader. This aggressive Absence is not inscribed, as was Constancy, on the body of the textual source in her role as character, but is inscribed in the lack of the lover's bodily presence in a last series of letters. So will writing be all Lucy will ever have of him again. At this point the relation between the novel's two culminating personifications reads like the inexorability of a mathematical equation: Absence + Constancy = Memory.

"Those years of absence! How I had sickened over their anticipation," we find in the first paragraph of "Finis," followed by a simile that is soon itself to be literalized: "The woe they must bring seemed certain as death" (42: 593). A sentence later this foreboding abstraction is personified in the male gender as alter ego of the male presence whose loss it embodies: "The Juggernaut on his car towered there a grim load. Seeing him draw nigh, burying his broad wheels in the oppressed soil—I, the prostrate votary—felt beforehand the annihilating craunch" (42: 592). Though Paul Emanuel's absence is installed here as an anthropomorphic harbinger of death, neverthe-less the three years of still hopeful separation turn out to have been far worse in anticipation than in the actual event; indeed, in the assurance of his love from afar, "Reader, they were the three happiest years of my life" (42: 593). This is in large part, we as readers may readily guess, because the feared onslaught of Absence has taken another form: the aura of the man in his letters, written in the "full-hearted plenitude" (42: 593) of his affection. "By every vessel he wrote," Lucy records, in a grammar that elides cause and effect, source and conveyance, so as to distend the verb "wrote" into a designation that spans inscription and delivery, edging the latter toward a mystified presence in reception.

But his own appointed vessel never comes, despite the narrator's tempo-rary retreat from fatality into the historical present tense. "And now the three years are past: M. Emanuel's return is fixed" (42: 495), writes Lucy—in a final distancing of even the declared lover by mere surname. There is no comfort for long in this phase of the remembered past, though, since Lucy's recurrent "nightmare" of storm and drowning now begins to "repeat" itself in waking tempest. Six paragraphs from the end of the novel, she is thus precipitated into the immediate scene, the unmediated sense, of anxiety, for "wander as I may through the house this night, I cannot lull the blast" (42: 595–96). As merely an actor in the scene, it is absurd to imagine that Lucy *could* "lull" the storm; it is only as an omniscient discursive agent, elementing the tempest in the present tense of discourse rather than event, that she—the narrating "I"—could conceivably exercise veto power over, even while rehearsing, the fatal course of the storm. "Peace, be still!" (42: 596) begins the third paragraph from the end, as if the vocative grammar marks Lucy's admonition to herself as the momentum of retrospect is carrying her implaca-bly toward the tragic disclosure. Yet by the next sentence it seems otherwise, as if the imperative has been an injunction from above, proleptically quoted and unfulfilled—a case of narrative omniscience extrapolated, as it were, to the providential plane. "Oh! a thousand weepers, praying in agony on waiting shores, listened for *that voice,* but it was not uttered" (my emphasis). They await the cosmic command to the winds and waters themselves to "be still," the fiat of "peace," the merciful voice of calm. Who then, or what, speaks in the present-tense imperative mood at the opening of the next sentence, again without "characterizing" quotation marks—and to whom? "Here pause: pause at once." Is it the imagined voice of providence again, perhaps, the roar of the elements announcing its own surcease? Is it this time, rather, the readers who are addressed, asked to relax our engagement with the textual melodrama, to back off and calm down? Or is it, as we suspected before, the narrator telling herself to halt the forward drive of plot?

For at least the next stretch of imperative grammar, the third possibility looms largest, as if the narrative agency is summoning its own cessation: "There is enough said. Trouble no quiet, unkind heart; leave sunny imaginations hope." In the double grammar of that last jussive clause, heard as utterance rather than read as unpunctuated phrasing, the truth of the text will out: the fact that plot now leaves behind (in the genitive sense) "sunny imagination[']s hope." Even without the junctural ambivalence of possession versus plurality, the narrative alternative to death is figuratively coded as a hope whose metaphoric epithet, "sunny," is itself symptomatically transferred from the meteorological realm—in what thus amounts to a radical subjectivizing of alleviated inclemency by which the cause of hope, the subsided tempest, is materialized in the induced effect of a brightening optimism. This irony, along with the homophonic shadow play of the phrase—this compound adumbration of the truth from within imperative grammar—leads directly to the superficially concessive gist of the paragraph, where again the lexical sequence may be found destabilized: "Let it be theirs to conceive the delight of joy born again fresh out of great terror, the rapture of rescue from peril, the wondrous reprieve from dread, the fruition of return. Let them picture union and a happy succeeding life,"[12] with the twofold valence of "succeeding" as both "following" and "successful." Apart from such clear-cut double *meanings* as we find operable in a word like "succeeding," those grammatical ligatures of the plural sibilant loosened in the process of aural reading at "sunny imagination[']s hope" may well accrue to a sense of the text read aloud at the Victorian hearth, that reduced and domesticated simulation of the epic commonality. And just such pertinent phonemic ambiguity may again be activated, against the graphic grain, for the homophonic clue in the spurious hope of rescue "after great [t]error," where a vocalized elision—undermining the narrator's stagey elision of the death scene itself—would tell the truer tale of great error in false hope.[13] In the terms of those early narratological essays by Kristeva, the loop of composition is found here to defer the loop of thematic event—and to do so by intruding upon and derailing it. The novel has become all talk, no action. In the process, the warping of its own language has the further effect of adumbrating Kristeva's own later work on the buckling of the symbolic order under pressure from the irruptive "semiotic" pulse of rudimentary signifying energies.

In the manuscript version of this next-to-last paragraph, there is a final sentence deleted in proof that also cuts both ways. "So be it," the optimistic vision had originally concluded—suggesting not just "let there be those who choose to hold out such hope," but "let there be for them this version of the story, complete with its happy resolution in reunion."[14] In short, the performative force of this locution, realizing its own representation, doing what it says, is cleared away to keep the alternative ending, though worded, always unrealized. The place of such suspended confirmation is a tear in the plot and a fraying of the discourse, a gap, a blank: the absenting of "Absence" himself as a personified figure is displaced to the incarnation of an unsaid Death. From the general interplay between the discursive here-and-now and the retrospective there-and-then, the textual operation has narrowed to the all but undecidable oscillation between the empty adverbial shifters of "*Here* pause" and "*There* is enough said"—the latter, in its deployment as syntactic filler, barely retaining any deictic force whatever. Here when? There where?

All that remains is the indirect suggestion that Lucy has lived on past the deaths of the plot's main participants: "Madame Beck prospered all the days of her life; so did Père Silas; Madame Walravens fulfilled her ninetieth year before she died." After several preceding paragraphs in the at once melodramatic, oneiric, and iterative present, the text now returns to the historical preterite of chronicle, with the only remaining ambiguity being (in contrast to the mentioned death of Madame Walravens) whether "all the days of [Madame Beck's] life" means "her life so far" or her life as already lived out. A similar and far more potent ambiguity, within the fluid tense structure of retrospect, has shadowed a passing emphasis early in this last chapter: "I thought I loved him when he went away; I love him now in another degree; he is more my own." More my own dead, here and now, remembered as I write? Or more my own as I too well recall waiting for him that fateful day? In any case, the latter possibility cannot suppress the former. From the vantage of retrospect, this is what her present-tense comparative could not help but evoke: a phase of possession ("my own") in excess of being, a denial of the Other in the apotheosis of Absence, a rewriting of death as merely another "degree" of life.

Indeed, even the dead within the plot may seem still available to the very discourse—as address—that frames it, if not that discourse to them. After Lucy's litany of longevity and death in the rest of the cast, her last word in the novel is "Farewell." Good-bye and good riddance, as addressed to the departed or departing cast? A sentimental flourish answering at last, years later, to the notably unreciprocal close of the engagement chapter? "We parted: he gave me *his* pledge, and then his farewell. We parted: the next day—he sailed" (41: 592; my emphasis). Or is Lucy's closing "Farewell" (in a nonsequitur that nonetheless seems more likely) addressed to her audience instead, the apostrophized reader invoked one last time, in valediction, at the final point of convergence between the gendered personification of "Absence" (the embodied figuration that is character itself) and the personified inscription that "my reader"—the phrase, the figment—always entails? Is this valedictory inscription therefore located to close the supposed distance between death-bound(ed) story and life-evacuating address? If so, we are led to suspect that during this long "Absence" of love, it is the narrator's desire for the readers, for us, that is all she has had left. And if this is the case, then the momentary and passing—though by the logic of antecedence, quite tempting—sense that the second-person address does in part incorporate the rest of the principals as valedictory recipients, taken leave of along with Paul Emanuel deep in the past, would only confirm our suspicion that in saying good-bye to us she is speaking across a rift as absolute as that of the grave.

It is thus that death comes to the narratee.

## VI

Rounding itself off in this way, however, the text rounds back on its own plot: to a scene of retrospective storytelling that serves, as microcosm, to reconfigure en route the encompassing motives of narration and inscribed audition. This is Miss Marchmont's story, of and by her, an early episode of which we have had no reminder until the "Finis" chapter, whose opening includes the mention of a modest legacy that finally reaches Lucy from one "Mr. Marchmont" (42: 593), cousin of her first employer. This "return" of Miss Marchmont in the form of a posthumous remembrance may well direct our attention to an endowment more deeply bestowed at the original scene of her death almost four dozen chapters before: the narrative impetus itself, death in the offing as the structuring antithesis of life writing, of autobiography, of fictional retrospect.

The reverberations of the episode with Miss Marchmont, as Lucy's mentor in the erotics of retrospect, are first registered obliquely in the chapter immediately following the old woman's death. Its dead-metaphoric title, "Turning a New Leaf," is inflected with an actively punning sense when Lucy, as narrator, parenthetically mentions—the first and last such clue in the novel as to the far distant point of her retrospective vantage—that "my hair which till a late period withstood the frosts of time, lies now, at last white, under a white cap, like snow beneath snow" (5: 105). The shifter "now" locates the point in time at which the "leaves" of retrospect, one after another, are being inscribed by an authorial agency whose name as character, in the further punning of "snow beneath snow," now seems a figuration of her state as discursive agency. But why should we be informed belatedly of the narrator's far backward glance upon already unfolding events at this particular turn of the plot? The answer rests both with the specific nature of Miss Marchmont's preceding retrospect and with Lucy's imputed role as audience to it, anticipating her manipulation of us as readers years after Miss Marchmont's dying tale of death.

Remembering the accidental demise of her lover on the eve of their intended marriage, Miss Marchmont calls up a fully narrativized form of this tragic past, "its incidents, scenes, and personages" manifested "with singular *vivid*ness" (4: 98; my emphasis). Recalled to it as we are by the allusion to her deathbed legacy in the "Finis" chapter, this vivification of the past bears an unmistakable isomorphic relation to the novel, as memoir, that contains it. Like Miss Marchmont's tale of would-be marriage and its fatal alternative, *Villette* too seems to subscribe to the familiar Victorian paradigm of death versus life as a closural determination. But in displacing that death from the protagonal agency to the intended marital partner, the novel obviates the fully disjunctive nature of the governing opposition—in part so as to emphasize the difference *within* the marital alternative between its regenerative and end-stopped aspects, in part to insinuate death as a prerequisite for full possession ("he is more my own now"). These maneuvers of displacement and hedged negation are not required by Miss Marchmont's tale, though, since its narra-tor-protagonist dies—unlike Lucy?—without ever regaining consciousness from the gathering peace ("She composed herself as if to slumber" [4: 101]) that follows in the immediate aftermath of her narrative: the fatal retelling of a death that long ago killed her chance of love.

For Miss Marchmont, the entire past is sublimated, in its absence, into the personification of desire. This takes shape in a way that anticipates the erotic displacement of Lucy's own later life writing. "I love Memory tonight" (4: 98), admits Miss Marchmont uneasily, commandeering Lucy as a confes-sor figure willing to audit a litany of superannuated desire. The invested narrator thus attempts to render her listener a mere function(ary) in the economy of narrative as purgation. "What do you think, Lucy, of these things? Be my chaplain and tell me" (4: 101). As with a reader rather than an auditor of a narrative, however, a reader whose invoked responses can never genuinely be circulated back through the textual system even when courted rhetorically—and even when sometimes ascribed, textually inscribed—Lucy remains mute: "This question I could not answer: I had no words" (4: 101). Neither do Lucy's readers, Brontë's readers, have words— except as they are put into our mouths. So with Lucy as disburdening audience: "It seemed as if she thought I *had* answered it," because Miss Marchmont's "Very right, my child" does all it needs to do—sustaining the narrative momentum as a pseudo-interlocutory contract.

Sympathetic audience to Lucy's own later and inclusive confession, into which this scene is recursively folded as a combined experiment in narrational and enunciative "closure," we are more like therapists than confessors or "chaplains," silently taking in without response or absolution. But all the while Memory, externalized as plot, is the reader's own object of desire too. So that any yearning for an ending happier than Miss Marchmont's, with its protracted gap between the death of a lover and the death of desire, may seem to participate in an ultimately closed circle: one whereby the fictions of the teller, once shunted off onto the auditor as narrative expectations, are then projected back upon the narrator herself as the revealed wish fulfillment, the sublimated and substitutive desire, out of which all narrative issues. To recall our preceding equation, Constancy + Absence = Memory, we can now rephrase the existential logic as a textual one: Absence + Rehearsal = Narrative, which is to say, returning to Kristeva: Life/Death + Narrator/ Addressee = "Bounded Text." In part prepared by that early personification of narrative "Memory" as passional object, this is an equation transcoded within the textual economy of *Villette* to the level of reader engagement itself, where it is manifested as the eroticized dynamics of reading toward closure.

## VII

Having arrived at Brontë's defiant—under the guise of pliant—closure, we have apparently run up against a decisive crux of textual deconstruction, where the differend threatens to replace the end, where the life/death paradigm is left open for our own fantasized mobilization in the syntactic axis— as unwritten plot. Such a radically differential sense of this ending may be taken, as I suggested above, to reverse the ordinary mechanisms of romantic fiction, whereby a protagonist plays out the fantasy life of the reader. Brontë's conclusion arranges instead for the discourse to project onto its reception the return of a repressed desire thus purged by displacement from the site of writing—with such force of displacement, indeed, that the plot itself suffers the recoil as an indeterminancy of closure. On the other hand, the differential ending might well subserve a feminist reading of the novel—of the novel as in its own right feminist—by suggesting that the closure of the female *Bildungsroman* cannot properly depend on a man, that a woman's story can exist either way, with or without. Or it might ratify those critiques of the closural paradigm itself that expose the deathlike stasis in marital end-stopping. In this sense the ending poses a rhetorical question: Even if reunion and subsequent marital unification were clung to by some imagined readers as the outcome of the story, what would *not* saying so in detail mean but that, formally speaking, there is nothing more to say? However we take it, or let it *take us in*, the most revealing fact about this closure is that it does just this: that the reader is, as it were, con-scripted by discourse as an agency of plotting.

It is at this point that I would return us to Kristeva's two "loops" of fictional structuration, thematic and compositional, in order to determine once and for all the interaction of the life/death bracket with the speaker/ addressee circuit. For at just the moment when closure is thrown open to the seeming contingency of reading, the narratee is in fact entirely constrained by the very form of the novel's address as a directed discourse. To be sure, the narrative does not, will not, say whether Paul Emanuel has died, yet the very process of its telling *enunciates* the exclusion of the only alternative to such a death. This is as hard to specify as it is to miss. Once the shifters of discursive emplacement have been foregrounded in the imperative formula "Let it be theirs to conceive," the enunciative position is itself tacitly "split" (Kristeva's term again, but for discourse now rather than plot) into the narrator of "third persons" (not linguistic "persons" at all, according to Benveniste)[15] and the addressor of the second person—not even us any more for sure, some presumed collectivity, but rather me reading, the "zero-degree narratee" who alone can produce every instance of the book as text.[16] By constitutive linguistic fact—rather than just emotional "constitution"—they who could convince themselves to think otherwise about the hero's fate (let us say, contemporaneously, those other and always more sentimental Victorians) are not here, then, at all—not here *now*—in the I/you circuit, the circuit of reading. They are not addressed by the text. It is therefore not *this* text that they are reading, that their reading produces, even if they hold in their hands the last volume of a three-decker novel by this name. The return of "community" as unifying addressee—a culturally consolidating ideal never more than partially banished, according to Kristeva, by the transformation of epic into novel—is here privatized in the pitting of me against them, not even them as readers, but just an abstract plurality of dupes likely to be fooled by a story to whose text they in fact, as grammar has it, can claim no present access.

What we are thus confronting at last, on the exacerbated occasion of closure in *Villette,* are the outer rather than the inner limits of formalism, where issues of representation, death, and closure intersect those of enunciation and address, to engage, gloss, and recast each other. At this point of convergence, what we find is that tensions developed within, but also foundational to, the novel as a plotted duration cannot be resolved on its own structural terms—though they can be structured *toward* a resolution. The site of conflation between narrational and discursive models is in fact grammar itself, the structure of tense that in the case of *Villette* permits a merger between the artificially restored present of the climactic past scene ("The sun passes the equinox; the days shorten, the leaves grow sere; but—he is coming" [42: 595]) and the perpetual present of second-person address ("Here pause"), even if only an address of the "I" to its own narrational motives. Indeed, if we reimagine the semiotic square by which Jameson accounts for the blind spots of a text's ideological parameters—reimagine it as a metatextual grid in which we find plotted a text's own ideology of reception—we might then be in a position to assess the way the systemic exchanges of plot are implicated, even replicated, at the outer boundaries of the discursive system.

The "neutral term" in a network of full narrational or thematic opposition—here the contrary axis "neither alive nor dead"—might in this sense be found manifested at the level of narrator/narratee in the form of a refusal to say more: an incomplete disjunction that would amount to announcing that "neither will I call him dead nor pretend that he is alive." But when that refusal is translated, transvalued, back to the thematic antithesis of life/death, it is remanifested as transcendence, in other words not as avoidance but as resolution in both senses: heroic determination and logical synthesis. Attained thereby is a position beyond life and death, above and beyond, a locus which, when projected back upon the complementary discursive rather than narrative circuit—as if through a recursive loop that becomes a textual loophole—appears as the quasi-transcendent position equally distant from life and death: the perpetuation-within-absence incident to the place of text, of closure *sub specie aeternitatis.* Each of us, in turn rather than collectively, holds the place of Paul Emanuel's "Absence," both by "admitting" it—as if it is ours to inscribe—and by being now where he last was to Lucy as reader of his letters: on the far side of a writing that knows its own basis in absence. To apprehend this is not to deconstruct the text in some monolithic manner, exposing its operation as mere inscription, but rather to recognize the competing models that have decentered it—stretching it unstably across the separable but overlapping systems of narrative and addressed discourse so that its thematic of death will therefore, when all is over, not stay put in plot.

It is by this route, I find myself saying again, that death comes to the narratee, in an evacuation reciprocal to that of the enunciating subject.

And so we can now redesignate the quadrants of our earlier analytic diagram in such a way that its constitutive subdivisions will also make plain the interdependence of story and discourse: laying bare, in particular, those collusive resolutions by which a tension in one network is worked out of the system only by being transferred to (or foisted off onto) another set of coordinates. As previously blocked out, the aspects of duration, finality, timelessness, and eternity—by which the meanings of the story are mobilized across a signifying grid—can now be found "transliterated" into the functions of that system itself in its formal coherence, as follows (fig. 2): *duration = plot; finality = closure; timelessness = pattern* (internal repetition). In the remaining space of the elusive complex term, the resolution achieved by the presence-within-absence of "eternity" (embodied in the deathless idea rather than the person of the remembered lover) is rechanneled, with full rhetorical force, into the discursive system as the reader's own reanimation of the life/death axis—both as it polarizes Lucy and Paul (first and third person) and as it subsumes Lucy under the retrospective aspect of her own mortality. Hence, in a shorthand that matches the text's short-circuiting of parallel systems, *eternity* (formal permanence) = *reading*. At this point, in other words, the epic recuperation of duration into transcendent "meaning" (the depersonalized form of a theological absolute in Kristeva) is translated instead, novelized, into an interpretive productivity, each activated reader privileged individually to feel what others are permitted to miss.

The implications of this spread wide. In *Villette* we come not so much upon another mode of self-reflexivity in fiction as upon its formal reconception. Plot requires the return of its own repressed, the return of discourse, for closure, even as discourse—become an oscillating field of subject positions (between "I" and "you/me")—must be "narrativized" in order to achieve any resolution of its own. In our quadratic mapping of plot, we originally charted, in effect, a clockwise movement from the finality of the Miss Marchmont episode, through the time-serving neutrality of Lucy's wait for love, to the engagement to Paul Emanuel, with its promise of the contradiction of denial in fulfillment, and on to his unsayable death, completing the square as a

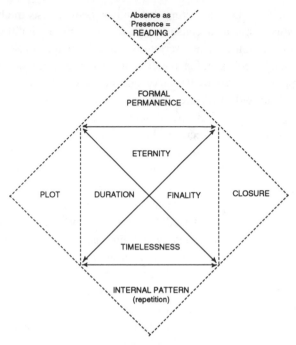

Figure 2.

vicious circle in which the heroine returns—now exclusively as narrator, functioning for the last paragraphs entirely in the discursive circuit—to approximate again the place of Miss Marchmont, an elderly spinster with a tragic story to tell, determined upon a submissive but engaged response. And so it is that at the apex and convergence of the two systems, narrational and discursive, each the transumption of the other, the specter of absence-as-presence (the figure, that is, of death and inscription together) can be functionally reinscribed as the figure of reading itself. In this manner Brontë's novel structures its plot, and plots its structure, toward a *formally defined* point of contact with the receptive agency outside the text. Such is the doubly "blind," because always invisible, point of internalization by the reader. It marks thereby that twin vanishing point of both story and address where we may well spot the cultural agendas not only internal to narrative but complicit in its telling as they are unloaded upon the text-as-produced. This is the text, in other words, as generated through the linguistically constrained engagement of a narratee fully written into the novel's closural dynamic.

But the narratee, finally, of what? *The Professor, Jane Eyre, Shirley:* these are all we have of the professor, Jane Eyre, and Shirley. Brontë's last title is more unflinching yet. No Lucy Snowe here. Located on no map of any country, Ville/ettc designates that pseudonymous, femininized, diminuitive, topography-free, utopic nowhere, always foreign and somewhat estranged— a book by any other name. Within its borders, at least its limits, after years of promulgating English language and literature in a working space mortaged to the local "bookseller" (41: 589), at last a retrospective narrator who withholds her name from the title, a "placeless person" (5: 103) as she once calls herself, has undertaken in "this hour" to "repeat" the "nightmare" of past loss—with all that lost past to be recovered only through the addressed responses of a reading strategically correlated with her story. Where Jane Eyre can be said to create a simulacrum of herself in *Jane Eyre*—her "life"— by contrast the titular, fictive space of Villette is all that Lucy, in a word, produces. Villette, then, as well as the book by its name, can denominate nothing more nor less than the site of a writing, where, for all the shows of vested autonomy, its relentlessly conscripted readers, even when all is over, are left residually to the text's devices rather than their own. But then to be moved is, after all, a passive construction, even when this is what we are brought by a text to produce it as causing in us.

## Notes

1. On the emotional superfluity of the Victorian death scene as a socialized conversion of erotic energy see, for instance, John Kucich, whose chapters "Storytelling" and "Endings" also speak to the relation of death and closure at stake in the present investigation. This same relation, in connection with the erotics of reading itself—as implicated in a kind of formal "death drive"—is explored by Peter Brooks. More recently, and in connection with nineteenth-century poetic figuration, death has been considered by Jay Clayton as a lacunary moment in representation, a gap of sheer figuration; see especially 96–102 on *Wuthering Heights*. My own introduction to *Death Sentences: Styles of Dying in British Fiction,* also aligning Victorian fictional practice with romantic poetry, surveys the interrelations among death, representation, and closure as they touch on poststructuralist issues of textuality and absence. These are matters I have since pursued further in their bearing on encoded reading and response, more in the vein of the present essay, in "Leaving History: Dickens, Gance, Blanchot," and in " 'Beckoning Death': *Daniel Deronda* and the Plotting of a Reading."

2. See, for instance, Sylvère Monod.

3. In this latter respect, the process by which a reader is widely, and loosely, said to be "inscribed into ideology" has been formulated as a version of Althusserian "interpellation" by Catherine Belsey; see especially 56–63. Where my topic intersects such an approach is precisely in an effort to *de*metaphorize the concept of "inscription," investigating instead the exact linguistic maneuvers by which, within a semiotically encoded circuit of response, the reader is simultaneously written in and written off by Victorian texts.

4. See Elizabeth Gaskell. Following a chapter in which Gaskell includes a letter from Brontë pleading with her not to make the heroine of *Ruth* die at the end ("And yet you must follow the impulse of your own inspiration. If *that* commands the slaying of the victim, no bystander has a right to put out his hand to stay the sacrificial knife"; 24: 391), Gaskell records how Brontë had told her "that Mr. Brontë was anxious that [Charlotte's] new tale should end well. . . . But the idea of M. Paul Emanuel's death at sea was stamped on her imagination, till it assumed the distinct force of reality. . . . All she could do in compliance with her father's wish was so to veil the fate in oracular words, as to leave it to the character and discernment of her reader to interpret her meaning" (25: 399–400).

5. If Brontë had set out to travesty by reversal the Dickensian style of dying, she could hardly have been more exact in her arrangements. In the classic case of Little Nell, prototype for many of his later death scenes, Dickens allowed his populace to wallow in lament while sheltering them in the assurance of their own freedom from perversely willed participation; the death was so inevitable that even the public outcry *in advance* could not forestall it. A decade later, this outcry is written into the text by Brontë, not just anticipated but pre(in)scribed; what is more, death in the face of this very resistance, death acquiesced in by us nonetheless, is therefore supposedly rendered voluntary, all responsibility for its acknowledgment laid at our own (exit) door.

6. Citations in the text are from *Villette*, ed. Tony Tanner.

7. My sense of the emotional tonality of Brontë's conclusion coincides up to a point with the feminist reading provided by Brenda R. Silver. I would agree both that Lucy is finally appealing on the last page, in her direct address to the reader, to "the community she herself has created to grant credence to the highly unconventional conclusion of her tale" (110) and that we are to believe she prospers without Paul Emanuel (in his absence, though in and through the memory of his love, I might add) during the intervening years between his death and her narration. Indeed, it is for just these reasons that my own analysis can be taken to begin with the question, Why, even though her *life* goes on, is her *narrative* so precipitously over with this distant and unnarrated death?

8. The essays in question, "The Bounded Text" and "Word, Dialogue, Novel," appearing back to back in Kristeva's *Desire in Language,* are Kristeva's attempt to sieve Bakhtinian theories of dialogism through a more rigorous grid of logical and semantic oppositions. Though the first of Kristeva's indirect meditations links the subject/addressee structure to the bracketing fictional poles of life and death—as tandem support systems, one might say, for what she calls the novel as "ideologeme"—discussion of the interplay of enunciation and utterance is reserved for the second essay. It is my purpose here to reconvene these issues more closely.

9. Kristeva's unspoken reliance on the "square of opposition" in analytic logic ties her work directly to that of Algirdas Julien Greimas collected three years in advance of the original French publication of her 1969 essays. Greimas's collection has since appeared in English as *Structural Semantics.* Kristeva's sense of disjunctive

and nondisjunctive functions in the conceptualizing of literary structure also anticipates the full deployment of Greimas's "semiotic square" in *Du sens,* much of which
has more recently appeared in English as *On Meaning*. This volume has an instructive
foreword by Fredric Jameson, who has also applied Greimas's semiotic narratology
to Balzac and Conrad with notable success in *The Political Unconscious,* esp. 154–
84, 253–57, and 275–80. For further discussion of this method, see the issue of *New
Literary History* lately devoted entirely to "Greimassian Semiotics," vol. 20, no. 3
(Spring 1989).

10. One of Jameson's chief "recommendations" in the application of Greimas is
that the four primary terms "need to be conceived polysemically, each one carrying
with it its own range of synonyms . . . none of them exactly coterminous with each
other, such that large areas of relatively new or at least skewed conceptuality are
thereby registered." See Greimas, *On Meaning* xv–xvi. It is in this spirit, in working
out a semiotic grid for *Villette,* that I depart somewhat from the "dialectical algorithm"
in *Structural Semantics* by which Greimas approaches the dichotomy of life and death
(L and non-L, D and non-D) and its various correlates in Bernanos's fiction (see
especially 263–65, 269–70, 280, 285, and 293–95).

11. This phenomenon has been noted in criticism, of course, but never in the
sense I am advancing here, in which personification of the character's attributes—as
the reductio of fictional character itself, and further of identity per se—operates on
the same discursive level as the personification of the reader. Tony Tanner has a
useful brief discussion of the "world of abstractions" in the novel in his introduction
to the Penguin edition (41), but he makes no distinctions, in his list of almost two
dozen such material embodiments, either between the gender of these personified
figures or between those that reify abstractions in general, including his examples of
Fate, Destiny, and Time, and such far more frequent personifications that objectify
aspects of existence presumed internal to consciousness—themselves often feminized
by Lucy—as the "hag" Disappointment, Hypochondria, Presentiment, Conviction,
and so forth (or from his own list—most of them neuter rather than feminine in
context—Curiosity, Spirit, Impulse, Conception).

12. As if these potential readers of happy endings should not have had their fill
with the two stagily framed instances of Victorian closure, complete with nuptials
and a compressed summary of the "succeeding" domestic harmony, that Lucy has
already interrupted the main plot to expatiate upon: namely, chapters 37 and 40, "The
Happy Pair" (Paulina and Dr. John) and its ironic counterpart, "Sunshine" (Ginevra
and de Hamal).

13. It is this activation of phonemic overtones by the reading act, an act understood
as the coproduction of textual discourse, that I pursue at the microlinguistic level in
*Reading Voices*. Including numerous other contingent (but nonetheless thematically
charged) instances of the Victorian proclivity for such homophonic shadow play,
examples in particular from *Jane Eyre* and elsewhere from *Villette,* this study may
be taken as a companion piece to the macrolinguistic account of conscripted reading
toward which the present essay is aimed.

14. *Villette,* ed. Rosengarten and Smith, 715; see description of the Sterling manuscript and proof sheets of the first edition, "Introduction," xxxvii ff.

15. See Emile Benveniste, 196–204. In the subsequent chapter that builds on this discussion, "Subjectivity in Language," Benveniste comments on the interplay between the subjective person and the nonsubjective person, *I* and *you,* in a way that bears directly on that dialogic circuitry that Kristeva sees "occluded" by traditional narrative, an open interchange where the addressee "becomes my echo to whom I say *you* and who says *you* to me" (225).

16. The term is from Gerald Prince. Benveniste also provides indirect support for my sense of the text at this point when he closes his essay "Relationships of Person in the Verb" with the assertion that only "the 'third person,' being a non-person, admits of a true plural" (204). In the concluding passage from *Villette,* the singular negotiations of person across the narrator/narratee axis thus structurally exclude whatever might be—plurally, and elsewhere—"theirs to conceive."

## Works Cited

Belsey, Catherine. *Critical Practice.* New York: Methuen, 1980.

Benveniste, Emile. "Relationships of Person in the Verb." *Problems in General Linguistics.* Trans. Mary Elizabeth Meek. Coral Gables, FL: U of Miami P, 1971. 195–204.

Brontë, Charlotte. *Jane Eyre.* Norton Critical Edition. Ed. Richard J. Dunn. New York: Norton, 1971.

———. *Villette.* Ed. Tony Tanner. Baltimore: Penguin, 1979.

———. *Villette.* Ed. Herbert Rosengarten and Margaret Smith. Oxford: Clarendon, 1984.

Brooks, Peter. *Reading for the Plot: Design and Intention in Narrative.* New York: Knopf, 1984.

Clayton, Jay. *Romantic Vision and the Novel.* Cambridge: Cambridge UP, 1987.

Gaskell, Elizabeth. *The Life of Charlotte Brontë.* London: Smith, Elder, 1877.

Greimas, Algirdas Julien. *Du sens.* Paris: Seuil, 1970.

———. *On Meaning: Selected Writings in Semiotic Theory.* Trans. Paul J. Perron and Frank H. Collins. Minneapolis: U of Minnesota P, 1987.

———. *Structural Semantics.* Trans. Daniele McDowell, Ronald Schleifer, and Alan Velie. Lincoln: U of Nebraska P, 1983.

*Greimassian Semiotics.* Spec. issue of *New Literary History* 20.3 (1989): 523–799.

Jameson, Fredric. *The Political Unconscious: Narrative as a Socially Symbolic Act.* Ithaca: Cornell UP, 1981.

Kristeva, Julia. "The Bounded Text." "Word, Dialogue, Novel." *Desire in Language: A Semiotic Approach to Literature and Art.* Ed. Leon S. Roudiez. Trans. Thomas Gora, Alice Jardine, and Leon S. Roudiez. New York: Columbia UP, 1980. 36–63; 64–91.

Kucich, John. *Excess and Restraint in the Novels of Charles Dickens.* Athens: U of Georgia P, 1981.

Monod, Sylvère. "Charlotte Brontë and the Thirty 'Readers' of *Jane Eyre*." Brontë, *Jane Eyre:* 496–507.

Prince, Gerald. "Introduction to the Study of the Narratee." *Reader-Response Criticism: From Formalism to Post-Structuralism*. Ed. Jane Tomkins. Baltimore: Johns Hopkins UP, 1980. 7–25.

Silver, Brenda R. "Reflecting Reader in *Villette*." Ed. Elizabeth Abel, Marianne Hirsch, and Elizabeth Langland. *The Voyage In. Fictions of Female Development*. Hanover, NJ: UP of New England, 1983. 90–111.

Stewart, Garrett. *Death Sentences: Styles of Dying in British Fiction*. Cambridge: Harvard UP, 1984.

———. " 'Beckoning Death': *Daniel Deronda* and the Plotting of a Reading." *Sex and Death in Victorian Literature*. Ed. Regina Barreca. London: Macmillan, 1990. 69–106.

———. "Leaving History: Dickens, Gance, Blanchot." *Yale Journal of Criticism* 2.2 (1989): 143–82.

———. *Reading Voices: Literature and the Phonotext*. Berkeley: U of California P, 1990.

■

# Lacan, the Death Drive, and the Dream of the Burning Child

## *Ellie Ragland*

### The Death Drive: Freud and Lacan

The way Jacques Lacan rereads Sigmund Freud's account of the dream of the burning child shows vividly where he advances beyond Freudian impasses in understanding both the death drive and representation. Lacan argues, moreover, that the death drive can take on its fuller meaning only in light of a new theory of representation. In Lacanian teaching representation and the death drive are connected by a fundamental link. All perceptions and thoughts are, according to Lacan, representations constituted around originary losses such that loss itself takes on a central, even centering, function in life. Indeed, language, desire, behavior, and affect are positioned around palpable loss at the center of all things human.

In "Analysis Terminable and Interminable" (1937), Freud wrote that castration anxiety was one shoal upon which psychoanalysis, teaching, and government all run aground. This impasse makes these "impossible professions." Lacan began where Freud dead-ended. Castration anxiety is not the obstacle human impossibilities coalesce around, but the *effect* of losses functioning as the organizing principle of all life. The myriad effects produced by this reality place a palpable void at the core of being. The death drive appears in the repetitions, or familiar despairs, to which people cling at all costs to stop up the void. Put another way, the first objects an infant sees, hears, or touches are presentations introjected as primary symbols. But for symbols or things to become language—to be verbally re-presented— they must disappear as omnipresent object. The disappearance gives rise to loss insofar as the mother says no to ongoing satiation. The infant grasps that the symbol is not stable, not *there,* not reliable. Moreover, the symbol or image leaves an empty place in its wake, thus making absence the condition for meaning or language to signify something. As Saussure pointed out, such referents usually arise binarily or differentially; that is, in reference to another signifier, in between which something lacks.

Thus, for the young child, a bobbin reel, a mother's face, an elephant, the sun, and so on, are "here" only in relation to being "gone." *Da!* takes on meaning only in terms of *Fort!* The "subject" represented by the signifiers one to the other is not the symbol as the thing-in-itself but the gap left by the fading of fullness or presence of something that was there and is no longer. These symbols underlie all subsequent efforts to represent objects (person, thing, or event) as projections of any individual's reality, which Lacan calls fantasy. But these projections are neither presentable nor graspable in a finally objective and transparent meaning, unless that meaning is pried out. Lacan equates the introjected Ur-objects or symbols with Freud's someThing thought to be pressed down under (*Urverdrängt*) ordinary repressions or forgettings. Certain of these objects are characterized by seeming to be joined to, yet separable from, the body qua organism. For example, the voice has a disembodied quality that suggests that at some level it is separable from the vocal cords. The eye that looks is not the same as the gaze that judges. An alphabetic letter is not the same as its potential effects—to wound, evoke, and so on—once used in a word. Insofar as primordial objects— person, image, thing, or event—are forever lost to memory, they do not exist as memory objects. And they have life at all only because the real effect of their loss ensures that other things, both objectal and experiential, stand in as semblances for their would-be a priori existence. Based on this theory, which joins representations to the death drive as effects of loss in memory that appear enigmatically as symptoms, Lacan attributes to unconscious desire and to the real of effects the role of organizing all human life.

Lacan placed the object at the heart of psychoanalytic understanding, but he gave it an entirely new twist by departing from the sociological, phenomenological world of visible objects in his explanation of what *it* is. In Lacanian theory seeing, being, talking, thinking, reading, writing, feeling, and perceiving are all organized in networks of meaning and affect around a hole or void that pierces through the weave of introjected representations. The palpable existence or positivizable reality of a hole in the center of being and meaning pushes individuals to keep filling this hole, lest they be confronted with any one of its many anxiety-producing faces. We know that individuals ceaselessly take in the world around them piecemeal, while unconsciously striving to maintain the illusion that inconsistencies or discontinuities play little role in their daily lives. Wallace Stevens wrote that we live by "necessary fictions," looking for "a new knowledge of reality" (166). The *objet petit a* is the name Lacan gave to the remainder or surplus of the real in *jouissance* that denotes the continual interference of loss and disunities in our lives, the more-than-pleasure in "enjoyment" (*jouissance*) that points to some meaning beyond sense data or visible objects. Lacan's real object dwells in the margins, at the edges, just beyond conscious fantasies.

This real thing makes holes in discourse, blockages of symbolizations, that Lacan calls *troumatique* (Miller, "Microscopie" 57). Lacan's real is always traumatic, partly because its structure or ordering is that of knots made up of disjointed, fragmented pieces of our "selves"—unsymbolized meaning—that appear as *jouissance* effects. In this context we encounter Lacan's innovative theory that the *objet a* is the subject as a response of the real. At any given moment a person *is* a gaze, a voice, a pack of phonemes, and so on. As such, the subject is not a whole being who picks up whole words and uses them neatly and rationally to re-represent himself or herself. Rather, parceled-out, broken-up, separated pieces of body, language, thought comprise the subject in the real. And so Lacan says the subject's cause is always already loss, a lost cause. It should not come as a surprise, then, that he viewed all human activities and systems of thought as idealized fantasies of wholeness we invent or create to give ourselves the comfort of believing in a Oneness of resolutions within consciousness. The anxiety attendant upon the human reality of loss (and its remainders) is not physically bearable, except intermittently. But it is theoretically bearable and even helpful in understanding our texts, our poetics, our politics, and our lives.

The innovation in Lacan's theory of the death drive lies in his positing loss as the reverse of the real order of "knowledge" that produces an object, the *petit a,* which in turn people seek in a quest for satisfaction. But the far more radical implication of the theory is this: Lacan finds the cause of biopsychic energy in this unassimilated obstacle—the *objet a*—that is lost qua memory or object but returns as "drive" or partial drive. Individuals continually encounter the paradox of being driven to seek satisfaction by going around the real object that, by definition, they cannot reach in any final way. Lacan's linking of *jouissance* to the death drive is neither metaphor nor fiction nor the postulation of a future impersonal project of being-toward-death, then. Rather, the markings of the real traumatic events are created. An inability or refusal to understand certain events for what they mean, for the personal devaluation implicit in them, make of traumata knotted, unassimilated meanings. As untranslated remainders, such knotty material becomes parasitical archaic letters that constitute death *material*. These letters (Lacan plays on *l'être* as the letter of being) maintain a power of death over life because *and simply because* they are present—embedded in flesh, in-*corp*-orated, repeated in behavior and myth—but are inaccessible to reflection, contemplation, or undoing.

Lacan finds the death drive everywhere in Freud's work, even though Freud officially distanced himself from this theory when he could not explain it. Lacan came to see death in drives or discrete bodies of meaning that control our destinies and write upon our bodies qua organisms. As such, the death drive is far more powerful than some abstract awareness that points to a mere animal fact of life. Death effects both hide and show themselves at the same time because they emanate from the object Lacan denoted as everyone's most intimate cause: the *petit a* that is neither inside nor outside us. Insofar as lives are organized around the *objet a*—not a real object, but a logically inferred constellation of *jouissance* effects—libidinal consistencies alternate between continuity and discontinuity, supporting the death that shows its real face in the symptoms we love more than ourselves. Although the *objet a* is not in itself a symptom (except as symptom of an excess "enjoyment"), symptoms cluster around it. The gaze, for example, becomes symptomatic if one refers to the voyeurism of a Peeping Tom. Lacan described symptoms as metaphors: enigmatic, substitute meanings that stand in for lost or unassimilated meanings. The symptom is a sign that something is awry, that something is not symbolized. Whether a symptom is visible on the body or in repeated acts that do not necessarily wish our good, it conveys the message that its cause is opaque. Lacan views symptoms as constituting a structural imaginary that dwells alongside the ego. Symptoms are unconscious fictions we cling to because they protect us from confronting the traumatic real that installed them in the first place as split-off meanings. Symptoms show the *jouissance* of death effects around which our egos organize crusades, fighting others rather than reconstituting our desires or rethinking our ideals and closures, with the possibility of dissolving or refashioning our symptoms.

## The Development of Lacan's Theory of the Death Drive

In his reading of the death drive, Lacan stressed that the word kills the thing, a Hegellian proposition he took up as early as his mirror stage article (1949). Lacan argued that once the word refers to a thing or an object, that object is lost to consciousness in any pristine form of "normal" conscious knowledge of it. Any empirical reality of the object first presented (breast, elephant, the mother's voice, tree, penis, and so on) is thereafter only tangentially re-presentable. Moreover, any re-presentation of it will of necessity be transformed or distorted. No Ur-lining of the subject by primordial objects that *cause* desire will ever find a correspondence between inner and outer objects. No unifying trait will ever be identical to itself. As infants build ever more complex meaning systems, representations of objects make up a growing body of evokable references. These reference "objects," already presented somewhere, are never directly sayable or graspable as totalities. Insofar as they are re-presented in language at all, they are transformed into signifiers that depend on a gap between grammatical meaning and real referent. Put another way, language opens up onto a certain void in any field constituted as reality.

In *Seminar II* (1954–55) Lacan first presented the death drive as a symbolic-order murder of the image or object by the word.[1] He explicated *Beyond the Pleasure Principle* in *Seminar II* to argue that the death drive is an imaginary-order masking of the symbolic order by repetition behavior that extends beyond the pleasure principle—a paradoxical principle that does not always give pleasure. In 1959–60 in *Séminaire VII* (*L'éthique de la psychanalyse*) Lacan introduced the notion that *jouissance* was what one found "beyond" the pleasure principle: "beyond pleasure," but carried back and forth between pleasure and displeasure in the object he called the real object (*la chose*) as causative of an energy. Insofar as the real object qua object is always lacking in any pure form, it is a permanent *ab-sens* unattainable in any final resolution or permanent satisfaction. Thus, any encounter with the real will always be an encounter with the death drive, the *more* than us in us that is at that moment irreducible to meaning or satisfaction. In *Seminar XI* the "drive" is portrayed as a montage of *objet a*. In desiring or aiming at these heterogeneous libidinal objects, one finds reminiscences of what causes one to desire in the first place, objects of desire that include

> the mammilla, faeces, the phallus (imaginary object), the urinary flow. (An unthinkable list, if one adds, as I do, the phoneme, the gaze, the voice—the nothing.) For is it not obvious that this feature, this partial feature, rightly emphasized in the objects, is applicable not because these objects are part of a total object, the body, but because they represent only partially the function that produces them?

During the 1960s Lacan elaborated his theory that the drive always misses the object qua object of total harmony and full pleasure. When the *objet a* functions as the object of drive energy, it points to a near miss, to loss, to an encounter with the real, the dream navel where what is seen is not exactly it (*la chose*). Representation is not mimetic or repressive, then, but a "holding the place of," a potential meaning. Rather than raw sexual id, drive is a montage of body/meaning associations by which sexuality participates in psychical life in a way that conforms to the gaplike structure that *is* the structure of the unconscious.[2]

Lacan's structural topology teaches that death is not the Other, but effects produced by the hole in the Other, from which the *objet a* emanates. Lacan equates the *objet a* as limit with the *Zwang* or constraint he postulates as a positivized negative, a kernel of excess *jouissance* (see Zizek). From the mid-1960s on, Lacan equated the death drive with the *jouissance* effects produced by the *objet a* that is both subtracted and expelled from the overlap of body and meaning in the various orders (real, symbolic, imaginary). The burning child dream, reinterpreted by Lacan in *Seminar XI,* is of particular interest because it holds the pivotal place where he begins to understand death and representation as connected in a fundamental way where meaning joins the body. Sexuality is constituted by partial drives (the gaze, the voice, the void, etc.) that link repressed (Other) signifying chains to the real of the body in a drive to interpret or recreate the missing Other (*Seminar XI* 181). But what does this mean? It means that we—as subjects—are not unified. It means that sexuality unites us to things and each other intermittently and in encounters that range from the least to the most. Although each person's partner always remains the Other sex, encounters with others are necessary lest we come face to face with the void *in ourselves.*

But these encounters are paradoxical because, even though necessary, they are painful—fraught with the real of fragmentation and loss that gave rise to them as partial drives in the first place. One consequence of locating the death drive in the real is that it coexists on several planes. But no linear narrative or binary opposition can bring together all the pieces in any one system. Lacan tries to map the multilinear by a new psychoanalytic logic. With Lacan, there is no longer an Eros versus a Thanatos. Thanatos gives rise to Eros, which tries to screen out Thanatos, renamed the *objet a* by Lacan, or the pseudo-*Dasein* of the subject when denoted as object.

But how does Lacan get to his multilinear logic via Freud's texts? In 1920 Freud discovered two new elements in *Wiederholungszwang:* First, that what the patient repeats is opposed to the pleasure principle; and second, that the compulsion to repeat lies at the heart of the death drive (*Beyond the Pleasure Principle*). In Lacan's rereading of Freud, a piece of life is retained and relived there where memory is lacking, but relived as an *inertia* rather than as a pristine memory. Insofar as it—the inertia or *jouissance*—resists memory, it does not come from the Other, which does not resist memory. Rather, Other or unconscious meaning insists, always trying to assimilate its knowledge to conscious meanings (Aparicio 36). In *Seminar II* Lacan not only took great care to show how the notion of the symbolic functions at the heart of the analytic field, he also argued that the homeostasis—or inertia— of the Freudian pleasure principle obeys a death drive, not a drive that is pleasurable because it reduces tensions. Rather than think in terms of conflict and biopsychic drives (often called instincts in English), Lacan noted that the compulsion to repetition revealed the symbolic as itself autonomous. Thus the compulsion to repeat shows the circular functioning of a repressed discourse beyond the ego; it is a discourse excluded from the subject in which he or she is nonetheless included (Aparicio 41–42). But as already noted, Lacan did not actually link the real to repetition until *Seminar XI* (1964), when he distinguished between the real *jouissance* inertia that always returns to the same place (*Wiederkehr*) and the repetition (*Wiederholung/automaton*) of signifying chains. In *Seminar XI*, Lacan wrote that the real is apprehended in one of its many unconscious prototypes in the dream in that it *repeats* something whose referent lies "beyond." And the point "beyond" that pro- vokes an awakening is an encounter with the real, a stumbling over an *objet a* that marks the limit of assimilated knowledge.

In summary, then, the Lacanian death drive is the traumatic knowledge we all possess but have not assimilated in memory, fantasy, or dreams. If we all possess a knowledge or knowing that is by definition not speakable, this is the sense in which the Lacanian real is an impossibility or impossible to bear. Paradoxically, it is an impossibility that never ceases not writing itself. Thus it returns into all arenas of human life with shattering force. It (does not) write(s) itself most particularly as an enigma on the human *body*, which Lacan distinguishes from the biological organism per se. In its oscillation between *parole* (word) and *écriture* (unconscious text), the body is structured by and for meaning, then, meaning that turns into an enigma at the level of the real.

Because knowledge of the real is familiar, albeit not directly available to conscious understanding, it infers paradox in all life acts. As early as "The Agency of the Letter in the Unconscious or Reason since Freud" (1958) Lacan says, "We are used to the real. The truth we repress" (169). Discourse is bordered by the real that appears in bits and pieces, as the unexpected or the uncanny. And the real destroys the linearity language imposes on us, showing us that neither meanings nor images are fixed in any innate syntax or grammar, nor in any simplistic binarism. The real is anamorphosis that shows things as other than they seem to be, as living inconsistencies. Yet these words do not encapsulate the horror effects of the real that Lacan called *jouissance* effects. We humans are caught in the paradox of loving what gives us libidinal consistency, even if it kills us. In this sense *jouissance* is narcissistic cum symptomatic, rather than narcissistic cum selfish or specular (Musso 41). Any smashing of the egotistical familiarities by which we protect the symptoms we love more than ourselves destroys the "necessary fictions" we live by. Lacan found a basis for his conceptualization of the death drive in "Analysis Terminable and Interminable," where Freud suggests that even if we learn to *faire avec* ("do things with") our symptoms, we do not get rid of them. Indeed, Freud was pessimistic about the chances of abating human suffering simply because he thought the someThing in us that wants to suffer is stronger than any wish to change. Lacan was not so pessimistic, because he learned how to approach *das Ding* he called the *objet a*.

Lacan interpreted the mythical father in *Totem and Taboo* (1912) as Freud's early intuition of the real power of a dead figural father at the base of mental and identificatory functions. But Lacan had no actual father in mind. Rather, the interplay of language and identification constitutes verbal myths in which one Ur-father is an exception to the rule of castration or lack. These build up individual egos (narcissistic ideals and myths) and superegos (responses to the gaze of others, as well as to one's own internalized ego). Yet fictions that support a sense of ego consistency are continually performed by the real that creates inconsistencies at the interface of all the orders: conventions (symbolic), identificatory fusions (imaginary), and drives (real). In the order of the real, desire and law conflict to produce *jouissance* that circumvents both, tying humans to the contradictory logic they try to get around in the imaginary and symbolic.

This becomes clearer in the difference between Freudian and Lacanian theory of dreams. Lacanian "drive" is made up of two kinds of energy: meaning as a repressed body of signifiers from which we speak and act (the Other); and *jouissance* as the residual effects or trauma accumulated in the human task of trying to unify being, body, and speech despite the fact that unity is to be found only in social lies and myths. We try to mend losses and inconsistencies and deny lack, through language and libido. Language and libido are grafted onto the biological organism in tandem, giving Lacan reason to speak of two deaths: the animal one and the signifying alienation imposed on the organism that becomes a particular subject's *cause* or *jouissance*. It should not be surprising that the second death sometimes causes the first death in ways that Lacanians do not find "natural." Death, then, is a clear focal point for looking at Lacan's discovery that there is a failure in representation itself, its first instance being a failure of any innate unity of body parts or mental processes. Indeed, dreams dramatize the failure in representation that Lacan equates with the second death.

## The Burning Child Dream

In chapter 7 of *The Interpretation of Dreams,* Freud recounts that among the dreams reported to him, one in particular claimed his special attention. It was told to him by a woman patient who had heard it at a lecture on dreams. The content of the dream made such an impression on her that she "proceeded to 're-dream' it; that is, to repeat some of the elements in a dream of her own, so that, by taking it over in this way, she might express her agreement with it on one particular point." Freud goes on:

> The preliminaries to the model dream are as follows. A father had been watching beside his child's sick-bed for days and nights on end. After the child died, he went into the next room to lie down, but left the door open so that he could see from his bedroom into the room in which his child's body was laid out, with tall candles standing around it. An old man had been engaged to keep watch over it, and sat beside the body murmuring prayers. After a few hours of sleep, the father had a dream that *his child was standing beside his bed, caught him by the arm and whispered to him reproachfully: "Father, don't you see I'm burning?"* He woke up, noticed a bright glare of light from the next room, hurried into it and found that the old watchman had dropped off to sleep and that the wrappings and one of the arms of his beloved child's dead body had been burned by a lighted candle that had fallen on them.
>
> The explanation of this moving dream is simple enough and, so my patient told me, was correctly given by the lecturer. The glare of the light shone through the open door into the sleeping man's eyes and led him to the conclusion which he would have arrived at if he had been awake, namely that a candle had fallen over and set something alight in the neighborhood of the body. It is even possible that he had felt some concern when he went to sleep as to whether the old man might not be incompetent to carry out his task. Nor have I any changes to suggest in this interpretation except to add that the content of the dream must have been overdetermined and that the words by the child must have been made up of words which he had actually spoken in his lifetime and which were connected with important events in the father's mind. For instance, "*I'm burning*" may have been spoken during the fever of the child's last illness, and "*Father, don't you see?*" may have been derived from some other highly emotional situation of which we are in ignorance. But, having recognized that the dream was a process with a meaning, and that it can be inserted into the chain of the dreamer's psychical experiences, we may still wonder why it was that a dream occurred at all in such circumstances, when the most rapid possible awakening was called for. And here we shall observe that this dream, too, contained the fulfillment of a wish. The

dead child behaved in the dream like a living one: he himself warned his father, came to his bed, and caught him by the arm, just as he had probably done on the occasion from the memory of which the first part of the child's words in the dream were derived. For the sake of the fulfillment of this wish the father prolonged his sleep by one moment. The dream was preferred to a waking reflection because it was able to show the child as once more alive. If the father had woken up first and then made the inference that led him to go into the next room, he would, as it were, have shortened his child's life by that moment of time. . . . Hitherto we have been principally concerned with the secret meaning of dreams and the method of discovering it and with the means employed by the dream-work for concealing it. . . . And now we come upon a dream which raises no problem of interpretation and the meaning of which is obvious, but which, as we see, nevertheless retains the essential characteristics that differentiate dreams so strikingly from waking life and consequently call for explanation. (*Interpretation of Dreams* 509–10)

Freud goes on to say that not enough is known yet to produce the logical explanations that would make psychical processes of such dreams, processes that trace back to something already known. The processes of dreaming must be left in suspense, he concluded (549–50). To summarize, Freud says that the dream was *caused* by an external physical stimulus, the glare of light. Moreover, the words the father hears must have actually been spoken by the son during the fever. "Father, don't you see?" remains enigmatic for Freud. For him the meaning of a dream is, above all, that it fulfills a wish. Freud saw the wish of the father as clear: that his son not be dead. But the "logic" of such a dream escaped Freud, leaving a gap between his depiction of the unconscious as knowing neither contradiction nor time and his interpretation of this dream as an unconscious production that wants to make the future into the past (see his essay "The Unconscious"). Indeed, even at this simple level the dream would already be a contradiction in terms. Yet Freud was ever careful in his logic. A dream like this was enigmatic enough—although apparently clear—not to merit the label "psychical process." It can only be called a wishful fulfillment.

Lacan will point out decades later that a wish has content and motivation and so, of necessity, language. The unconscious is structured not only like a language, but by language. Since Freud did not understand how language could dwell in an unconscious place, he could not answer his own questions regarding this dream. Lacan viewed dreams as lexical systems of meaning that follow the laws of the signifier that inhabits us, subjecting us to its preeminence. Whether the signifier represents image, word, gesture, name, and so on, it re-presents a subject for another signifier in the oppositional relational chains of associations where one thing has meaning only in reference to something that precedes it (an echo of an introjected presentation or symbol), and it takes on its shadow function of retroactively pinning down a meaning only in reference to a lost symbol. Although signifiers structure elemental meanings that are "suspended" as potential meanings, since they return as language—as signified effects—they *seem* to arise from themselves. Yet no language is natural. All language is referential, not only to itself, but basically to an empty set or void. But because it is not generally understood that the referent of language is first and foremost the void, the processes that allow it to function as a binary system seem complete within themselves. Yet if one sees language as time travel, it always infers the place it comes from, the gap in time necessary to leap from a memorized sound, image, or word to the act of speaking it. Lacan called this momentary interval, which infers a split second between speaking or thinking and memory, the unconscious or discourse of the Other. If we always draw on something partly graspable, but graspable only in parts, it should not be surprising that the unconscious is that which infers lack and fading in all language acts, as the intentionality of desire.

In this context dreams would not be a lure to a figurative semiology where the visible is what it seems in some ever-shifting pattern of cultural codes or rhetorical iconologies. Rather, dreams follow the laws of the signifier insofar as language makes meaning by binary oppositions joined to the relations implied in such oppositions, extended by the functions of metaphor (substitution) and metonymy (displacement). Looked at in this way, one can understand Lacan's claim that the unconscious is not hidden or repressed. Rather, he came to understand the unconscious in terms of the profound and extensive functioning of desire via metaphor and metonymy. But Lacan does not follow Roman Jakobson's claim that metaphor and metonymy are rhetorical tropes, set apart from poetic functions Jakobson finally decided must be autonomous.

Rather, metaphor operates dream thought as the desire that runs throughout language via substitutions. The displaced libido that blocks the realization of desire is metonymy, carrying the *jouissance* effects that surface between sounds, words, persons, things, and events of every kind. Dream signifiers articulate unconscious meaning as it fades into the unsymbolized region Lacan named the real, the order from which drives return with the force of libidinal energy, aimed not so much at someone or something as at the satisfaction of a desire. Such ideas shed light on Freud's confusion about wish fulfillment. If you wish for something, you wish *because you do not have it*. You wish for the satisfaction of resolution. In the wish you can fantasize or hallucinate something that appears to bring satisfaction with it. But the resolution in pleasure is illusory, just as is the issue of where the fantasized dream object comes from in the first place. "Nothing will come of nothing," Lacan says, quoting King Lear's words to Cordelia (*Séminaire VII* 146).

Freud saw no problem here where Lacan finds one. To wish for something is to say that something is lacking in reality, whether dream or fantasy is the mode of expression. For Freud, wishing is a childlike act, an instance of "pathology." Moreover, it is an act complete in itself. The wish fulfills the pleasure principle, providing in fantasy what is missing in reality. In rethinking the act of wishing, Lacan makes a distinction not only between pleasure/fantasy and reality, but also between dream content and dream structure. Wishing has a structure, or an order(ing) as well as a content. To wish for or desire something that is absent is precisely to state that something *is* absent. Insofar as desire functions by endless repetitions, which become substitutions—the law of metaphor points to a prior referent, the law of metonymy—Lacan does not see each desiring act as a discretely contained drama, focused on a particular object or event. Desire is, rather, a permanent function in subject structure. Arguing from various mathematical propositions, Lacan claimed that identity can never be One with itself. The "at least one" point of exception, be it thought, image, trait, fantasy, or whatever, indicates a grounding in something put in that seems already there, *as if* "inside," so to speak; some excess that goes beyond mere wish or satisfaction in pleasure. This excess can quickly turn into anxiety or painful repetitions of someThing that does not wish one's good. Thus this Thing (Lacan's *objet a*) is eradicated from conscious knowledge, but returns anyway to split apparent unities.

In further differentiation from Freud, Lacan hypothesized that sleep was a way to prolong a dream, not in order to maintain a state of pleasure, but to hold on to a state between consciousness and unconsciousness where one can defer a displeasure to be encountered in waking life. In this state the dreamer denies the reality of a future displeasure by disguising the something lacking. Thus the displeasure appears in starker and darker terms on awakening. This would hold true for any pleasurable dream. We desire what we lack. And what everyone lacks—except someone in a state of psychosis—is the Other that contains one's treasury of signifiers and the "objects" one imagines having lost. Signifying material and the effects of loss coalesce in layers of meaning ensembles, where signifiers propped up against the *objet a* allow us to think (Miller, "Preface" 12). Unconscious signifying chains surround the referent of loss, itself the catalyst to the building of egos, meaning systems, desires, and ideologies whose goal is *to close out intimations of loss*. Lacan refers not to lost objects per se, as we remember, but to loss as that which detotalizes our perception of images, our words, all our belief systems, and all our acts as well as our illusion that we are whole beings and bodies.

Loss occurs first in relation to the separations that give birth to desire by enforcing myriad cuts and interventions in the seemingly continuous space of space itself. A cut may appear in a glance of the eye, a flick of the tongue, a lowering of the eyelashes, a sigh, a word, removal of the breast or nipple from an infant's mouth, a silence cutting into a world of speech, a scream, a sacrificial cut on the body made in admissory denial of the losses we cannot bear. In any case, we quickly identify ourselves with objects that fill up the void. In this sense Lacan speaks of the subject as a cut, an identification with a separable object. Cuts go all the way back to the first separations— birth, weaning, toilet training, walking, speaking—that link the structure of separation to that of alienation (language and *jouissance* imposed on us) as organizing agents of lack and loss. The remainder of *jouissance* (ecstasy or agony)—affect produced by effect—left over from a cut valorizes the *objet a* not assimilated in memory or signifying chains. In-*corp*-orated, these objects in-*form* our language. They can always be found in the drama of any fantasy as an *objet a*—a cause of desire—toward which a fantasy aims in a moment of hoped-for satisfaction that turns sour when it must be repeated. Or they surface in yet one more missed encounter where the face of the real appears when we stumble over unfulfilled desire, and we quickly block it out to avoid facing the painful nature of the fleeting encounter.

One sees that Freudian wish fulfillment and Lacanian realization of desire are not the same thing. Moreover, Lacanian desire, insofar as it is the desire for the Other, is inscribed in a code to which the dreamer—once awake— has no access. Desire can become knowable only once deciphered through the fictionalized or distorted account of the dream narrated. Still, what relation does a dream have to desire, representation, or death? Freud thought representations were just the same as visual images, a combination of *Wunsch + Begierde* = *Vorstellungsrepräsentanz*. Yet Freud did not solve the problem of how visual images can have meaning in the unconscious if the unconscious has no words. Lacan did not take the picture to be the representation or the "thing." Rather, the Thing appears, if at all, in an intellectual act, in a use of language and intelligence meant to *avoid* recognizing some desire. This view raises many questions. Whose desire? Why avoided? How do you know when you recognize your desire or simply invent a new one? And so on. Lacan's point is simply that desire cannot be grasped outside speech and cannot be recognized or constituted outside the naming of it. Yet even though desire must be spoken to be "known," desire is not mind but, for Lacan, interpretation.

## Representation, Desire, and Repression

We know that Lacan did not take representation to be the picture, or even the image evoked by a picture with its various verbal attributions. That is, representation is an aesthetics neither of mimesis, of presence, of repression, nor of politics. Nor is re-presentation a rhetoric of tropes and figures. Although there is a juncture between repression and representation insofar as representations are suspended repressions—potential meanings—Lacan looks to Freud's essay "Die Verdrängung," translated as "Repression" (1915), to make sense of this juncture. In that essay Freud locates an originary moment, a repression after the fact, and a return of the repressed. Lacan agrees that these three different times or moments can be mapped in terms of the *jouissance* material that constitutes a subject in relation to desire. Basically, Lacan views repression as a *desire* not to know unconscious material. But repression is no more consistent than anything else. When subjects cannot fully represent something to themselves, repression momentarily lapses. Something falls from the Other in that moment. The subject is represented as an *objet a*. Such representations refer to a prior lack in identity, in the subject's signifying chains, such that the subject falls out of the chain from time to time as a missing link. What counts in representation—Lacan's version—then, is not the image, but the *petit a* that stands in for the lack in the image and breaks up all illusions of unity, a linearity of narrative, or a well-made subjectivity of perception.

Although desire is the desire to close out loss, the *objet a* that seeks closure also resists it. Simply put, the desire to re-press means that someThing presses back. This pressure is the energy that drives humans by a *jouissance* that is not biological per se and is constant (since inconsistent) only insofar as archaic remainders and unsymbolized effects are eternal. Lacanian *jouissance* effects reveal affects in the ego that unveil the pain in fixity and rigidity. The ego is in this sense inhabited by the death drive or enjoyment of pain that pierces the center of all being and representations, making itself the center. In this context one would read dreams backward, retroactively, to the narcissistic flow of fantasies that reach for the *objet a,* where bits and pieces of the real are caught at the impasses between conscious and unconscious life and can sometimes be assimilated as meaning. This real that empties into knowledge all the time as a palpably positivized negative is present in the dream in a way it is not in conscious life, where myth, symbol, words, stories, ideologies, desire, all keep us from confronting its naked horrors at the limit.

But what are these horrors? They are the moments of seeing past consciousness into the Other and beyond, into the power of desires that live in us like so many parasites and into the less than glorious causes that drive us. We encounter the naked real only in psychosis or in nightmares. Yet in conscious life the "return of the repressed" is the return of the real in a heterogeneous dissemination of the *objet a* intervening in language, images, and desire to produce gaps, fadings, moments of agony, the cutting effects of daily snubs, acts *manqués,* words committed, and so on. They are the discontinuities that reveal subjects as pieces of flesh, words, and dreams that are partial. The lack of unifying symbolization at the heart of matter(s) means that our real (not actual) bodies are fragments, image-inarily sewn together around a lump of nothingness that Lacan says is not no "thing." The irreducible object at the heart of every signifying chain makes us cling somewhat strangely, even desperately, to representations, words, and others in order to deny the alienations and separations that constitute us as creatures of *jouissance* who clothe ourselves in the paradoxical warmth of meanings and opinions that never quite eradicate lack or make up for loss.

What happens in life—and more acutely in the dream—is that meaning acquires an unreal aura that casts doubt on a normally logical explanation of the relation of signifier to signifier. In these moments meaning rejoins the real by the *objet a* that language only makes seem consistent (Ragland-Sullivan). Insofar as we discount the *objet a,* we must try to define limits to discourse by other means, by figures or by signifiers that pin down some meanings. But figures cannot say, nor can signifiers reveal, that the true limits of discourse are those of missed encounters, desiring encounters that flee even as they occur, showing the slip of mortality, the void, the hole in the field of knowing and being that sends us scurrying to totalize. The catch-22 is this: Repressed signifying chains in the Other function as a presence in knowledge but are closed off to the subject as to the meaning of intentionality cum desire. The Lacanian signifier does not relate to another consciousness, then, but only to another signifier. The subject is not a someone for whose benefit things are represented, but a missing link that is spoken or re-presented in its own blackout. The primordial character of the *objet a* disappears as well in the rituals organized around them. Everything works toward fixing consistencies that are still not dependable. Even rigid designators such as proper names are finally empty and meaningless except as they unify identity myths around a name and a lineage and in a position of desire.

What can the dream tell us about all this? Freud said we dream so we can keep on sleeping and thereby continue to enjoy the pleasure of an illusion. Lacan says the dream has the potential of showing the horror of the real at its navel. What does awake us, then, if not some external stimulus, as Freud said? As an empirical piece of evidence, the idea of external stimulus is hardly reliable, except in the most impersonal, haphazard of accounts. Lacan says we awake when we confront something just beyond the Other reality in the dream, that of the primal scene. But for him the primal scene is not parental copulation. Rather, he points to the claustrophobic desires and hurts closeted within family novels, those traumata that produce unassimilated, *almost* forgotten knowledge—the terror of the all too familiar. If, as Lacan argues, we really are bits and pieces of the real rather than whole subjects, and if we continually reconstitute ourselves in the eyes of others because we are not innately or autonomously whole—implicitly asking, "What do you want?" in our goal of winning love cum recognition—then it makes sense that what drives the life game is not life, but death. The idea of sometimes awakening from a dream in order not to know the terror of what is told there is not so nonsensical. The images, words, sounds, and movements of life lend a safety to consciousness that denies any fundamental link between being, desiring, and dying.

Lacan reread Freud's *Totem and Taboo* to mean that the father the sons wanted to murder is the paradigmatic Father: the "at least one" whose obscenity lies in the paradox of his embodying desire and law at the same time, his desire as the others' law. Freud never ceased asking what a father is. The answer Lacan found in Freud is a dead father ("The Subversion of the Subject . . . ," in *Ecrits* 321). The symbolic father is the signifier for a mark of law, a "no" to identificatory merger with the mother's body and being, spoken in the name of a differential signifier whose effect is purely and simply identifying with structural difference. A symbolic father can be any one of the names of the father, from "Daddy" to a river spirit. What interested Lacan was the Ur-Father, whom he called the real father, the one who signifies the paradoxical conjuncture of desire and law in each person (*Séminaire XXIII*).

Now this father is not the symbolic signifying father of law whose *name* knots the three orders, the knot itself giving rise to a fourth order. Rather, the real father is the dead father who returns to haunt us, to poison desire, to mock us with our inadequacies or theirs, in the form of *jouissance* obstacles that structure our desires in a language of the master, academic, hysteric (obsessional), pervert, psychotic, or analyst. Representations or signifiers cover up the real father whose name is the death that haunts us from before birth and beyond the grave. Although signifiers cut into the body, imposing the lack that gives rise to the desire Lacan called an Other place, objects also cut up the body. Objects separate the subject from its desire and from desired objects that seem precious *because* they are not full in themselves. If the subject is a response of the real, a discontinuity in the symbolic, then death is not just an allegory, analogy, or metaphor, but the *jouissance* effect we identify ourselves with, even as we lose ourselves in language, hiding out there.

### The Burning Child Dream Revisited

Now let us go back to the burning child dream, within a Lacanian purview. Despite its seeming clarity, the child reproaches his father, asking if his father cannot see that he is burning. We know that the Lacanian gaze and the eye are not the same thing, that seeing implies understanding whereas the gaze infers judgment or idealization. "Can't you see . . . ?" implies the gaze rather than the eye, the organ that seems to produce the gaze but actually shuts out the larger dimension of knowing related to seeing. The father "sees," Lacan thinks, that there is more reality in dreaming than in the light in the next room that supposedly woke him. Lacan does not agree with Freud that the boy's words—as repeated in the father's dream—refer to some actual statement the boy made about his illness. In *Seminar XI* Lacan asks a different question than Freud did: What caused the boy to die? He suggests that a missed encounter in reality lies burning somewhere in the father's unconscious knowledge and beyond, where cause is a real cause. The real father in the son's signifying knowledge would be the father who never dies. This obscene father—represented by consuming flames—never ceases to enslave a subject's desire by imposing his enjoyment (*jouissance*) on the subject as law. Children carry paternal or cultural superegos—or the lack thereof—as a dead weight on their shoulders. In our bereaved father's dream we hear only one sentence: the son's cry. "Don't you see? I'm burning" differs minimally from the Oedipal text, where Oedipus sees not the reality we all face—that of desiring the mother's continuing love and nurture—but the horror that he has murdered his father! The real that Oedipus cannot face is the realization that he occupies an impossible place: object of his own *jouissance* rather than subject of the law. In this death place, the horror is not that desire has won out over law, but that he has robbed himself of a viable name and position in the social order of possible positions: positions of exchange outside the family novel.

In the burning child dream the father sees what he had known before: that his son desires something (his mother, his father, his father's power, his father's death), or simply that he DESIRES. And the son burns from anger, jealousy, or passion. Indeed, the dream occurs before the father *knows* his son's arm is burning—whether the light from the fire in the adjacent room awoke him or not—but after some Other knowledge has come to him in the impotent cry of the son's passion heard, but unheeded, before his death. The horror of the real is that nothing circumscribes the subject there. The slits and rims of desire, the fragments of nostalgia, are nothing compared with the void edge of terror opened up by an ego unraveled onto anxiety's raw *jouissance*. In the real the *objet a* takes over. One is either swallowed up or persecuted by gazes or voices everywhere. The relief so commonly expressed on awakening from a dream comes from the realization that (unlike the psychotic) one has not after all fallen into the chaos of the real. To live as a piece of the real is to live beyond the limits of the law of the signifier that enables one to re-present oneself *as if* one were unified; to live beyond the law of metaphor that provides the capacity to substitute, and thus the comfort of a doubleness that appears as oneness: to live beyond illusions of unity, as if outside one's own body.

Lacan sees the father's dream as an act of homage to a missed reality that can no longer occur—except by repeating itself again and again in some never-attained awakening, where the real and symbolic brush directly against each other. In this scenario, repetition as fixity lies on the inverse side of desire (Other discourse), interrogating the time of repetition, which specifies itself only in relation to death (Sevilla 7 ff.).

In the synchronic structure of the signifying chain, one thing stands in for another, always referring to a before or an elsewhere. This function is, paradoxically, more hidden than the diachronic function where we see meaning referring to something laid down before. Lacan takes up the burning child dream in terms of the *jouissance* effects that lie outside the text. The dream is quite simply a voice pointing to an image that horrifies the father. Is it the fact that his son is dead that terrifies the father, as Freud thinks? Or did the horror come before the death, as Lacan suggests? Does the horror lie in the Lacanian theory of a splattering of libido in little haunting incests, murders, or other *jouissances* that lie outside social law but mark the scenarios of everyday life anyway? Why does Freud insist on the *moment* of an encounter with the father in a dream, *as if* by accident, as the same *moment* the boy caught fire? Lacan says the accident repeats something more fatal than the accident of the old man falling asleep beside a dead body.

The missed encounter of desire has occurred sometime between the father's dream and his awakening, a dream dreamed so that he would not formulate what he already knew but had never symbolized (*Seminar XI* 58–59). The dream is clearly not a pleasurable fantasy that his son is still alive. The son is not alive in the dream, but is horribly dead and burning, confronting his father with the real that Lacan writes in the axiom: "There is no sexual relation." This means that there is no sexual harmony possible between persons, insofar as there is a taboo against being One with the mother lest we become psychotic. Moreover, Lacan means, of course, not that there are no sexual relatings, but that in familial and tribal communities the polymorphous "perversity" of children's libidinal freedom confronts adults with desire as lack and *jouissance* as loss, calling into question the socialization of sexuality by superego injunctions. Indeed, Lacan's position is that such moments do not belong only to childhood sexuality, suddenly to disappear into neatly coded sexual repressions. Rather, in the greatest of innocence, children present themselves as "drives" to be sacrificed in ritualized gender ideologies in familial or tribal games. *This* is the "grimace of the real" in the dream where the child appears as burning. One might suggest that for loss of tribal rituals in contemporary life, we now have psychoanalysis, itself a symptom of modernity in Lacan's view.

Desire shows up in the loss expressed by an image at the cruelest point of an object, the object always referring to the partial drives Freud labeled "sexuality." If the power of these drives is omnipresent and overwhelming, making intimacy something we must generally hold at arm's length, it follows that in the contemporary West some "institution" (theory and praxis) would arise to name and try to tame what other cultures and our own ancient past named and domesticated as gods and devils: the real. Thus they made a place for *jouissance* effects in everyday life. It also makes sense that such unique encounters of what Lacan calls extimacy—where inside and outside join— occur in dreams. Dreams are repetitions of insistences and resistances. In the burning child dream "only a rite, endlessly repeated act, can commemorate this not very memorable encounter," Lacan says, "for no one can say what the death of a child is, except the father qua father, that is to say, no conscious being" (*Seminarr XI* 59). He means the real father of obscene *jouissance*. In Lacanian teaching the father qua father is the real father: the superego weight whose law is impossible to bear. In our text, the bereaved (imaginary) father's startled return to wakefulness is itself a representation of something that had already happened in the recent or even remote past.

Lacan said that when the signifier and signified knot together, a *point de capiton* or punctuation by the real occurs. Jacques-Alain Miller has called such moments *jouissance* effects or interventions of the *objet a*. Perhaps the same can be said of the compelling nature of the burning child dream, whether or not the dream ever occurred. Within the narrative, the father had to sleep. During this time, someone may have said that the boy looked *as if* he were asleep (i.e., not dead). We do know that people hear while they are sleeping. The father could have overheard such a remark and suddenly seen his son in a different light, so to speak. What we do know is that both Freud and Lacan reported a dream. Freud thought it concerned a straightforward wish but found that problematic to interpret. Lacan thought dreams were statements of unfulfilled desires (wants of the Other) and that Freud was a man of desire who recognized desire. In this context, what "falls out" of the dream is a voice, a firebrand, a detached sentence, bringing fire (passion) there where it falls on the sleeping father.

But the image of the flames blinds us to the fact that the fire bears on the *Unterlegt,* and *Untertragen,* the real (*Seminar XI* 59). What, then, is the correlative of the representation in the father's dream? Lacan answers that the dream is the counterpart of the *Vorstellungsrepräsentanz.* He does not mean a representing of a representation, but something taking the place of representation: the *objet a* that appears, essentializing subjects as semblances. This *objet* hollows out a place in the body and a void in linguistic meaning to be filled (*Seminar XI* 60). But what Lacan calls the "true representation"— the real father—is that of a forever-missed encounter with God. God has not been murdered in myth, as Freud claims, nor is he dead, as Nietzsche pronounced. God is another Name for the radicality of identification in Being. In this sense God is the real part of being that speaks us as if from beyond, as *jouissance* objects. Being is graspable in relation to the body, where the real appears in fragments and disappears, present only as a block of inertia that persists anyway, independent of signifying chains. That life and death are not opposed to each other, but that life twines itself around many potential deaths, may not now seem such a surprising idea. Insofar as humans have a representational deficiency for sexuality, and names that identity depends on cannot bear up under the weight put on them, the partner of every subject is the Other sex. That is, we desire our own *jouissance* whose presence is inferred by symptoms, the silence of the drives, signified effects that appear in repetitions and dreams. We desire *that* which is familiar, although it marks us as creatures of pain and insufficiency and so does not wish our good. In this sense the cut between the organic and inorganic marks the site of the death drive that returns us beyond the pleasure principle, returns fragments of our "selves" and each other to us as *objet a.* These cuts are commemorated by an impossible encounter of the body with the real of *jouissance,* where we are by definition thwarted.

In Lacan's hands a representation becomes the striking of a pose, something that seems to compete with the world of appearances. Language will not represent a referent. Language does not mediate between speakers, but carries the affect of *jouissance* effects. It also negotiates desire. In the burning child scenario, the dream works as a fantasy screen that hides something beyond language and also contains something primary and determinant where repetition functions as ritual. Thus, both awakening and the function of the real remain ambiguous. The noise or light that awakens the dreamer may *re-present* reality. But what wakes us in *the Other reality* hidden behind the lack of that which takes the place of the representation: *Trieb* or the *objet a*. For lack of representation, however, the drive is not there. It comes, then, in the *jouissance* that desexualizes desire, Lacan says, and joins up with narcissism. It comes in the awakening that resituates individuals in a consti-tuted and re-presented reality that carries out two tasks. First, the real has to be sought beyond the dream in what the dream envelops as hidden, behind the *lack of representation*. And behind this lack, there is only one representa-tive: a real that governs our activities, the real that is for each of us a *cause* (*Seminar XI* 60).

In the Lacanian rereading of the *fort-da* game, it is not the mother's leaving that causes a split in the infant's consciousness. Rather, the game is aimed at what is no longer there as re-presented. The game aims to close a gap opened up. Insistence on repeating—whether the repetition is a burning son's accusation, perhaps uttered only in a silent gaze, or a modest request that is not quite what it seems to say—shows us that inconsistency is the enemy we all battle (*Seminar XI* 195). The subject, merely a response or function of the real in internal exclusion to itself, thinks with its objects and thus is driven by the work of life, which is death.

Returning to the burning child dream, let me suggest that what wakes the father is his seeing what he had refused to see in his son's lifetime: his son "burning with desire." Did he see more? Did he sense himself sacrificing his son's desire on the pyre of family morality? Did he see that the father's Name bars the mother's *jouissance?* That law is artificial, an empty social construct? We cannot know this any more than we can know whether the dream occurred. But we can suggest that Lacan said something true about human beings: that we are above all desiring creatures. For Lacan the cause of desire, often antithetical to a given desire, is to achieve *jouissance* that produces yet more desire. Insofar as each creature's desire gives rise to ideological causes, causes whose logic may seem confused or irrational, the *objet a* allows a writing of the real to shine through the emptiness of symbolic and imaginary-order discourses, showing that representations occur because meaning re-presents (presents once more) a void reference in trying to cover over a hole that contains would-be secrets about who and what we are. Meanings and fantasies act like screen memories whose importance lies in their seeming substantivity. If we really are partialized pieces of drive (the *objet a*) that makes semblances of us all—apparently essentialized as creatures of *jouissance*—then such experiential essentialism will necessarily find a way to state itself in myth, meaning, and interpretation. The dream becomes paradigmatic of the human subject disseminated in images and words that fade into enigma or anxiety. And sometimes horror.

The limit is that of the missed encounter with the *objet a*, where mortality and death link meaning to the body through desire. So *jouissance* and desire materialize language through a logic of affect that lies closer to the realm of narcissism, the imaginary, and ego psychology than to classical biological drive theory or to the theory of economic history, where the material real takes objects to be facts. Nor is the Lacanian void total, totalizable, or negative; rather, it is a living presence whose effect is the human subject as itself a piece of the real: an *objet a*.

## Notes

1. See especially chapter 6, "Freud, Hegel and the Machine."
2. See *The Seminar of Jacques Lacan, Book XI: The Four Fundamental Concepts of Psychoanalysis* (1964), 176.

## Works Cited

Aparicio, Sal. "La forclusion, préhistoire d'un concept." *Ornicar* 28 (Spring 1984): 83–105.

Aubert, Jacques, ed. *Joyce avec Lacan*. Paris: Navarin, 1987.

Freud, Sigmund. *The Standard Edition of the Complete Psychological Works (SE)*. Trans. and ed. James Strachey. 24 vols. 1953–74. London: Hogarth, 1986.

———. "Analysis Terminable and Interminable." 1937. *SE* 23: 216–53.

———. *Beyond the Pleasure Principle*. 1920. *SE* 18: 7–64.

———. *The Interpretation of Dreams*. 1900. *SE* vols. 4–5.

———. "Repression." 1915. *SE* 14: 143–58.

———. *Totem and Taboo*. 1912. *SE* 13: 1–162.

———. "The Unconscious." 1915. *SE* 14: 166–215.

Lacan, Jacques. "The Agency of the Letter in the Unconscious, or Reason since Freud." 1958. *Ecrits*. 146–78.

———. *Ecrits: A Selection*. Trans. Alan Sheridan. New York: Norton, 1977.

———. "The Mirror Stage as Formative of the Function of the I as Revealed in Psychoanalytic Experience." 1949. *Ecrits*. 1–7.

———. *Le Séminaire de Jacques Lacan, Livre VII: L'éthique de la psychanalyse*. Text established by Jacques-Alain Miller. Paris: Seuil, 1986.

———. *Le Séminaire de Jacques Lacan, Livre XXIII: Le sinthome*. 1975–76. Unedited seminar, Jan. 20. Portions of this seminar edited and published in French in Aubert, *Joyce avec Lacan*.

————. *The Seminar of Jacques Lacan, Book II: The Ego in Freud's Theory and in the Technique of Psychoanalysis*. 1954–55. Ed. Jacques-Alain Miller, trans. Sylvia Tomaselli, with notes by John Forrester. New York: Norton, 1988. See especially chapter 6, "Freud, Hegel, and the Machines."

————. *The Seminar of Jacques Lacan, Book VII: The Ethics of Psychoanalysis*. Text established by Jacques-Alain Miller. New York: Norton, 1992.

————. *The Seminar of Jacques Lacan, Book XI: The Four Fundamental Concepts of Psychoanalysis*. 1964. Trans. Alan Sheridan. New York: Norton, 1981.

————. "The Subversion of the Subject or the Dialectic of Desire in the Freudian Unconscious." 1960. *Ecrits*. 292–325.

Miller, Jacques-Alain. "Microscopie." *Ornicar* 47 (1988): 46–64.

————. "Preface." Aubert, *Joyce avec Lacan*. 9–12.

Musso, Lydia G. "Breves punctuaciones acera de la psicosis." *Revista del cercle psicoanalitic de Catalunya* 9 (1989): 37–44.

Ragland-Sullivan, Ellie. "The Limits of Discourse Structure: The Hysteric and the Analyst." *Lacanian Discourse*. Ed. M. Alcorn, M. Bracher, and R. Corthele. Spec. issue of *Prose Studies* 11.3 (1988): 61–83.

Sevilla, Marc. "Rencontres intercales à Nice." *La Lettre Mensuelle: Ecole de la Cause Freudienne* 68 (1988): 7–13.

Stevens, Wallace. "Not Ideas about the Thing but the Thing Itself." *Poems: Selected*. Intro. by Samuel F. Morse. New York: Random House, 1959. 166.

Zizek, Slavoj. "Lacan and the Real." Unpublished paper for First Paris Seminar in English, workshop held in Paris, June 1989.

■

# Risky Resemblances: On Repetition, Mourning, and Representation

## Elisabeth Bronfen

> There are thus good reasons why a child sucking at its mother's breast has become the prototype of every relation of love. The finding of an object is in fact a refinding of it.
>
> Sigmund Freud, *Three Essays on the Theory of Sexuality*

### Repetition, Love, and the Death Drive

If Freud was right to claim that all love objects are refound, then love is based not only on repetition but also on loss. Lovers choose a desired object because they discover the resemblance to an earlier one, but they also mourn the old in the new. A paradox, then, seems to be inextricably embedded in an economy of love based on repetition. To recover a lost love object in the embodiment of another entails acknowledging precisely the loss that one is reinvesting libidinal energy to deny.

Yet repetition does not just imply a return to a previous point, in the sense of retrieving something lost, reiterating or relating a past event. Repetition also implies a plurality of events, a sequence of actions that relate to each other through resemblance. It thus implies that difference, deferral, and belatedness find themselves inscribed in the relation of the second term to the first. The repeated event, action, or term always contradicts its predecessor because, though similar, they are never identical; and though recalling the unique, singular, and original quality of the former event, the second emphasizes that it is *more than one*, a multiple duplicate, occurring at more than one site. Repetition describes a longing for an identity between two terms even as it stages the impossibility of literal identity.

To repeat, furthermore, implies that the second term doubles by copying the first. It is a citation, an imitation, an echo that renews or a reproduction that mocks. The relation between the two terms is, then, inscribed not only by a dialectic of similarity and difference, but also by reciprocity. Although the value of the latter term is dependent on the former because derived from it, the former exists as *recollection;* that is to say, only by virtue of the latter. Repetition not merely imitates but also reproduces something new out of an earlier body.

But what does repetition have to do with the psychoanalytic concept of the death drive? In an attempt to interlink psychoanalysis with semiotics, Rimmon-Kenan argues that repetition serves as a crucial node between the discourse of prose fiction and that of the unconscious. Though difference is in some sense always at the heart of repetition, she makes a distinction between *constructive repetition,* as a strategy emphasizing difference, and *destructive repetition,* as one emphasizing sameness. The former serves the pleasure principle, for it allows that repetition can be used to transform a passive position into an active one that achieves mastery over a disturbing, wounding event. Rimmon-Kenan emphasizes that whereas this form of repetition is constructive precisely because it works on a principle of difference, another form of repetition—based on undifferentiated oversameness, without variation—comes close to being a perfect repetition, an occlusion of approximation and distance. But this "complete repetition . . . is death or . . . beyond life and beyond narrative" (155). That is to say, a repetition that succeeds perfectly may be fatal because the space of difference between model and copy has been eliminated, collapsing both terms into one entity and abolishing the singularity of each separate term.

Indeed, if we return to Freud's *Beyond the Pleasure Principle,* we discover that his discussion of the death drive suggests several aspects of repetition. On one hand, the death drive uses repetition when it seeks to fragment and reformulate entities into new versions. Repetition is the process underlying life's detour toward death in an effort to avoid a fatal short-circuit. On the other hand, Freud's discussion of the compulsion to repeat also argues that "all repetition repeats an original identity that it seeks to restore: the lovers, their original unity; life, its original death" (Weber 150). The paradox is not only that the repetition traced by the death drive is either the source of division or what reduces tension and reproduces an earlier situation or unity. Rather, the paradox is that even as the death drive (or desire for death) articulates a triumph over temporality by returning to and thus repeating the preorganic inanimate condition of statis beyond division, it also supports a narcissistic desire for constancy, for a binding of energies and a reduction of psychic tension. Though this latter desire sustains life, it *also* strives to suppress alterity and to subordinate difference to identity. Because repetition, by producing perceptual identities or representations of resemblance, afford a rediscovery of the same, it supports *both* this narcissistic desire and a desire for death. Lacan, moreover, gives the interrelation of repetition, return, and sameness another dimension when he argues that what always comes back to the same place is the real. He thus suggests that what repeatedly returns in ever the same guise—or what the subject seeks to return to—is the facticity beneath and beyond images and symbols: death, as originary loss of the maternal body, of a full unity.

Weber, however, notes that the conscious subject cannot distinguish between an originary *fort,* a lost origin impervious to an exteriority, and its repetition in life, the *da* as a return of what is always already *fort.* For life to originate, the origin it departs from must in some way be disrupted, so that repetition can be conceptualized not only as a return to a movement before and beyond life but also as a form of departure, which produces "a *da* that is *fort:* elsewhere, and yet also here" (139). Repetition is, then, a double movement, both a return to something primary and the production of something new. Refining love objects as a trope for refinding the origin of unity and death is also an act of constructing representations that occlude the real origin, just as any surrogate love object never fully satisfies because, though similar, it cannot be identical. As my discussion of Alfred Hitchcock's film *Vertigo* will show, any primordial point of origin as the teleological aim of repetition can be thought of only from the position of belatedness, as a return to a point never known or, rather, known for the first time in an act of repetition that is based on difference.

Thus repetition articulates loss not only by enacting a *lost object* in the midst of difference, but also in the sense that the first repeated term refers to something that is, as Rimmon-Kenan notes, "not univocally a 'presence' but also, quite possibly, an 'absence' " (155). For what the child in Freud's narrative of the *fort-da* game repeats is not the mother but rather her *absence,* and it allows him to repress this experience of absence. Repetition is, then, a duplicitous rhetorical strategy, for what it enacts lies in the past. It is also different from— in fact quite possibly the first representation of—the *original* lost term. Thus repetition is also informed with novelty. In Rimmon-Kenan's terms repetition is "the first presence, the first 'performance' of the absence" (156).

Two points can then be isolated as central to my initial proposition that love is based on loss and repetition, suggesting a conjunction between the two terms. Repetition is inscribed by the death drive; in fact, it serves as one of its forms of articulation. At the same time, repetition can be seen as an attempt to counteract absence, loss, and death. Repetition suggests that, as a double of the lost object, the first object can return in a new form, thus questioning the uniqueness of the first term and implying that the loss is not irrevocable.

## The Psychic Process of Mourning and Refinding a Lost Beloved

In the following discussion I undertake a comparative reading of two texts in order to illuminate (1) how love, because it involves the repetition of loss, is intimately bound to the production of images; (2) how a love for images implies an exchange with revenants that places the lover in the position of the mourner; and (3) which position the beloved occupies in this process. Both Poe's story "Ligeia" (1838) and Alfred Hitchcock's film *Vertigo* (1958) revolve around the protagonist's loss of a first beloved and his refinding her in the body of a second woman whose death ends this plot of mourning and detection.

In both texts the man's initial response to the loss of his beloved is a form of melancholy: he withdraws from the world, his desire is invested in the dead. The world of the living regains his interest only when he sees that he can retrieve his *lost* love object by falling in love with a second woman who resembles the first. Because she is used as the embodiment of the first beloved, as the object through which the lost woman is refound or resurrected, the second woman's body also functions as the site for a dialogue with the dead, for a preservation and calling forth of the first woman's ghost, and thus for the articulation of necrophilic desire. Yet the reciprocity of original and copy is such that the second beloved can disappear within the process of repetition, subsumed under the representation of the first wife, who in turn may be just a copy of an original absent feminine body.

In general, the mourning process involves an identification between living mourners and the newly deceased in that both are situated "between the world of the living and the world of the dead" (Van Gennep 147). The interest of the mourners is either to *kill* the dead a second time as quickly as possible, so as to leave their shared position of liminality, or to preserve the dead and prolong their stay in the realm between. Mourning inspires ambivalence toward the deceased, a merging of love and hatred that, because of the identification between the dead and the living, can also be turned against the surviving self. What results is a merging of manic joy with depressive sadness. The accusation against the Other may turn into melancholic self-accusation; the desire for the dead Other may transform into a desire for one's own death, or the vengeance felt toward the Other may result in an exaggerated sense of triumph. Yet the core of melancholia, Karl Abraham argues, is significantly occupied by the loss of the mother. Not only, then, is the maternal body refound with each love object, but each process of mourning also repeats an originary disappointment engendered by this first loss.

In psychoanalytic terms the healthy trajectory from mourning to remembrance or commemoration is marked by a freeing of libidinal energies from the first lost object that must be reinvested in a second surrogate object, in whom may be perceived the image of the deceased, notwithstanding the introduction of difference. Successful mourning, one could say, is repetition as forgetting a lost object sufficiently to reinvest one's love in another, accepting the other as Other, even if the new beloved in part suggests the refinding of the former. John Bowlby distinguishes several phases of mourning: a period of numbing, distress, and anger followed by one of yearning and searching for the lost object, of thinking intensely about the lost person, calling for her or him, scanning the environment to find the lost one again, concerned only with stimuli that suggest her or his presence. After a phase of disorganization and despair, based on the recognition that the lost love object cannot be retrieved, a last stage of reorganization concludes mourning. This closure is a healthy failure by the survivor to preserve a continuing sense of the dead person's presence, a detaching of memories and hopes from the dead.

In the two texts to be discussed, however, repetition is such that a libidinal reinvestment tries to *coalesce* the refound object with the lost one. Here the memories of and hopes in the dead body are preserved precisely by a detour over another woman's body. For the *other woman* is chosen either because she is completely different (Poe) or because she uncannily resembles the first (Hitchcock). In this difference she clarifies the meaning of the first, much as a phoneme gains its value only through differentiation, as Saussure has shown. That is to say, if the difference between model and repetition is foregrounded, the double affirms the first woman's death, while she serves to deny death if what is privileged by the mourner's eye is an undifferentiated sameness. The second beloved is ultimately to become an identical substitute for her predecessor, yet such an achievement of oversameness requires blindness to the singularity of both women. Regaining a lost amorous unity, denying the narcissistic wound induced by death, occurs in the repetition of a beloved as an image, yet an image materialized at and over another body. Typical of the rhetoric of the uncanny in Freud's discussion of the term, a fatal blurring of the distinction between the imagined and the real occurs, in that a sublation of signifier into signified disaffects the difference between real materiality and semiosis.

For the second woman to repeat or double a predecessor means that she functions as a revenant in more than one sense. (1) She represents a dead woman; her body lodges and rematerializes a deceased person whom a mourner seeks to retain among the living. That is to say, *dead woman* is the semantic value she signifies for her lover. (2) She is denied her own body and is thus only a figure for a meaning other than herself, prematurely turned into a ghost, into a body without the soul or personality unique to her, into a living cipher for her lover's desired lost object. While she functions as a double, the second woman's uncanny resemblance to a dead woman signifies fatality, for the teleology of the narrative is that the exchange between mourner and second beloved ends in a second killing.

### The First Text: Poe's "Ligeia"

Poe's tale "Ligeia" is told in retrospect, the narrator writing after and in response to the death of his second wife, Lady Rowena of Tremaine, and the concomitant resurrection of the first wife over her corpse. That is to say, the narrative frame functions as the written repetition of the recent uncanny events in his life—"and now, while I write" (262). One could say that the narrator's act of textual representation qua recollection is thus clearly marked as an attempt to deny the absence of his beloved, since this gesture emerges precisely from an acknowledgment of his loss.[1] Invoking her name in order to bring "before his eyes in fancy the image of her who is no more," the narrator repeats a resurrection that will also be the topic of the narrative.

The unnamed narrator recalls that the body of his first wife came, even while she was alive, to pose an enigma to such a degree that it turned into the measure for his heuristic and imaginative abilities. The description he offers of her presents her in proximity to death, yet it does so in two very different ways: she lacks a fixed position in her social order, and her etheralized body signifies that she is no longer fixed in the realm of the living. He implies that for him she was always present as a name and an image, completely severed from any historical context. He cannot remember any external facts about her—how, when, or even where they first met. Cut off from any but his imaginary world, she is merely an image invoked by dint of a signifier; she is Ligeia, without a proper name that would place her within a specific kinship structure: "I have never known the paternal name of her" (262). Indeed, such a privileging of the name and image of the beloved over the woman's real body is found in all three phases of the tale, for the image takes the place of the model while she is alive, while she is psychically resuscitated during mourning, and while she is textually resurrected in his written narrative.

One could speculate on whether she may in fact never have existed, in which case the death of the second wife may have functioned as the performance of this absent wife's first presence. But even if such conjectures extend beyond the boundaries of the text, her invocation as a nongiven name, Ligeia (referring back to other literary women poised between the human and the divine—a dryad in Virgil's *Georgics,* a siren in Milton's *Comus*), invokes the idea that for the lover she is from the start always already a representation, her presence arising out of an originary absence. For the narrating lover she is *no body* because devoid of alterity, because, as I will analyze in more detail, she is a body image and a name, reproduced by and thus dependent on his spectatorial gaze.

Ironically, in contrast to the narrator's inability to present any external facts about his first wife, his memory never fails him in respect to "the person Ligeia." Yet this description of her appearance also presents her in conjunction with death by emphasizing her ethereal being, her more than human, enigmatic perfection. She seems to be positioned between life and death, entering his closed study "as a shadow," her hands of marble, the beauty of her face superlative, like "the radiance of an opium dream" (263). Precisely because she seems to embody an uncanny blurring of real and image, Ligeia serves as the object of his obsessive gaze. By analytically exploring her body, imaginatively fragmenting it bit by bit, he hopes to gain access to the answer her strangeness poses. Yet the fascination of this enigma seems to be contingent upon its always eluding his grasp, making the *living* Ligeia ultimately not accessible. That is to say, from the start Ligeia exists primarily in the imaginary register of the narrator. Here she traces the figure of death because she is conceived as an inanimate signifier (not a contextualized body) and because her body is treated like an inanimate substance that his gaze fragments. At the same time, as Barthes argues, to scrutinize the loved body means to search. Such speculation arises from the belief that the mechanical cause of desire is situated in the adverse body. It can be explained by an observation that fragments the body. Barthes, therefore, likens the lover's scrutinizing gaze to "the process of fetishizing a corpse" (*Lover's Discourse* 71).[2]

Above all her other body parts, the narrator privileges Ligeia's eyes as the source for his analytic abilities but also as the cause of their failure. His "intense scrutiny of Ligeia's eyes" becomes tantamount to speculating on metaphysical truths, for in the way that "Ligeia's beauty passed into my spirit, there dwelling as in a shrine, I derived, from many existences in the material world, a sentiment such as I felt always aroused within me by her large and luminous orbs" (265). Yet full knowledge remains beyond his reach, approaching and then departing again. Though he explains that he has incorporated Ligeia's beauty into himself, in a formulation that significantly presents her as a sacred dead body, because enshrined in his spirit, he stresses his dependence on her. In respect to knowledge, the narrator assigns Ligeia the position of the maternal body: "I was sufficiently aware of her infinite supremacy to resign myself, with a child-like confidence, to her guidance through the chaotic world of metaphysical investigation" (266). She offers the promise of satisfying his desire for knowledge while simultaneously defying its fulfillment on two scores. He believes her learning to be so superior to his own that only her readings can render the mysteries of the world transparent to him. At the same time, her body literally functions as the site where a fundamental enigma could be solved.

To lose Ligeia to death, then, means losing that figure through which a promise of gaining absolute knowledge seems to be secured. In his depiction of her death he interprets her last living moments as a "wild longing . . . an eager vehemence of desire for life," and the poem she writes, "The Conqueror Worm," is a call to defy death by virtue of one's will (268). Ironically, it seems as though Ligeia's death was the result of her husband's fatal appropriation. His usurping gaze not only reduces her to one meaning—that of a figure signifying absolute truth—but also reduces her to a meaning from which she is alienated. For she is merely the body at which his truth, but not necessarily hers, is reflected and secured. Furthermore, her death not only liberates him from his dependency on her but tests the omnipotence of his thoughts. Once he recollects the absent Ligeia in memory by the power of *his* will, he is no longer "a child groping benighted" when deprived of her intellectual tutelage. Rather, he now fully possesses the knowledge she had; "I revelled in recollections of her purity, of her wisdom. . . . Now, then, did my spirit fully and freely burn with more than all the fires of her own" (272). By implication, her absent body resurrected in spirit satisfies his will to knowledge more fully than her living body could.

The knowledge at stake is one surrounding death, for it involves reveling in the recollections of the deceased, calling her name aloud as if "I could restore her to the pathway she had abandoned—could it be forever?—upon the earth" (272). It involves, in short, a defiance of death's irrevocability and the impossibility of mastering death through knowledge. It is not incidental that Ligeia's *strangeness* is from the start connected with her liminal position between life and death. Alive, she has a truth that is beyond worldly knowledge; but she will not yield it. Thus she not only marks the limit of mortal knowledge but also metonymically represents that truth that is beyond. Once dead, she becomes the site where the mourning narrator can prove his imaginative will. Denying that she is now inanimate and absent brings about a second kind of liminality. If as a living woman she always already belonged to the Other world because of the knowledge she represents and the insubstantiation of her body, as a dead woman she again hovers between the two realms because he will not let her die. Although she is bodily absent, his imagination repeats her presence as a remembered image. If we recall that Freud interpreted the *fort-da* game as a scenario of mastery over absence and potential death, it seems that, as a representation, Ligeia is completely possessed by her lover since he can revive her at his will, precisely because he is possessed by her ghost.[3] Though in the process of his recollection he fragments her into many body parts, he does so to reconstruct a satisfying image of wholeness, now fully reliable because solely dependent on his ability to imagine. Given that it was the image, as signifier for his wholeness, that he loved all along, the absence of her material body logically affords pleasure. And yet the story he tells is that mourning this image requires its rematerialization, first as another body and then as a text.

That the possession of truth, the solving of an enigma, and a triumph over death are interconnected is metaphorically enacted in the repetition of Ligeia at the body of his second wife. It is certainly not incidental that the narrator omits all description of Ligeia's corpse and turns immediately to the second phase of his story—the unhappy marriage to Lady Rowena, Ligeia's physical opposite. Just as the fervor of Ligeia's love became clear only under the auspices of the threat of life's opposite—"But in death only, was I fully impressed with the strength of her affection" (267)—so too it is the difference of Rowena that allows the narrator to delineate and thus realize the meaning Ligeia has for him. Only in the presence of his utterly different second wife can he reassemble the memory image of his first wife; but because the trajectory of this undertaking is to reach a perfect and fatal repetition and to foreclose difference between the two, its result is a move beyond life.

Giving way to a "child-like perversity" and a hope of alleviating the sorrow of lost wholeness, he furnishes rooms in a way that suggests a fantastic destablization of any difference between the real and the imagined, the animate and the inanimate, by virtue of phantasmagoric effects induced through lighting and artificial wind currents behind draperies. In these bridal chambers, which are also the shrine of his first wife, he doubles his corporeally present bride with the recollected dead girl. This process of making the dead Ligeia present by a continual invocation of her name seems to drain the living Rowena, until an exchange occurs in which the latter becomes ever more like the invoked first wife, herself losing bodily substance. In this attitude of melancholic mourning, which one could describe as Bowlby's second phase of searching and yearning for the lost love object, it seems as though the narrator uses the name Ligeia to repeat a form of usurpation in respect to Rowena that he had already enacted in his epistemological appropriation of his first wife. The reciprocity contained in this repetition of one wife by her opposite is such, then, that the mourning husband desires the first dead body as a way to deny death yet in the same gesture causes death to reemerge in the form of the second wife's corpse. At the same time, though the process effaces the second wife, the first wife can be preserved at the expense of, but also only by virtue of, the body of her predecessor.

The culmination of this exchange is Rowena's actual death. If he needed Rowena's difference to define and secure those qualities that make Ligeia perfect for him, he now literally uses her body to recall his dead wife, undoing her death by giving her a second birth. A second point of complementary action resides in a narrative inversion: whereas Ligeia's process of dying was described but not her corpse, Rowena's movement of death is eclipsed while her corpse is excessively described in the famous scene of transfusion. Each time he remembers Ligeia as he sits next to Rowena's corpse, the figure of the dead Rowena seems to come alive; each time he physically reanimates the body, it falls back into stillness, until he is so fatigued by these efforts that he completely gives in to his fantasy and the image of Ligeia rises out of the body of Rowena.

This end, of course, poses several questions for the reader. Are we to see this resurrection of a dead woman as a trope for the fact that the protagonist can love Rowena only as a perfect repetition of Ligeia (that is, a belated statement of his love, induced by an opium dream and to be articulated only through the displacement of one body for another)? Or is this a trope for his inability to love a corporeal woman, desiring exclusively an intellectual relationship, and one, at that, which privileges the image over any concrete presence? Or is this an opium-induced, wish-fulfilling dream representation concerning the triumph of his will to knowledge and his creative imagination that defies the limits of natural mortality?

In one sense the doubling of one wife by another, by metempsychosis, is meant to prove a continued existence of the soul after bodily decay and thus serves to soothe the mourner about his own fear of mortality. What is assured in this resurrection is the repossession of a lost love object, implicitly a repetition of the maternal body, which promised infinite knowledge and at which the child first experienced a sense of unity and wholeness. At the same time, this doubled corpse—the dead Rowena/the resurrected Ligeia—

functions as a conglomerate of real and figural death, in that Rowena's actual demise also signifies the death of her two predecessors, the maternal body and the *first* wife. Furthermore, because a representation always points to the absence on which it is grounded, always articulates its difference from the original term, its rhetorical value is duplicitous. The resurrected corpse signifies the split within the self, the primary castration by death that grounds life even as she is used to re-present the narcissistic wholeness of the mother-infant dyad.

In the act of repeating a first dead woman in the figure of a second one, then, the surviving lover desires death even as he attempts to deny it. The repetition enacted at the body of the second wife, aimed at making her identical to the first, both succeeds and fails. To make them the same means structurally eradicating all difference and division between the two women, a move from doubleness to oneness. This is possible only when the body double is exactly what it signifies, when the space between copy and model is unambivalently obliterated, when it is dead like the model it repeats. But as such a figure of death she becomes completely Other and defies any unity with the survivor. What is thus ultimately eliminated is the disturbing and threatening factor of hesitation, the hovering between anxiety and desire. Put another way, this motif both articulates the fascination with the revenant materialized over a living representative of the dead and stages an imaginative triumph over the intellectual hesitation it induces.

One could say that what the narrator reproduces in the bridal/death chamber is an uncanny representation, a scenario that enacts the analogy between portrait and revenant. The emergence of the image of the first dead wife within the narrator's psychic reality involves the denial of loss engendered by an acknowledgment of loss. The production of this image signifies an escape from the mutability of the material world into the illusion of an eternal image repertoire, even as the resurrected body signifies an elusive, intangible, receding entity. Thus this representation obliterates and articulates mutability in the same gesture. The uncanniness of this representation resides in the fact that it both is and is not the living body of Ligeia, neither image nor body, neither living nor dead, neither absent nor present, neither the model nor the copy. It enacts a moment of ambivalent undecidability par excellence as it points simultaneously to the refinding of a lost object, with its ensuing erasure of death, and a perfect repetition as the presence of death.

Yet this second death also marks a closure of the protagonist's uncanny exchange with the dead, ushering in a new phase in his mourning. Realizing that the lost object can be retrieved in the form of a mental image confirms his belief in the omnipotence of his thoughts. The story's frame implies that from this experience of the uncanny he gains the canny satisfaction that he is in possession of a reassuring image, endlessly composable, completely reliable—that of Ligeia's person as the "one dear topic . . . on which my memory fails me not" (263). She is now at his disposal, severed from the danger of mutability that had threatened both Ligeia's body and her double's. If she was initially the cipher and key to an inaccessible knowledge of the Beyond, the security of this image reassures him that he now has power over and knowledge of death.

Repetition, then, in the duplicitous manner described above, both is inscribed by death and is its apotropaic charm. Repetition of the first wife at the body of the second enacts a fatal stasis of oversameness, while the repeated invocation of the name Ligeia throughout the story stages absence. At the same time, both the body double and the free-floating signifier Ligeia are used to show that death is not irrevocable because a first lost object can be returned to the living. The response to the uncanniness of the collapsing of a model and her repetition, of the imagined resurrection of the former and the real death of the latter, is one of putting closure on liminality. It is as though the narrator needed the second wife to prove the strength of an imaginative mastery over death, to enact the triumph over death occasioned by a literal translation of a dead body into a resurrected image. After this experience, he seems to have found the answer to the enigma posed by Ligeia's ambivalent presence between the Here and the Beyond and can bury both wives' bodies under the image and name of Ligeia, of whose possession he is now assured. The new fixing of semantic boundaries is such that resemblance shifts to the purely figural level and needs no further literal enactment. The frame of the story presents the successful exchange of *uncanny ambivalence,* or intellectual hesitation, for *canny uncertainty.*[4] The latter term implies a reassuring distinction between what is certain and what is not, while the former engenders (as one of death's articulations in life) a disturbing obliteration of the security of distinct meanings, even if it also entails the magic of a dead wife's literal return.

## The Dead Beloved Returned and the Representation of the Beloved: Two Moments of the Uncanny

Before turning to my second narrative, *Vertigo*—a cinematic repetition and differentiation of "Ligeia"—it is worth teasing out the theoretical implications of the questions so far raised by Poe's story. For the unrepresentability of death is such that it necessitates an unrolling of repetitions, both theoretical and narrative, a foreclosure of coherent and integrated conclusions,[5] as it also raises the issue of the particularity of death, of which Maurice Blanchot says it is unsharable even as it is also what each individual subject has in common with all other human beings. We must thus ask, Is this motif of the repetition of the death of the beloved a trope for the desire for death or the denial of death? Does the mourner desire the woman because she is a corpse/revenant, or does he force the second beloved to reenact the dead woman in an attempt to deny the irrevocability of death by denying its inscription on the body of the first beloved? As a double, the second woman dissimulates the presence of death even as she is also a sign of immortality beyond physical demise. These doubles thus embody both aspects of the death drive discussed, depending on whether similarity or difference is privileged. If the former, they enact the deathlike stasis of a return to an original unity; if the latter, they enact the principle of dissimulation, division, and nonidentity that splits any sense of wholeness. What remains undecidable is whether this repetition of the event of death is an excessive, because doubled, representation of the mourner's own death by virtue of a detour over two women's bodies, or an excessive exclusion of death. At the same time, the second woman's death raises the question whether we can distinguish between desire and denial; for by forcing a living woman to become the exact copy of a dead one, to literally embody a ghost, the mourner indicates a desire to transcend the limits of natural mortality. He also seeks to transcend the distinction between first and second, that is to say, the limit temporality poses. At the same time, he reproduces another uncanny return of the same, not only in respect to a lost woman but also in respect to her death, which the mourner had turned to repetition to repress in the first place.

Indeed, as Cixous argues, the uncanniness that repetition provokes suggests that "death is never anything more than the disturbance of the limits." What the double enacts is that, if what has been lost returns, nothing is ever lost, "nothing has even disappeared and nothing is ever sufficiently dead" (543). Even as a return of the dead at the body of a second woman apotropaically enacts that death is not irrevocable because the lost returns, what also returns is death itself. This gesture of repressing death betrays death everywhere. In Cixous's terms, to speak by resorting to the uncanny rhetoric of the double "is either to surmount it (thus to cancel it, to castrate it) or to effect it" (543). The compulsion to repeat the familiar in the unfamiliar, the known woman in the stranger, allows that other familiar value, mortality, which was to be repressed, to return as well. In his discussion of the uncanny, Freud notes that at the figure of the double, death returns as something known but defamiliarized by virtue of a substitution. In representations of a second beloved's death, repetition is an apotropaic gesture because it displaces death from the self, from the masculine position, by letting it return as the double of a feminine body. The beloved's body induces an intellectual hesitation about whether she is a sign for life's triumph over death or death's inhabitation of life; whether her presence signifies that a corpse has been resurrected or a living body turned into a corpse; whether the first beloved is alive or the living woman dead through repetition.

The crucial hesitation that her duplicitous presence induces, however, is about whether she is indeed the same as the deceased or different, a marvelous instance of the dead returned or merely a perfect imitation. For while the former instance of oversameness through repetition implies a canny identity that soothes the lover's desire for narcissistic wholeness, the latter similarity crossed with difference emerges as a disturbingly uncanny figure that must be expelled. The two women can be identical, with all difference eradicated, only when the second is dead. But once dead, she too is completely lost, completely Other, defying any belief in the recuperation of a lost unity, just as her uncanny presence thwarted such desires in that her dissimulation of death always also implied a division or split. What the second killing eliminates, then, is precisely the gesture of hesitation that left the spectating mourner suspended between bliss and mockery.

Another unresolved ambivalence set up by Poe's story is whether the dead woman is to be understood as a revenant, returning to feed on the living man's memory to preserve her own existence in the world. Does she draw him into her sphere of death and away from the world, making it impossible for him to reinvest his libido in another, living woman? If so, is this scenario to be interpreted as a form of mourning that prefers a preservation of the dead object, even if it means self-mumification or suicide, over an acknowledgment of loss? Or should one read the protagonist as embodying vampiresque traits? He draws the life out of a second living woman not only figuratively, in that she is to incorporate the inanimate representation of a dead feminine body, but also literally, in that he kills her in the process as she moves from *resembling* to being *identical* with the dead woman.

In the thematic paradigm I am concerned with, the second beloved is killed because she proves autonomous to the image of her lover's self, which she is meant to ensure—that is to say, because she thus embodies the way that misrecognition and difference is always inscribed in the illusion of finding a *lost* wholeness in and through the love for another. The killing, then, denies death's *castrative* threat to life as this threat shows itself whenever narcissism's stability is wounded. Yet ironically the *reproduced* dead body of the second beloved confirms death in its total identity to the first dead wife, confirms the irrevocable loss of a prenatal unity. However, though her death places the second woman outside the surviving lover's control, it also affirms his omnipotence of thought, since he can mentally reanimate her and continue the sequence of refinding and killing her in further surrogate bodies.

To raise one last theoretical point: This mourning plot ending in a second death also implicitly invokes the issue of representation and mimesis, given that the protagonist literally carves his image of the lost beloved with the material body of another woman. As Kofman writes, mimesis is necessary because life always already implies death and requires a mortal supplement so as to be fixed and take on shape. The feminine body, doubling a deceased, is a living representation of death, affording the mourner a fixture to death, in the double sense of a realized form and a displacement onto another feminine body. Yet as Kofman's linkage between the artist and the mourner, between representation and revenants, also implies, mimesis does not *fix* death in a canny sense alone. The duplicity of representation is such that it shows that life necessarily passes by death, lets death emerge and be repelled at one and the same time. Whereas images, repeating a lost object, help the mourner to assuage loss, Kofman argues for yet another conjunction between image and mourning. The resemblance any mimetic representation is grounded on is, in fact, the work of melancholy. It involves a duplicitous denial of loss because it acknowledges that the image emerges from an initial acknowledgment of loss and thus always also provokes its perpetual articulation. For the image of beauty, as it resonates with the lost perfect maternal body, allows us to escape from the elusiveness of the material world into an illusion of eternity (a denial of loss) even as it imposes on us the realization that this ideality is itself elusive, intangible, receding. Thus, because it is created based on the same elusiveness it tries to obliterate, what art in fact does is mourn such beauty, and in so doing it mourns itself.

In this ambivalent contingency on loss, art exemplifies the uncanny. Substituting for or doubling an absent object, it represents something that it both is and is not, while at the same time the beautiful form both is and is not eternal. The resemblance representation is based on involves similarity and difference; the second body stands in for but is not identical with its model, and it is precisely in this doubling that Kofman locates the analogy between representation and revenant. Both hover uncannily in a liminal zone, neither living nor dead, neither absent nor present; both stage a duplicitous presence, at once sign of an absence and of an inaccessible other scene, of a Beyond. Resemblance, she argues, topples all categories of oppositions that distinguish model from copy, the animate from the inanimate; it makes signs semantically indeterminate, meaning undecidable. Yet the anxiety that an experience of resemblance provokes in the viewer, because this resemblance points not only to the possibility of refinding a dead object but also to death, which is always a part of what the double signifies, can successfully be masked only by reestablishing fixed boundaries. These ensure that the living body resembling a dead body is truly dead, ensure that the portrait resembling an absent body is a figural, not a material representation; ensure canny Otherness. Not only, then, does a dead woman become a revenant because her image is preserved in and over the body of a second woman, but the image, because of the uncanny resemblance it evokes, is itself another form of the revenant. The second killing of a woman serves, then, as a trope for the reveiling of this fascinating and threatening resemblance that emerges when a deceased beloved returns at the site of a living representative of the dead.

## The Cinematic Repetition

The narrative theme of a man preserving a dead beloved in memory, resurrecting her by the power of his imagination, and able to complete his mourning only when this wife dies a second time has repeatedly fascinated writers and filmmakers.[6] I will, however, limit myself to a discussion of Hitchcock's *Vertigo*. In this film the resurrection of the dead beloved also requires the presence of a second, palpable body that the mourner can reinvest with desire by projecting his image of the lost woman, by making the second woman into his image of the first. As in Poe's tale, the similarity between the two women is forced into a relation of identity, fatal for the second one. The film, however, ends with the undecidable question whether this second death is a superlative gain or a double loss, a release from the first death that has successfully been worked through by virtue of the second or an instance of fatality, an act of compulsive repetition that could engender serial death. As such it discloses its own premises. As a metapoetic aside, if finding a love object is in fact a form of refinding an old beloved, by analogy finding a narrative theme seems to trace the trajectory of refinding a lost text. One crucial difference Hitchcock introduces in his cinematic refinding of Poe, even as he repeats the older theme, is that the beloved who is lost and refound is the wife of a friend and thus a forbidden lover. Furthermore, Madeleine is from the start a *revenant* because she is possessed by a dead ancestor, her great-grandmother Carlotta Valdes, so that her body is the medium through which this dead woman returns. The story begins when Madeleine's husband, Gavin Elster, asks his ex-detective friend Scottie Ferguson to follow his wife and watch her for fear she might kill herself, since Carlotta did so when she was Madeleine's age. Scottie accepts the job, fascinated not only by Madeleine's beauty but also by her suicidal attraction to death. She periodically falls into a trance, enters an Other world, splits herself in two, and suffers from amnesia when she regains consciousness. As Gavin Elster explains, "When she is in this state, she is no longer my wife."

Thus Madeleine's proximity to death sanctions a forbidden romance. Since when called by death she is no longer her husband's wife, she may be the protagonist's lover. Scottie desires Madeleine precisely because from the start she is not only an image of feminine beauty but, more important, a living representative of a dead woman. This morbid desire is duplicated when, having once stopped Madeleine from committing suicide, the detective fails to do so a second time, and she falls from a church tower and dies. In the second part of the film, the mourner refinds his dead beloved in a second woman, Judy. This second beloved serves as the body double of someone dead (Madeleine), who herself was conceived from the start as the double of the dead Carlotta Valdes. One could say she is a double revenant. Furthermore, in the first half Scottie not only falls in love with an image of perfect feminine beauty as it is enmeshed with the enigma death, but also confronts her with questions, probing her to disclose her secret. In the second half he refashions a second woman in the image of the first and again seeks to obtain the truth that she, as an embodiment of death, seems to harbor.

Hitchcock's film thus discloses that the desire resuscitation hides is the desire for a dead feminine body. To love a woman haunted by a ghost, and then a revenant of this *first* revenant, is to love a corpse with impunity, to embrace death by proxy in the figure of a woman returned and thus to do so without a threat to one's survival. Hitchcock explained, "I was intrigued by the hero's attempt to re-create the image of a dead woman through another one who's alive. . . . To put it plainly, the man wants to go to bed with a woman who's dead; he is indulging in a form of necrophilia" (Truffaut 243–44). The woman seems to oscillate between a husband (representative of the symbolic order) and a dead maternal body (the radically Other, the real of death whose access is barred to conscious knowledge). In this film, however, the protagonist, because he identifies with the divided, oscillating woman, is himself positioned between two points of reference. On the one hand he tries to *cure* Madeleine, so as to draw her away from the dead ancestor, and in this sense his desire for the haunted woman rivals not only the husband's but also the dead mother's. To cure here means to kill her fascination with death. But since this is also his fascination, the solution he seeks is a form of curing himself of death and ensuring his position as a survivor. On the other hand, courting Madeleine is a form of courting death, of identifying with precisely with position of nonexistence she embodies. As Modleski argues, "If woman, who is posited as she whom man must know and possess in order to guarantee his truth and his identity, does not exist, then in some important sense he does not exist either" (91).[7]

Yet this story falls not only into two halves but also into two plots, for here a romance plot is fatally intertwined with an economic speculation. The brilliant twist Hitchcock introduces is that the desired beloved is not merely an image and a revenant but in fact a masquerade, a false image, the dissimulation of a revenant. As the plot resolution shows, the Madeleine that the protagonist loved was always an impersonation by Gavin's lover, designed to cover the murder of the real Madeleine Elster so that the husband could inherit her wealth, with Scottie serving as the witness who would attest it was suicide. Furthermore, the woman he finds and forces to reenact the dead Madeleine is the same one who did the first impersonation, so that in making Judy into Madeleine he merely repeats the husband's gestures. The woman he refinds is indeed absolutely identical to the one he lost, yet both have been refashioned so as to function as a living representative of a dead woman, a materialized representation of death. Thus what this reversion deconstructs is the fact that an economy of love based on refinding a dead love object is a death-bearing illusion. As Spoto puts it, the relationship between Scottie and Madeleine must "involve a fraud and a deadly game, for the major theme of Vertigo is that a romantic fantasy is a dangerous hoax, potentially fatal" (335).

Given this second plot, Judy, unlike the Madeleine she represents, is not divided between her husband and her dead ancestor's desire, that being a scenario designed for Scottie's gaze. Rather, she oscillates between responding to two lovers' (Gavin's and Scottie's) desire, between being an accomplice to a murder and concealing this crime, and being an accomplice to a necrophilic love that in both parts of the tale reduces her to a materialized image of a dead woman returned. Faced with these two versions of love, real death emerges as a viable alternative. Whereas the first half of the story ends with a double death—the literal death of the real Madeleine and the figural *death* of the false *Madeleine* (the woman created by the husband for the detective)—the second half ends with the death of the real Judy as this also implies the death of the false *Madeleine* (now recreated by the detective for himself). The second death involves killing the double of the double, eliminating Judy masquerading as a false *Madeleine* who had been designed to dissimulate a real Madeleine while this real wife remains unseen throughout except as the *first* feminine corpse. It functions as the text's *mise en abyme*. What is thus also deconstructed in Hitchcock's version is that the image of the desired beloved can be a true image only once the death of the represented woman is confirmed. As de Lauretis argues, Madeleine's desire for (and identification with) the dead mother fascinates Scottie because it mirrors his own desire. Once Scottie discovers the hoax and Judy (Madeleine) turns out to be alive and real, the image she embodies is *untrue*. His search for the true image is not for the *simple image of woman,* but for the image of the dead mother represented and mediated for him by the revenant, as the constructed Madeleine. That Judy embodies the true image again only once she is literally dead implies that Scottie's desire is an impossible one—a true image of a dead woman from which all uncanny difference (death's rhetoric of life) is eliminated and must necessarily be inscribed by real death instead, placing the body once again beyond his grasp.[8]

Two important points distinguish the film from the novel it is based on, *Sueurs froides* by Pierre Boileau and Thomas Narcejac. Although the disclosure of the hoax marks the end of the novel, Hitchcock places it at the beginning of the second part, shifting his viewer's interest from the economic/murder plot to the romance plot. Whereas the novel ends, like Poe's text, in murder, the last death in *Vertigo* is the result of a second jump, whose motive is complex and ambivalent. My discussion centers on two questions. For what aim does the protagonist desire a dead woman returned? How does he respond to the discovery that she is the double of a double? That is to say, How does he resolve the uncanny hesitation the revenant enacts? Whereas in the novel murder occurs because the body double will not confirm that she is a revenant, the second death in *Vertigo* occurs precisely because such duplicity is to be resolved. The revenant of the revenant, once disclosed as a machination, must be destroyed so as to repress the sexual perversion this discovery also discloses. I will argue that Scottie provokes the fatal jump after Judy's confession because this shows him the void out of which his desire arose: the absence not only of any real woman but also of any real dead ancestor. Judy brings him face to face with his own death, which he has resorted to this romance to repress. If he must punish her for not being the living representative of the dead, he also punishes her for demasking both his necrophilic desire and his desire to conceal his own mortality, his vertigo being the symptom that marks an unsuccessful repression of it.

In a more rhetorical than thematic vein, the film also demonstrates how repetition not only is always inscribed by difference but also radically calls into question the notion of origins. For it emphasizes that there is no original beloved, only a woman repeating, by dissimulation, a woman haunted by a ghost, using no original living woman but rather the representation of a dead one, the portrait in a museum, as her model. That is to say, the Madeleine whom Scottie desires and chooses to refind is from the start not only a corpse but in fact the deanimated copy of a deanimated body, existing only in oral narratives of the past and in paint.

Whereas a portrait of Carlotta serves as the model for a series of surrogate love objects for the protagonist, a real masculine body stands at the beginning of the sequence of revenants and deaths: a dead policeman. As the plot unfolds, the reader learns that the reason Gavin chose Scottie as his exonerating witness is that Scottie left the police force because he suffers from vertigo. When he and another policeman were chasing a criminal over rooftops he was unable to follow, and the other man, turning back to help him, fell and died. Gavin is thus sure that Scottie will not follow Madeleine up the church steeple and discover the hoax—that he is throwing down the corpse of the already murdered wife.

Scottie falls in love with a woman who identifies with her great-grandmother, Pauline Lagerlac, while he is in the state of mourning his dead friend, while he feels guilty about the death of another and has been forced to recognize his own vulnerability before death. In Madeleine he believes he has found someone like himself, who knows that all the gestures of the survivor merely cover the underlying void. As he follows her on her visit to the cemetery where she learns, in an incomprehensible gesture, over the forgotten grave of Carlotta, to the rooms the dead woman used to inhabit, to the bridge where she jumps into the water, Madeleine is increasingly perceived as a mystery that he must pierce if he is to find peace. The unrest of the mourner turns into that of the detective/lover.

The second half of the film begins as Scottie—who is suffering from "acute melancholia together with a guilt complex" after Madeleine's suicide, which repeats and displaces the guilt induced by the policeman's accidental fall—sees Judy and recognizes her resemblance to the lost beloved he has been searching for everywhere. Hitchcock significantly changes the original story. He inserts a flashback at this point, from Judy's point of view, disclosing the murder plot even before the uncanny process begins of refashioning her into a perfect replica of the internal image Scottie has preserved of Madeleine. Giving the audience the truth about the hoax, he argues, lets suspense "hinge around the question of how [Scottie] is going to react when he discovers that Judy and Madeleine are actually the same person" (Truffaut 244). The crucial difference between the film and the novel resides in the way Scottie's response to his lover's confession implies an attitude toward death that lets him awaken with sudden sobriety from the fantasy of fulfilled necrophilic desire.

The romance plot in *Vertigo* allows Scottie fetishistically to invoke and avoid his own fall and articulates the ambivalent desire for and fear of falling qua dying. Madeleine's fallen body lies on the church roof in the same posture as the policeman's, and if her death in a sense displaces that of his friend, he identifies with both in his nightmare vision after his inquest, which engenders his momentary hospitalization for melancholia. His dream represents his body falling as the other two did, and in so doing it also imitates the dream of falling into the darkness of an empty grave that Judy as Madeleine recounted. That is to say, in fancy he repeats real and invented images of bodies falling to death until these two realms come together again when the fancied image is given reality in the last death.

Once he has rediscovered Judy, his courtship on the guise of dressing her again in the clothes, hairstyle, and makeup of the first Madeleine and teaching her the accent and gait of her predecessor, Judy does not resist Scottie's efforts to "make her over" into his fancied image. Indeed, she consents to her complete remodeling because she hopes to gain his love by virtue of his confirming gaze. She explains, "I'll do it, I don't care anymore about me." But already in the first half of the film, the impersonation she offered of a haunted woman was not independent. Judy's Madeleine does not know she is *possessed,* does not know about the strange visits to the graveyard, the hotel, the art gallery. This lack of knowledge places Scottie not merely in the position of the protecting spy, but also in that of the master analyzer who will scrutinize her gestures, her words, the dream material she offers him so as to "find the key," the "missing pieces" that will explain her symptoms. Preventing her from repeating her suicide transforms into a search for the truth she seems to harbor, a truth unknown to herself. The cure he ironically comes up with is that of remembering and repeating those gestures and scenes her dreams evoke until he gets her to return to the Spanish settlement Carlotta must have known. Here the murder hoax literally repeats the nightmare visions of falling, with which Madeleine has been feeding Scottie's imagination.

This scene is a successful representation of a successful suicide in which, for the spectator Scottie, the repetition of dreamed events transpires into their first actualization. Though the audience soon finds out that Judy never dies, that the Madeleine Elster never committed suicide, what Hitchcock's version implies is that Scottie's obsessional desire for truth drives the impersonated Madeleine to her death—this perfect repetition of dream material enacting the dissimulation of a fatal undifferentiated oversameness. Scottie seeks to cure by dispossessing the haunted woman; he wishes to kill the ghost of the dead mother and the power she seems to have over a living woman by uncovering a canny explanation for uncanny events. This desire for knowledge, for the *truth* about an event of death and a dead woman returned, informs the latter half of the film as much as does Scottie's necrophilic desire.

Furthermore, Hitchcock's film structurally exploits repetitions. Scottie (albeit unknowingly) repeats Gavin's scenario and is disconcerted about his lack of originality when he discovers this: "He made you over just like I made you over. Only better." Remodeling Judy into Madeleine haunted by a dead woman is meant to help him discover why she "ditched him for another guy" (as Judy puts it), namely death. In this second recreation, Judy once again becomes a tool, the body double at which he can kill his own possession by the dead woman. Because she realizes that he loves her not for her singularity but as the materialization of an image, she will dissimulate what was from the start a dissimulation. But this remodeling is also a form of psychic and social deanimation. In the transformation scene, which is staged as one long sequence culminating in the perfect repetition, her change in appearance is shown to be a kind of death on two scores. Once the costume, hair, face, and gait are perfect, the space between model and copy obliterated, Judy is like the dead Rowena, over whose corpse Ligeia rises, the image of the dead returned in the body of another. That is to say, she signifies a dead woman, yet in the process her own personality is *killed off*, since she is reduced to the substance with which this resuscitation can be modeled.

Once the transformation has been completed and Scottie can for the first time truly embrace her, an unconscious slip of the hand lets her don precisely the necklace that belonged to Madeleine and that Scottie duly recognizes from the painting of Carlotta. This move, I argue, can be understood in Lacanian terms as an *empty gesture,* as the beginning of a sequence of actions by which Judy signifies the recognition of her nonexistence, the void underlying her dissimulations. It signifies the beginning of her acceptance of her facticity. With the return of the piece of jewelry Scottie begins to realize that sleight of hand has been at play, and his second round of interrogation, which ends in a repetition of the fatal events at the Spanish settlement, is aimed at finding out the truth behind the woman's appearance. The confession he extorts from her is meant to clarify whether she is indeed a medium for a dead woman or a hysteric whose dissimulation can be solved. The solution Hitchcock gives is to show that her masquerade is twofold. It is the cover for a crime that can be solved to show that the woman is an imposter, her appearance false; this solution leaves Judy intact as a person in her own right, even if guilty of murder. But it also proves to be part of the hysteric's discourse, by which she plays the role of an object of speculation, impersonates an image for the male gaze to cover her lack in being; and this second disclosure leaves her faced with her nonexistence.

Sensing that the identity between the two women is the sign of a superlative hoax, Scottie wants to establish clarity by undertaking yet another repetition of the uncanny events, so as to put an end to all liminality and the intellectual hesitation it engenders. He explains to Judy that he needs her "to be Madeleine for a while. And when it's done we'll both be free." He wants to stop being haunted, wants to kill the ghost. He explains, "One doesn't often get a second chance. You're my second chance, Judy." The solution he believes her confession and the recreation of past events will offer is freedom from the guilt he felt about Madeleine's death as well as the guilt he feels for desiring to sleep with a dead woman. The repetition is meant to make him "free of the past," of the inscription of death, of the fatality and his own facticity that this implies, just as repetition was meant to cure Madeleine of her ghost. Yet where the latter brought about Judy's mock suicide, this brings about a real fatal jump.

The last shots of Hitchcock's film pose questions even as the detective and the mourning plot find closure. The oversameness in repetition indeed seems to free Scottie from one uncanny experience, that of death's presence in life. Judy's real death puts closure on liminality and duplicity. She is now identical with what she staged earlier on, and Madeleine, who has been cannily proved to be both a fraud and dead, can no longer haunt him. In one sense he overcomes his *castration* symptomized as vertigo (in this second attempt he does get to the top of the church tower), by castrating Judy, forcing her to be the tool and medium of his discovery of truth. He overcomes the death haunting him, the fallen policemen repeated in the fallen Madeleine Elster, by making Judy the *pharmakos,* letting her take death onto herself.

As in Poe's narrative, the aim of this last death is to eliminate uncanny hesitation, and the oversameness of repetition secures an identity between model and copy. Judy's corpse lying on the roof, dressed again by Scottie's hand, makes the first *figural* death *literal,* even as it confirms that, in Madeleine, Scottie loved the representation of a dead woman. Yet what the film leaves open is whether this last repetition is a triumph over death or a final subjection, whether Scottie is left in the posture of a madman, about to jump himself, or cured of his fascination and anxiety about death. Furthermore, the spectator in fact never sees Judy's dead body, only its reflection in Scottie's gaze, in the imitation of her fallen body that he, standing on the brink of the church steeple, slowly enacts by spreading his arms and legs as though he too were falling. As Stephen Heath argues, the act of producing representations functions such that the "sameness it asserts through the very fixing of difference" grounds and masks "a male domination, at the expense of woman" (112). Here difference is fixed in two senses: the difference of representation as the disturbing and uncanny articulation/concealment of death in life is effaced along with the difference that the living feminine body always poses to the masculine survivor's psychic representation of that body.

One last divergence introduced by Hitchcock, maybe in fact the most significant one, involves the question why Judy, as she sees the black outline of the nun approach, jumps to her death calling, "Oh, no." In his reading, Zizek suggests that *Vertigo* can be read as a film about the way sublimation is concerned as much with death as with an exclusion of sexualization. The power of fascination exerted by a sublime image always also announces a lethal dimension. Scottie loves Judy when she is idealized as Madeleine who is dead, and yet in this sublimation Judy is also already dead. For Zizek, the film uses its second part to enact the desublimation of the beloved object, to sap her power to fascinate from within, and her jump from the tower transforms into the realization of her diminution as sublime object in Scottie's eyes. Yet as I have also suggested, her jump, following her declaration of love ("I walked into danger and let you change me because I loved you") and Scottie's rebuttal ("It's too late. There's no bringing her back") can also be read as the ethical attitude Lacan connects with *subjectivization,* the *empty gesture,* with Judy's accepting without reserve the immanence of her own death, accepting that she is a victim of fate. Having fallen from being Scottie's idealized object of desire, she experiences the breakdown of her hysterical discourse. As the fascination Scottie feels turns into aversion, because her appearance transforms into mere dissimulation, one could say the mask he has loved and recreated proves tautologically to be indeed a mask, and he can distance himself from her and reject her.

After this fall, however, Judy recognizes not only that she has manipulated her lover, even as she seemingly lets herself be manipulated by him, but that she also is the object of fate's manipulation. Embellishing Lacan's definition of femininity, Zizek argues that woman's "power of fascination masks the void of her non-existence, so when she is finally rejected, her whole ontological consistency is dissolved. But precisely . . . at the moment at which, through the hysterical breakdown, she assumes her non-existence, she constitutes herself as a 'subject' " ("Looking Awry" 54). Judy's jump thus signifies an active act, a moment of subjectivity when she accepts the facticity of death she has so precariously been dissimulating throughout. In Zizek's terms, what is menacing about the femme fatale is not that she could be fatal for men but that she presents a "subject fully assuming her fate." I would add, it is the denial and repression of precisely this ethic stance that underwrites Scottie's behavior throughout this film. Furthermore, this form of feminine subjectivization always harbors a disquieting aporia. Even as it lets

Judy fall out of the illusion that any narcissistically informed images of wholeness procure, she always also repeats and fulfills the image of her model. In other words, even as she insists on her difference from any image Scottie may have formed of her, even as she confirms her subject position by embracing her own fatality, she also gives up her difference from the dead woman she was incessantly asked to repeat.

Both Poe's "Ligeia" and Hitchcock's *Vertigo* articulate the mourning lover's desire for excessive sameness as an image is given body. My comparative reading of these two texts—a first and a refound text—has emphasized that when a lost beloved is refound at the body of another, uncannily resembling the first, such repetitions deny the alterity of the copy, and if they are successful they also mean her mortification. These mourners resort to the force of death to cover the castrative wound to narcissism that an earlier instance of death had provoked. They reenact a real loss of their love object to repress the incision of the real, and they return by way of a second death to an illusion of their eternal stability, the revocability of death, the occlusion of facticity. The position of the mourner, however, also proves to be the position in which images are born and materialized. As such it serves as a recuperation of the mirror stage where, supported by the security of a wholeness with the maternal body, the child experiences its first jubilation at recognizing its own integrity over the images it has psychically formed. As Gaston Bachelard suggests, to love an image means unconsciously finding a new metaphor for an old love, the love for one's mother. As soon as one loves with all one's soul, it is this reality that is a memory. What ultimately emerges, both in the texts by Poe and Hitchcock and in my repetitive rereading of these texts under the auspices of theoretical discussion of mourning, of the death drive and of the uncanny, is the following. Repetition—the metonymic shifting of one's libidinal investment from one love object to the next (obliquely commemorating and forgetting the lost maternal body)—allows the new beloved to appear familiar and translates the beloved into a materialized image, yet it does so by the enactment of a second death. Repetition thus constellates a mode of representation called for by death even as it also serves as the apotropaic gesture used to ward off death.

## Notes

1. For another kind of discussion of representations of death in Poe see Kennedy.

2. See also D. H. Lawrence, who reads Ligeia's death as a form of being murdered by the husband's scientific observation, arguing that "to know a living thing is to kill it" (70).

3. See also Bronfen, "The Lady Vanishes" for a discussion of the *fort-da* game and the importance of the disappearance of the maternal body.

4. For a discussion of canny Otherness and uncanny difference within as two positions awarded to femininity in Western cultural representations, see Feldman.

5. See also Barthes's discussion of the twofold desire for coherence and disturbance in representations of death, notably in photography, in *Camera Lucida*.

6. In my book *Over Her Dead Body* I discuss further texts belonging to this thematic paradigm, which includes Villiers de L'Isle-Adam's "Véra," Maupassant's "La chevelure," Arthur Schnitzler's "Die Nächste," Gustave Rodenbach's *Bruges-la-Morte,* and Fay Weldon's *The Life and Loves of a She-Devil,* the last a feminist reversion of this theme.

7. Tania Modleski, in fact, argues that the image of the mother, dispossessed in life, assumes unlimited power in death. She reads Scottie's interrogation of Madeleine as a way to force her to turn her gaze away from the mother and acknowledge his supremacy.

8. See also Burgin 96–109.

## Works Cited

Abraham, Karl. *Gesammelte Schriften*. Vol. 2. Frankfurtam Main: Fischer, 1982.

Barthes, Roland. *Camera Lucida: Reflections on Photography*. Trans. Richard Howard. New York: Hill and Wang, 1981.

———. *A Lover's Discourse: Fragments*. Trans. Richard Howard. New York: Hill and Wang, 1978.

Bachelard, Gaston. *L'eau et les rêves*. Paris: José Corti, 1942.

Blanchot, Maurice. *The Writing of the Disaster*. Trans. Ann Smock. Lincoln: U of Nebraska P, 1986.

Boileau, Pierre, and Thomas Narcejac. *Sueurs froides*. Paris: Folio, 1958.

Bowlby, John. *Loss, Sadness, and Depression*. New York: Basic, 1980.

Bronfen, Elisabeth. "The Lady Vanishes: Sophie Freud and *Beyond the Pleasure Principle.*" *South Atlantic Quarterly* 88.4 (1989): 961–91.

———. *Over Her Dead Body: Death, Femininity and the Aesthetic*. Manchester: Manchester UP; New York: Routledge, 1992.

Brown, Norman O. *Life against Death: The Psychoanalytic Meaning of History*. Middletown, CT: Wesleyan UP, 1959.

Burgin, Victor. *The End of Art Theory: Criticism and Postmodernity*. London: Macmillan, 1986.

Cixous, Hélène. "Fiction and Its Phantoms: A Reading of Freud's *Das Unheimliche.*" *New Literary History* 7.3 (1976): 525–48.

Felman, Shoshana. "Rereading Femininity." *Yale French Studies* 62 (1981): 19–44.

Freud, Sigmund. *The Standard Edition of the Complete Psychological Works* (*SE*). Trans. and ed. James Strachey. 24 vols. 1953–74. London: Hogarth, 1986.

———. *Beyond the Pleasure Principle*. 1920. *SE* 18: 7–64.

———. "Mourning and Melancholia." 1918. *SE* 14: 237–60.

————. *Three Essays on the Theory of Sexuality*. 1905. *SE* 7: 123–245.

————. "The 'Uncanny.' " 1919. *SE* 17: 217–56.

Heath, Stephen. "Difference." *Screen* 19 (1978): 51–112.

Kennedy, Gerald J. *Poe, Death, and the Life of Writing*. New Haven: Yale UP, 1987.

Kofman, Sarah. *Quatre romans analytiques*. Paris: Galilée, 1973.

Lacan, Jacques. *Le Séminaire de Jacques Lacan, Livre II: Le moi dans la théorie de Freud et dans la technique de la psychanalyse*. Paris: Seuil, 1978.

Lauretis, Teresa de. *Alice Doesn't: Feminism, Semiotics, Cinema*. Bloomington: Indiana UP, 1984.

Lawrence, D. H. *Studies in Classic American Literature*. New York: Random House, 1923.

Modleski, Tania. *The Women Who Knew Too Much: Hitchcock and Feminist Theory*. London: Methuen, 1988.

Poe, Edgar Allan. *Poetry and Tales*. New York: Literary Classics of the United States, 1984.

Rimmon-Kenan, Schlomith. "The Paradoxical Status of Repetition." *Poetics Today* 1 (1980): 151–59.

Saussure, Ferdinand de. *Course in General Linguistics*. Trans. Wade Baskin, New York: McGraw-Hill, 1966.

Spoto, Donald. *The Art of Alfred Hitchcock*. New York: Doubleday, 1976.

Truffaut, François. *Hitchcock*. With collaboration of Helen G. Scott. New York: Simon and Schuster, 1983.

Van Gennep, Arnold. *The Rites of Passage*. Trans. Monika B. Vizedom and Gabrielle L. Caffee. Chicago: U of Chicago P, 1960.

Weber, Samuel. *The Legend of Freud*. Minneapolis: U of Minnesota P, 1982.

Zizek, Slavoj. "Looking Awry." *October* 50 (1989): 30–55.

————. *Tout ce que vous avez toujours voulu savoir sur Lacan sans jamais oser le demander à Hitchcock*. Paris: Navarin, 1988.

# Death and Gender

II

# Painting the Dead: Portraiture and Necrophilia in Victorian Art and Poetry

## *Carol Christ*

When Dante Gabriel Rossetti went to take his final farewell of his wife—dead, he feared, by her own hand—he thrust the manuscript of his yet unpublished poems into her coffin. He told Ford Madox Brown, "I have often been writing at those poems when Lizzie was ill and suffering, and I might have been attending to her, and now they shall go" (Doughty 303). Seven years later, trying to put together a volume of poems and unable to reconstruct those he had buried with his wife, Rossetti authorized the exhumation of her corpse. His friends gathered in Highgate Cemetery, where by the light of a great fire, the best protection they could devise against infection, they opened the coffin to remove the manuscript. Her body, they said, was wonderfully preserved, and one friend insisted that Lizzie's hair had continued to grow after her death, filling the coffin with its gold. In explaining the recovery of the poems to Swinburne, Rossetti attributed the act to Lizzie's will: "Art was the only thing for which she felt very seriously. Had it been possible to her, I should have found the book on my pillow the night she was buried; and could she have opened the grave, no other hand would have been needed" (Doughty 410).

The story of Rossetti's burial and recovery of his poems provides a vivid image of the connection that the nineteenth century made between art and necrophilia. When Elizabeth Siddal was alive, Rossetti and his Pre-Raphaelite brothers frequently painted her as dead or on the point of death—as Beatrice, Ophelia, the Lady of Shalott. When Rossetti had his poems taken from his wife's coffin, he played out in life what his art had already figured.

To paraphrase Poe, the most poetical of subjects were drawn from the dead body of a beautiful woman.[1]

As Rossetti's career itself suggests, the painted portrait is the most frequent vehicle through which nineteenth-century writers represent the connection of their art to the dead female body. Poe, not surprisingly, provides a paradigmatic image of this connection in his story "The Oval Portrait." The story concerns an artist who, caring more for his art than for his bride, paints a portrait whose tints "were drawn from the cheeks of her who sate beside him" (225). At the moment when he succeeds in completing the portrait that seems "*Life* itself" (225), his bride falls dead.

But even before the painter discovers the death of his bride, he grows "tremulous and very pallid, and aghast" (225) in looking at his work. Likewise the narrator, who discovers the portrait whose history he tells, must avert his gaze from the painting because it so "confounded, subdued, and appalled" him (224). The picture is so frightening, we are told, because of its "absolute *life-likeliness*" (224) of expression. In her study of the portrait in literature, Françoise Meltzer argues that the story thus formulates the taboo against an overly mimetic art (108).[2] But I think there is more than this to the fear the painter's work inspires. A Frankenstein of sorts, Poe's artist appropriates the female body in what he would like to believe is an act of autonomous creation, but the portrait that marks his triumph also records his depredation. The image he paints is a "mere head and shoulders" of a young girl; "the arms, the bosom and even the ends of the radiant hair, melted imperceptibly into the vague yet deep shadow which formed the background of the whole" (224). Like Perseus, then, Poe's artist, in token of his achievement, appropriates and displays a disembodied female head, from which the beholder instinctively averts his gaze.

Yet this is, quite literally, not the whole tale. "The Oval Portrait" begins by telling a story, to which we never return, about the narrator, who comes upon the portrait because he has forced his way into an Italian chateau.

> The chateau into which my valet had ventured to make forcible entrance, rather than permit me, in my desperately wounded condition, to pass a night in the open air, was one of those piles of commingled gloom and grandeur which have so long frowned among the Apennines, not less in fact than in the fancy of Mrs. Radcliffe. To all appearance it had been temporarily and very lately abandoned. We established ourselves in one of the smallest and least sumptuously furnished apartments. It lay in a remote turret of the building. Its decorations were rich, yet tattered and antique. Its walls were hung with tapestry and bedecked with manifold and multiform armorial trophies, together with an unusually great number of very spirited modern paintings in frames of rich gold arabesque. (223)

Taking "deep interest" in these paintings, the narrator prepares for bed in order to resign himself "alternately to the contemplation of these pictures and to the perusal of a small volume which had been found on the pillow, and which purported to criticize and describe them" (223).

The chateau is clearly a palace of art. The narrator, in contrast to the painter who works so literally from the life, is a belated and illegitimate guest in one of the smallest and least sumptuously furnished apartments in this palace, where he takes an intense interest in the criticism and description of the works of art that hang on its walls. The story thus begins in a self-referential literary context from which the history of the oval portrait removes us. That history, though it presents its own terrors, represses the anxiety of a belated and secondary literary habitation with which the story begins. To steal life itself is surely a more thrilling crime than to squat in one of the lesser apartments of Mrs. Radcliffe's chateau. What seems the mimetic triumph of the portrait diverts us from the initial narrative dilemma of the story, while giving it covert recognition. Much like the painter, Poe himself has based his art on female appropriation; but the portrait, while implying Poe's theft, provides a means of substitution and arrest for the problem of artistic identity with which the story began. Its apparent transparency—its Life itself—veils its more complex and literary origins.

Victorian poets contemporary with Poe use the portrait of the dead woman in similar ways. Tennyson's "The Gardener's Daughter," published in 1842, the same year as Poe's story, also ends with the portrait of a woman who, we discover in the last line of the poem, is dead. Like the oval portrait, the portrait of the gardener's daughter at once symbolizes the stylistic mode of the work and provides a substitutive resolution for the problem of artistic identity it begins with. As her name, Rose, suggests, the gardener's daughter is as much poetic mode as woman. The painter who narrates the poem goes off to see her with his fellow painter Eustace, in search of the material for a masterpiece. She is, Eustace tells him, the vision that will enable him to "climb the top of Art" and "work in hues to dim the Titianic Flora" (lines 31, 165–67). In lines originally composed for "The Gardener's Daughter" but later transposed to "Edwin Morris," Tennyson makes explicit Rose's kinship to the eroticized description of nature through which he portrays her.

My love of Nature and my love for her,
Of different ages, like twin sisters throve.
Her beauty with the growing season grew
Or seemed to grow, till drawn in narrowing arcs

The southing Autumn touched with sallower gleams
The granges on the fallows.
    (p. 564)

Rose is the picturesque, the absorption of the feminine subject to a landscape that seems—here I am quoting Hallam's description of Tennyson's early poetry—"evolved from it by assimilative force" (191). Much as Poe identifies the gothic with Mrs. Radcliffe, Tennyson identifies the picturesque as a feminine mode of poetry (Christ).

Tennyson uses the picturesque mode to arrest the progression of time. We first come upon the gardener's daughter as she tries to fix a fallen rose back onto the bush. This moment, as Herbert Tucker has also observed, provides an emblem for the poem's art (285), which seeks to reconstruct the past as if the future had not occurred. The poem tells the story of the artist's love for the gardener's daughter only to the point of her faltering words, "I am thine," and then it declines to go on, saying that memory has taken him thus far but love will allow him to go no further.

I had not stayed so long to tell you all,
But while I mused came memory with sad eyes,
Holding the folded annals of my youth;
And while I mused, Love with knit brows went by,
And with a flying finger swept my lips,
And spake, "Be wise: not easily forgiven
Are those, who setting wide the doors that bar
The secret bridal-chambers of the heart,
Let in the day." Here, then, my words have end.
    (237–45)

The speaker then presents the listener with the veiled portrait of Rose instead of the story that he declines to tell. All he has said thus far, he continues, has been just a prelude to the picture, which was painted "ere she knew my heart" (270). The poem thus seeks to convert nostalgia to anticipation and in the process links portraiture, and the picturesque style that is so frequently its vehicle and analogue, to the occlusion of narrative. The veil over the portrait suggests that there is repression involved in this transposition, the repression of death. Only in the poem's last line do we learn from the artist that Rose is dead, now merely the blessed memory of his age.

But the death of Rose is not the only death the poem represses. The subtitle of the poem is "The Pictures," and the poem contains two other portraits in addition to the one of the gardener's daughter: one of Eustace's beloved, Juliet, and the other a hypothetical portrait of Eustace himself, which is the poem's first mention of a picture.

> My Eustace might have sat for Hercules;
> So muscular he spread, so broad of breast.
>
> (7–8)

In the original prologue to the poem, published only after Tennyson's death as "The Ante-Chamber," the narrator describes a self-portrait of Eustace that resembles the hypothetical version with which "The Gardener's Daughter" begins. The description ends:

> This is he I loved,
> This is the man of whom you heard me speak.
>
> (14–15)

The narrator then relates Eustace's youthful hopes; he concludes:

> Yet he lives;
> His and my friendship have not suffered loss;
> His fame is equal to his years.
>
> (41–43)

He then introduces the portrait of the gardener's daughter.

> Step through these doors, and I will show to you
> Another countenance, one yet more dear,
> More dear, for what is lost is made more dear;
> "More dear" I will not say, but rather bless
> The All-perfect Framer, Him, who made the heart,
> Forethinking its twinfold necessity,
> Through one whole life an overflowing urn,
> Capacious both of Friendship and of Love.
>
> (45–52)

In his analysis of "The Gardener's Daughter," Tucker has pointed out the incessant doubling in the style of the poem, as if we are in the hands of a matchmaker gone wild. Tucker argues that this anxious doubling is a way of maintaining the illusion of fulfilled love that the poem seeks to sustain and in the end destroys (280–81). But the lines I have just quoted suggest another explanation for this doubling by connecting the idea of twinning with a complex emotional substitution. Eustace is obviously based on Hallam; the prologue was written in 1834, the year after his death. "The Gardener's Daughter" was begun in 1833, before Hallam's death, but completed the following year. The sequence of composition suggests that the portrait of the gardener's daughter, that other countenance made more dear by loss, comes to substitute for the loss of Hallam. The suppression of the death of the gardener's daughter throughout that poem shadows the suppression of Hallam's death in the poem's original beginning. In a process that is typical of his compositional habits in the years following Hallam's death, Tennyson retrospectively creates a plot of heterosexual loss to account for a grief associated with Hallam.[3] The elaborate structure of prologue, prelude, and veil that precedes disclosure of the portrait signals the substitution the poem employs. The story that the painter refuses to tell of the course of his love suppresses yet another story of loss, and the veiled portrait is itself a kind of veil. As in "The Oval Portrait," the apparent transparency of representation that the portrait offers provides a kind of cover story for a more complex transposition of artistic identity. The portrait functions almost like a screen memory, replacing a prior concern with some transformation that simultaneously blocks and expresses it. In Tennyson's case, however, the poem exposes its own substitutive strategies of composition in showing how the artist uses the portrait to recreate and repress the sequence of the past.

In his study of photography, Roland Barthes argues that the photograph always carries the sense of death by implying an anterior future. "In front of the photograph of my mother as a child, I tell myself: she is going to die: I shudder, like Winnicott's psychotic patient *over a catastrophe which has already occurred.* Whether or not the subject is already dead, every photograph is this catastrophe" (96). The photograph is thus a kind of *tableau vivant,* a still life, "a figuration of the motionless and made-up face beneath which we see the dead" (32). Victorian poets characteristically use the portrait in exactly this way; indeed, they often amplify the effect Barthes describes by constructing a narrative that represents and represses that anterior future, as in "The Gardener's Daughter," or by connecting the portrait itself to its subject's death, as in "The Oval Portrait." The artist in this way implicates his own artistic mode in this stilling of life, as if he, a lover of corpses, depends for his art on a deadly Orphic gaze.

In "My Last Duchess," published in 1842, another poem that centers on the veiled portrait of a dead woman, Browning explores the murderous impulse that can be at work in so deadly a portraiture. Obsessed by the desire to control his lady's "looks," the duke reduces her to the picture painted on his wall, which he alone reveals, "since none puts by / The curtain I have drawn for you but I." "My Last Duchess" confirms what I have been arguing about the portrait by giving the aesthetic impulse involved ironic and dramatic representation. The portrait seems to offer the duke a perfect transposition of life: "That's my last Duchess painted on the wall, / Looking as if she were alive." This transposition enables him to stop a train of events: "I gave commands; / Then all smiles stopped together. There she stands / As if alive." Despite the control the duke boasts over the portrait, however, his monologue reveals the very anxiety that he killed the duchess to suppress. The poem thus exposes the repression the portrait is based on.

Yet as "The Gardener's Daughter" and "The Oval Portrait" suggest, the portrait can function not merely to repress a story. It can also effect a transposition of identity, often centrally related to the writer's own sense of his art. A short poem, "Eurydice to Orpheus," written much later in Browning's career, reflects interestingly upon this process. The poem was first published in prose form in the catalog of the Royal Academy exhibition of 1864, where it described Frederick Lord Leighton's picture *Orpheus and Eurydice* (fig. 1).

> But give them me, the mouth, the eyes, the brow!
> Let them once more absorb me! One look now
>     Will lap me round for ever, not to pass
> Out of its light, though darkness lie beyond:
> Hold me but safe again within the bond
>     Of one immortal look! All woe that was,
> Forgotten, and all terror that may be,
> Defied,—no past is mine, no future: look at me!

The words Browning gives to Eurydice serve to identify Orpheus's look with the gaze of the painter. They thus connect the painter's task with mortification; the artist's gaze, in which he gives his subject the mouth, the eyes, the brow, kills her in one immortal look. This look seems to obliterate story: "no past is mine, no future." The portrait thus at once resists and represents the catastrophe of death, in this poem a catastrophe with a clear biographical component. Leighton had just finished designing Elizabeth Barrett Browning's tomb, and Browning associated his dead wife with Eurydice.

But Leighton and Browning do not imagine Eurydice as the unwitting victim of an Orpheus unable to resist the temptation to look back at his bride; this Eurydice actively solicits the look that will return her to the region of the shades. The poem recalls Rossetti's fantasy of Elizabeth Siddal's desire to return his manuscripts; Browning's Eurydice is eager to surrender the artistic subject that her dead body affords. In Leighton's painting it is Orpheus who resists, averting his gaze from his bride, who pulls him toward her. In Browning's poem, too, Eurydice wants to possess Orpheus. When she pleads, "Give them me, the mouth, the eyes, the brow," it is not clear whose

Figure 1. Frederick Lord Leighton, *Orpheus and Eurydice*. Leighton House Museum.

mouth, eyes, and brow she is soliciting. At the moment when Orpheus gives her identity with his look, Eurydice will hold his look as well. In painting and poem, she presses toward an absorption within him that he strains to resist. Because the painting inevitably implies the moment that we know will follow, when Orpheus's look returns Eurydice to Hades, its representation of the penultimate moment suggests the desire and fear at play in the mortification of the female subject. Like Porphyria's lover, Orpheus will free himself from her struggling passion when he clasps the dead body whose will he has accomplished. The painting thus implies that necrophilia may at once defend against a fear of female absorption and satisfy a desire for it.

There is no richer field in which to explore this hypothesis than the painting and poetry of Dante Gabriel Rossetti. Rossetti was obsessed with the relation of art to necrophilia, but his conception of that relation changes considerably over the course of his career. His early work uses the portrait of the dead woman to explore the ultimate inaccessibility of the subjects that art strives to represent. Later in his career he seeks to endow portraits of women with a fetishistic power that absorbs the beholder within a mortifying female gaze.

"The Portrait" provides the fullest articulation of Rossetti's early use of female portraiture. Like "The Gardener's Daughter," the poem concerns a painter's portrait of his dead love, a portrait in which he strives to recapture a moment before she knew of his devotion. The day after he has spoken his heart to his beloved, he decides to make the memory all his own by painting a picture of the blissful moment immediately before he spoke. To do so, he places his beloved among the plants in his room, "to feign the shadow of the trees" in the wood where the original scene took place. Unlike Tennyson, who tries to suppress the difference between reconstructive memory and event, Rossetti not only dwells upon the difference but uses it to define his poetic. He consistently figures the portrait in the poem as a mirror image or an echo without an original; it necessarily bespeaks absence and justifies a crepuscular, abstract imagery that minimizes referentiality.

> In painting her I shrined her face
>   Mid mystic trees, where light falls in
> Hardly at all; a covert place
>   Where you might think to find a din
> Of doubtful talk, and a live flame
> Wandering, and many a shape whose name
>   Not itself knoweth, and old dew,
>   And your own footsteps meeting you,
> And all things going as they came.
>     (19–27)

As these lines show, Rossetti does not associate the portrait, as Poe and Tennyson do, with transparency of representation. Rather, he creates a phantasmal poetic world that offers only a trace of the subjects whose presence it cannot sustain.[4] He closely skirts the limits of referentiality: talk is "doubtful," shapes do not know their own names, and identities double and collapse into sameness.

At the end of the poem, however, Rossetti imagines a different way of locating art in relation to its dead subject—that of eschatological fantasy. As the painter sits with his portrait, he anticipates an ultimate moment when

other eyes shall look from it
Eyes of the spirit's Palestine,
Even than the old gaze tenderer:
While hopes and aims long lost with her
  Stand round her image side by side
  Like tombs of pilgrims that have died
About the Holy Sepulchre.
  (102–8)

These final lines effect a transposition typical of much of Rossetti's art. He animates the phantasmal and absent object by identifying her with a powerful gaze, while he mortifies the speaking subject, first abstracting it to "hopes and aims," which he then transforms to pilgrims' tombs. This transposition resembles the strategy of "The Blessed Damozel," which also animates its dead subject, giving her both visual concreteness and the dominant voice in the poem, while her earthly lover speaks haltingly in occasional parentheses. In the picture that Rossetti painted years after he wrote the poem, she is the one who looks out from the gold bar of her picture frame, while her lover reclines below in a separate frame, a miniaturized and passive figure.

This configuration of the male and female is not typical of Rossetti's early painting, in which the dominant beholder is male. In his early compositions Rossetti tends to place a male and a female figure in the same frame; the man is usually larger and more powerful than the woman, who cowers before his gaze, as in *Ecce Ancilla Domine,* or *Found.* In the paintings that center on a dead woman—*Dante's Dream at the Time of the Death of Beatrice* or the studies for the never-completed *Lady of Shalott*—Rossetti pictures a man in the dominant position in the painting gazing at a woman on her bier.

In the portraits of women that he begins to paint in the 1860s, however, the structure of beholding changes dramatically. The woman, who appears larger than life, alone occupies a rather cramped spatial field and confronts the viewer with a startling direct frontal gaze. Many of the sonnets Rossetti wrote to accompany these pictures emphasize the power of this gaze to hold the viewer in its spell.

She muses, with her eyes upon the track
Of that which in thy spirit they can see.
  ("Venus")

Hers are the eyes which, over and beneath
The sky and sea bend on thee
  ("Sibylla Palmifera")

From her neck's inclining flower-stem lean
Love-freighted lips and absolute eyes that wean
The pulse of hearts to the sphere's dominant tune.
    ("Astarte Syriaca")

The pictures often center on a fetishistic representation of the woman's genitals—Pandora's box in *Pandora,* the pomegranate in *Persephone,* or the hand and dangling belt placed in the middle of the body in *Astarte Syriaca,* a composition repeated in the hand and belt beneath her prominent left breast (fig. 2). The sonnet that Rossetti composed for *Astarte Syriaca* calls the area clasped by these "girdles" "the infinite boon / of bliss whereof the heaven and earth commune" and tells us that the two angels at the top of the painting are compelling all thrones of light to be her witnesses. Yet they seem, rather, to be averting their gaze with the unnatural torsion of the neck so characteristic of Rossetti's painting. The portrait thus brings together the powerful impulses to look and not to look at a sexual object. It functions rather like the mirror of the Medusa that Rossetti described in a poem for a picture he never completed.

Andromeda, by Perseus saved and wed,
Hankered each day to see the Gorgon's head:
Till o'er a fount he held it, bade her lean,
And mirrored in the wave was safely seen
That death she lived by.

            Let not thine eyes know
Any forbidden thing itself, although
It once should save as well as kill: but be
Its shadow upon life enough for thee.

Rossetti's poem shows how the myth of the Medusa, like that of Orpheus and Eurydice, brings together the desire and the fear of looking. The object of desire and fear is similar in the two stories—the dead woman. Art can at once give the beholder such forbidden sight and shield him from its dangers, for it is not, in Rossetti's terms, the thing itself but its shadow upon life, the mirror of the Medusa. Rossetti's portraits of women function as such mirrors. Their snakelike hair, the fatal mesmerizing power he attaches to their sight, the tokens of genitalia that they bear all suggest the Medusa, but a Medusa appropriated by the artist, who, Perseus-like, controls its display. Like the portrait of the dead woman that figures so importantly as a literary source for Rossetti's art, these paintings allow the artist and his female subject to

Figure 2. Dante Gabriel Rossetti, *Astarte Syriaca*. City Art Gallery, Manchester.

share a single life. They thus suggest a similar transposition of gender through which the artist appropriates a female identity.

A picture by Burne-Jones of the scene Rossetti describes in "Aspecta Medusa" but never finished painting suggests the way the Medusa might effect such a transposition. The painting, titled *The Baleful Head* (fig. 3), shows Perseus holding the head of the Medusa over a well so that Andromeda can see its reflection. Three images are reflected in the well—the heads of Perseus, Medusa, and Andromeda. They are juxtaposed in such a way that the Medusa seems a middle term between the two lovers, capable of representing sexual difference to either one. Perseus could be showing

Figure 3. Edward Burne-Jones, *The Baleful Head*. Staatsgalerie, Stuttgart.

Andromeda a phallic token of his identity, or he could be comparing her face with the horrifying face of the Medusa. The androgynous and rather similar appearance of all three faces allows the Medusa's head to both call attention to sexual differentiation and make it ambiguous.

The heads of women that Rossetti painted so obsessively in the last twenty years of his life paradoxically function in a similar way as an androgynous middle term between man and woman.[5] Rossetti at once exaggerates all the signs of female sexuality—the full, slightly parted lips, the cascading hair, the fruits and boxes so prominently and temptingly held—while he distorts the female body so that it becomes phallic, in the elongated and muscular neck, the enlarged hands placed prominently at the picture's center, and the massive shoulders. These pictures are emphatically framed, not only by the gilt frames that Rossetti himself crafted for them, but by inset frames in the composition of many of the portraits and by inscriptions, making clear their status not as representations but as icons. Whatever success we attribute to these paintings, Rossetti imagined them, as the sonnets he composed for them testify, to have a fetishistic power to absorb the beholder's life.[6] This power, I think, is not merely a fearful image of female sexuality but a feminine projection of the artist's sexuality, thus rendered appropriate for the narcissistic reverie in which the subjects of the paintings are so frequently rapt. Rossetti's portraits of women thus identify art with a narcissistic and feminized sexual contemplation. The foundation of this identification had been laid much earlier in the century—with the association of poetry, in Keats and Tennyson, with looking at and euphemistically covering the sexually forbidden; with the identification of the picturesque and the gothic as feminine literary modes; and with the topos of the portrait of the dead woman. But what earlier writers had represented as art's appropriation of female life becomes in Pre-Raphaelitism an absorption within the female. This absorption enables artists to claim a different subject and emotional register for their work as well as to indicate the increasing marginalization of the poet from the masculine ethos and power of his society. The woman who previously had been killed into art now offers the passive spectator a fantasy of perpetual life.

The most powerful expression of this image of art is Pater's description of *La Gioconda,* which, it has often been observed, more appropriately describes one of Rossetti's portraits than Leonardo's painting.

It is a beauty wrought out from within upon the flesh, the deposit, little cell by cell, of strange thoughts and fantastic reveries and exquisite passions. . . . All the thoughts and experience of the world have etched and moulded there, in that which they have of power to refine and make expressive the outward form, the animalism of Greece, the lust of Rome, the mysticism of the middle age with its spiritual ambition and imaginative loves, the return of the Pagan world, the sins of the Borgias. She is older than the rocks among which she sits; like the vampire, she has been dead many times, and learned the secrets of the grave; and has been a diver in deep seas, and keeps their fallen day about her; and trafficked for strange webs with Eastern merchants; and, as Leda, was the mother of Helen of Troy, and, as Saint Anne, the mother of Mary; and all this has been to her but as the sound of lyres and flutes, and lives only in the delicacy with which it has moulded the changing lineaments, and tinged the eyelids and the hands. The fancy of a perpetual life, sweeping together ten thousand experiences, is an old one; and modern philosophy has conceived the idea of humanity as wrought upon by, and summing up in itself, all modes of thought and life. Certainly Lady Lisa might stand as the embodiment of the old fancy, the symbol of the modern idea. (122–23)

Pater here, like Rossetti, figures his ideal of aesthetic identity in a woman who contains within herself the capacity for a perpetual reincarnation that sums up all thoughts and modes of life in a continually delicate and various aesthetic experience. To claim a more limited lineage for Pater's Lady Lisa than he does himself, she is the fullest incarnation of the nineteenth-century portrait of a woman who subsumes and expresses the artist's identity.

. Women writers, as one might expect, show a complex response to this use of the female portrait. Christina Rossetti, for example, criticizes her brother's portraiture in the sonnet "In an Artist's Studio," in which she observes that "One face looks out from all his canvases . . . not as she is, but as she fills his dream"; but in her own poetry she repeatedly represents herself as the dead woman, laid out for viewing, as she is regarded by her lover. Here, for example, is "After Death":

> The curtains were half drawn, the floor was swept
>   And strewn with rushes, rosemary and may
>   Lay thick upon the bed on which I lay,
> Where through the lattice ivy-shadows crept.
> He leaned above me, thinking that I slept
>   And could not hear him; but I heard him say,
>   "Poor child, poor child": and as he turned away
> Came a deep silence, and I knew he wept.
> He did not touch the shroud, or raise the fold
>   That hid my face, or take my hand in his,
>     Or ruffle the smooth pillows for my head:
>     He did not love my living; but once dead
>   He pitied me; and very sweet it is
> To know he still is warm though I am cold.

In this sonnet Christina Rossetti gives a voice to the dead female subject of masculine regard, as if Tennyson's Elaine could speak from her bier. The poem, in a small way, exposes and subverts the gendered poetic topos I have been discussing. At the same time, however, it shows Christina Rossetti's very limited sense of where she can position a lyric voice and the scant mobility or warmth it allows her.

Elizabeth Barrett Browning also uses the portrait of the dead woman as a way of reflecting critically upon the images available to her. In the first book of *Aurora Leigh,* Aurora's knowledge of her mother comes from a portrait, painted after her death from her corpse. For Aurora, this picture

> kept the mystic level of all forms,
> Hates, fears, and admirations, was by turns
> Ghost, fiend, and angel, fairy, witch, and sprite,
> A dauntless Muse who eyes a dreadful Fate,
> A loving Psyche who loses sight of Love,
> A still Medusa with mild milky brows
> All curdled and all clothed upon with snakes
> Whose slime falls fast as sweat will; or anon
> Our Lady of the Passion, stabbed with swords
> Where the Babe sucked; or Lamira in her first
> Moonlighted pallor, ere she shrunk and blinked
> And shuddering wriggled down to the unclean;
> Or my own mother, leaving her last smile
> In her last kiss upon the baby–mouth
> My father pushed down on the bed for that,—
> Or my dead mother, without smile or kiss,
> Buried at Florence. All which images,
> Concentrated on the picture, glassed themselves
> Before my meditative childhood, as
> The incoherencies of change and death
> Are represented fully, mixed and merged,
> In the smooth mystery of perpetual life.
>      (1. 152–73)

The passage bears a striking resemblance to Pater's description of *La Gioconda* and thus suggests how fully Pater was working with a conventional poetic representation of woman. Here it is not merely the incoherencies of change and death that are transformed to the fantasy of a perpetual life, however, but fantasies about the danger of the look—in the stories of Psyche, Medusa, and Lamia. In each of these stories, looking in some way destroys the object of regard, although Aurora's mother is in a different position in each allusion—the Psyche who loses her beloved by looking at him, the Lamia who is destroyed by Apollonius's stare, the gorgonizing Medusa. The very differences among the stories keep us from forming a single image of Aurora's mother but lead instead to a sense of the danger of the look embedded within the structure of viewing that the portrait creates. Barrett Browning intensifies this sense of danger with the image of the Madonna stabbed with swords where the babe sucked and with Aurora's memory of her mother's dying kiss, both of which suggest that a child can consume the life of her mother by her loving contact. In this collection of images, Barrett Browning identifies a set of primitive fantasies about killing the object of regard with conventions of feminine representation. She thus associates the mortification involved in the nineteenth-century topos of female portraiture with maternal inaccessibility and loss.

Yeats's decision to place Pater's description of *La Gioconda* as the first poem in his edition of *The Oxford Book of Modern Verse* reflects the centrality that the framed woman had as a poetical topos for the Victorians. Much as Yeats makes *La Gioconda* a kind of gateway from the nineteenth century to the twentieth, so early modernist poets use the portrait to reflect upon their relation to the nineteenth-century poetic tradition—as in Pound's *Hugh Selwyn Mauberley* and "Portrait d'une Femme," Eliot's "Portrait of a Lady," and Williams's "Portrait of a Lady." These poems all use the portrait of a woman to reflect upon the gender identification of poetry as their authors try to establish a more masculine, and consequently gynophobic, sense of poetic identity. The way the titles of these poems refer to one another and to James's novel indicates their concern with intertextuality; the woman herself in each poem is seen as a textual creation. The lady in Eliot's "Portrait of a Lady," for example, represents a kind of aestheticism, "a worn out common song," against which the speaker poses his more masculine and modern counterpoint. The poem identifies the lady and the masculine speaker with different poetic registers. The man's attempt to escape the woman is reflected in an aggressive resistance to her vocabulary, a vocabulary far more characteristic of Eliot's early poetry than the masculine style to which he retreats. The poem, like Poe's "The Oval Portrait," thus absorbs its psychological subject to a question of literary tradition. The portrait of a lady becomes a way of placing oneself within a tradition that has become problematically femininized. Pound's "Portrait d'une Femme" uses its portrait in a similar way. The image he creates of the woman as a kind of aesthetic curio shop in which the debris of culture is deposited could well serve as a negative mirror of his own poetic and of his relationship to a feminized literary culture. Likewise, *Hugh Selwyn Mauberley* reflects upon the relation of its various personae for the poet to their nineteenth-century inheritance through Pre-Raphaelite portraiture. Finally, Williams's "Portrait of a Lady" suggests that he can approach his subject only through the effete representations of an overly refined artistic tradition.

> Your thighs are appletrees
> whose blossoms touch the sky.

Which sky? The sky
where Watteau hung a lady's
slipper.

I have used these modern examples to confirm the nineteenth-century convention that I have been describing. As these modern poems imply, nineteenth-century artists frequently use a portrait of a lady to reflect not only on feminine sexuality but on a feminized literary culture. For Victorian poets and painters, the portrait of a woman was inextricably connected with death. In part, this connection is just one element of the interest in stealing and animating corpses so characteristic of nineteenth-century literature. But the death that the portrait involves for its subject is specifically gendered in a way that suggests the desire and fear both of looking at a forbidden sexual object and of appropriating its life. The portrait implicates art in both of these desires. Like Orpheus, the artist goes down to the region of the shades and looks at the dead body of his beloved; like Perseus, he appropriates its head for his own.

## Notes

1. In "The Philosophy of Composition" Poe writes, "The death, then, of a beautiful woman is, unquestionably, the most poetical topic in the world" (369).

2. Meltzer argues more generally that textual portraits threaten the notion of representation because they so frequently define sites that rupture mimetic stasis. In the nineteenth century, whatever disruption of such mimetic stasis the portrait initiates always concerns gender.

3. I am thinking particularly of the genesis of *Maud,* which Tennyson tells us was composed backward from the lyric associated with his grief over Hallam's death, "Oh! that 'twere possible" (vol. 2, sec. 20, 571).

4. See McGowan, who also argues that "The Portrait" implies that Rossetti feels life and art are inimical (37–39).

5. See Riede, who also observes the androgynous character of the women in Rossetti's portraits (259). Gitter observes the androgynous character of Swinburne's Medusa but finds it idiosyncratic (952). I think that because the portrait always carries the possibility of gender transposition, it is easily adapted to a homosexual art, as in Swinburne's portrayal of the hermaphrodite or *The Picture of Dorian Gray.*

6. Stein argues that the sonnets Rossetti wrote to accompany his paintings "lull us into a condition of psychic receptivity to enable us to enter the magical realm of art" (143).

## Works Cited

Barthes, Roland. *Camera Lucida: Reflections on Photography.* Trans. Richard Howard. New York: Hill and Wang, 1981.

Browning, Elizabeth Barrett. *Aurora Leigh*. London: Women's Press, 1981.

Browning, Robert. *The Poems*. Ed. John Pettigrew. New Haven: Yale UP, 1981.

Christ, Carol. "The Feminine Subject in Victorian Poetry." *ELH* 54 (1987): 385–401.

Doughty, Oswald. *Dante Gabriel Rossetti: A Victorian Romantic*. New Haven: Yale UP, 1949.

Gitter, Elizabeth S. "The Power of Women's Hair in the Victorian Imagination." *PMLA* 99 (1984): 936–54.

Hallam, Arthur Henry. "On Some of the Characteristics of Modern Poetry and on the Lyrical Poems of Alfred Tennyson." *The Writings of Arthur Hallam*. Ed. T. H. Vail Motter. New York: MLA, 1943.

McGowan, John. *Representation and Revelation: Victorian Realism from Carlyle to Yeats*. Columbia: U of Missouri P, 1986.

Meltzer, Françoise. *Salome and the Dance of Writing*. Chicago: U of Chicago P, 1987.

Pater, Walter. *The Renaissance*. Cleveland: Meridian, 1961.

Poe, Edgar Allan. *The Selected Poetry and Prose of Edgar Allan Poe*. Ed. T. O. Mabbott. New York: Modern Library, 1951.

Riede, David G. *Dante Gabriel Rossetti and the Limits of Victorian Vision*. Ithaca: Cornell UP, 1983.

Rossetti, Christina. *The Poetical Works*. Ed. William Michael Rossetti. London: Macmillan, 1904.

Rossetti, Dante Gabriel. *Poems*. Ed. Oswald Doughty. London: Everyman's, 1961.

Stein, Richard L. *The Ritual of Interpretation*. Cambridge: Harvard UP, 1975.

Tennyson, Alfred. *The Poems of Tennyson*. 2nd ed. Ed. Christopher Ricks, 3 vols. Berkeley: U of California P, 1987.

Tucker, Herbert F. *Tennyson and the Doom of Romanticism*. Cambridge: Harvard UP, 1988.

Williams, William Carlos. *The Collected Earlier Poems*. New York: New Directions, 1966.

# Romanticism and the Ghost of Prostitution: Freud, *Maria,* and "Alice Fell"

## Sarah Webster Goodwin

> Determination is dead, indeterminism reigns. . . . If it was just a question of the primacy of exchange value over use value (or of the structural dimension over the functional dimension of language), Marx and Saussure have already pointed it out. . . . But if there is *equivalence* at the heart of the system the global system is not *indeterminate.*
>
> . . . The current system on the other hand is based on indeterminacy; it is driven by it; it is haunted by the death of all determinations.
>
> Jean Baudrillard, "Symbolic Exchange and Death"

## I

Somewhere near the middle of his essay "The 'Uncanny,' " Freud offers an example from his own experience to develop a point. It is the only personal example in the essay, and it is extraordinarily suggestive, both as a brief narrative and in terms of its position in his argument. The story sets up a complex network of associations among uncanny representations of death and of prostitution. Using those associations in Freud as my starting point, I will go on to argue that Freud is articulating, however guardedly, a view of prostitution that has been paradigmatic for Western culture since the late eighteenth century. The prostitute is akin to the corpse in the ways she

I thank Phyllis Roth, Douglas Wilson, John Anzalone, and Sonia Hofkosh for reading and responding to an earlier version of this essay.

inspires fears of—and desires for—contagion. In Freud, as in Mary Wolstonecraft and William Wordsworth, those fears and desires are frightening enough to be effectively submerged, a subtext written by association and implication rather than by overt statement. Reconstructing them, bringing into clear focus the ghost of prostitution, allows us to see more clearly one kind of pressure that haunts the text of romantic ideology. Put most crudely, it is the pressure of death by prostitution, which can also be read as the loss of intrinsic value in the industrial economy.

The rather strange appearance of prostitution in Freud's "The 'Uncanny' " is framed by—enclosed within—allusions to the death drive. At this point in the essay, Freud has been exploring the double as an aspect of the uncanny, citing Otto Rank's interpretation of the double as "insurance against destruction to the ego, an 'energetic denial of the power of death' " (*SE* 17: 235). Freud suggests that the double has powers of protection only in a primitive or infantile stage of development; thereafter, "From having been an assurance of immortality, he becomes the ghastly harbinger of death" (387). From this discussion of the double he turns rather abruptly to the function of repetition and recurrence in the uncanny, and this is when he tells his story. He introduces it as an example of the "uncanny feeling, which recalls that sense of helplessness sometimes experienced in dreams" (*SE* 17: 237). I quote what follows at length, because it bears close attention:

> As I was walking, one hot summer afternoon, through the deserted streets of a provincial town in Italy which was unknown to me, I found myself in a quarter of whose character I could not long remain in doubt. Nothing but painted women were to be seen at the windows of the small houses, and I hastened to leave the narrow street at the next turning. But after having wandered about for a time without enquiring my way, I suddenly found myself back in the same street, where my presence was now beginning to excite attention. I hurried away once more, only to arrive by another *détour* at the same place yet a third time. Now, however, a feeling overcame me which I can only describe as uncanny, and I was glad enough to find myself back at the piazza I had left a short while before, without any further voyages of discovery. (*SE* 17: 237)

The subsequent paragraphs return to the idea of the death drive, locating this narrative of the uncanny within the repetition compulsion and referring the reader to *Beyond the Pleasure Principle,* then completed but not yet published. Two points in particular interest me here: Freud locates an experience of prostitution at the heart of his idea of the uncanny; and prostitution appears in the closest possible proximity to death in its relation to the uncanny.

Is it prostitution itself, or simply the compulsive return, that makes Freud tell this story? Can the two be distinguished here? It is clear that Freud is returning not to any arbitrary place in the foreign city, but to a specific quarter; not just the "narrow streets," but the "painted women . . . seen at the windows" draw him back against his will. Indeed, the narrow streets themselves share the character of prostitution, both by metonymy—embodied in the expression "living on the streets"—and by metaphor, by the streets' unavoidable metaphorizing of the prostitute's body. Freud could hardly have been ignorant of Goethe's famous epigram that compares the breadth of Venice's canals to its whores' sexual parts. One wonders too whether he thought of the similarity between the women at the windows and the painted doll Coppelia, whose uncanny presence at the window in Hoffmann's "The Sand-Man" he tries hard to suppress during the whole first half of "The 'Uncanny.' " Finally, the Italian city here is itself a figure for the prostitute, as the foreign, feminine, somewhat exotic, swampy Babylon that it so often appears in German literature. (Mann's "Death in Venice" had been published seven years earlier, in 1912.) Here as elsewhere in Freud's essay, there are direct parallels between his claims for the individual and his claims for culture: the "early mental stage, long since surmounted" (*SE* 17: 236) may be *either* the "primitive" or the "infantile." The prostitutes—for Freud only in the plural, since they are real but he carefully avoids any individual contact—here preside over an entire system of binary oppositions, both personal and cultural. As the uncanny presence in a repetition compulsion, they also threaten that system.

What is it that the prostitute represents, then? Although it would be an overstatement to claim any undercurrent of obsession with prostitution in Freud's writing, it is something he returns to repeatedly throughout his long career. Perhaps the most far-reaching of such allusions occurs very briefly in Freud's notes on the Rat-Man case. He has been jotting down the patient's comments; he notes, "Also a play on my name: 'Freudenhaus-Mädchen' ['girls belonging to a House of Joy'—i.e., prostitutes]" (*SE* 10: 284).[1] Since Freud's essay on the uncanny is deeply concerned with demonstrating the relation between *Haüslichkeit* (domesticity), the *heimlich* (secret, domestic), and the *unheimlich* (the uncanny), it seems peculiarly meaningful that his own name should lend itself to such wordplay. Quite possibly his compulsive return to the prostitutes' quarter in the Italian city is also a return to an intimate part of himself. On some level, he is not only deeply drawn to the prostitutes, but identifies with them. A number of recent studies of Freud have noted the importance of money in the relationship between analyst and patient and have seen the analyst as being in some ways the patient's servant. As Jane Gallop aptly writes,

Whereas in other relationships both parties have an investment in seeing love not as a repetition but as unique and particular to the person loved, in psychoanalysis the analyst will want to point out the structure of repetition. What facilitates the recognition of the feeling as transference, as an inappropriate repetition, is the fact that the analyst is paid. The money proves that the analyst is only a stand-in. Rather than having the power of life and death like the mother has over the infant, the analyst is financially dependent on the patient. But in that case, the original "analyst," the earliest person paid to replace the mother, is that frequent character in Freud's histories, the nursemaid/governess. (212).[2]

In other words, as in sexual relations, money is the semantic marker defining the relationship. It is a point taken up too by Stallybrass and White, who note that the economic transaction at the heart of psychoanalysis troubles Freud and makes him anxious. That anxiety arises, they argue, from a fear of identifying with the maidservant, that hireling who is also a "source of sexual knowledge" but whose very wages indicate her actual powerlessness (162). To be paid as an analyst, then, is to put oneself in a position similar to that of these female figures who accept money in exchange for standing in for family members. Some of the emotional messiness of the situation gets tidied up in the theory of the transference. And yet in this *Freudenhaus*— not surprisingly—there is much that is repressed, that remains untold.

Indeed, in Freud's writings the prostitute is a mobile figure. She can be identified overtly with the mother, the daughter, the maidservant, the fiancée, and even the man. For the most part she is identical with prostitution: that is, to prostitute oneself, to sell one's favors, is to enter into the irreversible character of the prostitute. As Freud puts it in one of his essays, "The Psychology of Love," "In normal love the woman's value is measured by her sexual integrity, and is reduced by any approach to the characteristic of being like a prostitute" (*SE* 11: 167). This is a direct, almost mathematical equation. The translator disingenuously notes that "prostitute" is perhaps an unfair translation of the German word *Dirne* in this context: he writes that " 'Dirne' . . . is not well rendered by 'prostitute,' which in English lays too much stress on the monetary side of the relation" (*SE* 11: 167n). But what does the word "value" (*Wert*) allude to if not to monetary value? *Dirne* bears connotations of social class that differ somewhat from those of "prostitute"; *Dirne* originally referred not to a woman's sexual nature but to her social identity as a young girl, especially a country maid, and only secondarily, *abwertend* (derogatorily; literally, devaluing), as *Freudenmädchen* or prostitute (Wahrig 205). Social and monetary value directly parallel each other in this case; a woman's sexual integrity is defined in part—but very potently—by her social class.

And her social class is defined by her father or husband. It may be significant that in the paragraph preceding Freud's notes on *Freudenhaus,* he alludes to his daughter in unsettling, sexualized terms: "Another horrible idea—of ordering me to bring my daughter into the room, so that he could lick her, saying 'bring in the *Miessnick*' [A Jewish term meaning 'ugly creature'—trans. note]" (*SE* 10: 284). In this context the term *Freudenmädchen* takes on yet another meaning, more apparent in the translator's English version, "girls belonging to a House of Joy" (284): only his daughter could properly be said to belong to him. The passage is even more remarkable in light of Freud's fragmented notes in "Draft L" of the Fliess papers, written in 1897:

### The Part Played by Servant-Girls

An immense load of guilt, with self-reproaches (for theft, abortion, etc.), is made possible . . . by identification with these people of low morals, who are so often remembered by her as worthless women connected sexually with her father or brother. And, as a result of the sublimation of these girls in phantasies, most improbable charges against other people are made in these phantasies. Fear of prostitution . . . (fear of being in the street alone), fear of a man hidden under the bed, etc., also point in the direction of servant-girls. *There is tragic justice in the fact that the action of the head of the family in stooping to a servant-girl is atoned for by his daughter's self-abasement.* (248; my emphasis)

Again there is a sense here of the father's being responsible for the daughter's market value. Freud's definition of "normal" female sexuality seems finally to leave him uneasy. If a "woman's value" is measured by her "sexual integrity," why should a daughter atone for her father's "stooping" with her own "self-abasement"? When, in "The 'Uncanny,' " Freud describes his visit to that prostitutes' quarter in the Italian city, he notes that as he appears there unwittingly for the third time, his "presence was beginning to excite attention"; he seems on the verge of admitting that his presence there was beginning to excite *him*. In other words, Freud's definition and understanding of the uncanny have grown at least in part out of his feeling of unease with what his own model of the economy of female sexuality represses. And where he seems most uneasy—as his treatment of the Coppelia narrative in "The 'Uncanny' " also suggests—is in the impact of that economy on the life of the daughter.[3]

If the prostitute has a possible, implicit life as daughter in Freud's thought, she also has one as double, as harbinger of death. Freud interprets his own encounter with the prostitutes as an experience that "forces upon us the idea of something fateful and unescapable where otherwise we should have spoken of 'chance' only" (*SE* 17: 236); he concludes, in terms that remind us of his theory of the death drive, "that whatever reminds us of this inner *repetition-compulsion* is perceived as the uncanny" (*SE* 17: 238; his emphasis). The association perhaps makes more sense when we turn to one of his culminating points late in the essay, in which female sexuality is again at stake:

> It often happens that male patients declare that they feel there is something uncanny about the female genital organs. This *unheimlich* place, however, is the entrance to the former *heim* [home] of all human beings, to the place where everyone dwelt once upon a time and in the beginning. There is a humorous saying: "Love is home-sickness"; and whenever a man dreams of a place or a country and says to himself, still in the dream, "this place is familiar to me, I have been there before," we may interpret the place as being his mother's genitals or her body. In this case, too, the *unheimlich* is what was once *heimisch*, home-like, familiar; the prefix "un" is the token of repression. (245)

Thus, Freud implies, his return to the prostitutes' houses was a repressed turn toward home—and toward death, the womb where, he says, one is "buried alive." What the prostitute in particular seems to represent is the anxiety surrounding the connection between the repetition compulsion as an aspect of the death drive, on the one hand, and on the other, the compulsion to *substitute,* to replace, that is at the heart of his analysis. The prostitute is both a substitute for "real" intimacy and an encounter with one's own (the male client's own) replaceability, symbolized graphically in the money that accompanies and defines the exchange. An encounter with a prostitute thus is a metaphorical encounter with death for the male subject, since it is predicated upon his being dispensible, on his departing and being replaced. Sex for money smacks of death.

## II

The association of the prostitute with death was not Freud's idea; it had a long life before him and may already be seen implicit in the location of the Whore of Babylon in John's apocalyptic vision of the end. The fear, expressed by Rat-Man, of the danger posed by syphilitic infection strikes the psychoanalyst as "justifiable" (*SE* 10: 214) and is the primary reason usually given for the surveillance, control, and punishment of prostitutes in nineteenth-century cities. Recent research on the discourses surrounding prostitution in France and England has shown how far this was the case. According to Alain Corbin, the connections between the prostitute's body and the corpse were multiple and complex, some conceptual (the prostitute's body is "putrid," a "sewer," already rotting), some practical ("The proprietors of dissection theaters relied on purveyors for their supply of corpses. The

Faculté doctors used the prostitutes' bodies from the morgue"; 211). As Corbin points out, the prostitute, with her disease, threatens bourgeois culture and its "genetic patrimony" (212). Most obviously, the prostitute figures forth repressed and illicit desires, "depraved" sexuality, the woman's "unchaste" body, the animal that is on the margin of the human being, social intercourse as most crudely physical.

On the other hand, she is also a victim of that culture, herself "the symbolic synthesis of the tragedy of the times," a sign of the new urban pathology (Corbin 212). Thus she also represents the social repressed, the lowlife of the city's narrow streets and slums, its gutters and sewers. Her place on the city streets is consonant both with the place in the social hierarchy she represents and with the dissolution of hierarchies she engages. The streets are the marketplace, the locus of the crowds, the place of exchange, of buying and selling. They are thus the place where monetary value replaces intrinsic value, where the text too is a commodity.

The urban prostitute, though a distinct social type whose history parallels that of the city in general, also has a peculiarly nineteenth-century cast and cultural function. According to Lawrence Stone, bawdy houses abounded much earlier—in Elizabethan England, for example, where a certain amount of "casual, semi-professional" prostitution flourished (392). This is markedly different, however, from the carefully hierarchized, professional urban pros-titutes he records by the eighteenth century (392–93). Judith Walkowitz documents the system of nineteenth-century prostitution that emerged. The changes in the economy and the class system brought about during the Industrial Revolution affected the causes, the nature, and the social meanings of prostitution.[4] Perhaps paramount was the developing ideology of the market economy based on a consumer society. As Walkowitz puts it, "Living in a society where status was demonstrated by material possessions, women sold themselves in order to gain the accoutrements that would afford them 'self-respect' " (21). The act of prostitution comes to mirror the process of consumption, in which self-respect is reified in the consumed object, arbitrary signifier of perpetually receding fulfillment.[5]

Implicitly, in the prostitute, there is a parallel between commodification and disease or death. By the late nineteenth century, in the works of Félicien Rops, the prostitute is overtly a harbinger of death, her syphilis-stricken face and body an emblem of a diseased world. Rops is simply rendering an image that had gained wide currency in nineteenth-century popular graphics.[6] A century earlier, Blake anticipates Rops's images when he writes, in "Lon-don," of how the "harlot's curse . . . / Blights with plagues the marriage hearse." A liminal being who moves between social and psychological categories, the prostitute destabilizes systems, indeed threatens even the fundamental binary opposition between life and death. The prostitute as haunting presence is overdetermined: her body already the site of decay, she evokes death; and she is doubly repressed, as socially undesirable and as illicitly desired. She is thus both the alien, threatening Other and an aspect of the bourgeois self. To figure the prostitute—and not her clients—as the carrier of disease is clearly to project away from the collective self what is repressed inside it. Small wonder, then, that she comes to represent death itself, externalized but beckoning.

What is perhaps most deathly, most spectral, about her is that she represents the empty and infinitely mobile sign: female sexuality as the vehicle of avarice rather than of conceding desire.[7] In her, moreover, the woman becomes the subject, as well as the object, of her own exchange. Thus she destabilizes the comfortable "reality" of the bourgeois family, premised upon a legally encoded hierarchy of power and subjectivity.[8] At the same time, she holds a mirror up to it, exposing the market economy in the relations between the sexes. In the text that is haunted by the prostitute, there are no gifts—not even potlatch—only commodities.[9]

## III

It may be something of a truism that the male romantic artist suspected he was prostituting himself. Finely attuned to the market he was serving, he paraded his words above all for a scrutinizing and public crowd, one that bought his books in the streets and read about them in the newspapers and illustrated journals. It was Baudelaire, in the *Fusées,* who so notoriously asked, "What is art?" and answered, "Prostitution," articulating clearly what seems to have been in the air. If prostitution is an overt and complex figure in Baudelaire's poetry and in other contemporary works by French authors, it is an equally complex but rather more subtle figure in earlier British romantic texts. One might say that with Baudelaire, Balzac, and Flaubert something emerges that has long been a repressed aspect of romantic art.[10]

Thus the haunting: as the repressed haunts consciousness, as the exiled dead haunt the house of the living, the prostitute haunts the romantic text. Because she is repressed, her presence may well feel oblique, uncanny. There are numerous examples of such ghostly prostitutes; one thinks of the harlot Life-in-Death in Coleridge's "Rime of the Ancient Mariner," to name just one.[11] The two texts I will turn to here in order to sketch a recurrent pattern are Mary Wollstonecraft's *Maria, or The Wrongs of Woman,* and William Wordsworth's lyric "Alice Fell." Both, I will argue, are haunted by the prostitute and everything she represents. For the male poet she is doubly significant: as the uncanny but forbidden and strange home to which he is drawn; and as a figure for himself, caught in a diseased market of exchange where there is no reliable transcendent value. For the female subject, in contrast, the prostitute is the uncanny double, the body she does not know as her own, death dealing in ways she does not control. It is a prescribed role that haunts her as the predictable consequence of acts that challenge the code of propriety. Writing—especially writing for a large and popular audience—was one of them.

Mary Wollstonecraft's novel fragment *Maria, or The Wrongs of Woman* was written in 1797 (just five years before Wordsworth wrote "Alice Fell"); Wollstonecraft died from complications of childbirth before she completed the work. In it Wollstonecraft, herself an abandoned daughter who has had trouble making her way financially, writes about prostitution both as a threat (to Maria, the genteel protagonist) and as an actuality (in the life of Maria's jailer, Jemima). And like "Alice Fell," *Maria* is a haunted text, one with an excess of meanings that seem to emerge out of things impossible to say. It is a complex novelistic fragment, however aesthetically unsatisfying, and I will not try to treat it at length here. Instead I will point out some of the ways it complements and anticipates "Alice Fell" by giving a woman's account of the same cluster of problems. The pivotal similarity is their shared awareness that the female must be wary of seeming "gifts": the women in this novel live in a world where the gift bears the shadow of the compulsory exchange and where the home is haunted by prostitution, whose consequences are fatal.

This identity of gift and commodity, romance and prostitution, house and tomb participates in a series of mirrorings that inform every aspect of the novel. It culminates, with seeming inevitability, not with the *death* of the protagonist but with something if possible even more "fatal." Her elided death, undecided, is allowed to the reader but undelivered, a dead letter: in Mary Wollstonecraft's inability to finish the novel, despite months of uncharacteristic labor writing it, can be read her inability to finish off her heroine properly. In other words, this feminist author refuses to put her protagonist where the story inevitably leads her, in one of two places: a coffin or a connubial bed. The two versions of closure for this novel are mirror images, both deathly. And as if to underscore the undecidability, not only the protagonist vacillates between life and death, but also her daughter, the fictional reader to whom the mother addresses her first-person narrative. In some of the notes for the ending the daughter survives, in others she does not. Whatever ending one chooses, the uncertainty about the daughter's survival unsettles the whole narrative: since the novel is epistolary in form, the reader occupies the place of the kidnapped, absent daughter, potentially dead.[12]

*Maria* recounts events in the life of a gentlewoman who marries badly, out of ignorance and financial need. She discovers she dislikes her husband, the merchant Mr. Venables (his name alerts us to his allegorical function), who first uses what money she brings to the marriage and then stoops to trying to pander her to a friend. Outraged, she leaves him, taking her infant daughter. He has her captured and taken to a privately run insane asylum in a crumbling ancestral mansion. Again the metaphor is clear: in a typical romantic posture, the mansion in ruins represents the decline of civilization, figured as an aristocratic, patriarchal home. At the asylum, Maria falls in love with a gentleman, Darnford, who is unjustly held there. (Like Maria, Darnford meets a variety of endings in the sketches the author left behind: he is by turns traitor and trusted companion.) Embedded within Maria's story is the story of her jailer, Jemima, who is the protagonist's dark shadow, her double. Jemima recounts how, abused and abandoned, she worked as a prostitute and finally as a courtesan to raise herself out of poverty and illiteracy.

What Wollstonecraft argues all but overtly in *Maria* is that prostitution is not the woman's crime—that it depends on and grows out of the masculine culture of the marketplace. The market system itself assumes a set of values that are seemingly consonant with prostitution. Thus, for example, it is for Venables a seamless transition from speculating in business to pandering his wife. The public and private arenas mirror each other, just as pandering seems to him a reasonable extension of the economy of marriage. So important, so pervasive, is this particular mimetic metaphor that it is the key to the novel's structure of mirrors: *Maria, or The Wrongs of Woman* clearly repeats and inverts Wollstonecraft's *Vindication of the Rights of Woman*, just as Maria mirrors the author's name Mary (and the central problem of marrying), the very name Maria a near homonym for mirror.[13] Even—perhaps most significantly—the servant/prostitute Jemima's name incorporates miming, mimesis, her womanly body miming Maria's in their like commodified sexuality: Jemima's narrative of abuse, framed within Maria's story, is the downstairs version. Even more, Jemima's fortunes in marketing her sexuality have moved up and down with the same rapidity—and the same depressed outcome—as Venables's fortunes in speculation. These multiple mirrors do not reflect a free-for-all of meaning, a *mise en abyme,* so much as they imply a profound identity in dialectic between seeming differences: rights and wrongs, lady and prostitute, marriage and prostitution, business and prostitution, philosophy and fiction, novelist and character, even life and death, "original" and "image trace."

It is within this dizzying multiplicity of mutual substitutes that the novel reveals the existing social system as a trap for the woman. As Mary Poovey has shown, Maria's imprisonment throughout the extant portions of the book emblematizes not only the ways her movements and even her behavior are confined, but also the confinement of mentality that results from long enclosure. Maria intuits the possibility of another way of living and being, but it continues to elude her, even on the level of conscious awareness. Thus from the moment she is imprisoned her impulse is to find a man to rescue her.[14] The insane and ghostly ravings of the house's inmates, like Alice Fell's cry in Wordsworth's poem, voice an excess of meaning, something for which her world has no words. At one point Maria says, "Marriage has bastilled me for life" (103). But storming the marriage provides no way out: she merely discovers how deeply she is caught, in a prolonged series of repetitions. Arriving at the asylum, Maria notes, "I . . . perceived I was buried alive" (135). Even as Maria escapes from the asylum, an inmate with a "sepulchral voice" (141) detains her, cursing her and seizing her by the arm.[15] He too is there as an inarticulate excess. His gesture mimes that of the prostitute, although he is looking not to seduce her but to remind her of an affinity.

Maria's greatest affinity with the prostitute lies in her relationship with her uncle. He is the benign father substitute in all symbolic functions; it is he who arranges for and secretly bankrolls her doomed marriage to Venables, and he who repeatedly bails her out with money. He hovers over the first part of the novel with the aura of a Mr. Darcy, promising solutions and happy endings. But their relationship has its unsettling undercurrents. Maria narrates: "The evening before his departure, which we spent alone together, he folded me to his heart, uttering the endearing appelation of 'child.' . . . [He] yet requested me, most earnestly, to come to him should I be obliged to leave my husband" (105). There is more in this vein, making one thing clear: where Maria believes herself to be receiving gifts, she is in fact part of an ominous, unwritten exchange. The shift from gift to transaction with the uncle explicitly signifies an unfortunate fall: at one point, when he kisses her, she writes, "I started back, as if I had found a wasp in a rose-bush . . . and the demon of discord entered our paradise" (91). Maria's story is haunted by the sense that despite her impeccable "virtue," she must prostitute herself subtly to her uncle in order to obtain his help. She thus speaks from a position of uneasy doubleness: the story we read is one of purity martyred, but the uncanny voices of the insane are just one figuring of an unspoken transaction that the heroine repeatedly accedes to and performs, as the symbolic daughter in an Oedipal and patriarchal economy.

Writing seemingly from the daughter's position, Wollstonecraft twice kills the Father (Maria's father dies, then her uncle); but the longing for a Father, an orderly solution, a transcendent meaning not only remains, it virtually cripples the text by being implicated in the very genre of the sentimental/gothic romance that Wollstonecraft has elected to write, and that she cannot find a way to rewrite. The "feminine" genre here is as entrapped as Maria is.[16] Wollstonecraft's inability to finish can also be read, then, as a rupturing gesture, textual violence, however unintended or itself incomplete. What we learn from *Maria* is that the ghost of prostitution is death dealing in ways that Wollstonecraft herself seems to have been wrestling with. To the female subject her own body, her own discourse, is as though possessed by powers of destruction not her own. "Stooping" (to use Freud's word) from philosophy to the novel, to "feminine" writing for the marketplace, Wollstonecraft finds an uncanny double she cannot write into line.

Wordsworth's "Alice Fell" is not obviously about a girl's potential fall from innocence, but I will argue that the poem is haunted, more subtly than *Maria,* by the threat of prostitution.[17] The speaker of the poem recounts how he has ridden in a coach at night and heard an uncanny sound; it turns out to be the voice of Alice Fell, a young girl who is riding on the back of the coach and whose cloak has been caught in the turning wheel. She cries "bitterly," "as if her innocent heart would break"; asked by the speaker where she lives, she replies that she is "fatherless and motherless," and that she belongs to Durham. When they arrive at the post tavern, the speaker gives the host money to buy her a new cloak. The poem concludes with the speaker's sense of satisfaction: "Proud creature was she the next day, / The little orphan, Alice Fell!" It is a brief narrative, told, like most of Wordsworth's lyrical ballads, by an unreliable narrator. The poem is at least as much about his experience as about hers.

Her story, however, is the poem's more obvious subject, and it focuses on her hysterical attachment to the shredded cape. Her ghostly and inarticulate cry, pure intense emotion, occasions the poem and invites interpretation. The speaker tells us that she weeps "as if she had lost her only friend," and indeed her solitude and vulnerability are striking. What is implied, however, is that she needs a real friend and protector; the speaker's simile prepares us for his charitable gesture of replacing the cloak. But it does more. It subtly underscores for us the nature of Alice Fell's position: in her solitude she clearly needs a "friend," and the question remains open what kind of friend she will eventually get. The speaker is willing to make a gift to her without any seeming stipulation of exchange. His share of the deal is the satisfaction he derives from the experience; we see it in the self-congratulatory final stanza. He can be satisfied only if he pointedly does not take advantage of her in any way, but uses the narrative to reiterate her innocence and unfallen state.

The idea of Alice's real fall, the sexual fall from innocence, is kept offstage in the poem. It seems possible that the cloak itself alludes to it: this is the first step in the undressing of Alice. The cloak, we note, gets caught up in the carriage's turning wheel, whose movement is an inexorable as the fate it invokes. As David Simpson has pointed out, "Fell" may refer both to a skin or covering and to something fierce and wild.[18] Alice's cloak is central to the poem's concerns. A metonymy for the poor girl's virtue as well as her living body, it is her only friend, her only thing of value. She is described by the speaker as "half-wild," and in this light her cloak is what stands between her and full wildness. It is her emblem of civilization and also her protection, a sign of continued innocence. Perhaps one reason her grief "would not be satisfied" is because she apprehends the full nature of the threat in her position. She must fear gifts from strange men.

No overt allusion to a sexual threat appears in the poem, and the speaker is at pains to stress how childlike and innocent she is. Nor do we suspect him of suppressing lascivious thoughts. She simply seems too young. But that is part of the story's potency. What is a very young girl doing riding alone at night in a coach with a strange gentleman? How long will she be able to protect herself in such circumstances? How often will charitable gifts be offered without expectation of return? Part of the girl's significance lies in her marginality: she is a social outsider, "fatherless and motherless," outside the patriarchal system of protection and dowry, a human being in excess, whose very existence calls the viability of that system into question.[19] Alice's potential fall is fell, dire, threatening to our idea of human decency.

A look at the context in which Wordsworth wrote "Alice Fell" may lend some credence to this reading. The poem is very precisely dated beneath its title: "Composed March 12, 13, 1802.—Published 1807." These dates do not tell the whole story. Wordsworth conceived and wrote the poem at a time when he was in a state of some turmoil over his romantic affairs. He had recently decided to marry Mary Hutchinson, and their plans were in full gear. On 15 February 1802 he received a letter from Annette Vallon, the woman with whom he had had an affair in France some ten years earlier.[20] She had borne him a daughter, Caroline, whom he had never seen. After his return to England she had at first written him frequently, describing Caroline to him and begging him to return to France and marry her. Their correspondence was interrupted in 1795 because of the war between England and France. When the war ended, she wrote to Wordsworth again. The letter must have come like a cannon shot from the past.

The day after her letter came, Wordsworth apparently heard the story of Alice Fell told by his friend Robert Grahame. Six days later, on 22 February, letters arrived from Vallon and from Caroline, his daughter. On the twenty-fourth, Wordsworth wrote to Vallon, possibly telling her of his engagement to Mary. On 12 and 13 March, then, he composed "Alice Fell." One week later he had postponed his marriage and planned a trip to France to see Vallon and meet his daughter.

Without entering into the debate about just how important Annette Vallon was to Wordsworth's imaginative life, let me point out that she and their daughter were significant enough for him to drop everything and go to them for a whole month as soon as the opportunity came.[21] His biographer Mary Moorman carefully explains his behavior, stating that he obviously had intended to marry her, but that financial difficulties and later the war intervened. Moorman wants at all costs not to cast the poet as the wicked seducer who abandons the innocent girl to a wasted life. And yet even she acknowledges that the idea of that role must have haunted Wordsworth. A young woman of good family, Vallon had never married, doubtless—at least in large part—because of her illegitimate daughter. In the early years of their separation, when Vallon wrote him frequently and pleadingly, as Moorman speculates, he might have imagined the worst: "He was forced to sit, reading those heart-wringing letters of 'poor Annette,' as Dorothy called her, and face to face with the bitter thought that he was himself now a guilty party in a tragedy that might end, for Annette, as it had ended for those girls whose voices had haunted him in London streets and round the doors of theatres" (183–84). Here it is Vallon that Moorman transforms imaginatively into the disembodied voice of the prostitute. But in 1802, when Wordsworth's daughter was ten years old—a child, but on the brink of adolescence—he must have had some anxious thoughts for her future as well. Caroline was no orphan, but she was as good as fatherless (after Wordsworth's departure, in fact, Vallon used the name "la veuve Williams"). As Moorman indicates, Vallon may well have written to Wordsworth in 1802 partly to ask for "some financial provision" for his daughter, which would have strained his already meager finances just as he was about to marry (554). At stake was how far he felt himself her father and was able to fill those shoes, emotionally and financially.

Unlike the speaker in "Alice Fell," Wordsworth could not simply put down the money for a cloak and walk away, assured that the girl would be happier the next day. His daughter laid a vastly more complex claim on him. Feelings of guilt and anxiety for her future would no doubt have gone hand in hand. Without a father, without a clearly defined name and place in the patriarchal system, without a dowry, and with a mother whose own position was ill defined, what chance did she stand for finding financial security and happiness in marriage? And what chance was there that she could manage on her own? What father would have wanted to think his daughter was possibly headed toward prostitution?

Wordsworth was not specifically addressing these questions when he wrote "Alice Fell," but the circumstances are striking enough that we may think of them as contributing to the shape of the poem.[22] It clearly was written in the midst of turmoil surrounding the consequences of his suppressed affair with Annette Vallon. That affair was the occasion of repression in his own life and in his poetry, most notably in its awkward omission from the Prelude and in the way he at first allowed it muted representation through the episode of Vaudracour and Julia and then elided it.[23] As in the public debate over what kind of support townships were obliged to give their poor and their orphans, Wordsworth must have debated privately with himself at some length over the nature of his obligations to his daughter. Among other things, then, "Alice Fell" may be read as a concealed confession of doubts about his own response to his daughter. It gives oblique expression to his sense that the contemporary framework of male and female relations bears the mark of venal corruption.[24]

One of the problems in reading "Alice Fell" is discerning whether the speaker's gesture is in fact inadequate. The indeterminacy is itself telling. David Simpson makes the strongest argument for its adequacy and appropriateness, proposing that the orphan's needs must first, and primarily, be met on the material level: the poem is subtitled "Poverty," and that is the problem the speaker addresses practically. The poem allows this reading. Its final stanza invites it. But that stanza also finally withholds any certain judgment of the speaker's behavior, because the conclusion is only his hypothesis, and we do not know how far to trust him.[25] More important, there remains that haunting excess of the child's grief, which the material cloak itself does not fully account for.

The poem's opening quatrains set a gothic tone, complete with a dark night and a drowned moon; the speaker first takes Alice Fell's ghostlike cries for the moaning of the wind. This is imagery typically associated in the contemporary romance with ghosts, past crimes, and current terrors: the living dead. As Ann Radcliffe so notoriously does in her novels, Wordsworth explains his ghost rationally without dispelling its eerie effect. Alice's imagined "fall" takes her into a liminal space that is neither life nor death and is terrifying to consider. Her inarticulate, disembodied cry haunts the poem because what it expresses cannot be explained away. Poverty, here, is not a simple problem to be solved by cash. Instead, it represents a state of mind—one that the poet feels himself at times to have shared. Less vulnerable than an Alice Fell, he nevertheless was also an orphan who had been left without fortune, and at this moment, as he contemplated marriage and thought of helping his own child, he may well have felt even more acutely than before the distress of his own lack of resources. It was not until June 1802—several months after "Alice Fell" was written—that the distinct possibility arose of at last claiming his modest inheritance from the heirs of Lord Lowther. Until his inheritance was established, we see him constantly concerned with fiscal matters, including the viability of his poetry in the marketplace. "Alice Fell," like Wordsworth's other poems about marginal beings, gives voice to the orphan's experience in part because he seems to know it well: as part of his own. But it also draws quite clearly the line between her being and his. His is on the side of life.

I have been speaking of prostitution here as though the metaphorical act of selling one's soul—or one's disembodied principles—were comparable to the literal one of engaging in sexual activity, a meeting of bodies and of flesh in exchange for money. Clearly the two must be distinguished. Here is where we observe the limits of the text, when it encounters the body; the thought of the sheer physicality of actual prostitution can induce—in me at any rate—a visceral revulsion. There is a direct parallel in the revenant: as the ghost is to the corpse, so is the symbolic to the actual prostitution. Elisabeth Bronfen has written that the corpse is generally seen as "destabilizing," "calling forth strategies of recuperation."[26] Something comparable may be said of the prostitute: her venality and her diseased body corrupt, destabilize, spread their contagion.[27] As "Alice Fell" and *Maria* show us, the text—narrated story, composed poem, novel fragment, bearing the feminine name—is the gift engendered by the act of recuperation, a spectral excess of another kind.[28] The text, that is, substitutes for the prostitute (and for the unstable daughter) and emerges, however disembodied, as a stabilized utterance, an entity that at once recuperates the woman and compensates, or substitutes, for her. This is a gesture we recognize from the elegiac tradition that is so central to the function of the lyric in our culture. But it is here given a peculiarly gendered, economic twist.

It is by now commonplace to view Freud as in many ways a late romantic, a figure who put in the form of an analytic model, or at the very least articulated discursively, the basic romantic insights into the grounding of subjectivity in the obscurity of the unconscious. It is Freud who would make a *reasonable* claim for the death drive; Freud who, as Terry Castle has argued so suggestively, makes ghosts and specters the subject of an enlightened discourse, granting them a genuine reality in the psyche. In exchange, however, Freud's model occludes history—much as romantic poetry does in its attempt at transcendence. Jerome McGann has identified the quintessential romantic ideology with such an occlusion, and he sees Wordsworth as its primary embodiment: "If Wordsworth's poetry elides history, we observe in this 'escapist' or 'reactionary' move its own self-revelation" (91), he writes. And then: "The idea that poetry, or even consciousness, can set one free of the ruins of history and culture is the grand illusion of every Romantic poet" (91). It does not take much to locate Freud in this romantic tradition.

The position of the male romantic writer in the marketplace also bears kinship to that of Freud in the economics of his practice. Both offered for sale the knowledge of the body: they read its texts in the unconscious, in one's "real" experience that eludes and authenticates the masks that the social being presents to the world. But of course then the "authentic" becomes another mask, itself a fashionable one—in Walter Benjamin's memorable description of Paris fashion, a Mister Death. Analyses, translations, of the unconscious seem to be marked inevitably by a nostalgia for the real, which is encoded most emphatically in the feminine body, and most extremely in the corpse.

Curiously, prostitution may be a peculiarly apt metaphor for the romantic position vis-à-vis death, that tempter with a price. If it is, and if we are indeed still thinking from within the romantic ideologies, then working to understand it as a paradigmatic metaphor may bring us closer to a historical understanding of how we represent death to ourselves—of how our sense of death's power is implicated in the social structures of power within which we exchange our meanings. In the readings I have sketched here, prostitution is a metaphor for death, so that death itself is represented only indirectly. What I am suggesting, however, is that death finally is just what is at stake here: both in the actual narratives, in which the figures cling so tenuously to life, and in the figure of prostitution, representing the loss of intrinsic value and therefore of meaning and life in human relations.

## Notes

1. The phrase in brackets is the translator's.

2. Gallup is here developing a point made by Cixous and Clément, as she points out.

3. For a superb extended treatment of that economy, see Boose and Flowers.

4. For example, during the nineteenth century, "young single women were increasingly required to seek work outside the home and sometimes to migrate to nearby urban areas to find alternative employment. There, they were expected to fend for themselves, and not burden their family for support" (16). Stone also notes that the conditions of labor away from home were very unattractive and the work was ill paid (392).

5. For the parallels between romantic ideology and consumerism, see Siskin, especially his chapter "High Wages and High Arguments" (151–63). He argues there that "the turn to the kind of luxury consumption increasingly favored in the wage debate was being made, learned, and justified in the texts produced at that time" (158).

6. For discussion of those graphics, as well as some reproductions, see Goodwin, *Kitsch and Culture*. Bernheimer explores at some length this idea of the prostitute, seeing in her threatening presence a "challenge to male autonomy and power" that has been critical in the development of modernism, which he argues developed specific techniques in response to that challenge (272 and passim).

7. Note Baudrillard's use of the brothel as metaphor: "Everything becomes undecidable. This is the characteristic effect of the domination of the code, which is based everywhere on the principle of neutralization and indifference. This is the generalized brothel of capital: not the brothel of prostitution but the brothel of substitution and interchangeability" (128).

8. Walkowitz goes so far as to claim a certain feminist authority and independence for the prostitute: "Superficially, prostitution seemed to operate as an arena of male supremacy, where women were bartered and sold as commodities. In reality, women often controlled the trade and tended to live together as part of a distinct female subgroup. Prostitutes were still not free of male domination, but neither were they simply passive victims of male sexual abuse" (31). In other words, the social relations of prostitutes and clients fit no easy binaries, were not easily described by such overly simple phrases as "male domination" and "female passivity."

9. I am using *potlatch* here in the sense elaborated at some length by Marcel Mauss, who refers to social events in which seeming gifts are exchanged that in fact bear multiple meanings and incur responsibilities.

10. Sonia Hofkosh is the only scholar of British romanticism I know of who has attended to what she calls "the metaphor of the writer as whore" in that period (98). As she puts it, "Selling herself, she [the prostitute] represents the writer who depersonalizes his self-expression by marketing it; even more, her promiscuity, her failure to distinguish among men, endangers the very foundation of self-expression— the logic of personality and propriety by which men determine who they are and what they own" (99). Hofkosh in turn draws on the work of Catherine Gallagher, who has shown that Baudelaire's Victorian contemporaries too understood the writer's position in these terms.

I am grateful to Sonia Hofkosh for sharing with me her impressive work in progress on these matters; it touches on and richly develops many points in common with this essay.

11. On that harlot, see Goodwin, "Domesticity."

12. Mitzi Myers calls Wollstonecraft's "hints for an ending" an "oddly apposite do-it-yourself kit for the reader" (113). For more on the reader's place in this narrative, and a rich reading of the novel generally, see Tilottama Rajan 167–94, esp. 173–83.

13. Rajan (173) also notes a pattern of echoes between these two works.

14. Mary Poovey develops this point subtly in her extended discussion of the novel (95–113). But see also Laurie Langbauer, who proposes a much more complex function for romance in the novel's structure and for the novel's use of fragmentation and the inarticulate to convey a femininity that can be aligned with the Kristevian semiotic.

15. The man's "form was scarcely human," and his "ghastly eyes" recall the ancestral portraits in the house's staircase: when Maria arrives at the asylum, she recounts, "Large figures painted on the walls seemed to start on me, and glaring eyes to meet me at every turn. Entering a long gallery, a dismal shriek made me spring out of my conductor's arms" (134). These are gothic flourishes, but not gratuitous ones. The man and the portraits are represented as death dealing for a reason.

16. Mitzi Myers argues in detail that Wollstonecraft self-consciously chose a genre that is the opposite of enlightened philosophy and that is "customarily associated with the feminine" (108).

17. For another treatment of prostitution in this poem, see Goodwin, "Romantic Voice."

18. It is striking that in David Simpson's astute reading of the poem he goes so far as to point out that the "debate or choice between nakedness and clothing was a feature of the 'political' rhetoric of the times" (*Wordsworth's Historical Imagination* 181), without, however, noticing that the choice between nakedness and clothing is loaded very differently for a young girl than it is for a man. Similarly, he mentions that "fell" may refer to "the *fallen* state" (180; his emphasis), without noting that the fallen woman is in a rather different position from that of the generic postlapsarian man.

19. Simpson elaborates on how the poem engages the contemporary debate about how charity should be practiced. See also Heather Glen's readings of Blake's poems about orphans. Walkowitz, studying nineteenth-century prostitutes, stresses "the one striking feature of these women's social background, their orphaned status," which "may have released these women from the stranglehold of standard female socialization" (20).

20. This and the subsequent dates are drawn from Pinion's chronology, 45 ff.

21. Stephen Gill's recent biography is exemplary in the way it refuses to conjecture about what might have been going on in Wordsworth's mind at the time, even as he acknowledges the importance of the events. There is almost no record of Wordsworth's feelings about Vallon, either at this or at any point in his life. In fact, the very lack of record seems significant: not even Dorothy, who accompanied him to France and who kept a detailed journal the rest of the year, kept any written record.

22. Even the names Alice Fell and Annette Vallon seem to echo and complement each other, as Herbert Tucker pointed out to me.

23. For another recent (and complementary) discussion of the effects of these events on a different poem, see Simpson's "Public Virtues, Private Vices."

24. "Alice Fell" is in no sense a unique instance of these issues being raised in Wordsworth's poetry in this oblique way. Peter J. Manning's recent essay on "Poor Susan" discusses the ambiguous position Susan occupies on a Cheapside street at dawn and alludes to the social debates of the 1790s that were concerned with the status of just such figures. Alan J. Bewell, reading Wordsworth in the context of contemporary studies of witchcraft, argues that in several poems "abandoned women come to serve as the empirical medium for recovering origins" (365), figures for the poet and for something beyond and outside him. In another kind of article, Anne Rylestone has noted the preponderance of abandoned women in Wordsworth's poetry and argued for a biographical source for the violence done them. In each instance there is a telling ambiguity in the poet's relation to the female figure.

25. Simpson too backs away from certainty at the close of his reading of "Alice Fell": "It may be that, in the tentative though arguable gap that this poem opens between poet and speaker, we can see something of a Wordsworth who has things both ways, and who does not make it finally clear whether he endorses or ironizes the insight that Alice and others like her might be 'past all relief' " (*Wordsworth's Historical Imagination* 182).

26. In private correspondence. See also her book *Over Her Dead Body*.

27. On the prostitute's diseased body and the corpse, see Sander Gilman's essay in this volume.

28. Kofman reads the text as revenant, spectral excess, though she does not consider that as a gift. I am grateful to Elisabeth Bronfen for directing me to Kofman's work, and for her pervasive influence on my thinking about these matters. Although Bronfen does not to my knowledge write about gift theory, her thoughts about the corpse as an object of exchange have been especially influential for me here.

## Works Cited

Baudrillard, Jean. "Symbolic Exchange and Death." *Selected Writings*. Ed. Mark Poster. Stanford: Stanford UP, 1988.

Bernheimer, Charles. *Figures of Ill Repute: Representing Prostitution in Nineteenth-Century France*. Cambridge: Harvard UP, 1989.

Bewell, Alan J. " 'A Word Scarce Said': Hysteria and Witchcraft in Wordsworth's 'Experimental' Poetry of 1797–98." *ELH* 53.2 (1986): 357–90.

Boose, Linda E., and Betty S. Flowers, eds. *Daughters and Fathers*. Baltimore: Johns Hopkins UP, 1989.

Bronfen, Elisabeth. *Over Her Dead Body: Death, Femininity and the Aesthetic*. Manchester: Manchester UP; New York: Routledge, 1992.

———. "Pay as You Go: On the Exchange of Bodies and Signs." *The Sense of Sex:*

*Feminist Perspectives on Hardy.* Ed. Margaret R. Higonnet. Urbana: U of Illinois P, 1993. 66–86.

Castle, Terry. "Phantasmagoria." *Critical Inquiry* 15.1 (1988): 26–61.

Corbin, Alain. "Commercial Sexuality in Nineteenth-Century France: A System of Images and Regulations." *The Making of the Modern Body: Sexuality and Society in the Nineteenth Century.* Ed. Catherine Gallagher and Thomas Laqueur. Berkeley: U of California P, 1986. 209–19.

Freud, Sigmund. *The Standard Edition of the Complete Psychological Works* (*SE*) 24 vols. 1953–74. London: Hogarth, 1986.

Gallagher, Catherine. "George Eliot and *Daniel Deronda:* The Prostitute and the Jewish Question." *Sex, Politics, and Science in the Nineteenth-Century Novel.* Ed. Ruth Bernard Yeazell. Baltimore: Johns Hopkins UP, 1986. 39–62.

Gallup, Jane. "Keys to Dora." In *Dora's Case: Freud-Hysteria-Feminism.* Ed. Charles Bernheimer and Claire Kahane. New York: Columbia UP, 1985. 200–220.

Gill, Stephen. *William Wordsworth: A Life.* Oxford: Clarendon, 1989.

Glen, Heather. *Vision and Disenchantment.* Cambridge: Cambridge UP, 1983.

Goodwin, Sarah Webster. "Domesticity and Uncanny Kitsch in 'The Rime of the Ancient Mariner' and *Frankenstein.*" *Tulsa Studies in Women's Literature* 10.1 (1991): 93–108.

———. *Kitsch and Culture: The Dance of Death in Nineteenth-Century Literature and Graphic Arts.* New York: Garland, 1988.

———. "Wordsworth and Romantic Voice: The Poet's Song and the Prostitute's Cry." *Embodied Voices: Female Vocality in Western Culture.* Ed. Leslie Dunn and Nancy A. Jones. Cambridge: Cambridge UP, forthcoming.

Hofkosh, Sonia. "The Writer's Ravishment: Women and the Romantic Author—The Example of Byron." Mellor 81–92.

Kofman, Sarah. *Mélancolie de l'art.* Paris: Galilée, 1985.

Langbauer, Laurie. "An Early Romance: Motherhood and Women's Writing in Mary Wollstonecraft's Novels." Mellor 208–19.

Manning, Peter J. "Placing Poor Susan: Wordsworth and the New Historicism." *Studies in Romanticism* 25 (Fall 1986): 351–69.

Mauss, Marcel. *The Gift: Forms and Functions of Exchange in Archaic Societies.* Glencoe, IL: Free Press, 1954.

McGann, Jerome J. *The Romantic Ideology: A Critical Investigation.* Chicago: U of Chicago P, 1983.

Mellor, Anne K., ed. *Romanticism and Feminism.* Bloomington: Indiana UP, 1988.

Moorman, Mary. *William Wordsworth: A Biography. The Early Years, 1770–1803.* Oxford: Clarendon Press, 1957.

Myers, Mitzi. "Unfinished Business: Wollstonecraft's *Maria.*" *Wordsworth Circle* 11 (1980): 107–14.

Pinion, F. B. *A Wordsworth Chronology.* Boston: Hall, 1988.

Poovey, Mary. *The Proper Lady and the Woman Writer: Ideology as Style in the*

*Works of Mary Wollstonecraft, Mary Shelley, and Jane Austen*. Chicago: U of Chicago P, 1984.

Rajan, Tilottama. *The Supplement of Reading: Figures of Understanding in Romantic Theory and Practice*. Ithaca: Cornell UP, 1990.

Rylestone, Anne. "Violence and the Abandoned Woman in Wordsworth's Poetry." *Massachusetts Studies in English* 7.3 (1980): 40–56.

Simpson, David. "Public Virtues, Private Vices: Reading between the Lines of Wordsworth's 'Anecdote for Fathers.' " *Subject to History: Ideology, Class and Gender*. Ed. David Simpson. Ithaca: Cornell UP, 1991. 161–90.

———. *Wordsworth's Historical Imagination: The Poetry of Displacement*. New York: Methuen, 1987.

Siskin, Clifford. *The Historicity of Romantic Discourse*. New York: Oxford UP, 1988.

Stallybrass, Peter, and Allon White. *The Politics of Transgression*. Ithaca: Cornell UP, 1986.

Stone, Lawrence. *The Family, Sex and Marriage in England, 1500–1800*. Abridged ed. New York: Harper and Row, 1979.

Wahrig, Gerhard, ed. *Wörterbuch der deutschen Sprache*. Munich: DTV, 1978.

Walkowitz, Judith R. *Prostitution and Victorian Society: Women, Class and the State*. Cambridge: Cambridge UP, 1980.

Wollstonecraft, Mary. *Maria, or The Wrongs of Woman*. New York: Norton, 1975.

Wordsworth, William. *Poetical Works*. Ed. Thomas Hutchinson and Ernest de Selincourt. 1904. Oxford: Oxford UP, 1981.

■

# Writing as Voodoo: Sorcery, Hysteria, and Art

## *Regina Barreca*

> Death makes a firm dividing line between the present and the past. There they were, and now they aren't, and the knife slides firmly through the home-baked cake, dividing. This side, that side, then and now. There, see, isn't that real enough for you? And you were beginning to think, weren't you, that experience slipped along in some kind of continual stream, more or less under your control, at your behest? That'll teach you. Before death, after death. Now you see them, now you don't.
>
> Weldon, *Remember Me*

## Death and Women's Writings

Just in case you thought there was no distinction between representation and reality, there is death. Just in case you thought experience and the representation of experience melted into one another, death provides a structural principle separating the two. See the difference, death asks, see the way language and vision differ from the actual, the irrevocable, the real? See the way death and representations of death differ the way food and a menu differ? The substance exists apart from the bill of fare, described by it but not conjured up by it or inhabiting it.

An earlier version of this essay was presented at a 1989 MLA Convention Special Session on Sociological Approaches to Literature, organized by Mary Ann Caws. I thank Mary Ann Caws, Jane Marcus, and Margaret Higonnet for reading drafts of the essay, and I especially acknowledge the inspiration and direction of both Sarah Webster Goodwin and Elisabeth Bronfen.

Women writers have a particular relationship with death, creating as they do female characters who are unsure of any reality besides death. For a number of the characters created by writers as diverse as Fay Weldon, Jean Rhys, and Colette, death and only death confers meaning on an otherwise patternless existence. These three writers are emblematic of the way women's writings assert the existence of a particularly female relationship with death that is familiar, even friendly, while at the same time respectful and generous. Death and the female characters in these narratives have an excellent working relationship; the characters make offerings to death, and death in turn provides something for them. Women tend to write about death as if the lives of their characters are positioned always in relation to a final moment. Weldon, Rhys, and Colette intensify the theme that, for women characters especially, death confers validity on a life otherwise denied value or meaning.

Death is often the single certainty—the thing they are most sure of—in the lives of these women, and they hunt it out the way scholars seek a definitive document to substantiate an otherwise eccentric reading. Death acts as a shaping principle for an existence fraught with a fear of shapelessness: if nothing else can be relied upon, at least death provides a boundary. Although Weldon, Rhys, and Colette are not the only writers to delineate this pattern, they are representative of the ways women writers deal with death, power, and the intricacies of the causal, culminating relationship between the two.

Death, like adultery, makes women's lives interesting to men because it renders exotic what is otherwise seen as domestic. Women's lives are of little interest to men because they appear to be without progress, a series of repetitions and cycles. Elisabeth Bronfen, in an essay on the dead woman as muse, has shown that an otherwise "ordinary woman" is able to make an "impressive mark on the public realm" after her death, "since her gift to the poet is the removal of her body" (242–43). Death, however, marks women's time and space. If there is a boundary, then there must be a territory bound and, by extension, a form to the territory.[1] Death is the point at which self-referential and circular reasoning breaks apart, where the continuum of an apparently seamless Möbius strip is exposed as having two sides, where it is shown that, for example, wishing someone dead is rather different from killing him—although, as a number of the women writers discussed here illustrate, wishing him dead is at least a start.

## The Curse

In modern writers like Weldon, Rhys, and Colette, and even in slightly earlier writers such as Mary Webb and George Eliot, the power behind the woman's curse or prophecy is substantial. Her curse is given substance by the ways the world sees women as themselves cursed—by bleeding, by giving birth in pain, by weeping, women have earned the right to give body to their desires. It is as if they can mortgage their own deaths in order to give pain to others. Women willing to do this are dangerous because they refuse to acknowledge the boundaries keeping order—boundaries between life and death, power and powerlessness, magic and doctrine.

Women are dangerous to the cultural order because they are "cursed" in that their bodies cannot contain themselves—women pour forth milk, tears, and blood. (What woman has not heard menses called "the curse"?) Anthropologist Mary Douglas asserts that the production of such matter calls into question fundamental assumptions about the nature of boundaries, declaring that bodily orifices are vulnerable margins, that "matter issuing from them is marginal stuff of the most obvious kind . . . blood, milk, urine, faeces or tears by simply issuing forth have traversed the boundary of the body" (121). The power behind the female utterance in these writings is made substantial, given body, in a quite literal way: there is substance to a curse given with sufficient vehemence, particularly when it is backed up by an experienced, even if unconscious, understanding of the consequences.

The curse is the only utterance made by female characters in these texts to be given credence, to be acknowledged as important. It is the only language they use that has any impact on their lives. Naming—defining the world through words—has power over the universe and draws the universe into every life. Women have a particular and complex relation to language because they have for so long been barred from acting on their ambitions or rebellions that they have learned to turn to language as a way of dealing with and influencing the world. Their curses confirm their existence and, if successful, their importance. Curses, like promises, are speech acts, in that they embody the action they describe: the menu printed on the bread to be devoured. Like promises, curses cannot be revoked. You can no more take back "I wish you dead" than you can take back "I promise to be faithful." You can break a promise, but you cannot unmake it because the utterance is a completed action, a finished piece: shattering a glass bowl is essentially different from unmaking it.

A curse is complete because it embodies what it represents; it fuses utterance and action. Often the curses given by the characters in these works are the result of a promise broken, some direct result of another character's misunderstanding the terms of an agreement. Where a man might have thought a promise was merely a ritual assurance, to be given lightly and without considering the currency behind the words, a woman will have conferred upon the words a different value. For him the language is disembodied. For her the language constitutes not simple conversation but an event, and an event of considerable significance. These writings indicate that when women become the producers of signs, instead of merely themselves signs offered as exchange between men, their signs will do more than represent. A woman uses language differently from the way a man uses it, whoever she is; she has a different relation to the word.[2] When the promise he has given proves bankrupt, she responds with a curse that inverts the power dynamic. As the victim of his false language, she uses her language to kill him.

The skillful and effective curse is a power belonging to the vanquished, not to the victor. In part this power depends on the subterfuge of the vanquished, the camouflage offered by perceived insignificance. This is perhaps the most important connection between women's writings, death, and magic: the effectiveness of the female in all three depends upon the acknowledgment and use of a perceived powerlessness. Death and magic are the effective tools of those considered ineffective. The texts under discussion concern themselves with the power of those in apparently powerless positions: discarded wives, underpaid servants, abandoned lovers, and slaves. These figures are able to catalyze the liminality of their inscription within the larger social order to draw upon forces and mechanisms outside the orthodox belief systems.

Perhaps this accounts for the frequency with which curses bubble up in women's writings, curses that are catalytic as well as catastrophic. Curses are process as well as payment. The curse usually employs death as its best and final weapon in order to validate the currency of its language. Importantly, even when addressed aloud to their objects, curses are often misinterpreted because the listener constructs a meaning based on an undervalued assessment of a situation. Those who believe themselves safe are actually in danger. And as when someone is given a reassuring misdiagnosis by an incompetent physician, the consequences of false security can be grave.

Where a promise has to be renewed daily—where one action can destroy it (one moment of infidelity rendering twenty years of fidelity null and void, for example)—the curse accumulates power and typically offers death as a final point that actualizes once deferred meaning. Words are reinfused with magic, with incantation replacing explanation, conjuring replacing conjecture. In other words, the writers here all acknowledge the importance of language in structuring reality. Put another way, they wrote from the knowledge that words themselves matter and that language is a vital force, often the stimulus for far-reaching actions. These authors link acknowledging the central role of language to acknowledging the validity of female experience. The boundaries of what has been considered the "feminine world" are systematically revised and refigured. Actions themselves do not offer definitions: the words describing the actions become the central factor, and the way language frames a situation determines that situation. In defining a situation by naming and tagging it, by limiting and categorizing it, the words themselves are clearly both manipulative and powerful. Language is snapped into a rigid context, not unconnected to or disconnected from the real, with death performing the sacramental function of connecting the symbolic and the actual.

## Fun and Games?

If women are going to be used as magic, or to use magic themselves, then we can only hope that the magic is as powerful as possible. In Fay Weldon's *The Heart of the Country,* a chapter titled "Human Sacrifice" concerns "the virgin sacrifice" as played out in a small-town parade in 1986. In a manner emblematic of Weldon and a great many other women writers, "domestic rituals" of the harvest parade sort are spliced onto "serious rituals" of the killing women sort.

Weldon explains that virgin sacrifices exist "so the world could cure itself of evil and renew itself." She adds, typically, "I hope it works" (197). If a woman is going to be sacrificed, after all, the least we can hope for is an efficient and effective payoff. If women are going to be laid on the sexual, domestic, or spiritual altar, then we can only hope their final gestures hold meaning. Earlier Weldon's narrator has explained that "in the early days of carnival they'd like as not burn their chosen virgin to death. At first on purpose—later by accident on purpose. That was the point of the event. Burn a virgin, fire a barn, drown a witch. Clear old scores and start afresh! What do you think the carnival is about, fun and games? On no" (184). The contemporary social and cultural script dictates that only the "by accident on purpose"—the fun and games—version is acceptable, with the "on purpose" version remaining vestigial and shadowy, the way smoke remains in the air after a bridge is burned.

Death is summoned but not welcomed by these rituals, invited but not embraced, so that the experience of death is invoked without being irrevocably initiated. Death is supposed to be represented by the formal aspects of the ritual the way a foreign dignitary of great status sends a card of regrets when invited to a public function. The invitation is respectfully issued with no expectation that the dignitary will appear, and the card acts as sufficient acknowledgment of a cordial response. But in a Weldon novel there are very few rituals—verbal or otherwise—that remain in the realm of the purely representational. Rituals split and spill in Weldon's texts, becoming messy and uncategorizable until they blur into the "real" world of power and magic.

In the same way that there are no rhetorical questions in her works, so there are no rituals devoid of magic. Fun and games are laced with voodoo and sorcery of the most serious sort.

Curses abound in the heart of the country, for example, and these curses are not simply the symbolic manifestations of discontented existence that relieve the emotion that precipitated them even as they evaporate into everyday discourse. When somebody says "drop dead" in a Weldon novel, we start searching for the body. For example, Sonia, the sometimes first-person, sometimes third-person narrator, can curse a neighbor for the "particular sin of splashing the poor" (14) because the neighbor carelessly drives her Volvo through a puddle when she passes Sonia while taking her whining children to school. "God rot her," says Sonia aloud. "Rich bitch!" Weldon explains that "Sonia had been born a nice, round, pleasant thing. Her life and times had turned her sour, so now she could deliver a curse or two effectively. God heard. God sent his punishment on Natalie" (15). The punishment is fitting: Natalie's husband leaves her, the Volvo gets repossessed, and her children end up going to the same state school as Sonia's. Eventually they all walk through the rain together. Weldon also offers the possibility that Sonia's curses are connected to a larger establishment: "Or was it the Devil who sent his punishment? Natalie committed the sin of splashing the poor. Sonia cursed her. Misfortune fell on Natalie. Cause and effect? Surely not. Let's just say coincidence" (16). In Weldon's iconography, sins and curses are in opposition to cause and effect in the same way that the feminine and unofficial version of a ritual is in opposition to the masculine and authorized version—magic and voodoo versus fun and games.

## Writing as Voodoo

Writing as voodoo: sorcery, hysteria, and art. What are the connections? *Wide Sargasso Sea,* Jean Rhys's revision of the story of Bertha from *Jane Eyre,* is laced with voodoo as well as replete with women's pain and women's art. Rhys's heroine, Antoinette (renamed Bertha by Rochester), consults her servant/surrogate mother Christophine to find out how to use magic to recapture Rochester's affection. Voodoo is the alternative text created by the islanders, the text placed up against the artificial, perhaps unreal text of this place called England, the place Antoinette/Bertha does not (in her saner moments) believe actually exists: " 'England,' said Christophine. . . . 'You think there is such a place?' " (111).

Voodoo is fire and earth and air and water; mostly it is fire and earth. Voodoo as text is particularly interesting in terms of women's exclusion from the masculine "high culture" script. Maya Deren, a dancer, filmmaker, and writer who went to Haiti in the late 1940s to record voodoo rituals as art, writes in *The Divine Horsemen,* "I have come to believe that if history were recorded by the vanquished rather than by the victors, it would illuminate the real, rather than the theoretical means to power" (6).

Jean Rhys's novel is the story written by the vanquished. Voodoo is the residual power of the vanquished held by Antoinette/Bertha. It is the power and magic behind the fire she calls down on the house of her husband and his mistress. Voodoo is the text constructed by Antoinette/Bertha. Voodoo—if we see it as the reaction of the vanquished to the victor, the skill adopted by the marginalized figure, the figure closest to banishment and death—is the power held by women in women's texts. Voodoo, in a metaphorical sense, is what Catherine performs in *Wuthering Heights* when she writes all over the blank spaces in her Bible and tears the covers off her religious texts. Voodoo is what calls up Catherine's ghost and what makes her more powerful in death than in life.

One of the significant aspects of voodoo is its tacit recognition that those who have lived without power are not necessarily powerless in death. As Muriel Spark writes, "One should live first, then die, not die then live" (123), but that is not always possible. Voodoo recognizes the power of the vanquished once they are removed from the arena of life where their defeat was scripted by the forces of oppression: voodoo is about the powerless finding power in death.

Voodoo is connected to language through its stress on incantation, the magical combination of words. That language is powerful. As Fay Weldon explains, "One must be careful with words. Words turn probabilities into facts and by sheer force of definition, translate tendencies into habits" (*Fat Woman's Joke* 24). Words are connected to some boundary power, the dangerous power of the margin, the marginalized, the vanquished. Words are not, in fact, part of some infinitely deferred meaning. Meaning can be deferred only so long—at a certain point it flashes up and consumes itself in some actuality. To call death upon someone is to begin a process; women possess the nomenclature of mortality, the grammar of death, because they understand that the basis for naming and language remains magical. Logically or reasonably structured systems of cause and effect have no weight in the world of voodoo: you get sick and die because someone wants you dead. You die not of a disease, but simply of death itself.

## Heresy and Choice

Mary Daly wonders, "Why has it seemed appropriate in this culture that the plot of a popular book and film [*The Exorcist*] centers around a Jesuit who exorcises a girl who is possessed? Why is there no book or film about a woman who exorcises a Jesuit?" Daly leads us to consider the use of the idea of evil to victimize women. "It is a mistake," she writes, "to see men as pitiable victims or vessels to be saved by female self-sacrifice." She insists that women, in fact, have to exorcise the Father from themselves to become their own exorcists. She writes of the witch burnings during the fifteenth, sixteenth, and seventeenth centuries as connected to the growing role of the printing press, "upon developing technology and upon controlled access to officially acknowledged learning." She discusses the idea of women as possessing unlegitimized wisdom—healing, insight, power—and therefore being a threat to the growing class of professional men. These newly legitimized authorities sought to gain credibility for their officially recognized and hierarchically structured constructs of culture, which came to be seen in turn as the only "real" knowledge or wisdom.

The idea of heresy as choice is a point readily supplied by George Eliot in *The Mill on the Floss* when she describes the religion of the Dodson sisters as including no heresy, "if heresy properly means choice" (364). There can be no choice if the dominant system is to remain unchallenged. All choice/challenge has to be rewritten as heretical, as evil, as outside the bounds of acceptability. All challengers have to be inscribed as evildoers or madwomen, sorceresses, hysterics. Or as artists.

## Death and Desire

But voodoo works as an interesting metaphor for women's texts for a more specific reason: voodoo relies on the double frame whereby the "true" power of the voodoo spirits is placed under the aegis of "accepted" religion. Before a voodoo ceremony begins, there is an *action de grâce,* calling upon (usually) a Roman Catholic saint for a benediction on the ritual to follow.[3] This creates an acceptable, decorous surface text that makes voodoo seem to be enfolded within the dominant religion. Behind this decorous surface supplied by the vigil candles around the plaster saints, by the superficial adherence to convention, there is hidden from the "authorities" the nonbeliever, the true text of the ceremony. In the double frame of women's writing suggested by Gilbert and Gubar we can see the parallels. Women writers are like voodoo practitioners in their nodding or kneeling toward convention even as they seek to dismantle the system by finding and using alternative sources of power. Women, needing to express their desires and anger in a language alien to them, must rely on ellipses and lacunae. As Rhys's Rochester says of the island: " 'What I see is nothing—I want what it *hides*—that is not nothing' " (87).

Rhys makes this point most clearly when she describes the servant Christophine's room. Christophine is a slave, a present to Antoinette's mother on her wedding day. Christophine and Antoinette are very close—Christophine is more concerned with Antoinette's fate than anyone else in the book—yet Antoinette, when she comes near to understanding the source of her friend's power, is afraid to enter the servant's room: "I knew her room so well—the pictures of the Holy Family and the prayer for a happy death. She had a bright patchwork counterpane, a broken-down press for her clothes, and my mother had given her an old rocking-chair" (31).

Everything seems perfect for a servant's room. Religious, humble, used, useful, it appears both domestic and feminine. The passage continues, however:

> Yet one day when I was waiting there I was suddenly very much afraid. The door was open to the sunlight, someone was whistling near the stables, but I was afraid. I was certain that hidden in the room (behind the old black press?) there was a dead man's dried hand, white chicken feathers, a cock with its throat cut, dying, slowly, slowly. Drop by drop was falling into a red basin and I imagined I could hear it. No one had ever spoken to me about obeah—but I knew what I would find if I dared to look. (31)

After Antoinette asks Christophine to use her voodoo, known as obeah in Jamaica, she once again looks around the room: "But after I noticed a heap of chicken feathers in one corner," she writes, "I did not look round any more" (117). She understands without needing an explanation, and she is drawn to the possibility of employing voodoo for her own purposes. Why does Antoinette need voodoo? Rochester, after a period of intense desire and sexual exploration, no longer wants his wife in his bed. He is terrified by her sexuality, her intelligence, and her refusal to accept the role of a passive, conventional wife. Because he has discovered that she is named after her mad mother, Rochester always refers to her as Bertha. Changing both her names in marriage is also a form of magic. She tells him, "Bertha is not my name. You are trying to make me into someone else, calling me by another name. I know, that's obeah too" (147), but Rochester's is a form of black magic culturally sanctioned and translated into legal and religious terms. Rochester renames Antoinette and strips her of some of her power; yet he is intent on keeping her, despite his own lack of desire. "Made for loving," Rochester thinks of his wife: "Yes, but she'll have no lover, for I don't want her and she'll see no other" (165).

What recourse does Antoinette have? She asks Christophine to use magic to bring Rochester back to the marital bed. The servant at first refuses to use voodoo on Antoinette's behalf. Christophine explains, " 'When man don't love you, more you try, more he hate you, man like that. If you love them they treat you bad, if you don't love them they after you night and day bothering your soul case out. . . . A man don't treat you good, pick up your skirt and walk out. Do it and he come after you' " (110). This is enormously sound advice, but Antoinette understandably wishes to employ more desperate measures. " 'If he, my husband, could come to me one night. Once more. I would make him love me' " (113). Christophine warns her of the possible consequences, but she performs the magic.

Her voodoo brings Rochester to his wife's bed. But Rochester then uses the wildly passionate night as evidence of Antoinette's hysteria, as reason to classify her insane: "She'll . . . laugh and coax and flatter," he tells himself, "(a mad girl. She'll not care who she's loving). She'll moan and cry and give herself as no sane woman would—or could. *Or could* " (165). The depth of Antoinette's desire and her ability to give herself over to sexual passion terrify Rochester to the point that he must convince himself she is simply insatiable, which, when translated into the masculine grammar of the female body, is called "insane." In her essay "The Guilty One," Catherine Clément examines in great detail the relation between hysteria, sexuality, and sorcery. She discusses Freud's own awareness of the ways his patients replicated the behavior that damned women for witches in the sixteenth century. By examining the assumptions and questions of Freud, Mauss, and Lévi-Strauss, she suggests, as Lévi-Strauss suggested, that the sorceress, the hysteric, and the woman artist might all be linked by a "desire for disorder or rather for counterorder" (*Newly Born Woman* 30), some sort of balance against prevailing and confining orthodoxy. The powerful sexuality of both the sorceress and the hysteric must be roped and tied into a category: witchcraft or insanity. The *Malleus Maleficarum* declares that "all witchcraft comes from carnal lust, which in women is insatiable" (Kramer and Sprenger 127). The syllogism operating here is, "No normal woman experiences intense sexual desire / This woman experiences intense sexual desire / This woman is not normal."

In *Wide Sargasso Sea,* Rochester believes that he has been bewitched into a passion he cannot understand, and he attempts to reassert his self-control, paradoxically, by controlling his wife.[4] He needs to confine the woman who makes him come out of himself so that he can again possess himself; fearing his own abandon, he must truss her up in a motionless, positionless place. As Clément writes, the "feminine role, the role of sorceress, of hysteric, is ambiguous, anti-establishment and conservative at the same time. Anti-establishment because the symptoms—the attacks—revolt and shake up the public, the group, the men . . . [but] these roles are *conservative* because every sorceress ends up being destroyed, and nothing is registered of her but mythical traces" (5).

In Rhys's novel, Antoinette/Bertha's final gesture is to start the magnificent fire, the real consummation of her marriage to Rochester. She is absorbed into the moment of finality that he manages to survive, but her own life is what she has weighed as worth the price of the gesture. She sees the wall of fire as "protecting her" and sees death as "why I was brought here and what I have to do" (190). Death gives her life consequence. And—as happens to many heroines—once she is denied the possibility of love, death becomes her vocation.

## Death and the Story Line

Antoinette's death gives her control and a distinct story line. One consequence is that even as she destroys herself she becomes the focus of, and conduit for, spiritual, sexual, and psychological power in a way that she never was during her lifetime.

"It is as if Madeline's body, so little regarded in life, has in death become the focal point of some kind of group energy, some social concentration, some common search for consensus," writes Fay Weldon in *Remember Me* (158). Madeline has a great deal more power after death than she had in life, being a woman who, like Antoinette/Bertha, was considered half mad and unworthy of her husband's attention and desire. The point of Madeline's death is lost on no one, although the point of her life had been rendered meaningless by the trivial domestic rituals she performed, albeit badly, even while making them the object of her ridicule. Like that of the madwoman/wife of many texts, Madeline's death acts as the moment of her most definite power through the very force of its definition: "Ordinary life. Extraordinary death" (213). To her daughter, Madeline's death is her "best and final gift" (245), because she has written herself into her daughter's past instead of drawing on her future. When she is older, Hilary will be able to organize and thereby control her mother's story in terms of her mother's death, saying simply, "Oh yes. When I was a girl of fourteen I lost my mother. She was killed in a car accident" (155). In effect, Madeline substitutes her story for her life, knowing her daughter can survive and incorporate the story of Madeline dead but could not have withstood Madeline alive. The character chooses to fix herself into death.

In Eliot's *The Mill on the Floss,* Maggie is transfixed by the picture of the woman being tried for witchcraft: "It's a dreadful picture, but I can't help looking at it. That old woman in the water's a witch—they've put her in to find out whether she's a witch or no, and if she swims she's a witch and if she's drowned—and killed you know—she's innocent and not a witch, but only a poor silly old woman. But what good would it do her then, you know, when she was drowned?" (66). Maggie is compared to a witch because of her learning, particularly her way with words. Lucy says that Maggie's learning "always seemed to me witchcraft—part of your general uncanniness." It is interesting to note that women are accused of being uncanny or unnatural when they are too intellectual, as in Maggie's case, as well as when they are too physical, as with Antoinette.

It is true, however, that Maggie's physical self also contributes to the prevailing notion that she is not quite acceptable or natural. Maggie is often told that she is "half-wild" and "like a gypsy," alerting the reader to her liminal position in the social structure. Philip wonders why "Maggie's dark eyes" remind him "of the stories about princesses being turned into animals," in important contrast to the tales in which animals arc turned into princesses; she will become the woman made into the animal, whereas the traditional stories offer the salvation of the woman from the animal. Several people tell her that her unruly hair makes her look as if she "were crazy" (that last remark is from her brother Tom). Maggie's death by drowning would, in narrative terms, seem to declare her innocence. But it does so in the terms of magic, applying the system of judgment used for witches and deviants. Maggie is herself suspended between systems, unable to escape the iconography of witchcraft and so internalizing it. She drowns herself as Bertha burns herself, occupying the positions of both executioner and executed. "See," they seem to say, "we will give substance to language and, through death, render our own actions meaningful."

## Refusing Renunciation

How about a character saved from being drowned as a witch who, in a good voodoo way, both does and does not renounce her powers? Such a character is Prue Sarn from Mary Webb's *Precious Bane*. Prue is on the boundary of her early nineteenth-century society for a number of reasons; most important for our consideration is that not only does she read well and for her own pleasure and edification, but she writes for pleasure as well as to serve the needs of others. Prue has a powerful intelligence and an almost magical ability with words. Webb, in her preface to the book, in fact speaks of "conjuring" a story.[5] Prue knows that the particular combination of words has power and a signature, that language does more than reflect reality—that it creates it and is therefore magical. "You canna write a word even but you show yourself—in the word you choose, in the shape of the letters and whether you write tall or short, plain or flourished. It's a game of I Spy and there's nowhere to hide" (135).

Why was a woman like Prue given access to written language in the first place when, as she says, "us women . . . lead such lost and forgotten lives" (262)? Prue has a harelip. She is taught to read and write by the local sorcerer, Wizard Beguildy, and her association of language with magic weaves its way through the novel. As Prue says, "A wizard could not rightly be called a servant of [God], but one of Lucifer's men" (15), and yet Prue must connive a way to define her learning as part of God's greater plan.

Prue is marked by another trait defined as deviant for a woman: like Antoinette, she possesses great sexual passion. She is not neutered by her "deformity." That her harelip in no way impedes Prue's desirability is interesting for a number of reasons, not the least being Webb's identification of desire as a combination of the physical and the intellectual. Prue cannot be regarded as beautiful, but she becomes an object of intense sexual desire for the hero when he sees her, in a quite remarkable scene, "conjured up" by the sorcerer as an image of Venus in a pornographic tableau. Naked in the candlelight, with her face obscured by smoke and a thin veil, Prue delights in the idea that her sex and sexuality are under observation. She loves the fact that she is "crucified in nakedness" (116). She muses on being "a woman to whom it was said, "You'll never have a lover. Two men would have been my lovers that night if I'd willed it so. . . . I saw [his] shoulders stooped forward with the weight of his longing. . . . Under the red light my flesh was like rose petals, the shape of me was such as the water-fairies were said to have, lissom and lovesome" (116). The book ends with the conventionally handsome, sought-after hero kissing Prue "full upon the mouth" (288) after he has rescued her from being drowned as a witch by her benevolent townsfolk.

Kester, the hero, knows full well that he has seen her naked, offering herself for full view to men who have paid for the privilege. He also knows that she participated in the sorcerer's magic, and he is in love with her because she can write as well as he can. He seems to be able to connect the carnal and the intellectual, omitting the conventionally romantic valorization of the pretty or beautiful. He appears to love her for the very reasons most others would damn her: obvious intelligence and passion. Kester, a powerful man in his own right, equally passionate and intelligent, seeks to free from restrictive cultural conventions a woman who has powers of her own.

Prue knows that her defect has turned into a defection; she knows that "the worst crime of all, I stood alone" (280) is the reason she is accused of witchcraft and is why the locals scream, "she's so strong, because she's a witch!" (281). We return to the syllogism—she's so passionate because she's a witch. She's so smart because she's a witch. She has a dangerous, unacceptable power because she's a witch. The power of her sorcery lies in the fact that she hides her alternative vision behind a screen of convention, that she disguises her defection behind her defect. Prue is emblematic of the woman writer's portrayal of the apparently vanquished triumphing over the would-be victors; Prue uses the power of language and sexuality to direct death away from herself. The witch/sorceress/deviant woman has access to power because she understands how to conjure through language, how to delight in her own sexual passion and the sexual passion of others, and how to translate her marginal position into a position of control through art.

## Revenge Is the Best Revenge

In examining the nexus of writing, sorcery, and sexuality for women, one point becomes clear: women's use of their intransigent powers occurs in reaction to a perceived wrong committed against them or against their loved ones. Most frequently they are betrayed by lovers who consider infidelity or abandonment a minor issue, underrating the consequences of their behavior. The unfaithful man pities the woman he has abandoned, but he is not afraid of her; and it is through this misperception that he makes himself vulnerable to her latent strengths.

The unfolding of the revenge plot transforms nexus into praxis: the narratives depend on the reader's growing awareness of the uncanny methods the women use to secure their own ends. The readers, like the characters in the tales themselves, at first resist and are only gradually initiated into the unorthodox strategies used by the sorceress figure. In Colette's "The Rainy Moon," the first-person narrator gives "no thought to perils that might come from the unknown" and treats "ghosts with scant respect" (*Wayward Girls* 101) for the greater part of the tale. But during the time of her acquaintance with two women, the narrator uncovers a plot that one sister calls "a bit like a novel, only better" (113). One sister, the brooding, silent, mysterious sister, has "taken into her head to revenge herself" on her estranged husband.

There are few narrative clues preparing us for the advent of the revenge plot. Until almost the midpoint of the novella, the narrator has been discussing the relation between her own writing and an earlier unhappy love affair. She refers to her new typist, Rosita, who in a surprising coincidence lives in a flat she herself once possessed. Rosita, a fairly nondescript young woman, lives with her enigmatic sister who is apparently miserable over the recent loss of a lover.

The story abruptly introduces a new element when the narrator asks if she might visit the melancholy sister to offer her comfort and reassurance.

The typist replies, " 'I don't see why you should go and say how d'you do to a murderess.' " When asked by the narrator, quite appropriately, " 'Whom has she killed?' " Rosita replies, " 'Ah, Madame, it's not done yet, but he's going to die. . . . When she realized he did not love her any more, she said to herself: "I'll get you." So she cast a spell on him' " (120). One must remember that this is Paris in the thirties, and there is a great deal of talk about cafés, hats, and novels. There has been nothing to prepare us for voodoo.

The narrator laughs—as we might expect, given the lack of narrative context for such a remark—but Rosita rebukes her: " 'Anyone would think you really didn't know what you were laughing about' " (121). Her remark implies that the narrator is already part of the woman's world that understands the gravity of such things, and that to laugh at such serious matters is a betrayal of the sex. The narrator suggests to her typist, " 'We're not living in the Middle Ages now. . . . Think calmly for a moment,' " but Rosita resists being confined within a system that reduces her careful and observant remarks to absurd and speculative ramblings. She argues, " 'I am thinking calmly, Madame. I've never done anything else! This thing she's doing, she's not the only one who's doing it. It's quite common' " (122).

The narrator, who does "not care for the picturesque when it is based on feelings of black hatred," has dabbled in the "rich but limited music of old, ritual words" (124), but only for amusement or comfort, a séance given at a middle-class home, a form of "innocent, popular magic" (123). But when she faces the prospect of a young woman determined to make her estranged husband die through magic and voodoo (even as she eats fresh cherries from the vendor and goes out to use the telephone), she is frankly startled. Acting as a mirror for the reader's reactions, asking all the legitimate questions one by one, the narrator is met with the voice of women's passion that cracks the acceptable veneer. When explaining her sister's mission, for example, Rosita drops her social mask: "Her refined, high-class saleslady's vocabulary had gone to pieces" (128). The typist can function as an ordinary woman in ordinary circumstances, but given her sister's practice of black magic, she herself begins to lose control. She becomes further and further marginalized, unable to carry out her usual routine.

Indeed, the man dies. He dies, the tale makes clear, because even though he has been warned by Rosita, he had dismissed his well-wisher as an ignorant, powerless woman. " 'He told me he'd had enough of one crack-brained woman,' " Rosita explains, " 'and that the second crack-brained woman would do him a great favor if she'd shut up' " (130). Rosita, who harbors her own affection for the man, is frustrated by his dismissal of her warnings. She states, in furious resignation, that even " 'the most intelligent men can argue like imbeciles, seeing no difference between fantastic made-up stories and things as real as this . . . as such deadly machinations' " (130).

The narrator realizes that what she is hearing from Rosita is not nonsense, but the accumulated force and vision of "widows who had willed the deaths of the husbands who had deserted them, from the frenzied fantasies of lonely women" (131). She asks herself whether, despite a critical understanding of the world bought at the expense of her youth and fine-tuned with her own sensitivity and skepticism, the forces that "procured love, decided life and death, removed that lofty mountain, the indifferent heart" are not in fact simply the "whisperings, an obtuse faith, even a local custom" (131).

The power of life and death certainly seems to have been held in the hands of the sister, who is seen in the final line of the story wearing "the white crepe band of a widow" (135). Belief in her own powers gives her the right to summon the forces of the universe to her side. The narrator cannot do as much because she does not believe, even as she illustrates. She leaves the women to "their stifled, audacious, incantation-ridden lives where witchcraft could be fitted in between the daily task and the Saturday cinema, between the little wash-tub and the frying steak" (134). Incantation replaces cause and effect; magic replaces science and sequence. Witchcraft is like housewifery: a series of undervalued and easily overlooked tasks misunderstood by a culture that remains essentially blind to its effects because it has been relegated to what is considered a feminine domain. And if witchcraft and housewifery are equally women's work, then we can assume that neither is ever done.

Women's power has learned to exist in the confinement of such moments, between the washing up and the lying down, in the interstices of such places. Women's magic works because of the dangers they are willing to evoke, to summon up and take upon themselves as well as impart to others. They have found themselves excluded by the social order that gives them neither permanence nor importance. Only death will give them these, and with death they will deal. Denied love, they choose death as their vocation. Denied access to those areas of knowledge considered credible, they will deal with the incredible. The sorceress and the hysteric embrace the incredible and substantiate it by invoking and risking death, and the artist gives their incantations and cries substance by inscribing them. Like the voodoo priest, a woman might hide the cock with its throat cut behind the clothespress, but the power—even when hidden—remains.

## Notes

1. In *Divine Horsemen: The Living Gods of Haiti,* Maya Deren writes in her first chapter, "Death, as the edge beyond which life does not extend, delineated a first boundary of being. . . . Death is life's first and final definition." She goes on to explain: "But death we recognize not so much by what it is as by the fact that it is not life. As the land and sea define each other at the shore, so life and death define each other by exclusion" (23–24). Death, then, can give shape to a woman's life that might otherwise seem shapeless or placeless: "Everywoman must inevitably find that she has no home, no where," stresses Sandra Gilbert in her introduction to *The Newly Born Woman.* "Central to Cixous's thinking, and to Clément's,[is] this sense of metaphysical alienation" (xvi).

2. In "The Guilty One," Clément investigates the points made by both Michelet and Freud concerning a woman's relation to the past, to the repressed: "It is because the sorceress is the bearer of the past that she is invested with a challenging power" (*Newly Born Woman* 9). Can it be, then, that women can go so far back into the past that they bear with them some of the savage magic of language?

3. For a fuller discussion of this issue see Metraux, particularly the chapter titled "Voodoo and Christianity."

4. In the context of a discussion on Lévi-Strauss and Freud, Clément argues that women are "perceived by culture, by men who take on its value, as disorder. That is why women, who are still savages, still close to childhood, need good manners— conventions that keep them under control. They have to be taught how to live" (*Newly Born Woman* 29). This argument suggests the one made by Mary Douglas in *Purity and Danger.* Douglas claims that cultures insist on patterns of demarcation in order to create the appearance of order: "It is only by exaggerating the difference between within and without . . . male and female . . . that a semblance of order is created" (4). Douglas also maintains, "All margins are dangerous. If they are pulled this way or that the shape of fundamental experience is altered. Any structure of ideas is vulnerable at its margins" (121), rendering, one may assume, the marginalized vision of women particularly dangerous.

5. I thank Paula Kot for calling my attention to this point in Webb's preface.

## Works Cited

Bronfen, Elisabeth. "Dialogue with the Dead: The Deceased Beloved as Muse." *Sex and Death in Victorian Literature.* Ed. Regina Barreca. London: Macmillan, 1990. 241–59.

Cixous, Hélène, and Catherine Clément. *The Newly Born Woman.* Trans. Betsy Wing. Minneapolis: U of Minnesota P, 1986.

Colette. "The Rainy Moon." *Wayward Girls and Wicked Women.* Ed. Angela Carter. New York: Viking Penguin, 1989.

Daly, Mary. *Gyn/Ecology: The Metaethics of Radical Feminism.* Boston: Beacon, 1978.

Deren, Maya. *Divine Horsemen: The Living Gods of Haiti*. New York: McPherson, 1953.

Douglas, Mary. *Purity and Danger: An Analysis of the Concepts of Pollution and Taboo*. London: ARK, 1966.

Eliot, George. *The Mill on the Floss*. London: Penguin, 1979.

Gilbert, Sandra, and Susan Gubar. *The Madwoman in the Attic: The Woman Writer and the Nineteenth-Century Literary Imagination*. New Haven: Yale UP, 1979.

Kramer, Heinrich, and Jacob Sprenger. "The Malleus Maleficarum." *Witchcraft in Europe, 1100–1700: A Documentary History*. Ed. Alan C. Kors and Edward Peters. Philadelphia: U of Pennsylvania P, 1972.

Metraux, Alfred. *Voodoo in Haiti*. New York: Schocken, 1972.

Modleski, Tania. *Loving with a Vengeance*. New York: Methuen, 1984.

Rhys, Jean. *Wide Sargasso Sea*. New York: Norton, 1982.

Spark, Muriel. *The Hothouse by the East River*. New York: Viking, 1973.

Webb, Mary. *Precious Bane*. New York: Dial, 1924.

Weldon, Fay. *The Fat Woman's Joke*. London: Hodder and Stoughton, 1967.

———. *The Heart of the Country*. New York: Viking, 1987.

———. *Remember Me*. New York: Random House, 1976.

■

# Women in the Forbidden Zone: War, Women, and Death

## Margaret R. Higonnet

What can a woman writer have to say about war? Why is the canon of American writers about World War I exclusively male? War, thought Hemingway, is "one of the major subjects and certainly one of the hardest to write truly of," especially if one has not "experienced" it. To "see" war, he continued, is "quite irreplaceable." His literary canon accordingly includes Tolstoy and Stendhal, taught by revolution and Napoleon; only one woman, Charlotte Yonge, figures briefly with her sketch of Thermopylae in *Men at War,* the anthology of war descriptions and memoirs Hemingway edited.[1]

What does it mean to "see" war? Must the war writer "man" a gun turret and read the mud fields through its sights before "he" can write with a pen?[2] Homer, we are told, was blind; in postwar years, the French ritually paraded down the Champs Elysées their mutilated and blinded soldiers in testimony to their war sacrifice. Why does Hemingway, who served as an ambulance driver, so often insist on what he calls "the big wound"? The ultimate proof that one has seen action in war is to be mutilated or even dead. We might define war as the politically sanctioned inflicting of wounds and death by one body of soldiers (usually male) on another. War involves the communal experience of death. Paul Fussell and Eric Leed have helped us understand the way this ultimate confrontation shapes a homosocial, even at times homoerotic, and aesthetically elect community. In the twentieth century not only seeing combat but dying in action have become paradoxical prerequisites to the writing and certification of war poetry. The annotations to many anthologies of "lost voices" suggest that the direct experience of death itself offers the highest guarantee of a war poet's authenticity and interest.

Does death have a sex? Death, it seems, is indeed what differentiates men from women in wartime.[3] In "Before Action," a poem written two days before his own death, William Hodgson prays, "Make me a soldier. . . . *Make me a man.* . . . Help me to *die*" (Hussey 78–79; my italics). War has always been a ritual that initiated youths into manhood. With the Great War of 1914–18, war and death became a rite of passage to poethood as well.

If war and death are understood to define manhood (and manly poetry) they also by opposition define womanhood. In this symbolic economy, to escape from death threatens the manhood of the war survivor, as Sandra Gilbert has shown in her study of the veteran writer's fear of impotence and feminization, "Soldier's Heart." Although in the past most thinking about war has been governed by the double helix of gender, reflection on that discursive dichotomy should make it possible for us to escape its reductive regime. On the surface, however, a masculinist and militarist ideology dictates that womanhood be identified with peace and life, positive values. For a woman to write about war, then, might seem an oxymoron.

It is not altogether surprising, therefore, that Hemingway imagined Willa Cather had derived the battle scenes in *One of Ours* (1922) from a movie about the Civil War, *Birth of a Nation*—war seen at third hand. He commiserated ironically with her lack of knowledge: "Poor woman, she has to get her war experience somewhere." In fact, Cather was inspired by the letters of two soldiers and a doctor's diary, as well as by trips to French battlefields and many interviews with returned soldiers.[4] Similarly approving the attack on Cather's best-seller by reviewers, the critic Frederick Hoffman concluded that readers wanted "the horror and the boredom of the war" "from men who had been there and had fought in or at least experienced the war" (90). Although Cather herself had once thought a "battle yarn" should be "manly," her faith in the imagination was such that she proposed the form for any woman writer who wished to overcome the limitations of feminine subjectivity (O'Brien 184, 186).

We must interrogate Hemingway's fetishizing of military service and Hoffman's sexist materialism. We must ask again, Can a woman writer "see" war? On a purely material level, World War I was not only a "total" war that engulfed civilian populations, but the war that marked a turning point for European and American women's active, institutionalized involvement in a major theater of war. Nonetheless, in spite of women's mobilization as ambulance drivers, nurses, and couriers at the front as well as in more protected auxiliary and volunteer functions farther back, beside male support forces, women were still understood to have remained "behind the lines." Since America entered the war late, American women writers symbolically suffered from a double distance and therefore disability in representing the war.

Governing the symbolic polarities between war and peace, death and life, men and women are spatial metaphors that ground the separability and purity of these concepts. Place has startling resonance in our definitions of war. War defiles men by forcing them to cross a doubly physical boundary, both geographic and corporeal, between life and death.[5] Does a woman writer defile war itself by traversing boundaries between domestic and public arenas? Central to the question whether a woman can write about "war" is the distinction between the battlefront and the home front, a distinction that may make little sense in total war. What is the political agenda of a woman who writes a "war novel" about the "home front"? Does "seeing war" mean witnessing the deconstruction of a physical landscape into muddy chaos? If seeing clearly means recognizing a pattern at a broader sociopolitical level, which patterns count as historic or poetic or both? Which are unutterable? Social order and transgression, central themes in women's works on this subject, are at stake in the prohibition on women's writing about war and about the ostensibly communal, masculine experience of death.

One of the areas that calls for inquiry, then, is that mapped by tropes of femininity in time of war. Do tropes built on "womanly" activities of reconstruction such as sewing or nursing necessarily reinforce the stereotypical opposition between women and war? If poetry is a more "feminine" genre than prose, do male poets become femininized and female poets hyperfeminized in their attempts to represent war? How can a woman steer between the Scylla of "feminine" but jingoistic receptivity and the Charybdis of "feminist" but unpatriotic resistance?

In fact, as Jean Elshtain has said, neither woman nor war is a self-evident category (x). Do we see war as an action, a time, a political and social process, or a place? If we look closely at texts that record the experience of World War I, we find very significant slippages between war and peace, between masculinity and femininity, between death-dealing and life-giving functions, as well as between positive and negative values. War, according to a familiar political formula, makes peace possible; peace, according to a number of women writers, masks gender war. A soldier at times seems to accede to a fuller, androgynous humanity through the experiences of nursing, physically intimate comradeship, and finally the reception of a death wound. Women, by contrast, masculinize themselves in new uniforms and new roles. Avant-garde, futurist literature plays militaristically with an identification of peace with passivity and death, while a more complex war poetry may locate in the grave the only peaceful refuge from the horrors of the trenches and the hypocrisy of civilian society. The fetishistic war death to which countless monuments were constructed at the end of the war loses its boundaries when set in a context of death by influenza, the explosion of a munitions factory, starvation, or mental death. As John Peale Bishop wrote, "The most tragic thing about the war was not that it made so many dead men, but that it destroyed the tragedy of death" (Hoffman 85). This blurred outline of death, which challenges political justifications and our belief in individual choice, in turn entails a slippage in the figure of the hero and of the boundaries between men and women.

The blurring of dichotomies between men and women, war and peace, death and life provides a hallmark of women's writing about war. Such slippages are important for several reasons. First, they may explain why women's writing on war has been virtually illegible. Quite deliberately, the slippages help us see the falsity of a worldview based on gendered polarities. Last, they help us see how the buried contradictions of our shaping images actually sustain destructive mythologies, including the ideologies of war.

Every woman writing on the subject of war finds herself forced to address these polarities. In her preface to a volume of women's poetry, Judith Kazantzis condemns the "atavistic feeling that war is man's concern, as birth is woman's, and that women quite simply cannot speak on the matter." Yet even Kazantzis concedes that, by millions, "men in the Great War had to die and women did not" (xxiii).

Because women were barred from the ultimate rites of war, they became its symbolic stakes, what war was fought for. Opposed to the battlefront in daily discourse was the home front—even in the European context, where the two might not be separated at all. We cannot be surprised at the resentment men sent to the trenches felt against idle "butterfly ladies" and jingoistic "girls with feathers."[6] Thus the notorious poem "Glory of Women," by Siegfried Sasson, mocks women who "worship decorations" and "believe that chivalry redeems the war's disgrace" (Silkin 132). Similarly, e. e. cummings, in "my sweet old etcetera," ironically contrasts a soldier who lies dead in the deep mud with the warmongering members of his family:

aunt lucy during the recent

war could and what
is more did tell you just
what everybody was fighting

for . . .

. . . my

mother hoped that

i would die etcetera
bravely of course
            (Silkin 140)[7]

Facing a fallen friend whose corpse will rot away, the speaker of Harold
Monro's poem "Carrion" distinguishes the loyal comradeship of men (and
their marriage with death) from the embrace of women: "No girl would kiss
you. But then / No girls would ever kiss the earth / In the manner they hug
the lips of men: / You are not known to them in this, your second birth"
(Hussey 94). One ironic diversion of the opposition between dying male
soldiers and living female survivors, then, is this suggestive contrast between
the second birth men enter in battle, a birth into truth and transcendence, and
the more ordinary realm of birth governed by women. The primary concepts
of life and death drawn upon to describe the war experience turn out to be
peculiarly reversible, as Eric Leed has observed (77).

    In a symbolic transfer of resentment not only against the civilians at the
home front but also against the body politic of the enemy, male writers in
their bitterest moments describe Britannia and Germania as sick women.
Thus Eden Phillpotts celebrates the war as a form of surgery against the
"cursed canker that doth foul" a female "Germania" (Hussey 104). Finally,
death, pain, and war itself become female. "Desolation broods over all,
/ gathering to her lap / her leprous children" (Herbert Read, "Ypres," in
Hussey 111). Ironically, it is because women preserve life and preserve their
lives that they become death dealers and death becomes feminine.

    Not only men but women writers themselves may perceive the nation's
sacrifice of its young men, while most women remain protected at home, as
a form of moral imprisonment in inactivity. The dilemma was particularly
acute for those women who also opposed the war. The black poet Alice
Dunbar-Nelson, who taught at Howard High School in Wilmington, Dela-
ware, voices in her poem "I Sit and Sew" the frustration women have
universally felt when left on the home front, without power to alter the course
of a war ravaging the lives of men. Moreover, as she pointed out in her essay
"Negro Women in War Work," women of color were barred from many
local Red Cross organizations, and none were accepted for service overseas
(376–78). Her sewing, she laments, is "useless," an "idle patch" on worn
clothes that cannot mend the great rent war has torn in the world. She dreams
of war and "grim-faced" men "gazing beyond the ken / Of lesser souls,
whose eyes have not seen Death." The soldier's confrontation with death
makes him superior to civilians left to continue with trivial daily tasks.

Yet the poem moves beyond what we would today call survivor's guilt. Part of the power of Dunbar-Nelson's poem comes from the dialectic between the soldier's empowerment by death and the woman's potential empowerment in his hour of need. She responds to a call from the fields of woe for her powerful assistance, across the barrier of conventional social role assignments according to gender and race. She aches with desire to go to the battlefield, its wasted fields and grotesquely writhing wounded men, for it is there that her stitches and patches can bind up the wounds of the living, that she can do what is needful for the dead. Buried in her image of stitching are two larger metaphors, one of nursing the wounded, the other of curing a world that wastes lives through its violence and racism. Implicit in the notion of cure, then, is a critique of the war and the social order itself. Whereas the first two stanzas seem to be stitched together by the paired lines: "I sit and sew. . . . But—I must sit and sew," that refrain is inverted and wrenched in the final line: "God, must I sit and sew?" By moving a single word, Dunbar-Nelson turns what was a rule into a question. Her questions, in turn, led to her pacifist work in the twenties for the American Interracial Peace Committee.

In a similar vein of criticism, Amy Lowell wrote in 1916 to a friend, "War is foreign to our instincts, completely alien to our ideals and desires. I regard this war as a social illness" (Damon 420). We women (it is understood) instinctively desire peace and life. Yet a mixture of guilt and horror speaks in Amy Lowell's poem on the mobilization of Harvard College students. As the young men parade in front of an aged Marshal Joffre, whose chest glitters with "silly decorations," the speaker foresees

The young bodies of boys
Bulwarked in front of us
The white bodies of young men
Heaped like sandbags
Against the German guns.

This is war:
Boys flung into a breach
Like shovelled earth.
    ("In the Stadium")

Death is the unspoken cost of "our" protection: it means that bright young men have been reduced to mere matter—human sandbags. A feminine life can shred her garments, but she is helpless to alter the political orders that cause the deaths of men.

To think such thoughts is very painful, and many women wrote about other wars in order to work out the meaning of the current war. In "Patterns" (1916), for example, Lowell projects the losses of World War I back onto the loss of a woman living in an earlier time. The speaker, who walks composedly down "the patterned garden-paths" in brocaded gown and powdered hair, is herself "a rare / Pattern" both in her outward appearance and in her self-controlled behavior. She conforms to a socially imposed pattern in two ways. As the speaker threads through the garden, she dreams of her fiancé, giving us a first glimpse of conflict. We see the contrast between her stiff brocade and the seething desires within her bosom: she "wars" not to betray her dream of her lover's caresses. Then, however, we learn that he is not simply absent: she has just received word of his death in action. She will remain stiffly guarded by her buttons and hooks. "For the man who should loose me is dead, / Fighting with the Duke in Flanders, / In a pattern called a war." Their marriage "would have broke the pattern" of their lives in separation, would have brought the heat and motion of life and procreation.

Peace, then, is like a disorderly "maze" of personal freedom, set against the clipped, artificial garden and the mutilating "pattern" of war. One may well ask, with the speaker in her closing line, "Christ! What are patterns for?" (75–76). Saving life or dealing death? By describing a social "pattern" that rests on war and death, Lowell calls the social order itself into question. She seeks to find the pattern according to which the materials of war can be cut out and resewn or reseen. Hers is an impulse toward artistic representation and preservation of a demilitarized artistic zone.

The new patterns of imagist art were Lowell's contribution to the cause of peace and life, against the war fever.[8] Quite literally, Lowell paid to send libraries of modern poetry to soldiers' training camps. Her poem "Peace" (1919) epitomizes both the contrastive vividness of "imagist" poetry and what many would read as a feminine response to war, an optimistic hymn to the Armistice. In its entirety, "Peace" runs:

Perched upon the muzzle of a cannon
A yellow butterfly is slowly opening and shutting its wings.
    (228)

The motionless threat of the first line conceals death itself lying in wait. But the frozen word "perched" is undone by the peaceful motion of the verbs in the second line, the leisurely stretch of a natural ephemerality, emblem at once of the passage of time and of the immortal soul.

If peace and life are implicitly feminine in Lowell's poetry, they become more explicitly so in Edna St. Vincent Millay's antiwar "Apostrophe to Man"

(1934). This poem, addressed to "homo called *sapiens,*" implies that war flows from the greed of social institutions dominated by men.[9] Writing in 1934, "on reflecting that the world is ready to go to war again," she ironically foreshadows the end of the race: "Detestable race, continue to expunge yourself, die out." For Millay, the connection between capitalism and war is clear: "build bombing airplanes," crowd, encroach, "commercialize / Bacteria harmful to human tissue. Put death on the market." The market needs war, so men make it.

These antiwar poems we have been looking at by Dunbar-Nelson, Lowell, and Millay tend to construct peace as a woman's text—but they also express a sense of woman's impotence, her imprisonment in trivial social tasks and patterns, her ineffectual beauty, like that of a butterfly. Insofar as they reinscribe the polarity between active, dying men and passive, living women, they reinforce the prejudices I cited in beginning this essay.

If we turn to women's fiction, a more complex image begins to emerge, possibly because the more expansive form permits a more ironic and detailed description of women's relationships with fighting men, as well as a closer scrutiny of the political plot of war.[10] "Death" in this second group of texts no longer is the privileged domain of war or the badge of manhood. It may come unintentionally, quietly, in pathetic isolation. Moreover, the political terrain of War, it turns out, stretches from the battlefront all the way to the cornfields of America. If women's novels about the Great War are written under the shadow of death, the death they show us often takes unexpected and unheroic forms.

"Pale Horse, Pale Rider," by Katherine Anne Porter, may superficially remind us of the theme of survivor's guilt. Miranda, Porter's autobiographical heroine, lives in a boardinghouse and struggles to survive on a wretched journalist's salary. Economically marginal but employed as a result of the war, she falls in love with Adam, a young soldier about to leave for the front. The story opens with a dream: she must outrun death, the pale rider (270). She awakens to remember the war, which menaces her future with Adam. The two have scarcely begun to know each other when they both catch influenza: Adam nurses her briefly, then also succumbs. At the worst of her fever Miranda has a second dream, in which arrows pass through her before they strike and kill Adam (305). But the fever breaks, and she realizes she has outrun death.

Because her near-death experience has united Miranda to Adam, Porter succeeds in drawing the line between life and death in a fresh way. When Miranda returns, Lazarus-like, to consciousness after the bout with influenza, she feels "condemned" to a dull world of "objects and beings meaningless, ah, dead and withered things that believed themselves alive!" (314). She feels like a walking corpse in a world that has lost its meaning. The immediacy of her sense of death aligns her with Adam rather than separating them. Furthermore, through the flu epidemic that decimates the troops, Porter underscores that death may come to soldiers in wartime from causes that are not heroically military: in that Adam deliberately risks exposure, his role of nurse is a "feminine" instance of courage. In Porter's rewriting of the script of wartime death, as experienced on the home front, the encounter with physical death joins lovers rather than dividing them, and it sets them apart from the moral death of a jingoistic society. Porter's vision thus demystifies a fetishized "manly" death as well as the arbitrary distinction between feminine home front and masculine battlefront.

In the other three texts I discuss here, by Willa Cather, Edith Wharton, and Mary Borden, death remains a central problem of representation. For Cather and Wharton, it is the seduction of battle heroics that they must confront as women writers, and both deal with that seduction ironically. For Borden, who directed a mobile hospital under the French at the front, the artistic difficulty will be the most complex of all.

Set against a large economic framework in Willa Cather's novel *One of Ours,* the war penetrates only gradually into the consciousness of Midwestern America. Her protagonist, Claude Wheeler, an idealistic Nebraska farmer, seeks in vain at home for the meaning of life, finding it finally in luminous bravery and male comradeship. Although Cather shows us battle through her hero's deluded eyes, she makes sure we also see the dark backdrop of a brutal war and does not simplistically glorify the war from a nationalistic perspective.[11] In the first part of the novel, set in the Middle West, she suggests that sinister political and economic motives may have fueled the war and shows the chauvinistic persecution of German neighbors. In the second part, she fully develops the cost of the war in lives lost not only at the front, but also behind the lines, owing to accidents and influenza.

Life on the Great Plains, as one of Claude's friends comments, seems like "death in life" (308). In fact, as spoken by his rigid, sexless wife, Enid, Claude's name sounds like "clod." He is only a lifeless piece of humanity responding to the voracious demands of the land, an insignificant and even alien partner to his wife. When he closes up the house he had built for her, he reflects, "The debris of human life was more worthless and ugly than the dead and decaying things in nature." "How much better it would be if people could go to sleep like the fields" (223). One of the lines of poetry that springs to mind when Mrs. Wheeler looks at her restless, frustrated son, with his glimpses of "bright uncertainties," is Hamlet's "rest, rest perturbéd spirit" (69). Claude will indeed find that rest in the grave.

When war breaks out we face other types of death, both heroic and pathetic. Soldiers die of influenza in mid-Atlantic, the victims of poor distribution of medical supplies as well as of purveyors' greed. An armless soldier and his French girlfriend cling in an embrace "so long and still that it was like death" (1198); the soldier's wound has "clear wiped out" his memory of women back home (1201). The death of the past constitutes the erasure of woman. Cather describes in some detail conditions in the trenches; at the final battle of the Moltke trench, a defensive cement bulwark is built over the liquefying bodies of the dead. Most moments of death are curtly reported. A soldier strikes a match; a few pages later, we read that the light gave the distance to German shellers and he died for it. For some death comes as an escape, as to the swaggering flying ace Victor, who finds "a death like the rebel angels" (375). For Claude as well, war and death signify release from marriage and meaningless tasks.

Yet Cather makes sure that we demystify this death at the end. We may recall that no-man's-land is "a dead, nerveless countryside, sunk in quiet and dejection" (364). The dead, however, will not stay sunk: a large boot projects from the side of the trench, as does a dark German hand, grotesquely reaching out in appeal. These dead return, in spite of all efforts to cover them with mud and escape their signal reminders. Claude's mother consoles herself that Claude died with "beautiful beliefs," but she herself "can see nothing that has come of it all but evil" (1296). Other men like Claude who survived the war returned to America only to be disillusioned by the "meanness and greed" of the social structures they had fought to preserve; and they have quietly taken their lives. For the sensitive soldier, to survive meant suicide.

Such an ending was doomed to be misread. In lieu of an analysis of his own, Frederick Hoffman quotes Percy Boynton on Cather: "The truth about warfare has been rediscovered of late. I have yet to find a soldier who has been long at the front who has read the book without a feeling of revulsion at the concluding chapters. Barbusse and Dos Passos, Remarque and Hemingway, are more likely to be to their taste. The death of Miss Cather's hero has been to them the snuffing of a candle rather than the apotheosis of a lover of democracy" (90). Boynton said more than he knew. The ironic frame Cather places around Claude's heroic illusions does not cater to a taste for apotheosis.

In *A Son at the Front,* Edith Wharton maintains a more systematic distance from the heroics of the battlefront, since her narrative filter is the soldier's father, who stays behind the lines in Paris. Wharton's decision to write from behind the lines has strategic importance. It alters the picture we have of the war and of death, both of which traverse the line of battle. Though herself made a chevalier in the French Legion of Honor for her relief work, Wharton satirizes the selfish concerns and profiteering of civilian society, which she depicts as deeply implicated in a political economy of war.

Wharton's strategy interrogates our generic definitions. Should "war poetry" or the "war novel" focus only on battle scenes and above all on death? What does it mean to privilege such material, to give it exclusive value? One of the flaws that critics have found in Wharton's novel is her focus not on the battlefront but on what war does to civilian relationships. Most of Cather's novel, too, takes place before Claude reaches the front. Why, we may begin to wonder, do women's works about war significantly realign the focus from military to social structures?

Wharton, like Cather, explores the ambiguity of death. The young men who have seen battle return as a mystery to others: they are both familiar and unrecognizable, both "new" and "dimly familiar," uncanny bearers of the sign of death. George's smile marks him as different—"transubstantiated" in the word of his friend Boylston. "He was like a traveller returning after incommunicable adventures to the place where he had lived as a child" (310). Such a soldier has become mercurial, like Mercury a messenger from the other world, no longer completely human, and like Mercury also, often changeable and unpredictable in mood.

A *representation* of death draws the line between the battlefront and the home front. The closest friend of this young soldier, an American named Boylston, comments that he does not know how returned combatants feel, any more than if they were "dead" (390). George's father agrees, as he keeps watch over his badly wounded son: "If he were dead he could not be farther from me"—"so deeply did George seem plunged in secret traffic with things unutterable" (402). The patient bears on his face a sign, a mysterious look that shows him to be "inaccessible to reason, beyond reason, belonging to other spaces, other weights and measures, over the edge, somehow, of the tangible, calculable world" (359). Inscribed on George is the unreasonableness of war itself, but also the unreasoning, seductive siren call of a self-sacrifice that might purge the loss of his men. Until the "job" of winning the war is finished, he can have no real life. "We chaps haven't any futures to dispose of till this job we're in is finished" (383). In some sense to be at the front is to be in a suspended state of not yet but already dead.

War erases individuality, and the Great War did so most spectacularly, because it deployed a technology that permitted more extensive destruction at greater distances. Individual death blurs into a mass of deaths, "great red mounds of dead." The cries of the wounded turn into a "white voice," "a nauseating scream in a queer bleached voice," "as featureless as some of the poor men's obliterated faces" (278). In the face of such depersonalization and pain, the actual moment of death loses its meaning.

Having been to the front and witnessed the appalling conditions of the trenches and the unspeakable suffering of those next to him, George yearns for quiet and monotony, a stasis that in itself resembles death. At the same time, he cannot relinquish his task: "We seem to be sealed to it for life" (383).

This quest for stasis—and one could describe the desire to halt the Germans as another thirst for stasis—takes on aesthetic form in two scenes that frame the novel. Early on, the first night that Campton has his son with him in Paris, he watches George asleep, a sheet modeling his flank and legs. Fascinated by the "happy accident of the lighting," he links the image to "a statue of a young knight I've seen somewhere," and starts to sketch it. Then suddenly his pencil stops. "What he had really thought was: 'Like the / *effigy* of a young knight'—though he had instinctively changed the word as it formed itself" (53–54).

A parallel scene closes the novel. George is dead, and after stubbornly resisting a request to design a monument, Campton finally accepts, after realizing that "George had been; George was; as long as his father's consciousness lasted, George would be" (423). Using materials that are the archetype of life itself, Campton picks up some lumps of clay, spreads out his fragmentary sketches of George, and begins. Campton's artistic work is emotional work as well, a sorting out of images in the mental portfolio as well as the pictorial portfolio. He plays with the bits of memory, as with the bits of clay, like Freud's little grandchild who played with a spool, saying *fort-da* in a game that helped him work through and master the death of his mother.

Yet this task of reconstruction does not mean that survivors draw artistic power from the dead, as Sandra Gilbert has argued. Sardonically, Campton grins "at the thought that he had once believed in the regenerative power of war" (334). A bitter humor and protective irony seem the only shields against paralyzing despair. Wharton and Cather both point out that a long death lingers after the armistice. Whether the ones left behind are fathers, as in Wharton, or mothers, as in Cather, their own survival without the beloved son carries no meaning. It is life in death.

Already in the face of the soldier George Campton, we have read death as the uncanny: the familiar/unfamiliar, what we know but cannot consciously acknowledge, which occasionally peers out at us from behind its mask. This death assumed a particularly horrid mask during the Great War. It came as a female figure to some—a point recorded by Mary Borden, herself serving as a nurse just behind the front lines.

When Borden published her sketches written during 1914–18, she "called the collection of fragments 'The Forbidden Zone' because the strip of land immediately behind the zone of fire where I was stationed went by that name in the French Army. We were moved up and down inside it; our hospital unit was shifted from Flanders to the Somme, then to Champagne, and then back again to Belgium, but we never left 'La Zone Interdite.' "

The story "Moonlight" is Borden's most allegorical description of her confrontation with death at the front. This sketch opens on the troubling scent of new-mown hay, which threatens the nurse's wartime mentality, according to which the lullaby of cannon fire is "natural" and soothing. For a nurse to survive in her borderline zone, she must block out all memories of normal life: "The war is the world" (52). The inhabitants of Borden's forbidden zone are patients, surgeons, and three others: pain, life, and death. The nurse fights against pain's vile lust for men's bodies until death comes, "the peacemaker, the healer" (54).

The nurse's business, as she tells us in another sketch ("Blind"), is to create "a counter-wave of life" (143) in the bodies brought to her. But the bodies have been disassembled by war: "three knees have come in, two more abdomens, five heads" (135). The station huts are named for their contents— the abdominal ward, Knees, Elbows, and fractured Thighs" (59). "There are no men here, so why should I be a woman? There are heads and knees and mangled testicles. There are chests with holes as big as your fist, and pulpy thighs, shapeless; and stumps where legs once were fastened . . . and parts of faces—the nose gone, or the jaw. There are these things, but no men" (60).[12] Instead of proving men's masculinity, war makes men lose it.

War and nursing both engage in the struggle at the threshold between life and death. Because war so often is understood as a question of borderlines, it becomes symbolically identified with other thresholds of initiation, into sexuality and death. Such initiations provide the heroic themes of a Hemingway or an Erich Maria Remarque. But in Borden's account, death and femininity become empty riddles. The death and dehumanization that lurks in these men's bodies threatens her with psychic death and desexualization. The narrator comments on another nurse: "She is no longer a woman. She is dead already, just as I am—really dead, past resurrection. Her heart is dead. She killed it. She couldn't bear to feel it jumping in her side when Life, the sick animal, choked and rattled in her arms. . . . She is blind so that she cannot see the torn parts of men she must handle. Blind, deaf, dead—she is strong, efficient, fit to consort with gods and demons—a machine inhabited by the ghost of a woman—soulless, past redeeming, just as I am—just as I will be" (59–60). Death no longer resides on just one side of a corporeal line.

Even more important, psychic death has corrupted those who are organizing the war: metaphorically, the politicians and generals carry the infection to the others. Social policy dictates this mass experience of individual suffering, for pain "is a harlot in the pay of war" (62). The officer who drives by in his padded touring car, busy "calculating the number of men needed to repair yesterday's damage, and the number of sandbags required to repair their ditches," does not see the horrid scene in the hospital huts. His militarism makes him "blind, deaf, and dead as I am." In the political economy of territorial gains, life and death no longer count.

In sketch after sketch, Borden ponders what the creature is before her. "They did not look quite like men. One could not be certain what kind of men they were" (24). These creatures have no eyes for what is around them; all they can see is the death before them. "Why, if they are men, don't they walk? Why don't they talk? Why don't they protest?" (114).

These sketches, obviously, protest against the war and what it does to the men who are in Borden's hands. The nurse who wields needles and scalpels may appear to be in a position of power. In a sexual role reversal, she tells us in "Conspiracy" how the wounded soldier helplessly and obediently submits to her: "We dig into the yawning mouths of his wounds. Helpless openings, they let us into the secret places of his body" (120). She "flaunts" her "paraphernalia," her blankets, tubs, and gauze "things" in the face of the dying man's "mysterious exhaustion" ("Paraphernalia" 124). In another sketch titled "Blind," she shows off her "lovely new needles" and exults in her power like a wizard, flashing knives against the invisible enemy, on "the second battlefield" (142, 147). When half a man's brain comes off with his bandage, she takes refuge in the "business" of sorting out the living from the dead.

But Borden's bitter language makes it impossible to mistake the nurse's power over these men for a glorious thing. "Blind, deaf, dead—she is strong, efficient, fit to consort with gods and demons—a machine" (59). To stand at the threshold of the supernatural is to be polluted, and this nurse typically has a bloodstain on her apron, clammy sweat on her face, like the gangrenous slime of her patients. She can continue to function only by ceasing to think. And ultimately, her work seems futile: "Death is inexorable and the place of death is void." "What have you and all your things to do with the dying of this man? Nothing. Take them away" (124, 126).

Moreover, her power to heal is subverted by the system within which it is set; not only must she repress her feelings, becoming a "ghost" of herself, but she must acknowledge that her task is not to save a life but to heal a body so it can be thrown back into the trenches again until it is dead. "We conspire against his right to die" (119). Both her own living work and those she works to preserve alive have been converted into parodic versions of death.

The nurse's work is mechanical because her patients are interchangeable parts in a vast machine of war, and because her task itself must be repeated, repairing those parts until they are irreparably broken. War, the nurse-narrator tells us in "Conspiracy," is "carefully arranged." A trope borrowed from the domestic arena of feminine chores takes on grating power: "It is arranged that men should be broken and that they should be mended," like clothes one mends when they come back from the laundry "as many times as they will stand it" (117). "And we send our men to the war again and again, just as long as they will stand it; just until they are dead, and then we throw them into the ground" (117).[13]

By focusing on the way these women writers deal with the problem of death, we can begin to see into and past the stereotype of the "lady writer" for the *Ladies' Home Journal,* with which they were so often identified. First, we can see that such women were extremely conscious of the line war had drawn between them and men. Even though women were organized into auxiliary forces and served as nurses, drivers, and couriers in the "Forbidden Zone" at the risk of their lives, these writers still recognize the primary sacrifice of life exacted by war as male. This is true even of Mary Borden, who never mentions attacks on medical staff other than the occasional lost roof.

In turn, however, by virtue of their symbolic exclusion from military sacrifice, the women cited here are led to a critical perspective on the social "pattern" that ritually exacts individual deaths as a price for social and political gain. Again and again they point to the economics of war, to what Millay calls "death on the market." War will drive up grain prices for the farmer. For the general, as both Lowell and Borden tell us, soldiers, like sandbags, are just matériel to be "calculated."

Confronting this economy, we may begin to ask about our implicit *canon of death:* Is death in the trench of greater value than death on a transport ship or death from influenza in camp? Is the mystique of death a form of madness, a justification after the fact of the social disease we call war?

The classic war novel by a man focuses intensely on the test of character in the face of death and physical suffering. It brings to life climactic experiences of individualism amid blood brotherhood. Though such experiences mark Cather's novel, she and the other women writers analyzed here have a broader social focus. Wharton in particular reexamines the way war brings men together in the face of loss, by ironically anatomizing John Campton's jealous homosocial relationships with his son and his son's stepfather. She estranges us from the young soldier, Campton's son George, whose motives are masked from us. By leaving this character enigmatic, she encourages us to ask whether his sense of being wedded to his men and to death is not a kind of war fever.

Furthermore, the thematics of these women's novels are social rather than military and individualist. One of the immediate consequences in narrative technique is an ironic flattening of character. Wharton, as a result, has been condemned for shallow characterization, for inability to penetrate beneath the surface to the real springs of moral action. But she relocates "moral action" from the individual to the social level. We need to reassess the criteria that have been used to elevate the male war novel and ask whether the ways these women undercut motivation and break up the social mosaic do not contribute to the female versions of a modernist aesthetic.

Finally, in Mary Borden's work we find the woman's identification with life—her double identification as woman and nurse with the saving of life—called into question. Does saving a life simply mean prolonging the war? Does it mean supporting the political machine that will throw the body back into a trench again and again until it is dead?

Because these women write about death and war satirically, bitterly, and with great honesty, they must be taken seriously, as they have not been in the past. One reason they have not been included in the canon of war poetry and novels, I believe, is that critics did not expect to find such social criticism and such profound pessimism in the works of women. They could not acknowledge the satire in Porter, Wharton, and Cather, whose texts, like the fragments of Borden, are about the debasement of language in the mass orchestration and obfuscation of men's deaths. Their writing infringed on a forbidden zone of male experience.

## Notes

1. *Green Hills of Africa* 70–71. Stephen Crane poses a problem for Hemingway, since he wrote *The Red Badge of Courage* "before he had ever seen any war," yet it is "one of the finest books of our literature." *Men at War* 10.

2. See Claire Tylee's excellent discussion of the "unexploded mine" of the concept of "war poet." She traces the erasure of women's war writings from anthologies, the

myth of trench experience and combat brotherhood as prerequisites to composition, and the contradictory critical views of cliché in war verses ("Verbal Screens" 128–33).

3. In *Death and the Right Hand* the anthropologist Robert Hertz argues for a systematic alignment of women with death (and the left hand) in primitive cultures. The *social* activity of warmaking, however, is exceptional in aligning death with men.

4. In short, Cather made use of the same kind of materials Stephen Crane drew on, but only in Crane's case could Hemingway accept such a secondhand procedure: "But he had read the contemporary accounts, had heard the old soldiers . . . talk, and above all he had seen Matthew Brady's wonderful photographs" (*Men at War* 10).

5. In his probing study of the "liminality" of war, Eric Leed finds that "invisibility, death, burial, and pollution" describe the soldier, who is caught in a marginal zone between two social categories (18). He concludes that "war experience is nothing if not a transgression of categories" (21), in which death becomes a dash or a continuum rather than a slash between life and not-life.

6. Crosbie Garstin, "Chemin des dames," and E. A. Mackintosh, "Recruiting," (Gardner 42, 111).

7. The lines from "my sweet old etcetera" are reprinted from *IS 5 poems by e. e. cummings,* edited by George James Firmage, by permission of Liveright Publishing Corporation. Copyright © 1985 by E. E. Cummings Trust. Copyright © 1926 by Horace Liveright. Copyright © 1954 by E. E. Cummings. Copyright © 1985 by George James Firmage.

8. "I believe that the world needs poetry more than it ever needed it. . . . most people are lost in the maelstrom which the war brings" (Damon 415).

9. The scornful apostrophe reads as an unmistakable indictment of modern society. Yet there remains ambiguity: it is addressed to "homo called *sapiens*." Does the speaker exempt the female sex as a separate "race"? Millay surely was aware of the complicity of women propagandists in the war fever of 1914.

10. There is no room here to explore the political gap between American women's poetry and prose on World War I. Perhaps the desire to impose poetic form upon the recalcitrant material of war, however critical their vision, impels these writers to have recourse to familiar tropes.

11. Part of the ambiguity of Cather's novel lies in her oscillating point of view. The narrator's voice can be distanced from Claude's belief in heroic action, but the focus also moves to a close-up view of Claude, immersed in the comradeship that sustains him in battle. Such oscillation in perspective may have, ironically, won Cather the Pulitzer Prize for patriotism.

12. On Borden's depiction of physical debasement and desexualization through war, see the excellent articles by Tylee and Marcus. Marcus calls attention to the connection between Borden's blistering analysis and Elaine Scarry's work on pain, in which she identifies injury as a measure of military success and demonstrates the

propagandistic erasure of death and pain through military calculations and metaphoric displacements of the individual body.

13. In an extension of the wizard motif, the nurse becomes a witch, who "fattens" the soldier until he can be consumed by war. Gilbert misreads Borden's satiric voice as an expression of survivor's guilt (224).

## Works Cited

Borden, Mary. *The Forbidden Zone*. 1929. New York: Doubleday, 1930.

Cather, Willa. *One of Ours*. 1922. *Early Novels and Stories*. New York: Viking, 1987. 939–1297.

Damon, Sam Foster. *Amy Lowell: A Chronicle with Extracts from Her Correspondence*. Boston: Houghton Mifflin, 1935.

Dunbar-Nelson, Alice. "I Sit and Sew." *Norton Anthology of Women's Literature*. Ed. Sandra Gilbert and Susan Gubar. New York: Norton, 1985. 1337.

———. "Negro Women in War Work." *Scott's Official History of the American Negro in the World War*. Ed. Emmett J. Scott. N.p., 1919.

Elshtain, Jean Bethke. *Women and War*. New York: Basic, 1987.

Fussell, Paul. *The Great War and Modern Memory*. New York: Oxford, 1975.

Gardner, Brian, ed. *Up the Line to Death: The War Poets, 1914–1918*. London: Eyre Methuen, 1964.

Gilbert, Sandra. "Soldier's Heart: Literary Men, Literary Women and the Great War." *Behind the Lines: Gender and the Two World Wars*. Ed. Margaret Higonnet et al. New Haven: Yale UP, 1987.

Hemingway, Ernest. *Green Hills of Africa*. New York: Scribner's, 1953.

———, ed. *Men at Warr*. 1942. New York: Berkeley, 1948.

Hertz, Robert. *Death and the Right Hand*. Trans. Rodney and Claudia Needham. Glencoe, IL: Free Press, 1955.

Hoffman, Frederick. *The Modern Novel in America, 1900–1950*. Chicago: Regnery, 1951.

Hussey, Maurice, ed. *Poetry of the First World War*. London: Longmans, 1967.

Kazantzis, Judith. Preface. *Scars upon My Heart: Women's Poetry and Verse of the First World War*. Ed. Catherine Reilly. London: Virago, 1981.

Leed, Eric. *No Man's Land: Combat and Identity in World War I*. New York: Cambridge, 1979.

Lowell, Amy. *The Complete Poetical Works of Amy Lowell*. Intro. Louis Untermeyer. Boston: Houghton Mifflin, 1955.

Marcus, Jane. "Corpus/Corps/Corpse: Writing the Body in/at War." *Arms and the Woman: War, Gender and Literary Representations*. Ed. Helen M. Cooper, Adrienne Auslander Munich, and Susan Merrill Squier. Chapel Hill: U of North Carolina P, 1989. 124–67.

Millay, Edna St. Vincent. "Apostrophe to Man." *Norton Anthology of Women's Literature*. Ed. Sandra Gilbert and Susan Gubar. New York: Norton, 1985. 1565–66.

# History, Power, Ideology

III

# Euripides' *Alcestis:* How to Die a Normal Death in Greek Tragedy

## *Charles Segal*

Euripides' *Alcestis* (produced in 438 B.C.) allows us an extraordinary glimpse of how men and women in classical Athens might have responded to a wife and mother's death in the house. The play begins with the divinities Apollo and Thanatos (Death), but as soon as they exit at line 76, we enter a fully human world and witness the emotional consequences of a major death in the family: conflict, escape, denial, and the feelings of loss and guilt. The play presents a veritable anthropology of death, a kind of miniature encyclopedia of attitudes and responses, from the heroic self-sacrifice of the wife— established at once as the touchstone against which all other reactions to death are measured (cf. 83–85)—to the unthinking self-centeredness of the husband and the children's sense of helpless loss.

In looking at the play as a cultural document, we must of course be aware of the filter of artistic representation. The play is concerned with telling its story in its own dramatic form, not with giving us a catalog of cultural attitudes. But because Euripides gains much of his dramatic effect by playing his fabulous myth off against a fairly realistically depicted set of cultural practices and attitudes, we can observe how the latter are condensed into clearly defined literary topoi or plot motifs, such as the lament scene, the commemorative ode, and the unexpected rescue.[1] Even in their abbreviated or stylized form these motifs offer important clues to cultural attitudes.

The Greek tragedies, moreover, not only are great works of art, they are also cultural texts, which were presented before the entire citizenry of Athens at the state festivals. It is legitimate, therefore, to look at this play not just as an autonomous, self-reflective literary and linguistic construct but also as a dense symbolic representation of social behavior, reflecting a culture's way of dealing with a recurrent crisis in human life.

The ancient Greeks, realists about human nature in war, politics, sex, and economic exchange, are skillful dissimulators, in their art and literature, about the physical necessities of their lives. Rarely, for example, do the details of farming and the country enter literary representation in the way they do in Roman writers like Virgil or Varro. So it is too with birth and death.

The Greeks' reticence about the normal process of dying is analogous in some respects to their reticence about the details of sexual behavior (see Foucault 38–43). Both are due in part to their tendency to hierarchize and generalize and to place values above individual activities. Death in war, for example, is subsumed under the ideal of the noble death of the hero-warrior and his undying fame in song (Vernant, *L'individu* 41–79). It is only the more popular literary forms, such as comedy and the satyr play—forms that appeal to the "lower" segment of the populace (see Plato, *Laws* 2.658c)— that permit such details. Comedy indulges freely in accounts of the bodily functions of eating, digesting, and excreting that tragedy largely excludes, but it says relatively little (as one might expect) about dying. Tragedy, like epic, has deaths aplenty, gruesome details included, but these are generally the extraordinary, heroic deaths of great figures like Ajax or the quasi-heroic suicides or self-sacrifices of women like Antigone, Deianira, Jocasta, Phaedra, or Iphigenia.[2] The *Alcestis* is virtually unique in classical literature for its account of a normal death in the house.[3]

When they do deal with death, the Greeks show their characteristic lucidity. Thanatos, the personification of Death, is not an unspeakable monster, like the Italic Orcus or *letum*. He has a human shape; and he appears on vases (especially in the sixth century B.C.) with his gentler brother, Sleep (Hypnos), conveying the body of the dead warrior to his homeland for burial, as he does for Sarpedon in *Iliad* 16 (cf. the illustration of this scene on the celebrated vase by Euphronius in the Metropolitan Museum, New York). Hesiod suggests a sharper contrast between the "mild" Sleep and the harsh Death, of "iron heart" and "pitiless breast," but even the latter is not a figure of utter terror (*Theogony* 758–66).

In the *Alcestis* Thanatos is rather buffoonish. He carries a knife or sword, but he uses it to consecrate his victim to the underworld, not to cut flesh. "Murderous Hades," against whom the chorus invokes Apollo later in the play (225), is more ominous.[4] Heracles, the closest of all the characters to the mythical world, describes Death as wearing a black robe (843) and wanting to drink the bloody offerings by the tomb (844–45, 850–51). These are not pleasant features; yet this Death also has "ribs" that Heracles can squeeze with his brawny arms to make him surrender his victim (847–49). For the truly horrifying face of death, the demonic image of sheer terror, the Greeks use the female figure of Gorgo, the petrifying mask of death (see Ramnoux 50–54; Vernant, *La mort* passim and *L'individu* 117–29; Loraux and Kahn-Lyotard). The threat of her appearance from the depths of Hades after the visions of heroes and heroines fills Odysseus with "green fear" and terminates his exploration of Hades (*Odyssey* 11.633–35).

It is striking how rarely Greek literature presents the process of dying a natural death. Warriors die in battle in the epic or in violent circumstances in tragedy. The *Iliad* recognizes virtually no death other than death in war (see Loraux, in Vernant and Gnoli 32–33). The *Odyssey* takes a wider view (e.g., in the death of Odysseus's mother not from illness, as she says, but from longing, *Od.* 11.197–203), but it offers little detail. The peaceful death of King Polybus in Sophocles' *Oedipus Tyrannus* is a foil to the violent consequences that this news has for Oedipus himself (cf. *Oed. Tyr.* 941–70, especially 960 ff.). This lack of attention to ordinary death is perhaps due to the Greeks' emphasis on life, on the realm of the living rather than the dead. "There is nothing more precious than one's life," Alcestis says (301), echoing the sentiments of Homer's Achilles (*Il.* 9.408–9); and for all the glory she receives, no one in the play doubts that life is better (see Burnett, "Virtues" 259). Though tombs are prominently located in cemeteries just outside the city walls, there is nothing like the vast cities of the dead such as that of the Etruscans at Cerveteri, with its painted and sculpted homes and furnishings for the deceased. Even the dead person is more important as an exemplar of cultural values among the living than as an individual being who has a separate existence in the otherworld. This is one of the ways, as Vernant suggests, that the Greeks "socialise and civilise death . . . by turning it into an 'ideal type' of life" (Vernant in Humphreys and King 287; see Vernant, introduction to Vernant and Gnoli 12–13). We see the process in Homer, the commemorative epigram, Pindar, and of course the funeral oration of the fifth and fourth centuries B.C.

The tendency to subsume personal death into idealized representation is also clear from the grave stelae and white-ground lekythoi of the late fifth and early fourth centuries B.C. Here an idealized version of the living person engages in a characteristic activity. A young girl plays with a pet bird; a mother holds her child; a hunter looks at his spear and dog; older men converse with their living kin. Death is not denied, and there is often a moving pathos in the contrast between the fact of death in the stone slab and its depiction of the fullness of life that has been lost. But these representations seem more concerned with life than with death per se.

Why should death have so extensive and realistic a treatment in the *Alcestis?* I can only offer some speculations. First of all, the play was probably intended to substitute for the buffoonish satyr play that each dramatist usually presented after his three tragedies.[5] Euripides can make the experience of death so vivid because it is going to be overthrown by life. He exploits a double fantasy of escaping death: having someone die in one's place and forcing Death to dislodge his victim. But the effectiveness of the surprise ending depends on our first being immersed in the atmosphere of dying and grieving.

Then, more generally, Euripides is constantly exploring issues of contemporary society by stripping away the heroic patina of the myths he inherits. He does this, for example, with marriage in the *Medea* and *Andromache* and with war and politics in the *Hecuba* and *Trojan Women*. The story of Alcestis provided the opportunity to study death in a domestic setting in a similar vein. Possibly, too, the mixture of sadness and levity enabled the poet to present sensitive material with greater distance and objectivity.

In a celebrated ode of his *Antigone,* performed only a few years before the *Alcestis,* Sophocles had warned that despite its brilliant intellectual achievement, the human race had still devised no remedy against death (360–62). Euripides' play does in fact allow the escape from death that Sophocles leaves as the last residue of untamed nature. This triumph is doubtless due less to the glory and confidence of Periclean Athens, then at its height, than to the pro-satyric nature of the play. The motif of overcoming death is embedded in the myth. Apollo, grateful to Admetus for his hospitable treatment, has granted him the privilege of allowing someone else to die in his stead. Admetus's wife, Alcestis, has offered herself, and the day of her death has now come. The everyday quality of gradual death in the first third of the play is the foil to the fairy-tale rescue of the heroine by Heracles, who thus rewards Admetus for his (dubious) decision to conceal the truth of his wife's death and receive his old friend into the house as a guest.

Euripides uses his audience's familiarity with the rites of mourning and burial to depict the inevitability of death—only, in the last scene, to turn everything upside down with Heracles' rescue of Alcestis. The pro-satyric play, unlike the straight tragedy, can have it both ways. It provides a moving reflection on dying and grieving; and it also feeds our wishful thinking that the dead can somehow be recovered.

At one level the drama plays with the wish fulfillment of its opening scene. After apparently blocking the fantasy by demonstrating onstage the harsh necessity of inescapable death, it turns the tables and suddenly has a hero defeat death after all. At another level the play carries us from a fairy-tale denial of death to a painful recognition by Admetus that Alcestis's sacrifice is impossible: the life left to him is in effect worse than death. On this ironic reading of the play, which has wide support, the deus ex machina effect of Heracles' salvation of the house only enhances the unreality and undercuts the myth.[6]

By placing an indefinite period between Apollo's offer of a substitute victim and her actual dying, Euripides creates a mood of brooding and anxiety as this house waits for death (see Lesky, *Alkestis* 55). By dividing into two—namely, Admetus and Heracles—the man who receives the gift of a surrogate victim and the folktale hero who wrestles with Death, he also introduces an ironic view of Admetus that enables him to question some of the traditional gender divisions involved in death and dying. Finally, by introducing a long and painful scene of conflict between Admetus and his father, Pheres, he places the situation of dying into the larger context of the extended household or *oikos*. The introduction of Heracles also creates another set of conflicts, between the duty to mourn and the obligation to receive outsiders under the traditional ties of *xenia*, guest-friendship between aristocratic males of different cities (see Rosenmeyer 235–36).

## The Fated Day: Time and Mortality

In counterpoint to the fairy-tale and folktale aspects of the play stands the language of tragic inevitability, the "necessity" (*ananke*) of the final ode (962 ff.). In this perspective, which tragedy inherits from Homeric epic, death is the defining term of the human condition. It delimits the "portion" (the Homeric *moira* or *aisa*) that the Fates (Moirai) spin out for each of us at birth (cf. *Odyssey* 7.197–98, 24.28–29).

The play opens with this stern perspective on death, appropriately presented through the remote, if sympathetic, Olympian Apollo. "On this day," he says, Alcestis is "fated to die" (*peprotai,* 20–21). Apollo's verb *peprotai* implies the distant, mysterious, unbending world order that fixes the life span of us all. It recurs when the servant confirms the hopelessness of Alcestis's situation (146–47):

*Cho.* Is there then no hope to save her life?
*Serv.* No, for the fated day exerts its harsh compulsion [*pepromene hemera biazetai*].

Recognizing that "the appointed day" was at hand (*ten hemeran kyrian,* 158), the servant says, Alcestis prepared herself accordingly. In a dense phrase of its opening lyrics the chorus describes her death as the "abrupt doom," the "shorn-off portion" (*moros apotomos*) that is "drawing near," with no hope of averting it by prayer (118–21).

This concern with the day reflects the Greeks' basic definition of the mortal condition. Man is *ephemeros*, the creature of a day, an unstable being whose life can be undone in the single revolution of the sun (Fränkel passim; Wankel 129). He is the mortal creature who is ushered out of life on the "apportioned day," "fated day," or "pitiless day" of his end, in the recurrent Homeric formulas *aisimon emar, morsimon emar, nelees emar.*[7] In the *Alcestis* this "fated day" is the frame for the hopes and fears of the mortal characters who live in the precious and limited flow of ongoing time.

The opening scenes draw their pathos from this approach of the "fated day." Apollo has saved the house "up to this day" (9) and announces that the awaited end will come "on this day" (20). The chorus knows—we are not told how—that this is the fateful day, *kyrion emar* (105); and the servant echoes their words later for Alcestis's own recognition of the same moment (*hemeran ten kyrian*, 158). When Apollo, in the prologue, describes Death as "watching for this day on which she must die" (26), Euripides is not making a joke about inappropriate bourgeois punctuality, as one critic suggests,[8] but is invoking the epic and tragic mood of death's inexorability. Death greedily awaits the hour when he may seize his victim.

Death appears as the frozen moment of the "right now" (322) that Alcestis sees terminating the rhythmic succession of days, months, and years (320–22): "For I must die, and that woe is coming not tomorrow, nor the day after; but at once [*autika*] shall I be reckoned among those who no longer exist."[9] To Admetus, however, she holds out the promise of the "time" (*chronos*) that will "soften" his pain (380), a commonplace echoed, with multiple ironies, by Heracles in the last scene (1085). Admetus, in his scene with Alcestis, dwells on his "year-long grief" and the "lifetime" (*aion*) for which he will remember her sacrifice (336–41). Soon after, he decrees public mourning for "the twelve moons that come to fullness" as the months pass (431); and the chorus then predicts Alcestis's fame "as the circling season of the Carneian [festival's] month comes around at Sparta" (447–51). For Alcestis, this extended seasonal time is obliterated by the single day of the opening scenes. Only at the end does the reckoning of days once more take on meaning for her as Heracles stipulates the "coming of the third light [of day]" as the end of her required silence (1146).

The inexorability of the day in tragic time is also the foil to the satyr play's victory over death. In the prologue Apollo tells how he tricked the Fates to save Admetus (12), a deed that he would reenact in persuading Thanatos to "postpone" Alcestis's imminent death (50, reading *ambalein*, after Bursian). Thanatos, however, is adamant about the impossibility of Alcestis's reaching old age (52–53).[10] Heracles, soon to be the vanquisher of Death, is also the champion of extended mortal time, urging Admetus to "postpone" his grief until the remote time (as Heracles thinks) of Alcestis's death (*es tot' ambalou,* 526). His notion of the single "day" is just the opposite of the doomed woman's: forget about tomorrow, he tells the mourning servant (784), and "reckon the life of the individual day as yours, all else as fortune's" (788–89).[11] His foil, in turn, is the old Pheres, who hoards the remaining "time" of his life and makes a niggardly "reckoning" of the long period below and the brevity of life's sweetness here (691–93; see Burnett, "Virtues" 270). Perhaps deliberately distancing himself from the brutal immediacy of Alcestis's death, he speaks not of the "fated day" but, somewhat euphemistically, of the "fated chance" (*ten pepromenen tuchên,* 695) that Admetus has transgressed or outlived by Alcestis's sacrifice. For him life at any cost is precious, even in the exiguous quantity left to him (722 ff.). The old, we see, fear death just as much as the young; it always comes too soon, no matter how much life one has had (cf. 711 ff.).

If the folktale frame of the play enables us to escape the inexorable death of full tragedy, the ending restores us, paradoxically, to the normality of dying at one's appointed time. Alcestis's return is a victory over death (and Death), to be sure, but it also suggests Admetus's mortality. Apollo's offer is now canceled out; no one will now get a second chance at life (see Gregory 268–69). Everyone in this world will henceforth die on schedule, just as they would have before Apollo's intervention. The Necessity of the last ode, then, so melodramatically overthrown in the moment of Heracles' gift onstage, remains triumphant in the long term; and the characters live within the limits of the human condition, mortally ever after.

## Physical Decline

Despite the mythical apparatus behind the events, Alcestis's death has a natural physical cause. This is a *nosos,* a disease, that, as in the contemporary medical treatises of Hippocrates, follows a predictable course over time. Early in the play Apollo refers to Alcestis's dying by the verb *psychorrhagein* (19–20), "letting the soul break loose" at the final gasp. The servant repeats the word in our first human account of her condition (143). In the same speech the servant reports her as "wasting away and being extinguished by disease" (203) and as "still breathing a little" (205). The chorus repeats the former phrase as it laments "this best of women, who is being extinguished by disease" (235–36).

However common in real life, this situation, as we noted earlier, is rare in tragedy. The opening scenes of the *Hippolytus,* a decade later, show us Phaedra's illness, but this is shrouded in mystery and is not quite a physical illness. Even in a play like Sophocles' *Oedipus at Colonus,* where the protagonist is old and infirm, the actual process is kept at a distance. In this miraculous end, in fact, the hero departed "without illness, in no pain" (1663–64). The dying of Euripides' Hippolytus and of Sophocles' Heracles in the *Trachinian Women* are, of course, more drawn out, but these are still violent deaths, outside the house.

In Alcestis's case we are shown the physical weakness in her last moments as Admetus asks her to raise her head and she answers that she would if she had the strength (388–89). "My eye in darkness becomes heavy," she had said just before (385). Euripides exploits the pathos of the scene in the child's cry, "Look, look at her eye[s] and her stretched-out hands" (399). It is assumed that she will die surrounded by her family, even the small children, from whom nothing is hidden.[12]

## "Tame Death": Alcestis's Preparations

The play is interested in Alcestis's death more as a social process than as the series of predictable physical crises described, for example, by the Hippocratic writers or by Thucydides in his account of the plague (see Buxton 20). Despite her weakened condition, Alcestis makes the rounds of her house, "stands" before the altar of Hestia, the goddess of the domestic space of the household, and "goes to" all the other altars (162 ff.). Prepared and accepting, she takes this final farewell of the house in its ritual aspect. Then, in her first onstage speech of the play, she makes practical provision for her children's future. She speaks of her death with matter-of-fact simplicity as she makes her last request (280–81): "Admetus, for you see how matters stand with me, I want to tell you what I wish before I die."[13]

In the following lines she refers to her dying in the same direct, nonmetaphorical way (284–85). She uses metaphor only in the familiar expression, again reflecting the real situation, of "not looking on the light" (282). Closer to the end, she self-consciously marks the division between herself and the living: "You may speak of me as being nothing any longer" (387; cf. 320–22, 381). The stark "I exist no longer," *ouden eim' eti,* is her final utterance before the last syllable, "farewell," *chair'*—spoken, we may surmise, with a failing voice (cf. 385, 388–89). To be "nothing," however, holds no particular terror; "nothingness" is simply the absence of life.

As the exemplary wife, Alcestis does all she can to mark the ritual closure of her relationship with the house and its gods (162 ff.). She takes a tearful personal farewell of her children and her household servants (189 ff.). She fulfills her role as mother by providing as best she can for her children's future, the subject of her only extended speech in the play (280–325). She is realistic about Admetus's grief, which she knows "time will soften" (381). This combination of acceptance, realism, and preparation corresponds to the "tame death" of Ariès's medieval Christian. Death has its place within the framework of life. It is a transitional process to be accomplished in regularly marked stages of disassociation from both the sacred and the secular parts of life. There is grief but also completion.[14]

## Between Life and Death

In a prolonged death from illness, what is the point that definitively separates the living from the dead? For the lexicographer Hesychius, as in the classical philosophical tradition generally, death is the moment of "the soul's separation of the body."[15] Nearly every culture, however, has a more personal gesture or a sign to mark this crucial transition. In the pagan world it is often the covering of the face, as at the end of Euripides' *Hippolytus* or Plato's *Phaedo* or at the death of Caesar in Plutarch's *Life*. For Jews it is turning the face to the wall; for the medieval Christian it is composing one's features and crossing the arms on the chest (see Humphreys in Humphreys and King 263–65; Ariès 13 ff., especially 21–26; Vernant, "Death" 258; Garland 15–16).

In the *Alcestis* the gods of the prologue have absolute clarity, but the mortals wait in anxiety and uncertainty. Thanatos closes the prologue by entering the house for the definitive ritual act of cutting off a lock of Alcestis's hair, thus consecrating her to the gods of the lower world (74–76); but this solemn sign of death's power remains invisible to the choristers, who enter immediately after with questions about what is happening. Puzzled by the silence in the house (78–79, 93), they listen for the wailing, breast-beating (86–87, 104), libations, or cutting of the lock of hair (98–103) that would signify this transitional moment. The servant reports Alcestis's still suspended state between life and death (141 ff.); but her description of Alcestis's prayer to Hestia for her children, her visiting of the household altars, and her address to the marriage bed constitute the personal gestures that have set the process of dying under way.

Euripides, of course, is giving us only a general sketch, which he manipulates for his own purposes. Thus the long scene between Admetus and Alcestis enables us to witness the husband's solemn promise, which he will break at the end. To make Admetus's later deception of Heracles possible, it is necessary for the greater part of the domestic rites to have been completed, so that only the carrying out of the corpse and the actual burial remain (cf. 513).

Even within these limits imposed by the plot, however, the movement of the play is governed by the funeral ceremonies that divide Alcestis from the living. Thus the transition to the second stage of the action occurs as Admetus is carrying the body "on its final road" from the house to the tomb (606–10). Here he meets Pheres, who is bringing a gift for the tomb's adornment, to help escort Alcestis on her way to the dead ("Receive this adornment, and let her go beneath the earth," 618–19). Admetus's brutal rejection of this gift makes the funeral ceremony the focal point for the unity of a household soon to be shattered. The immediate effect, enacted before our eyes, of disowning his father is to exclude him from the funeral rites (629–32) and thus from the intimate affairs of the *oikos*.

With Pheres' exit after this bitter scene, the funeral rites resume. The chorus's prayer for Alcestis's kindly welcome in the lower world moves her further from the living (741–44). Hinting that the noble fare better in Hades than the base, they install her there seated beside Hades' bride, Persephone (744–46), a step toward her honor as an underworld *daimon* in their last ode (1004–5).

The contrast between this sad, ritualized farewell and Heracles' feasting introduces the next scene, the latter's discovery of the truth (747–860). We return to Admetus, however, as he enters his widowed house, having (he thinks) definitively consigned Alcestis to the realm of death (861–934). The rituals of separation here continue to be the vehicles of emotional intensity. There is a poignant retrospective glimpse of the funeral ceremony as Admetus asks the chorus why they prevented him from leaping into the tomb (897–902). This violent gesture is his last point of resistance to accepting Alcestis's disappearance. In his next speech, sadder and wiser, he grasps what her sacrifice means and how little is left of his life (934–61).

The chorus's last ode, on the invincible power of Necessity, renders definitive this separation between living and dead (963–1005; see Riemer 107–18). Admetus is now reestablished in his present condition of widowed and mourning husband, and Alcestis is now fixed in her status as one of the dead. The chorus's closing prayer to her inaugurates her new existence as a local deity of the underworld (1004–5). Once more, ritual seems to be sealing the tragic ending, as a foil to the surprise Heracles has in store.

The visual experience of the funeral rites is reinforced by the sound, as the play alternates silence, mourning, songs of lament and celebration, the weeping in the house, and the revelry in Heracles' guest chamber. The odes that establish Alcestis as one of the honored dead emphasize the music that transmits her glory to the future (446–54). The music of "Apollo of the beautiful lyre" on Mount Pelion drew the wild beasts with Orpheus-like magic (569–87). This supernatural music, with its power to cross the division between god and beast, contrasts with the play's final reference to songs, wherein the chorus finds only the confirmation of absolute Necessity, the finality of death (962–65). Not even the "voice of Orpheus," recorded on the Thracian tablets, holds a remedy for this (967–70). Yet Apollo's Orphic music at the center of the play points both forward and back. It points back to Admetus's impossible wish for a musical Orphic persuasion that could win Alcestis back (357–62) and forward to Heracles as the Orpheus figure who will in fact accomplish this miracle (cf. 850–53).[16]

Another set of contrasting songs defines the sense of loss. Admetus, returning to his "desolate bed," juxtaposes the joyful wedding song of the past with the wail of the dirge in the present (915–25). He thereby sets Alcestis's adult life as a woman between its two major transitional points, but only from the point of view of his grief. Finally, the silence in the house that ushered in the uncertainty of Alcestis's place between living and dead at the beginning is balanced by her silence at the end (1143–46). Still dedicated to the gods of the underworld, she has the tabooed quality of the corpse (see Garland 47, 101; Riemer 100–103). Admetus's taking her hand (1117–18) must have sent shock waves through the audience, for he is reaching out to touch what might be a veiled figure of Death itself, "an apparition of those below," as he says warningly (1127).[17] We are reminded of Apollo's departure in the prologue to avoid this touch of mortality (22–23). In any case, he may not have a conversation with her. Ritually separated from the living in the course of the play, Alcestis must be ritually (as well as physically) brought back from the dead. Formally consecrated to Hades by the gesture of Thanatos at the end of the prologue (74–76), she has no identity among the living until the period of deconsecration and reintegration is over (see Betts). Thus not only may she not speak, she also, in a sense, has no name. Admetus calls her "my wife" (1131, 1133), but he never says "Alcestis."

Alcestis's veil, appropriate to mourning, is the sign of her continuing marginal status, between life and death (Buxton 21). It is also a reminder of another transition, the bridal ceremony, in which the removal of the bride's veil in the so-called Anakalypteria, "the rite of uncovering," marks her passage to a new status. The play's final scene, then, unites these two principal transitional moments in the adult woman's life, the day of her marriage and the day of her death (see Halleran).

For Admetus, reentering the house after the funeral, the wedding day was a sad and remote memory of a lost joy (912–25). Now the marriage day and the funeral day once more come together, through gestural imagery, in a very different mood. Heracles presumably removes Alcestis's veil when he tells Admetus, "Look at hcr, and see if she somehow seems to resemble your wife" (1121–22). To remove the veil is also to repeat the wedding. Thus the play replaces the tragic ending of loss with the familiar comic ending of a rite of marriage. This "wedding," however, keeps the muted tones of tragedy. The restorative echo of the wedding day comes together with the horror and awe attaching to the dead in Hades. One can scarcely imagine a more powerful scenic image of the interpenetration of life and death, joy and fear.

Weddings are noisy; Alcestis remains silent. In strong contrast to the music, singing, wailing, and reveling earlier in the play, this silence keeps the awesomeness and solemnity of death in the foreground. The separation between living and dead is fundamental to the Greek sense of the order of the world. This barrier, like that between immortal gods and mortal men depicted in the prologue, must remain intact. Heracles, himself a demigod and destined to reach Olympus, has the privileged role of mediating between these separate realms on both sides. But for Admetus the passage is full of horror and uncertainty: this veiled woman may be "an apparition from the lower world" (1127). As he reaches out to touch her, he feels as if he is "cutting off the Gorgon's head" (1118), an allusion to the extraordinary heroic deed of Perseus in confronting this dread monster. The Gorgon, we recall, is the ultimate terror of the realm of the dead for Odysseus, the face of Death as utter, paralyzing fear.[18]

Once in the grave, the deceased has no more story. The *Alcestis*'s final ode on Necessity, with its virtual epitaph for the heroine (995–1005), seems to be moving us toward this tragic closure. Greek tragedies often end with the rites of burial that mark the death as the definitive ending, both of the life and of the play. In this case, however, there *is* more story. After the interment the play enacts a tale of "surprise" and "unhoped for wonder" (cf. 1123, 1130, 1134, 1160). By juxtaposing this epitaph with the entrance of Heracles, moreover, Euripides suggests that this additional story will be told not on the funeral monument or in its musical equivalent, the commemorative songs of funeral cult, but in the play itself, with its fairy-tale surprise conclusion (995–1005). In characteristic Euripidean fashion, this ending plays off ritual against art, life against literary form, and calls attention to art's own special power, embodied in the fiction of this play, to overcome death (Segal, "Cold Delight").

## Resisting Death

While the rituals that separate the dead from the living provide the controlling rhythm for much of the play, they also provide the field for representing a healthy resistance to death. In the mythical framework this resistance is embodied in Apollo and Heracles.[19] Apollo is a champion of life. His "tricking of the Fates" to save Admetus recalls other trickster figures who evade death by their wits, for example, Sisyphus and Prometheus (see Gregory 261). His son Asclepius has restored the dead to life; and the god himself has defended Admetus from the Fates and tries to convince Death to wait. On one hand, he can simply walk away from death as a *miasma* (pollution) that, like Artemis in the *Hippolytus,* he must avoid (22–23); on the other hand, he is willing to engage with Death himself in a long, agonistic encounter.[20]

Heracles, with his earthy appetites and boisterous hedonism, strength, and confidence in himself, embodies a joyous gusto for living (755 ff., 782 ff.). Borrowed from the comic stage, he embodies a comic spirit of renewal and vital energy in a potentially tragic setting. He is thus the present analogue, onstage, of the remote, victorious Orpheus, whom the play mentions several times (357–62, 967–69). He in fact succeeds in doing by force what Orpheus accomplished by persuasion (850–54; cf. also 1127–30).

The ordinary mortals resist death by refusing to give up life. The chorus, anxious for news of Alcestis, hopes for respite from Apollo the Healer (90–92) or his son Asclepius (122–31). Even after their hope in prayer and sacrifice fails (cf. 119–21 and 133–35) as the servant describes Alcestis's gestures of farewell (158–98), they continue to invoke Zeus and Apollo for some way out (213–35, 455–59). Their final ode on irremediable Necessity marks the definitive acceptance of death (963–110; cf. 965–66 and 221).

The chorus thus embodies a healthy social response to death: resistance and hope as long as these are feasible, then a realistic acceptance. In the same vein they offer traditional and conventional consolation to Admetus: death comes to all, he is not the first to lose a wife, his weeping can do no good, his lot is hard, but he must endure and still has life to enjoy (416–19, 871–77, 889–94, 926–34).[21] This conventional wisdom can do little for Admetus, whose anguish is at its height in the lyrics and speeches immediately preceding this ode (861 ff., 878 ff., 895 ff., 912 ff., 935–61).

The chorus's personal sympathy, however—first for the lately departed Alcestis in the ode of 435–76 and later for the grieving Admetus (especially in the lyrical exchanges or *kommos* of 872–77 and 889–94)—is a necessary and expected part of the community's support for the mourner and should not be dismissed as empty convention.[22] Like all conventions in such circumstances, the content may be less important than the gesture itself. The mourner is not to be left alone, emotionally or physically, especially at the critical juncture of reentering the bereaved house (912 ff.). Euripides' chorus performs the socially expected task of the family and community at such a crisis.

## Emotional Responses: Separation and Survival

For all her acceptance of death, Alcestis still grieves fully. She weeps over her marriage bed (176–85), and she is soon joined by all the servants and her two children, who hang on to her dress and weep (189–93). This weeping goes on throughout the play and in fact becomes dramatically important in the contrast between the wailing and the feasting in the house (760 ff.). At the moment of death, the elder child has a short song of grief (393–415), a dirge or *threnos,* punctuated by Admetus's comment that Alcestis can neither see or hear them and that they are all "stricken by the heavy misfortune" (405–5). "With you gone, mother," the boy concludes, "the house is destroyed" (414–15). The sentiment is appropriate to the child, whose stage presence, unusual in its speaking part, keeps before us the catastrophe for the house as a whole and not just for Admetus (cf. 189–96).[23] The child sings with utter simplicity, in contrast to Admetus's elaborate rhetoric of the scene before, with his promise of the statue in his bed and his reference to Orpheus (348–68; see Rosenmeyer 231).

In both his case and Alcestis's, the intensity of grief does not remain at the same pitch throughout. It follows an alternating rhythm between moments of total surrender to the emotions of sorrow and calmer, more reflective periods. Thus Alcestis enters with a song (in lyric meter) expressing her terror of dying (244 ff.), but soon after she makes her long, well-reasoned plea for her children's future (280 ff.; cf. especially the repetitions in 269 ff. and 285 ff.). Admetus can conceal his suffering before Heracles in the important central scene between them (476–545) and rationalize his decision to receive a guest-friend in these circumstances (551–67). Yet at Alcestis's tomb he is so distraught that he has tried to throw himself into the grave (897–902). The contrast is due to some extent to the dramatic conventions, which demand of the characters long, well-articulated speeches and must also present in linear sequence elements that in real life can be simultaneous (see Seeck 50–51). Yet Euripides may also be drawing on observations of the ebb and flow of feelings over the long process of grieving.

The repetitions of Alcestis's farewells, first in intense lyrics, then in dialogue meter (268–72 and 385–91), contribute to the gradualness of this departure, so that it leaves an impression of greater solemnity and duration (see Seeck 45–47). The repetitions also deepen our sense of being onlookers at something both powerful and mysterious, for we do not in fact know when

Alcestis is going to die. The moment of her departure is as uncertain to the spectators as it was to the chorus at the beginning of the play. For all we know, Alcestis might not die until, say, line 600 (instead of at line 392). That she does not die when she says she is going to at 270–72 leaves us in some suspense about her statement at 385 ff. Death's consummation is beyond human prediction.

## The Consolation of Fame

In the epic tradition the tomb is the locus of the hero's posthumous fame (cf. *Il.* 7.86–91), and the chorus perhaps adopts a version of this commemorative attitude in singing that Alcestis's tomb is not to be considered merely the burial place of an ordinary mortal but will draw the reverence of passers-by in their honor for her sacrifice (995–1005; cf. 435–54).[24] Unlike the Homeric "imperishable glory" or the Christian belief in Resurrection, however, this is presented as having very little palliative effect. The servant regards the tomb as a permanent memorial when he describes it to Heracles as a prominent landmark of "polished" stone (*xestos*) on a main road just outside the town. It is like the monuments of Euripides' own day that can still be seen in the Kerameikos cemetery just outside Athens's Dipylon Gate (835–36 and see Dale ad loc.). But we see a very different aspect of this tomb when Admetus would throw himself into its "hollow ditch" (*taphron es koilen*) to lie beside Alcestis in death (898–99).[25] For him, in this moment of utter desolation, the tomb is neither elevated nor of stone, but the cavity in the earth where the mortal remains lie buried. It does not point to a glorious future in the cultural memory, like the "marker tomb," or *sema,* of the epic hero, but it elicits the most intense identification possible with the death and absence of the beloved in the present moment.

## Mythical Death

Pervading and interacting with this more or less realistic representation of dying and grieving is the assumption that the dead go to Hades, a gloomy, forbidding, sunless place of nonlife (cf. 360–61, 437, 457–59, 952–53). When Alcestis repeatedly says that she is "nothing" or "does not exist," therefore, she does not mean her total annihilation so much as the cessation of real life as she has lived it on the earth. What survives in Hades is the feeble shade, wandering in darkness, reduced to a minimal state of energy and consciousness, a zero degree of existence. In *Odyssey* 11, the fullest account of the underworld in early Greek literature, the dead in Hades regain consciousness and the power of speech only when they drink the blood of Odysseus's sacrificial ewe (11.29 ff., 89 ff., 390), although the poem also allows some kind of gloomy interchange among the ghosts in the so-called Second Nekyia (24.19 ff.). Having relatively little formal doctrine about the afterlife (with the exception of a sect like the Orphics), the Greeks easily admit inconsistency.

Alcestis assumes that she will be "nothing" after death; but Admetus, for a moment, can imagine a shadowy underworld household that he will share with Alcestis; and he will ensure this by having himself buried in the same coffin: "Wait for me there [for the time] when I die," he says, "and make ready the house to share the dwelling with me" (363–64). Nowhere else does the play envisage such a posthumous extension of their married life, nor does Admetus again mention it as a possible solace.

A meeting in the afterlife is within the limits of possibility for a fifth-century audience. Antigone reflects that her burial of her brother will make her arrival in Hades dearer to her mother and brother below (Sophocles, *Antigone* 897–903). In a darker vein, Oedipus defends his self-blinding by citing the repugnance of looking on his mother and father in Hades (*Oedipus Tyrannus* 1369–74), drawing on the common belief that he will arrive below with his body in its current state. Euripides' Polyxena, in the *Hecuba,* asks what message she should carry to her dead brother and father in Hades (422–23). In Pindar too, as in Homer, the dead can take joy in good news of children or descendants still among the living (Segal, "Messages"). Only rarely in tragedy does this motif play a major role in assuaging grief. Alcestis herself, as we have noted, views death only as her nonexistence.

Admetus's statement, therefore, is a rhetorical presentation of his highly emotional state at this point in the play, although the exaggeration (cf. 357 ff.) also contrasts sharply with the simplicity and practicality of Alcestis's speech just preceding. His closing lines, then, with their promise of domestic reunion, are a denial of that death, a momentary flicker of hope that will fade when the loss fully sinks in (see Dale xxii ff. and at 365–66). As in his later impulse to throw himself into her grave (897–902), the funerary rituals channel emotion but also release and intensify it.

At the moment of her death he cries out, "Take me with you below" (382) and says that he is "destroyed" if she leaves him (386); but of course she is dying precisely to keep him from being "destroyed." Just before, he promises that he will be buried with her in the same coffin, "for not even in death may I be apart from you, the only one faithful to me" (367–68). Yet her "faithfulness" consists in choosing the death that separates them. It is a contradiction of which Admetus will become aware only at the end of the play. At one level, this motif transfers to the male the response that Greek tragedy generally attributes to the woman: the wish to join a spouse in death.[26]

It is a wish that Euadne makes literal in plunging into her husband's funeral pyre (Euripides, *Suppliants* 990–1071). Thus it reflects the play's tendency to invert male and female roles in its heroism of Alcestis's sacrifice and the passivity of Admetus's acceptance. Psychologically, this motif also expresses the unreality that her death, contemplated at a distance, has had for Admetus.

The dying person herself has a very different vision of the mythical Hades. Admetus mentions the underworld landscape, with Pluto's dog, Cerberus, and Charon's boat (360–61), but only as a part of his unreal wish for Orpheus's magical voice. Alcestis, however, experiences this landscape as one of fearful separation and disorientation. Charon will drive her brutally across the horrid marsh of the Styx to the nameless dead on the other side (252–64):

> I see the two-oared boat in the marsh; the ferryman of corpses, Charon, with his hand on the pole, is already calling me: "Why do you delay? Hurry up! You are keeping me." Hastening me along with such remarks, he makes me hurry. . . . Someone is driving me, driving me on—don't you see?—to the hall of the dead, winged, glancing beneath his dark-eyed brows. What will you do? Let me go! Alas, utterly miserable that I am: this is the road on which I go forth.

Her repeated cries depict the frightening experience of death as violent separation. Euripides makes us see the dying person's fear and existential isolation. Charon, or "someone," is forcibly pushing her to join the mass of the dead, the *nekyes* (253, 260).[27]

This swarm of the unindividualized dead is similar to what Homer's Odysseus perceives both at the beginning and at the end of his journey to Hades (*Odyssey* 11.36–43, 632–33); and in both cases "green fear takes hold of him" (11.43, 633). Odysseus's fear, however, is a living man's sensible precaution to save his life. Within the play, Heracles has no fear of Hades' "sunless halls," which he is prepared to enter (851–54). Euripides may have found it more acceptable culturally to project the dread of Hades upon a woman and thereby to make it easier for the male audience to experience such fear vicariously. Whether or not there were women in the audience, the judges, as Euripides knew, were all male.

Alcestis's terrifying vision of Hades makes clear the price she pays for her heroic death. Her first words are an invocation to the remote presences of the sky and sun: "O sun and light of day and heavenly swirlings of the rushing cloud" (244–46). She thus conveys at once her different perspective on the world of the living,[28] and this becomes intense in the vision of Hades soon after. Admetus stands by, in anguish at this scene (257–58, 264–65), although his sympathy seems to be more for himself and his children than for Alcestis. Her parenthetical "don't you see" (259) deepens the pathos of this gap between her and those she is leaving. Death is a mysterious journey;[29] it is surrounded by the awesomeness of the unknown. To die is to enter a strange world, hidden from those in life. The chorus will later refer to this "sunless house," its "black-haired god," and Charon as the ferryman of the dead (434–44); but the details of Alcestis's passage are not frightening and in any case are tempered by their praise of her as "best of women" and her future honors in cities like Athens and Sparta. For Alcestis herself, there is no such mitigation.

Euripides obtains his two most pathetic responses to death through this mythology of the lower world: the sheer terror of Alcestis's vision of Charon and later the child's simple cry, "Mother has gone off below; she is no longer under the light of the sun, father" (393–94). Judging from Aristophanes' *Frogs,* such images had enough vigor in the popular imagination to be effective onstage (see *Frogs* 180–315). Yet, the mythology of death has a positive side too, particularly in Orpheus's presumably successful journey to Hades (357–62), where Charon and his oar are also mentioned (361). And this mythical passage is the exemplar of a happy return journey from the underworld that will be completed at the end of the play (cf. 850–55, 1123 ff.).[30]

## Death and the House

When Plato alludes to the myth of Alcestis and Admetus in the *Symposium* (179b), he contrasts it with that of Eurydice and Orpheus as a myth about eros, sexual love. In Euripides' play, however, eros has no explicit role. This is a play about death in "the house of Admetus," the phrase with which Apollo opens the play (1; cf. also 9 and 41). We approach the main figures only gradually, through those who are concerned with the fate of the house: first Apollo, then the chorus, and finally the grieving servant, who surveys the emotions and gestures within (183–98). Alcestis's first act is to bid farewell to the parts of the house that belong especially to her role as wife and mother (162–88); her last is to ensure her children's future (304–19). Early in the play we meet the grandparents (290–94), whose rejection of the sacrifice occupies the powerful scene at the center of the play. There is also a brief reference to Alcestis's family of origin (730–33).

Alcestis never directly attributes her sacrifice to love for Admetus (cf. 282–310). It is not that she does not "love" him in our sense of a wife loving her husband.[31] She does in fact say, in reviewing her decision, "I did not wish to live torn away from you" (287); and her verb, *apospastheisa,* does convey pain at the thought of separation. But she goes on at once, in the next verse, to add "with the orphaned children," so that she still seems to be thinking of their life together as parents rather than as a devoted couple per se.

The play is concerned with the family rather than the couple. The appearance of a child with a speaking part on the stage indicates this concern. Such a role is unusual in Greek tragedy. The closest parallel is the lament of the children of Euadne and Capaneus after the former's suicide in Euripides' *Suppliants* (1123–64), another play about a wife's sacrificial death. In *Alcestis* the boy's song of grief (393–414), which has been carefully prepared for by the servant's account of the weeping children in 189–91, is perhaps the family's most immediate response to the actual moment of Alcestis's death. The chorus of Thessalian elders sympathizes primarily with Admetus. The boy, repeating the chorus's word, "she is gone" (394; cf. 392), reminds us of the larger reverberations of her death. He not only weeps over his own orphaned life (396–97) but also includes his sister and father (406 ff.), and he can even sympathize with the latter's loss of joy in marriage and the companionship of old age with his wife (411–14). His closing sequence of direct addresses to sister, father, mother and his reference to the day of marriage and to old age (412) run the gamut of intimate relations within the house. "House," *oikos,* is the last word of his song: "With you gone, mother, the house has perished" (414–15).

This poignant little song thus recreates the totality of the house under the sign of the loss felt by its most vulnerable members. The child enacts onstage the emotional solidarity that the house *should* have, the sympathy that its members should feel for one another. The directness and simplicity of his grief contrast with the rhetoric of Admetus in the preceding scene (especially 348 ff.) and also with his instructions for elaborate public and private mourning immediately after (422–34). Throughout Alcestis's dying Admetus bemoans his loss primarily in I-statements and makes only a brief allusion to the children (388, 390). Earlier, too, Alcestis asked him to avert the evils of a stepmother for the *children* (304–10), but Admetus replied with a promise about a *wife* for himself (328–33; see Seeck 51 ff.). The boy's song elicits from him a brief expression of solidarity in family suffering (404–5): "You two [children] and I are smitten by heavy misfortune." Admetus is not unfeeling about the children. He refers to their suffering at the end, "crying for their mother as they fall about his knees" (947–48). But the grief of children is not as interesting to the Greeks as it is, say, to the Victorians. The emotional world of childhood has yet to be discovered.[32] The remarkable thing is perhaps that this little scene exists at all.

The boy's song, though brief, is also an important foil to the scene with

Pheres (614 ff.). The two father-son relationships stand in striking contrast. Both contain expressions of sympathy for Admetus (411 ff., 614). But in Pheres' case initial solidarity fragments into bitter hostility. We see the house becoming divided around the figure of the dead woman. Death brings out its latent tensions as well as its potential solidarity. Pheres in fact shifts his position on Alcestis from heroic praise (620–24) to the cynical view that Admetus has found someone foolish enough to die in his place (728; cf. 698–701, 720). When Pheres refers to Alcestis's kin, Admetus's in-laws, it is his parting shot, a warning of retribution from her family (731–33).

The play has hinted at these tensions earlier in more or less open criticism of, or at least disappointment with, the refusal of Admetus's parents to die for their son (cf. 290–94, 336–41). But it is quite another thing to see the son disown his father to his face (629–72). As a number of critics have suggested, the scene shows the emotional instability and egotism of Admetus's character.[33] But Euripides is also exploring the limits of a hypothetical situation, the disintegrative effect on a household of allowing a person to escape his own mortality through another's sacrifice.

The father's passing on of the patrimony has its other side in the son's obligation to look after his father in old age and perform the burial rites when he dies. From Homer on, the father's loss of this "nurture" in his old age, the *threptêria,* is considered one of the great misfortunes of life (see *Iliad* 4.477–79, 17.301–3). Admetus's angry abrogation of these duties (662 ff.) gives this scene its shocking effect and contributes to our growing doubts about his character.[34] The sudden swing from his elaborate performance of the rites for Alcestis to this refusal of rites for his father reflects the rifts this house begins to show. It is also an indication of those generational conflicts that one sees—more humorously but no less seriously—in Aristophanic comedies like *Clouds* and *Wasps*.

Admetus's expectations of his father and the latter's refusal in particular become catalysts for a wider range of tensions within the patriarchal family. The son resents his duty to look after his aging parents and arrange for their funeral (662–68). The father resents relinquishing his authority and his property to his son (681–90). The father can extend his existence only via the son and heir to whom he leaves his property (655–57). But bequeathing his property does not palliate the fact of his own mortality.

Transmission of property through patriarchal inheritance is only a second-best solution to death. The father-son conflict here reflects in dramatic form the double bind of mortality that Hesiod sets out in a famous passage of the *Theogony* (603–12). Either a man marries and has the care and expense of supporting a wife, or else he dies without heirs and his property falls into other hands.[35]

The other side of the dilemma is also reflected and then idealistically glossed over in the basic situation. The wife, once she has produced male heirs, is the most expendable member of the household, the one most easily "sacrificed" (see Vellacott 101 ff.; Vickers 117–19). In this sense too she is the "outsider," in the pretext that Admetus uses to discount the mourning for her and thus extend hospitality to Heracles (532 ff.). A measure of truth underlies Admetus's prevarication in this scene: she is, with Pheres and his wife, the closest to being extraneous to the house. The Thessalian elders and later, more cynically, Pheres praise her as the ideal wife (460–65, 473–75, 620–29), the "best of women." But this claim rests, of course, on her self-effacement before the needs of her husband.

The (male) spectators could thus find in the play the validation both of the ideal wifely role and of the superior value of the male in the household. They also could see, acted out before them, the tensions between generations, particularly between grown son and aged father, that the patriarchal property system brought with it.

Pheres begins his rebuttal of Admetus's claims by enumerating the possessions he is bequeathing to him, including the kingdom and his lands (681–88). He asks, in effect, Do I have to give you all this and die for you too? (cf. 682). In thus listing the obligations they have to each other, each reveals his latent resentment of them. Admetus resents his old parents' continuing hold on life. His emotional response may well be acting out what adult males in the audience feel but are ashamed to confess. He has, in effect, no answer to the old man's demonstration of his own right to live other than to threaten to withdraw his support: Just wait till you need me, he tells his father (719).

Pheres, however, is not cast in the heroic mold either. No sacrifice for him. Yet he needs his son and heir and has no counterthreat to Admetus's act of disowning him. All he can do is to look outside his own family to Alcestis's kin and their possible demands on Admetus (730–33). The move is perhaps a sign of his desperation and frustration. His allusion to her family of origin, unique in the play, is also a reminder of that other side of her life. Yet its very isolation may indicate how little the family of origin is in fact involved and also how much of "life" the austere dramatic form excludes.

The contrast between this scene and what follows is just as harsh as the contrasts in father-son relations implied in the child's song at Alcestis's death. Admetus turns from banishing his father and mother from his house forever (734–38) to placing Alcestis's body on the pyre (739–40). The funerary rituals in the background function as an ironic frame for the action, for Pheres entered with a funeral gift for this very burial (614–18).

## Death the Revealer

We cannot, of course, be sure that Euripides meant his audience to view Admetus's experience as a model of coming to terms with death. It is possible, as Carlo Diano suggests, that this play, like so many tragedies, served as a kind of memento mori, a meditation on death that prepares us for the suffering it brings, a kind of "art of avoiding pain," *techne alypias* (Diano, "Euripide" 130 ff.). Admetus is the *gennaios,* the wellborn man of noble and generous feelings, who will not weep before Heracles. But tragedy does finally sanction the open expression of such grief, as Admetus lets forth "springs of tears" from his eyes (1067–68) before a sympathetic Heracles (cf. 1081), rather like the "floods" of tears that Alcestis is described as shedding early in the play (183–85; see Segal, "Female Death"). This response perhaps suggests a model for possible audience reaction and, as Diano suggests, may even anticipate Aristotle's *katharsis,* or at least one view of *katharsis.* In the chorus's finale in the *Hippolytus,* the shedding of "many tears" is not only "a common grief for all the citizens" (1462 ff.) but perhaps also a bond of shared emotion and sympathy for the community established by the theater (Segal, "Theater" 69–70).

In any case, by allowing the audience to identify with both the dying person and the mourning survivor, the play is able to explore the range of emotions involved both in dying and in grieving for death. This double focus may be one of the reasons critics are so divided in their sympathies between Alcestis and Admetus. Euripides wants us to identify with both. But he does so without sentimentalizing or glossing over the problems, tensions, and conflicts that a household suffers in such a crisis.

The heart of this exploration is the shifts in Admetus's attitudes that we have examined above. In this respect Euripides remains true to the deeply held belief of classical antiquity that the experience of death, one's own and that of loved ones, is the final test of character. A life acquires its clearest meaning only in the light of death.[36]

Tested in this way, Admetus's life is found wanting.[37] Not only does he find his survival meaningless, but he has been shown a coward, as he himself acknowledges (955–59).[38] He will be remembered for his ignoble behavior, whereas Alcestis will live on in the cultural memory as a kind of heroized ancestor (445–54, 995–1005). She wins the "good fame" or *eukleia* generally reserved for males like Heracles (cf. 173–74, 290 ff., 742, 938, 999 ff., 1092). Admetus taunts Pheres with cowardice and with the failure to win the repute of a noble death (642, 648, 717, 725); in fact, the insult applies equally to himself, as he recognizes at the end of the play (954–61).

Admetus makes another discovery, also deeply rooted in antiquity and given philosophical formulation by the thinkers central to the classical tradition—Socrates, Plato, Aristotle, Epicurus, and the Stoics—that the mere prolongation of life is not an end in itself. Continued physical existence is meaningless unless the resultant life is based on values like honor, altruism, and love. This is something Alcestis knew from the beginning. Were this a tragedy of "late learning," like *Antigone* or *Hippolytus,* Admetus's late discovery would, of course, be too late. But the fairy-tale ending enables him to survive his discovery and thereby to become a little more deserving of a reborn Alcestis.[39]

## Notes

1. On Euripides' tendency to compose in terms of such more or less isolated motifs see Seeck 157 ff.

2. See in general Loraux, *Façons* 31 ff., 41 ff., and passim. The closest parallel to the situation in the *Alcestis* is the death of Deianira in Sophocles' *Trachinian Women,* whose address to her marriage bed closely resembles Alcestis's (*Trach.* 900–935 and *Alc.* 175–91). It is likely that one of these versions is dependent on the other, but the question of which came first is still much discussed. For a recent survey and bibliography see Riemer 84–103.

3. The centrality of the theme of death in *Alcestis* is widely recognized: see Beye, "Alcestis" 126–27; Rosenmeyer 210–13; Diano, "L'Alcesti" 71–72; Burnett, *Catastrophe* 28; Gregory, especially 260 ff.; Bradley passim; Seeck passim; Lloyd 124–25; Garner 59–60. The focus of these studies, however, is generally on the dramatic structure of the play, not on attitudes toward dying per se, as in the present study.

4. See Loraux, *Façons* 36–37 with note 19 on p. 106, who rather exaggerates this quality of Death as "tranchante ou sanglante," especially in 74–76. Seeck 32 suggests that the notion of Thanatos as consecrating the dying person to death may have been Euripides' own invention. On the traditional representations of Death see Grillone 39–40, with note 1.

5. That the *Alcestis* is a substitute for a satyr play is the consensus of modern scholars and probably the view of ancient scholars as well (Hypothesis II, ad fin.): see Lesky, *Alkestis* 84n86; Dale xviii ff., and recently, Seidensticker 129 ff. and 137 ff., as well as Conacher, "Structural Aspects", 73–74. There are occasional arguments for its being a regular tragic offering, e.g., most recently by Riemer, with a useful review of previous scholarship, 1–5; see also Lesky, *Greek Tragic Poetry* 209 and Von Fritz 263–64, 312–21.

6. This "ironic" view is probably now the majority opinion, at least in recent Anglo-American scholarship: so, with variations, Beye; Bradley; Conacher, *Euripidean Drama* 133 ff.; Nielsen; Rohdich 23 ff., 32–33; Smith; Von Fritz.

7. E.g., *Iliad* 11.484 and 587, 15.613, 21.100, 22.212; *Odyssey* 16.280. Cf. also the reflections on the coming "day" of Troy's destruction in *Il.* 4.164, 6.448, 21.111, etc. Cf. also the famous passage in Lucretius, *De rerum natura* 3.898–99 on death as the "single hostile day" (*una dies infesta*) that takes away all life's joys.

8. So Rosenmeyer 214, whose paraphrase, "He's come on the dot of the hour," destroys the motif of the fatal day and misleadingly gives the line a "bourgeois quality" (Rosenmeyer's phrase).

9. I adopt what I think is the most plausible meaning for line 321 where, despite the efforts of interpreters, the manuscripts' "to the third day of the month" yields no satisfactory sense. Diggle, in the Oxford Classical Text, plausibly regards *mênos* as corrupt.

10. Cf. 49, where the language of orders and necessity also suggests the inexorability of the epic and tragic death: Death says that he is "appointed" (*tetragmetha*) to "kill whomever it is necessary."

11. The rhyming effect of 782–85 is doubtless intended to add a humorous touch to this scene of the philosopher Heracles. It may well evoke the mood of a skolion, or drinking song, as Riemer 49 suggests.

12. Compare the scene in Lucretius 3.466–69 of the family members gathered around the bed of the dying person.

13. For parallels to this last wish of the dying person see Seeck 51 ff.

14. Cf. Andromache's suffering at the lack of such closure at Hector's death on the battlefield in *Iliad* 24.742–45, since thus in dying he "did not speak to her a close-set word that [she] might remember nights and days pouring forth tears."

15. Hesychius, s.v. *thanatos: chôrismos tês psychês apo tou sômatos*. For discussion see Brendel 10.

16. Euripides is probably drawing on a version of the Orpheus myth in which Orpheus succeeds in winning Eurydice back from the underworld. Virgil's version, in the fourth *Georgic,* in which he loses her by the fatal backward glance, is not firmly attested before Virgil. For discussion see Segal, *Orpheus* 16 ff., 69, 155 ff. Cf. also Heracles' contrary-to-fact wish in 1072–74.

17. The reference to the Gorgon in 1118 of course adds to the mood of terror: see below. Bradley 125 suggests that the veiled woman may serve as "the symbolic figure of death which is at last apprehended and through direct, physical contact, overcome." In my view, however, there is more fear and less victorious heroism here than Bradley suggests. Halleran 126 ff., defending the passage, whose authenticity has occasionally come under attack, also points out how it echoes the ritual of betrothal and thus suggests a remarriage that restores the integrity of the house. See also Buxton 21–23.

18. Admetus's Gorgon is, of course, not in Hades, as Dale rightly points out, ad loc. Even so, the Gorgon in this context may evoke this horrific side of the underworld. That connection would be stronger if one kept the reading of the manuscripts, *karatomôi,* and translated "as if at the Gorgon whose head is cut off." There are difficulties with this text (see Dale); but Vernant's studies of the monstrous head

(especially *La mort* and *L'individu* 117 ff.) may make us doubt Dale's confident assertion, " 'A beheaded Gorgon' in any case would have no terrors" (at 1118).

19. For different characters' attitudes toward death in the play see Smith in Wilson 48–51.

20. On Apollo and death in the prologue see Bradley 114–15; on the contradictions in Apollo's contact with death (and Death) see Seeck 31.

21. This traditional consolation of death's universality is as old as Homer (e.g., *Odyssey* 1.353–55). For later examples see Lattimore 250 ff., with the passages cited in note 286, p. 251; also Wankel passim, especially 146–49.

22. Rosenmeyer 218–19, for example, seems to me to go too far in regarding this consolation as comical.

23. Dyson 17 notes that this is the longest speaking role of a child in Greek tragedy.

24. For the form of 995 ff., that the tomb in the earth is not a real memorial to the dead, cf. Simonides' epigram on the Spartans (no. 531 Page) and Thucydides 3.42.3

25. Garner 64 also suggests a possible echo of the heroic burial of Hector and his "hollow grave" (*koilen kapeton*) that ends the *Iliad* (24.797). It is possible, of course, that this reflects on the heroism of Alcestis; but it is equally possible that we are to reflect on the contrasts with the Iliadic situation and the contrasts with Admetus. Sophocles echoes the Homeric phrase with fewer ironies in *Ajax* 1403. Cf. also *Alc.* 433–35 and *Il.* 19.320 ff.

26. On the union in death see Loraux, *Façons* 53–55 and Seeck 78. The motif, however, is not restricted to women: cf. Theseus's death wish in *Hippolytus* 836–37. For the widespread topos of union in death in funeral epigrams, see the extensive examples in Lattimore 247–50.

27. For the "nameless dead" see also Hesiod, *Works and Days* 154. The reality of Charon for the fifth-century imagination is indicated also in the depiction of this figure, with his bark, next to the tomb on the white-ground lekythoi of the late fifth century. On these vases, however, Charon has none of the terrifying aspect that so disturbs Alcestis here: see Shapiro 649–50, with fig. 21. Possibly the literary work can allow the expression of anxieties that must be repressed in the objects used in cult. On the scene of Alcestis's vision of Charon there are good remarks in Lesky, *Alkestis* 74 ff., Nielsen 96, Rosenmeyer 212 and 225, and Von Fritz 304.

28. Compare Ajax's similar address to the powers of nature in the moments before his suicide: Sophocles, *Ajax* 845–65.

29. Death's "leading" Alcestis below (47 and 73) also implies the recurrent image of death as a journey (124–27, 263; cf. 379, 393–94, 610).

30. See in general Smith in Wilson 50–51. In addition to Orpheus, the play cites the figure of Asclepius as a restorer of the dead. In the background too is the myth of Protesilaus, a young warrior, newly married, who gains the right to return to his still living bride for a single day. This latter myth was the subject of a play by Euripides, the *Protesilaus*. The motif of the statue in 357 ff. is another connection between the two works: see Dale on 348–54.

31. Some interpreters accuse Alcestis of coldness and even of emotional black-mail: cf. Beye, "Alcestis" 122 ff. and *Alcestis* 78; also Rosenmeyer 226–27. But this kind of psychologizing does not take account of the conventions of the play or the cultural attitudes toward death, especially the importance of the family and the dying wish. For some sensible observations see Seeck 65–72 and 83–89; Lesky, *Greek Tragic Poetry* 211 and 216. For all her concern with her children, Alcestis has made it clear that she is dying for Admetus (178; cf. 434).

32. For example, in *Iliad* 6.390–493 and Sophocles, *Ajax* 485–582, which is closely modeled on it, the presence of the child serves primarily to heighten the pathos and tragedy of the relationship between the parents.

33. For useful recent discussion and bibliography see Seeck 104–8 and Riemer 155–56; also Rosenmeyer 238–39; Conacher, "Rhetoric" 7–9 and "Structural Aspects" 79; Blaiklock 2 ff. A more positive view is taken by Burnett "Virtues" 265 ff. and Lesky, *Greek Tragic Poetry* 215–16.

34. There can be little doubt that Admetus's character is tarnished in the scene with Pheres: see, for example, Rosenmeyer 238; Conacher, "Rhetoric" 8 and "Structural Aspects" 79; Riemer 155–56. For other views see Rohdich 32 ff., Bergson 11–13, and Dyson 21–22.

35. See Vernant, *Mythe* 191–94; Arthur passim, especially 72–75.

36. The idea is deeply embedded in classical thought. The most famous formulations are perhaps in Herodotus 1.32 and Sophocles, *Trachinian Women* 1 ff.; see also Cicero, *Tusculan Disputations* 1.30.74 and the extended discussion in Aristotle, *Nicomachean Ethics* 1.10 (1100 a10 ff.).

37. The question of Admetus's "success" or "failure" at the end continues to stimulate discussion. I incline to the more ironic readings of, e.g., Rohdich 42–43 and Seidensticker 151; for the more positive view of the "test" of Admetus see, e.g., Burnett, *Catastrophe* 45–46 and Lloyd 129.

38. From a psychological point of view this confession of cowardice and future ill repute is an aspect of the self-abasement common in mourning, what Freud describes as "a lowering of the self-regarding feelings to a degree that finds utterance in self-reproaches and self-revilings, and culminates in a delusional expectation of punishment" (Freud *SE* 14: 244). In Admetus's case the self-punishment takes the form of imagining his loss of his good name.

39. This essay was prepared during a fellowship at the Center for Advanced Study in the Behavioral Sciences in Palo Alto, California. I am grateful for financial support at the Center, which was provided by the National Endowment for the Humanities (RA-20037-88) and the Andrew W. Mellon Foundation.

## Works Cited

Ariès, Philippe. *L'homme devant la mort*. Paris: Seuil, 1977.

Arthur, Marylin B. "Cultural Strategies in Hesiod's *Theogony:* Law, Family, Society." *Arethusa* 15 (1982): 63–82.

Bergson, Lief. "Randbemerkungen zur Alkestis des Euripides." *Eranos* 83 (1985): 7–22.

Betts, G. G. "The Silence of Alcestis." *Mnemosyne* 4th ser. 18 (1965): 181–88.

Beye, Charles Rowan. "Alcestis and Her Critics." *Greek, Roman and Byzantine Studies* 2 (1959): 111–27.

———. *Alcestis by Euripides: A Translation and Commentary*. Englewood Cliffs, NJ: Prentice-Hall, 1974.

Blaiklock, E. M. *The Male Characters of Euripides*. Wellington: New Zealand UP, 1952.

Bradley, Edward M. "Admetus and the Triumph of Failure in Euripides' *Alcestis*." *Ramus* 9 (1980): 112–27.

Brendel, Otto. "Observations on the Allegory of the Pompeian Death's-Head Mosaic." *The Visible Idea: Interpretations of Classical Art*. Washington, DC: Decatur House, 1980.

Burnett, Anne Pippin. *Catastrophe Survived: Euripides' Plays of Mixed Reversal.* Oxford: Oxford UP, 1971.

———. "The Virtues of Admetus." *Classical Philology* 60 (1965): 240–55. Rpt. in E. Segal 254–71.

Buxton, R. G. A. "Euripides' *Alkestis:* Five Aspects of an Interpretation." *Papers Given at a Colloquium on Greek Drama in Honour of R. P. Winnington-Ingram*. Ed. Lyn Rodley, Supplementary Paper 15. London: Society for the Promotion of Hellenic Studies, 1987. 17–31.

Conacher, Desmond J. *Euripidean Drama: Myth, Theme and Structure*. Toronto: Toronto UP, 1967.

———. "Rhetoric and Relevance in Euripidean Drama." *American Journal of Philology* 102 (1981): 3–25.

———. "Structural Aspects of Euripides' *Alcestis*." *Greek Poetry and Philosophy: Studies in Honour of Leonard Woodbury*. Ed. Douglas E. Gerber, Chico, CA: Scholars, 1984, 73–81.

Dale, A. M., ed. *Euripides, Alcestis*. Oxford: Clarendon, 1954.

Diano, Carlo A. "L'Alcesti di Euripide." *Euripide: Letture critiche*. Ed. Oddone Longo. Milan: Mursia, 1976, 70–78.

———. "Euripide auteur de la catharsis tragique." *Numen* 8 (1964): 117–41.

Dyson, M. "Alcestis' Children and the Character of Admetus." *Journal of Hellenic Studies* 108 (1988): 13–23.

Foucault, Michel. *The Use of Pleasure*. Vol. 2 of *The History of Sexuality*. Trans. R. Hurley. New York: Pantheon, 1985.

Fränkel, Hermann. "Man's 'Ephemeros' Nature according to Pindar and Others." *Transactions of the American Philological Association* 77 (1945): 131–45.

Garland, Robert. *The Greek Way of Death*. Ithaca: Cornell UP, 1985.

Garner, Richard K. "Death and Victory in Euripides' *Alcestis*." *Classical Antiquity* 7 (1988): 58–71.

Gregory, Justina. "Euripides' Alcestis." *Hermes* 107 (1979): 259–70.

Grillone, Antonino. "Vita e realtà quotidiana nell'*Alcesti* di Euripide." *Atti dell'Accademia di Scienze Lettere e Arti di Palermo* 4th Ser. 34 (1974–75): 39–61.

Halleran, Michael R. "Text and Ceremony at the Close of Euripides' *Alkestis.*" *Eranos* 86 (1988); 123–29.

Humphreys, S. C., and Helen King. *Mortality and Immortality: The Anthropology and Archaeology of Death.* London: Academic, 1981.

Lattimore, Richmond. *Themes in Greek and Latin Epitaphs.* Illinois Studies in Language and Literature. vol. 28, nos. 1–2. Urbana: U of Illinois P, 1942.

Lesky, Albin. *Alkestis, der Mythus und das Drama. Sitzungsberichte der Akademie der Wissenschaften zu Wien,* Phil.-Hist. Klasse, vol. 203, no. 2. Vienna, 1925.

———. *Greek Tragic Poetry.* Trans. M. Dillon, New Haven: Yale UP, 1983.

Lloyd, Michael. "Euripides' *Alcestis.*" *Greece and Rome* 32 (1985): 119–31.

Loraux, Nicole. *Façons tragiques de tuer une femme.* Paris: Hachette, 1985.

———. "Mourir devant Troie, tomber pour Athènes." Vernant and Gnoli 27–43.

Loraux, Nicole, and Laurence Kahn-Lyotard. "Mort: Les mythes grecs." *Dictionnaire des mythologies.* Ed. Yves Bonnefoy. Paris: Flammarion, 1981, 117–24.

Nielsen, Rosemary M. "Alcestis: A Paradox in Dying." *Ramus* 5 (1976): 92–102.

Page, D. L. *Poetae Melici Graeci.* Oxford: Oxford UP, 1962.

Ramnoux, Clémence. *La nuit et les enfants de la nuit.* 2nd ed. Paris: Flammarion, 1986.

Riemer, Peter. *Die Alkestis des Euripides. Beiträge zur klassische Philologie* 195. Frankfurt am Main: Athenäum, 1989.

Rohdich, Hermann. *Die Euripideische Tragödie.* Heidelberg: Winter, 1968.

Rosenmeyer, Thomas G. "Alcestis: Character and Death." *The Masks of Tragedy.* Austin: U of Texas P. 201–48.

Seeck, Gustav Adolf. *Unaristotelische Untersuchungen zu Euripides: Ein motivanalytischer Kommentar zur "Alkestis."* Heidelberg: Winter, 1985.

Segal, Charles. "Cold Delight: Art, Death, and Transgression of Genre in Euripides' *Alcestis.*" *The Scope of Words: In Honor of Albert S. Cook.* Ed. P. Baker, S. W. Goodwin, and G. Handwerk. New York: Peter Lang, 1991, 211–28.

———."Female Death and Male Tears in Euripides' *Alcestis.*" *Classical Antiquity* 11 (1992): 139–54.

———. "Messages to the Underworld: An Aspect of Poetic Immortalization in Pindar." *American Journal of Philology* 106 (1985): 199–212.

———. *Orpheus: The Myth of the Poet.* Baltimore: Johns Hopkins UP, 1989.

———. "Theater, Ritual, and Commemoration in Euripides' *Hippolytus.*" *Ramus* 17 (1988): 52–74.

———. *Tragedy and Civilization: An Interpretation of Sophocles.* Cambridge: Harvard UP, 1981.

Segal, Erich. *Oxford Readings in Greek Tragedy.* Oxford: Oxford UP, 1983.

Seidensticker, Bernd. *Palintonos Harmonia: Studien zu komischen Elemente in der griechischen Tragödie.* Hypomnemata 72. Göttingen, 1982.

Shapiro, H. A. "The Iconography of Mourning in Athenian Art." *American Journal of Archeology* 95 (1991): 629–56.

Smith, Wesley D. "The Ironic Structure in *Alcestis*." *Phoenix* 14 (1960): 127–45; Rpt. in Wilson 37–56.

Vellacott, Philip. *Ironic Drama*. Cambridge: Cambridge UP, 1974.

Vernant, Jean-Pierre. "Death with Two Faces." Trans. Janet Lloyd. Humphreys and King 285–91.

———. *L'individu, la mort, l'amour*. Paris: Gallimard, 1989.

———. *La mort dans les yeux*. Paris: Hachette, 1985.

———. *Mythe et société en Grèce ancienne*. Paris: Maspero, 1974.

Vernant, Jean-Pierre, and G. Gnoli, eds. *La mort, les morts dans les sociétés anciennes*. Cambridge: Cambridge UP, 1982.

Vickers, Brian. *Towards Greek Tragedy*. London: Longmans, 1973.

Von Fritz, Kurt. "Euripides' Alkestis und ihre modernen Nachahmer und Kritiker." *Antike und Moderne Tragödie*. Berlin: De Gruyter, 1962. 256–321.

Wankel, Hermann. "Alle Menschen müssen sterben: Variationen eines Topos der griechischen Literatur." *Hermes* 111 (1983): 129–54.

Wilson, John R., ed. *Twentieth Century Interpretations of Euripides' Alcestis*. Englewood Cliffs, NJ: Prentice-Hall, 1968.

■

# Beheadings

## *Regina Janes*

The French Revolution saw two kinds of beheadings. Through the little national window of the guillotine, one kind looked toward our own time and the technological perfection of impersonal violence. The other looked back a much longer way, past Temple Bar to the heads of Pompey and Pentheus or those of Ahab and the sons of Thyestes. Heads held aloft on pikes, posted on bridges, gates, and walls, or heaped beside a tent are far more ancient than the guillotine and far more widespread in their geographic dispersal. But the guillotine, like other works of human art, has accrued meanings more complex than the simpler work of human hands that severs a head and impales it on a phallic pike. For contemporaries, both the guillotine and the pike symbolized the Revolution, but they also occupied distinct, though overlapping, semantic spaces. Heads on pikes were the product of primitive, popular violence (or justice); the guillotine was the mechanism of revolutionary, institutional justice (or violence). Pike and guillotine shared the multiple, culturally determined meanings that belong to the public display of severed heads. Both evoked contradictory responses—horror in some quarters, relish in others—linked by the usual continuum, fascinated horror, queasy relish, and the shrug of indifference. But the guillotine was new. It was an instrument of public order, and almost at once it acquired a spectacular history that knotted it inextricably to the most controversial period of the Revolution. As Tristram Shandy might have said, it was a new whim-wham inserted into reality. One way or another, every observer had to accommodate it, and reality had to be reshaped to fit it in, precisely because the guillotine was an instrument of order that generated (what seemed to many) disorder.

242

The first beheadings of the Revolution took place on 14 July 1789 when the heads of Flesselles and de Launay were promenaded on pikes in the gardens of the Palais Royal.[1] As Bertier and Foulon followed, an observer across the Channel remarked that "the old Parisian ferocity has broken out in a shocking manner" (9 August 1789, Burke, *Correspondence* 6: 10). To this observer there was nothing new or surprising in the capacity of crowds for murder, and he would be the first in a long line of authors and artists to exploit that capacity for violence in order to denigrate the Revolution.

For the better part of a century, men of Burke's class had been congratulating themselves on the improvement of modern manners relative to both violence and sexuality. Circumscribed ever more narrowly, the legitimate uses of violence had visibly diminished. What such changes meant, Montesquieu, Adam Smith, and Adam Ferguson were prepared to explain: commerce civilized. The exigencies of exchange softened the manners of men and improved the treatment of women. The late eighteenth century was no peaceable kingdom, but by the time the Bastille fell, violence had become what it remains in modern Western sociology—an aberration to be accounted for (Hirschman passim). Whatever view of human nature one held, whether one followed Hobbes or Rousseau, whether one preferred culture or nature, violence required explanation. For the advocate of culture, the progress of society had rescued mankind from Hobbes's state of nature where the war of all against all raged on. For the advocate of nature, society had corrupted and deformed the innocence of peaceable, cooperative, equal man. It was not nature, but "the new-born state of society" that plunged mankind into the same "horrible state of war" (Rousseau 249).[2] Whether one preferred society and progress or nature and simplicity, violence belonged to the Other.

In the *Reflections,* Burke deprives the crowd of any motivation—ideological, political, or economic—for its violence. The violence stands alone, isolated, irreducible, and incomprehensible. Like the other bodily functions and vices, this violence squats at the Augustinian base of human nature, grotesque, sordid, and inseparable from the column. It can be hidden by draperies or it can be chained up, but it is always there: "The *old* Parisian ferocity has *broken out*" (emphasis added). When Burke describes the activities of the crowd during the October days, his metaphoric categories label the violence as they remove it from sympathetic understanding. The similitudes identify the crowd's behavior as part of the repertoire of human behaviors, but a part that we would perhaps as soon see expunged from the realm of possibility and relegated to history or remotest anthropology.

From history and remote anthropology Burke pulls his metaphors, and they swarm into the present to defile it. The march from Versailles, with the royal family led by the Garde Nationale and the women of Paris, is likened to "a procession of *American savages,* entering into *Onondaga,* after some of their *murders called victories,* and leading into *hovels hung round with scalps,* their captives" (159; emphasis added). If Burke's similitudes begin in anthropology, they end in the classical ages. The vilest of women are "furies of hell," and to sum up all the horrors of those days, Burke reaches for another classical reference: "Theban and Thracian Orgies." This classical, religious debauch is also violent, sexual, and specifically female. Led by severed heads and surrounded by shrilling women, the procession parodies a civilized triumph, the celebration of a just victory. Monstrous, every element is out of nature, out of place, out of time, out of order. But Burke, whose affinities with radicalism have often been pointed out, catches an element of the scene that most apologists for the Revolution have chosen to ignore these two hundred years. Although he would have his depiction repel us, Burke shapes the exuberance and the uncanny pleasure of those who cut off the heads and put them on pikes.

Friends to the Revolution of Burke's class, then and now, have evaded its violence by restoring the ideology Burke excises. They provide the people with a respectable motivation for acts of violence, usually retaliation against oppression, and they attribute the people's excesses to a culpable but comprehensible fury on release from oppression. Entirely absent is any sense of the pleasure of violence. If the fact of violence is acknowledged, the horrid details are dropped. For Paine, the mob's cutting off the head of the baker François and presenting it to his wife on a pike becomes only "the affair of the unfortunate baker" (17 January 1790, Burke, *Correspondence* 6: 73).[3] An unfortunate baker indeed, and one would not know from Paine the form his misfortune took. Philip Francis speaks in generalities of "the fury of the populace," "the crimes of individuals," "the loss of a *single* life, in a popular tumult," but he describes more specifically the scourgings, dragoonings, and galleys of the ancien régime (3, 4 November 1790, Burke, *Correspondence* 6: 153–54; emphasis added). Or Anacharsis Cloots, the cheerful atheist, reminds us early in 1790 that not so very many heads have been lost: only "dix ou douze têtes" when there are "douze ou quinze siecles d'oppression à venger" ("ten or twelve heads" and "twelve or fifteen centuries of oppression to avenge" (12 May 1790, Burke, *Correspondence* 6: 113).[4] The oppression takes up where the heads leave off—at twelve, less than a head per century.

Modern historians are equally predictable in their choices. Alfred Cobban, who would prefer that there should have been no Revolution, deploys violence as rhetorical decoration, artfully, wittily, and horribly. Albert Soboul,

Georges Lefebvre, R. B. Rose, and Lynn Hunt ignore it almost entirely, while popular historians such as Christopher Hibbert wring all they can from pathetic and shocking events. More interesting is the tact of George Rudé. In *The Crowd in the French Revolution,* Rudé does not obscure the fact of murder, and he names many of the victims: de Launay, Bertier, Foulon, François, the two gardes du corps at Versailles (56, 76, 78, 227). But only de Launay and the two gardes du corps have their heads cut off. The rest are merely murdered. That is a little odd, but more interesting is what Rudé does with the heads when they are cut off. Nothing. Nothing more is done with them or to them. The pikes are excised. There is no promenade. One might well wonder why anyone went to the considerable trouble of sawing through bone. Removing the promenade removes the celebration and denies the perpetrators of violence their pleasure. It also removes the threat explicit in the action.

When the people cut off and displayed the head of a "traitor," they made the "sovereignty of the people" more than a pretty compliment. They enacted that sovereignty by exercising a traditional prerogative of the European sovereign. (This meaning is, of course, culturally specific. Although severed heads always speak, they say different things in different cultures.) By the period of the Revolution, the display of severed heads had long been one of the commonest ways a European sovereign demonstrated his power to his subjects. As part of his responsibility to control public violence, he reserved to himself and his officials the right to take and to display heads. Simultaneously he asserted his right to violence and showed his subjects one consequence of their tampering with his order. By the mid-eighteenth century, such displays were usually confined to the heads and body parts of rebels or traitors, such as Damiens, the unfortunate assassin. In earlier periods, display was used for more common offenses, and the heads of thieves adorned sixteenth-century bridges. When the sovereign displays a head, he shows it not to his equals but to his people. They are the objects of that display, both as raw material and as audience. Their heads are the heads that are elevated, and it is they who must learn the lesson taught by them.

When the rabble cut off the heads of the king's officers, they have redefined themselves as the sovereign people. Literally and physically, they have seized the ultimate power of the sovereign. Instead of learning, they teach. It is a disturbing lesson to those identified with the old order; it is an invigorating lesson to those who identify with the new. As for those identified with the old order who believe they identify with the new, they ignore the lesson or palliate it. Many supporters of the Revolution desired to see no changes beyond their own admission, and that of their class ("the best," as

Wordsworth described them), to power, prestige, influence, and participation. The lesson of the heads is that there has been a fundamental change in social hierarchies and the distribution of power. Article 3 of the Declaration of the Rights of Man and Citizen declared that the people were "the source of sovereignty." But taking a head transforms the *menu peuple* from the passive "source of sovereignty" to the active executor of sovereign power.

Here and there, beyond such transparent acts as taking the Bastille or storming the Tuileries, burning a manor or demanding the heads of the Gironde, there are traces of the people's awareness of their subversion and appropriation of sovereignty. After the first paroxysm of excitement, the man who hacked through de Launay's neck with his cook's knife was frightened. Dénot feared punishment, and he justified the act as self-defense. Then, as time passed and customs changed, he decided he should put in for a medal and made the act his boast (Rudé, *Crowd* 56). He had committed not a shameless mutilation for which he should be punished, but a patriotic act for which he should be rewarded. Dénot's taking off de Launay's head had originally been represented to him as an act of personal justice. In the fray that led to de Launay's death, "It was you he hurt," they told him. Finally, however, Dénot justified himself by his service to his sovereign, the people.

The people's subversion and appropriation of power appear in numerous prints that stress the exuberance of popular decapitations. These were, maugre Cloots and Paine, not decapitations to be hidden, but decapitations to be flourished, to be brandished under the nose of power. Among the more popular subjects of revolutionary prints was the double decapitation of Bertier de Sauvigny and his father-in-law Foulon. Thrusting the head of Foulon on its pike into Bertier's face, the crowd had chanted, "Baise papa, baise papa," and anonymous printmakers loved the joke.[5] But there was another father whose head had still to be appropriated.

The principal head taken during the Revolution was the king's. No active, insurrectionary pike figured in that grand moment of subversion, but of the countless prints that represent the event, the most radical retain an emphasis on the people's direct manipulation of the king's head. More bourgeois revolutionary images handle the king's head more carefully and provide an image of the authority that is to replace the king's. Today, the most frequently reprinted image of the king's execution shows a great panorama of troops, scaffold, and massed crowds, while off to the left a tiny *bourreau* or headsman holds up a tiny head to the crowd (fig. 1). This "historical" image renders the king's fate and the transfer of authority from a remote, off-center angle. Put in perspective by the dignified, orderly masses of troops and people that dominate the scene, the king's fate is not central, but it is decisive.

Figure 1. *21 January 1793, the Death of Louis Capet in the Place de la Révolution, Presented to the National Convention 30 Germinal by Helman.* Paris, Bibliothèque Nationale (BN), C48616.

His head is held up; his authority is destroyed. At the same time, the destruction of one authority is more than offset by the weight of orderly troops and people to whom authority is now visibly transferred. Such is the image preferred by many historians of the Revolution. By contrast, the most radical of revolutionary prints sweeps away troops, crowd, scaffold, all save the king's head and the hand that displays it (fig. 2). In profile like the head on a coin, Louis's head is held by a graceful hand and forearm with plebeian buttons on the cuff. The hand grasps the head by the top curls; the neck drips blood, and the title is a warning: *Matière à réflection pour les jongleurs couronnées* (A subject for crowned jugglers to reflect upon). The message is unmistakable: the people have power over this head.

Because handling the head represents power over the head's former owner, royalist prints do not share the radicals' pleasure in playing with the king's head. Nor do they make the good order of the people en masse the focus of representation. Preferring not to depict the separation of the king's head from his body, royalist prints frequently show the king standing on the scaffold before his execution or in the heavens after it. Even when the king

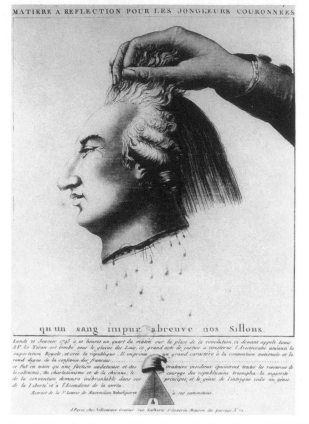

Figure 2. *A Subject for Crowned Jugglers to Reflect Upon.* BN, B86253.

is placed in the guillotine in a pro-monarchical print, the artist usually refrains
from severing his head. In Gillray's *The Zenith of French Glory, the Pinnacle
of Liberty,* the image is dominated by the figure of a gibbering Jacobin with
a fiddle (fig. 3). Perched on a lamppost that holds a few hanged priests, the
ragged revolutionary is watching the guillotining of Louis XVI at the lower-
left center of the print. Revolutionary disorder rejoices at the end of the old
order, but the head is not yet severed. It rests expectant at the base of the
guillotine, as it does in many serious accounts of the "massacre of the French
king." Reality was different. When royalist prints omit the holding up of the
head, they censor the real transfer of authority.

Royalist prints that do record the handling of the head represent the
bourreau as a figure of horror or as a kinsman. In a much-copied German
print, the bourreau as a wild-haired Medusa lunges at the crowd with the
king's head, horrified and horrifying. In Isaac Cruikshank's *The Martyr of*

Figure 3. James Gillray, *The Zenith of French Glory, the Pinnacle of Liberty,* 1793. BN, B26573.

*Equality,* Philippe Egalité, once the duc d'Orléans, takes off his plumed helmet to the head he holds. In every case, no matter what the political identification of the artist or his work, all are agreed that what is done with the head is of the utmost importance.

Why should separated heads have such power, as they do, "multas per gentes et multa per *tempora*"? Freud tells us, "to decapitate = to castrate" ("Medusa's Head," *SE* 18: 273–74),[6] but the equation is not perfect. There is no tradition of lofting severed genitals on pikes and carrying them about the city. For good or for ill, genitals do not identify their owners. Once they have been detached, there is no way to tell whose they were. (The test case is David's dowry of foreskins. They do not tell us or Saul that David killed Philistines. They tell us and Saul that David killed—or converted—many men who were neither Jews nor Egyptians.) Precisely the opposite is true of heads. The head tells all. It identifies itself, and it speaks, to the extent of its previous owner's ability, a silent narrative of fallen greatness and mastery transferred. On its face, the head carries our social identity: the lineaments that enable us to recognize members of our species as such and to tell one of us from the next, to differentiate members of the species.[7] Human infants focus on faces from their first days of life, and the first abstraction they recognize is a human face: a hairline, a chin line, two eyes, and a mouth. Those phallic substitutes, noses and ears (vide Sterne and Swift), are otiose.

The prestige of the head is mirrored in contempt for the body without a head. The body without a head is a body without a name. Perhaps the most powerful and familiar evocation of that fact is Virgil's:

> Jacet ingens littore truncus
> Avulsumque humeris caput, et sine nomine corpus.
>     (*Aeneid* 2.557–58)

(This was the end of Priam: "The huge trunk lies on the shore, / the head torn from the shoulders, and the body without a name.") Priam's nameless body, rubbish by the seashore, is the final, personal embodiment of burning Troy, fallen Pergamum. Against this obliteration, the next line thrusts an affirmation of the survivor against such unnaming. Aeneas's next line begins, "At *me* . . . " (emphasis added). Burke seems to recall the effect of the Virgilian passage when he warns Mrs. Crewe in 1795 against sympathy with the dead Mme Roland: "They've cut off the head of this bold, intriguing female Regicide—and now they shed Crocodile Tears over her headless Trunk" (*Correspondence* 8: 303). With all Mme Roland's character and all her actions in her "bold, intriguing" head, Burke cuts off her head again. He would have us see only the "headless Trunk," contemptible and unempowered. The equations head = name = identity; body = nobody = rubbish are aristocratic: they assume that the head had an identity worth noting.

Like other detached body parts, ambulatory hands or forlorn feet, a detached head is a sign we privilege. As a sign, it can enter into a variety of discourses, and its meanings will derive from the discourse(s) of which it forms a part, from the tribal to the psychoanalytic, from the developmental to the discursive. Wherever it appears, a severed head is a sign in a discourse over which that head exerts no power and no control.

Severed heads figured, as we have seen, in two revolutionary discourses. More powerful, pervasive, and persistent, the guillotine's discourse subdued that of the pike, although it never succeeded in repressing the memory of the pike. More specific to the Revolution, more paradoxical in its origins, the guillotine also owes its relative success as an emblem to the efficiency with which it reduces the visibility of human violence.

The discourse of the pike is fundamentally a simple one. The pike had been the weapon of the common foot soldier, of the "poor bugger who possesses only a pike," as *Père Duchesne* put it (No. 117, Boime, in Cuno, *French Caricature* 78). By the eighteenth century it was being superseded, and revolutionary prints of national guardsmen show them carrying the smarter, more up-to-date bayonet. Old-fashioned, primitive, common, simple, and cheap, the pike was an apt instrument for the people to use when they sought to show their old masters that the mastery had changed hands. The pike used to uphold the old order now held the dead old order up to its still-living face in the promenade, a simple, gruesome paradox. For counterrevolutionaries, pikes were equally well adapted to represent the horrors of that transfer of mastery.

Since pikes must be held up if they are to display heads, graphic representations are committed to showing someone holding the pike, and the argument of almost any print can be inferred from who is doing the holding. The delights of overturning the repressive old order emerge in the exuberant revolutionary prints that show a particular, albeit anonymous, sansculotte shaking his Foulon at Bertier. Far less unsettling are the popular revolutionary prints that show the heads rising from a sea of pikes and bayonets, with the individuals who actually hold the pikes submerged in "the people." Distributed in orderly ranks, the people display the heads their justice has exacted, but they are not actively questing for more. The pikes are present, but they are for the moment still. Invoking the discourse of the people's insurgency, expiring Jacobinism cried, "Resurrect the pikes," in 1795, when it was too late. The pikes had been broken by the guillotine, the new machine that not only cut off the heads of the leaders of the sansculottes, but also replaced their pikes as emblem of the Revolution among revolutionaries and counter-revolutionaries alike.

The guillotine originated as a technical solution to a practical problem. The practical problem, however, was not simple: it had been created by the intersection of egalitarian and humanitarian ideals and promoted by a powerful desire for public order. In the new criminal code of 1791, the Constituent Assembly decreed that decollation would henceforward be the punishment for all capital crimes. The bourreau, Henri Sanson, protested that present technology, the sword, was inadequate to meet the projected demand. Each decollation would require one or two swords, and any number of successive executions would put a severe strain on the headsman. The Assembly appointed Dr. Antoine Louis to pursue the suggestion of a decapitating machine made by Dr. Joseph Ignace Guillotin in 1789. After meticulous experiments at home and extensive research abroad into such decollating machines as the Maiden at Edinburgh and the Halifax gibbet, Dr. Louis and Sanson produced a machine that was first used on a thief in April 1792. Nicknamed at first "Louisette" and "La Petite Louison" for Dr. Louis, the machine soon took her name from the voice that had suggested her rather than from the hands that had designed her.

The Constituent Assembly's motives for decreeing decollation as the punishment in all capital cases were egalitarian and humanitarian. Early in the discussions of reform of the criminal code, it had been determined that along with other privileges and exclusions, differential sentencing based on the rank or quality of the criminal was to be eliminated. All crimes of the same kind should be punished by the same sentence. For crimes for which the penalty was death, it was proposed that the punishment be decapitation (Assemblée Nationale). The effect was not only to eliminate social differences in dying, but also to level upward. Decapitation had been reserved for aristocrats. Now all citizens would be treated to an equal and honorable death.

Paralleling the egalitarian argument was a humanitarian one. When Guillotin presented the projected reforms in the criminal code to the Assembly, he proposed at the same time "un simple mécanisme" to effect the decapitations. Such a mechanism, he argued, would permit a punishment less cruel and less painful than hanging, hitherto the commonest mode of execution. With his death delivered more efficiently, the victim would struggle less and endure less agony. Such a machine would enable the state to kill citizens without hurting them. By 1795, the painlessness of the guillotine had been called into question. Doctors disputed the cessation of sensation when the spinal column was severed. Much debated was Charlotte Corday's blush when the executioner slapped her severed head. But the positive aspects of the guillotine as an implement for inflicting the death penalty were sufficient to keep it in use in France until 1977, when it was last employed. (The death penalty was abolished in 1981.) Foucault manifests a lingering admiration for the machine when he describes decapitation as reducing "all pain to a single gesture, performed in a single moment—the zero degree of torture" (33). For many the guillotine embodied the best of the Enlightenment in capital punishment.

Seconding the egalitarian and humanitarian arguments was a powerful desire for public order. In the debates on decapitation, both those who opposed it and those who favored it argued from its effects on the populace at large. Those who opposed it, such as the Abbé Maury, argued that decapitation was too bloody a mode of execution, that it would accustom the people to effusions of blood and render them "féroce."[8] Against the negative effect on character, those who favored decapitation argued that decapitation would have a positive effect on the people's actions. A decapitating machine would control the exercise of popular violence and restore control over violence to more conventional custodians. As the duc de Liancourt put it, a decapitating machine would lend itself less easily to popular vengeance and irregular application than did bloodless hangings (Croker 532). His observation was greeted with applause by his fellow deputies. With a decapitating machine, violence would be reinstitutionalized and immobilized.

Unspoken but clear to all were the various ways formal decapitation would contribute to public order. A machine restored control of public punishment to the established authorities. Removed from their role as actors, the people would be returned to their traditional position as spectators, while the authorities tended the mechanism and managed the delivery of victims from trial to prison to place of execution. Developed by the Constituent Assembly, the machine would represent the people's justice, but that justice would not be exerted directly by the people. Fundamental to these good effects was the immobility of the machine. Unlike pikes, decapitating machines are stationary. They do not perambulate palaces and streets. They cannot surge threateningly and randomly through the ways and still do their work. On the days the guillotine walked, forced by a crowd to remove to the place du Carrousel or the Champs de Mars, the work was delayed.[9] Nor did these implications of the guillotine's fixity pass unnoticed. From radical quarters there came persistent, unanswered demands for portable guillotines and multiple stations.

Finally, crowning the project was the technological magic of the machine qua machine. Egalitarian, humanitarian, and still, the machine had the peculiar virtue that it effaced the headsman. When the *Ancien Moniteur* praised the humanity of Dr. Guillotin in making his proposal, it was the impersonality of a machine that was singled out for admiration. Displaced from a person to a machine, the act of death became the product of justice itself: "comme la loi" (*Ancien Moniteur* 18 December 1789). In this new age the machine, like the law, disguised human agency and human responsibility.

At first the guillotine lived up to expectations. The people nicknamed it, flocked to see its initial use, and registered disappointment at the spectacle. It was too quick; there was nothing to see. Equal, humane, stable, legal, and boring, the guillotine was, for the Assembly, a complete success. As the Revolution lurched toward violence in the summer of 1792, the guillotine soothed sensibilities exacerbated by other horrors. Although the fact is often forgotten, the guillotine was innocent of the worst atrocities of the Revolution, from the September Massacres at Paris to the drownings at Nantes and the shootings of Lyons. The guillotine at least preserved the individuality of the victim, the dignity of death inflicted one at a time.

Soon, however, the people began to make the guillotine their own. Although the neighbors complained about inadequate drainage, others were not troubled by the puddling of blood, and the guillotine became a place of popular resort. More important, radical elements, from the sections up to Danton and Robespierre, began to direct the guillotine's use for their own political ends. From the fall of the Gironde to Robespierre's last speech, the radicals' means included intimidating, or attempting to intimidate, the Convention. When the deputies turned on Robespierre, they turned on the guillotine as well. In July 1795 there was considerable discussion as to how to celebrate the anniversary of 9 thermidor. While controversy swirled over speeches and places, one proposal of the organizing committee found immediate acceptance: the Convention ordered that there should be no more executions in the place de la Révolution (*Ancien Moniteur* 23 messidor, l'an 3 [11 July 1795]).[10] That order removed the guillotine from its place at the heart of the Revolution and consigned it to the periphery. In that gesture of removal, the guillotine was riveted to the Terror, that period of great hopes and great disappointments when the guillotine had been at the center of the (place de la) Révolution.

For a brief period, the guillotine belonged to the people. By those who lived with it, the socially egalitarian guillotine was domesticated, miniaturized, familiarized, familialized, feminized, and sanctified, as "our holy mother" or "the patriotic razor." It was the little national window of the national domus. Those who saw their neighbors at the window reduced whatever terrors it held by fitting it into the order of things in a subordinate and controllable position, associated by nicknaming with houses, barbers, women, children, and religion.

For a brief, halcyon period between the execution of the king and the acceleration of the Terror later in 1793, the guillotine was a neutral implement, as the *Annual Register* suggests, or a playful adjunct. Early innocent, charming, and small representations of the guillotine do exist. The miniature guillotine was a pet. It served as a paperweight or a child's toy or, smaller still, as women's hair ornaments and earrings. Children have long been given toy swords, guns, and lasers to play with, and women have worn bodkins and ornamental swords as brooches. But neither have been often supplied with miniature gallows, blocks and axes, or electric chairs. The practice has been attributed to a gruesome levity that is peculiarly French, but it is also possible that the intricacy of the mechanism fascinated and that the identification of the machine with the people's justice—their own, not the king's—made it less alien.[11]

Among the most fruitful and familiar of the guillotine's domestications is her feminization. Like her elder sister the gallows, the guillotine also bore the nickname "la veuve" as long as she was in use, and she was always female: Louisette, La Petite Louison, La Guillotine. Lemuel Hopkins in 1796 called his American democratic dirge "The Guillotina," carrying the femininity into English as far as he could. Carlyle sputtered at the impropriety of naming a beheading machine "la guillotine" as if it were M. Guillotin's daughter (1: 115; pt. 1, bk. 4, chap. 4, "The Procession"). He could have saved his outrage: his fellow Scots had anticipated the French with their own beheading machine, called "the Maiden." The last man to die by the Maiden, the earl of Argyle in 1685, declared "as he pressed his lips on the block, that it was the sweetest maiden he had ever kissed" (Croker 542).[12] Behind "la veuve," who has consummated her affair, and "the Maiden," who sheds her first blood, is the guillotine as a gaping, single-toothed vagina dentata. The man who flirts with her attempts to retain or assert his sexual dominance. The elegant innuendo or crude joke insists on amorous foreplay before the opportunity for play is foreclosed. (The desire for domination and the insistence on self-assertion underlie both of Danton's famous closing re-marks—You will not be able to prevent our heads from kissing in the basket; show my head to the people, it will be worthwhile.)

Although other capital implements have been feminized and thence slipped into a dynamic of sexual interaction, only the guillotine has been explicitly eroticized. The *tricoteuses* knitting around the guillotine domesti-cated it: they turned the scaffold into the family hearth. Those women who wore guillotine earrings or hair ornaments eroticized the guillotine by associating it with female sexual display. But if the guillotine could be used by women as an erotic adjunct, it was also turned against them.

Just as the guillotine replaced the carnival of the people's violence with the immobile, institutional violence of established authority, so its representa-tions acted to repress disorderly feminine sexuality. Cruikshank's hideous Republican belle with her guillotine earrings is familiar, as are his counterrev-olutionary Mariannes, drunken, blowsy "furies of hell." But other explicit eroticizations of the guillotine remind us that in the family drama taking place on the scaffold, the authority masked by feminization is masculine. It is not mother up there going chop, chop, chop, but father. It is the state.

In a few explicit eroticizations of the guillotine, the guillotine is replaced by (as in Dickens's Mme Defarge) or, more usually, linked with a sexually inviting female body. Such depictions emphasize the parallels between female anatomy and guillotine geometry and set up a tense oscillation between desire and destruction.

One of the few images of this kind to emerge in the revolutionary period assaults Marie Antoinette (fig. 4). The queen stands high-bosomed and seductive, her right hand turned invitingly on her hip. Below her is a guillotine acting as cinch or stomacher for a very explicit piece of female anatomy, breasts, hole, pot. The image is in the tradition of obscene depictions of the queen, and its caption, "Ça ira," rejoices at the prospect of the fate the image proposes for her. No hostility is directed toward the machine. Instead, the skeletal guillotine, providing the frame and supports of the pictured flesh, shows the queen what she must come to. The grinning skull beneath the proud, painted face of living beauty: this is the modern version of that favorite Jacobean image. Although the explicit subject is an eroticized guillotine, the effect is to deeroticize the woman and to replace Eros with Thanatos.

A hundred years later, Adolphe Léon Willette made a parallel drawing that reflects the intervention of the Terror between the image of Marie Antoinette and his own time. On a scaffold, by night, a lamp above her inscribed "93," a strong, Phrygian-capped, entirely naked and entirely beautiful young woman leans against the guillotine, one arm akimbo, one supporting her head, with her legs arrogantly and tauntingly apart, one foot propped up. She reclines against the board to which victims are strapped, and she represents, shockingly, the Revolution as a young and experienced whore. (Reproduction obscures a certain wistful delicacy, an innocence, evident in the original.) The tension of the drawing, which is considerable, is relaxed by the inscription, for the inscription explains what part or aspect of the Revolution is embodied by this dangerously ambivalent body. In the inscription the woman speaks: "I am holy Democracy. I await my lovers" (fig. 5). Although the politics of the images of 1793 and 1887 are antithetical, the images share a few impulses: *épater les bourgeois* and upend the slut.

Images of the Revolution as a young and beautiful whore do not appear during the revolutionary period itself. When Marianne appears as a whore in counterrevolutionary engravings, she is old, deformed, and drunken: no sober man would buy. During the revolutionary period, the shocking function of the eroticization of the guillotine seems to have been filled by the beatification of the guillotine.

At first the beatification of the guillotine seems just a bad joke of the dechristianizers at the expense of the traditional hierarchies of church and state. It was that and more. In the new religion of the Republic, the guillotine became La Sainte Guillotine, to be decked in blue velvet and roses for

Figure 4. *Ah! Ça ira*. BN, P18363.

Robespierre's Festival of the Supreme Being. In the older and simultaneous iconography, blue is the color of the virgin, and the rose is one of her many emblems. La Sainte Guillotine had ambitions of rising; she was also called "our holy mother" (Cobbett 30: 1188).[13] If the guillotine made one uneasy, putting her in the pantheon was a way to placate and neutralize her. Safely elevated, she could be appeased by continual sacrifice and ritual attendance. Although she shocked and horrified the counterrevolutionary enemy, the good revolutionary sat safe in her shade.

As Daniel Arasse has shown, those aspects of the guillotine that had once seemed most positive—its rationality and its mechanical self-sufficiency—

Figure 5. Adolphe Léon Willette, *I Am Holy Democracy. I Await My Lovers,* 1887. BN, 89Cl39822.

became in themselves sources of revulsion. Mme de Stael turned the guillotine into a metaphor of the revolutionary government of the Committee of Public Safety to argue that events were out of anyone's control. The impersonal efficiency of the machine so praised by the *Ancien Moniteur* in 1789 was now turned against the machine: "Le gouvernement ressembloit à l'affreux instrument qui donnoit la mort: on y voyoit la hache plutôt que la main qui la faisoit mouvoir" (2: 141–42). ("The government resembled the hideous instrument employed on the scaffold; the axe was seen rather than the hand that put it in motion.")[14] The triumph of impersonality is a mark of technical perfection, but it is also deeply threatening. The independence of the machine suggests, in Paulson's memorable image, "that the machine would continue to cut off heads, as a pinmaker continues to make pins, as long as it is supplied with bodies" (in Cuno, *French Caricature* 58). In their first tentative steps, the liberating procedures of industrial capitalism joined in the dance of death.

For radicals of a certain stripe, of both the Left and the Right, there is nothing paradoxical about the guillotine. The scientific implement of the people's power, the guillotine illustrates what must happen when the people overturn the established order. "You can't make an omelette without breaking eggs." The radical Left embraces the necessity that the radical Right waves as a warning. For those who regard history itself as a movement of inexorable forces, sweeping mere human actors along, the guillotine is also an apt emblem. Impersonal, indifferent, and inevitable, history is a blade that cuts whatever interposes. Nor are its cuts to be questioned. They are only to be rationalized and understood: "When *we* are lashed, *they* kiss the rod, / Resigning to the will of God." For those who regard history as the continuing evidence of unintended outcomes, the guillotine is equally apt: an instrument of progress that produced great horrors, an embodiment of failed hopes and frustrated good intentions. As a paradox of the Revolution, the guillotine is a fit figure for the paradox of revolution.

Yet the guillotine is more than a figure. In its origins and its actions, the guillotine shaped the views of history that turn to it as emblem. Its technological and mechanical efficiency provided more than a metaphor; it supplied a conception. Without the guillotine, Carlyle's Terror could never have been so implacable or so remorseless. As texts so commonly do, the guillotine redefined the historical space it entered.

Of capital instruments in repose, only the guillotine so thoroughly reveals its threat while refraining from any actual display of violence. A gas chamber is only a room with ducts; an electric chair is only a chair with wires. The gallows noose, when it produces its full effect, always bears the burden of a body. To have any effect at all, the pike must sport a head. But the geometry of the guillotine is energetic. The blade is always there, potentially active, and requires only release from tension to execute its fell purpose. The guillotine is also discreet. It evokes violence, but it does not show it. More, it makes its point by itself, without any need for human actors to intervene or even to appear. The machine thus politely, if misleadingly, erases the humanity of violence.

The guillotine's persistence, then, derives from the same source as its existence, that "improvement of manners" on which the eighteenth century so prided itself. The ancient pleasures of violence recede from view as the machine erases the human hand. The carnival of the pikes falls to the order of the machine that controls and subordinates the vehemence of popular violence. The bloodless stillness of a waiting guillotine invites rhetoric—passionate, ironic, or frenzied—to twine around it or to break against it. Inhumanly passive, the machine challenges language, and language will always rise to the occasion. But the improvement of manners, while real, is also deceptive: it is only an improvement of manners.

Violence is still with us. Experimental psychologists will doubtless soon show how it is wired into the basal ganglia along with hand washing, territory surveillance, nest building, and Samuel Johnson's tics, but the sociologists have still to explain it. Although the improvement of manners controls the pleasure we take in violence, it eradicates neither the violence nor the pleasure. With its potential for blood, the guillotine provides a frisson for the dainty, the squeamish, the fidgety, those who would never make their hands wet or sticky by impaling a head on a pike. For those who prefer not to gaze upon severed heads, the guillotine mediates an ancient promise of violence and power. Those whose manners are most improved contemplate neither pike nor guillotine. They neither write such essays as this one nor read them to the end. For those of us who do, and those who have, the guillotine is a frame that invites us to contemplate and to control the human violence in which we are inevitably implicated.

## Notes

1. Jacques de Flesselles, merchant and acting head of the provisional government of the city of Paris, had denied ammunition to the crowds at the Hôtel de Ville. The marquis de Launay was the governor of the Bastille.

2. J. G. A. Pocock has shown how important the image of republican virtue was to the Revolution and in eighteenth-century thought (passim). Such virtue controlled both its own violence and others'.

3. More recently, Albert Soboul tells us much about the price of bread, but little about the hazards of baking it.

4. Translations are mine unless otherwise noted.

5. Lynn Hunt recently remarked on the "horror" of the prints that represented the deaths of Foulon and Bertier and moved promptly to a less grisly topic (in Cuno, *French Caricature* 35).

6. See also "A Connection between a Symbol and a System" (1916), *SE* 16: 339, and "The Taboo of Virginity" (1918), *SE* 11: 207.

7. Seagulls too can identify an individual human "predator," intent on banding their young, by facial features (Spear).

8. In 1791 Maury's argument was repeated by Lachèze.

9. The radical implications of movement have been explored in another context by Agulhon (88).

10. Mass deportations replaced mass guillotinings.

11. Certainly the oddest and most unexpected miniaturization of the guillotine is Wordsworth's. A child's toy, a windmill, replaces the guillotine exercised by the terrorists:

> They found their joy,
> They made it proudly, eager as a child
> (If light desires of innocent little ones
> May with such heinous appetites be compared),
> Pleased in some open field to exercise
> A toy that mimics with revolving wings
> The motion of a wind-mill; though the air
> Do of itself blow fresh, and makes the vanes
> Spin in his eyesight, *that* contents him not,
> But with the plaything at arm's length, he sets
> His front against the blast, and runs amain,
> That it may whirl the faster.
> (*Prelude* 10.363–73)

Ronald Paulson translates this image into "the monstrous child playing with the guillotine" (270). But Wordsworth's imagery refuses to allow the Terror to erase his earlier, more hopeful sense of the Revolution.

12. Sir Walter Scott's account, which Croker is using, is slightly less voluptuous: "He mounted the scaffold with great firmness, and embracing the engine by which he was to suffer, declared it the sweetest maiden he had ever kissed" (24: 281). Argyle's father, the marquis of Argyle, had been beheaded by the Maiden in 1660.

13. Remarked with horror by the earl of Mornington, January 1794.

14. The translation is that of George Rudé (*Robespierre* 126).

## Works Cited

Agulhon, Maurice. *Marianne into Battle: Republican Imagery and Symbolism in France, 1789–1880*. Trans. Janet Lloyd. Cambridge: Cambridge UP, 1981.

Arasse, Daniel. *La guillotine et l'imaginaire de la Terreur*. Paris: Flammarion, 1987.

Assemblée Nationale. *Journal des débats et des décrets* 1 Dec. 1789.

Burke, Edmund. *The Correspondence of Edmund Burke*. Ed. Thomas W. Copeland et al. 10 vols. Chicago: U of Chicago P, 1967.

———. *Reflections on the Revolution in France*. Ed. Conor Cruise O'Brien. Baltimore: Penguin, 1969.

Carlyle, Thomas. *The French Revolution*. 2 vols. London: Dutton, 1906.

Cobban, Alfred. *Aspects of the French Revolution*. New York: Braziller, 1965.

———. *A History of Modern France*. Vol. 1. Baltimore: Penguin, 1957.

Cobbett, William, ed. *The Parliamentary History of England from the Earliest Period to the Year 1803*. 36 vols. London, 1806–20.

Croker, John Wilson. "The Guillotine." *Essays on the Early Period of the French Revolution*. London, 1857.

Cuno, James, ed. *French Caricature and the French Revolution, 1789–1799.* Los Angeles: U of California P, 1988.

Foucault, Michel. *Discipline and Punish.* Trans. Alan Sheridan. New York: Pantheon, 1977.

Freud, Sigmund. "Notes on Medusa's Head." 1940. *The Standard Edition of the Complete Psychological Works (SE).* Trans. James Strachey. 24 vols. 1953–74. London: Hogarth Press, 1986. 18: 273–74.

Hibbert, Christopher. *The Days of the French Revolution.* New York: William Morrow, 1982.

Hirschman, Albert O. *The Passions and the Interests.* Princeton: Princeton UP, 1977.

Lachèze, M. *Ancien Moniteur* 4 June 1791.

Lefebvre, Georges. *The French Revolution.* Trans. Elizabeth Evanson, John H. Stewart, and James Friguglietti. 2 vols. New York: Columbia UP, 1964.

Paulson, Ronald. *Representations of Revolution.* New Haven: Yale UP, 1983.

Pocock, J. G. A. *Virtue, Commerce, and History.* Cambridge: Cambridge UP, 1985.

Rose, R. B. *The Making of the Sans-Culottes: Democratic Ideas and Institutions in Paris, 1789–1792.* Manchester: Manchester UP, 1983.

Rousseau, Jean Jacques. *Discourse on the Origin of Inequality.* "*The Social Contract*" *and "Discourses.*" Trans. G. D. H. Cole. New York: Dutton, 1950.

Rudé, George. *The Crowd in the French Revolution.* Oxford: Oxford UP, 1959.

———, ed. *Robespierre.* Englewood Cliffs, NJ: Prentice-Hall, 1967.

Scott, Sir Walter. "Tales of a Grandfather: Scotland." *Miscellaneous Prose Works.* 28 vols. Edinburgh, 1850–53.

Soboul, Albert. *A Short History of the French Revolution, 1789–1799.* Trans. Geoffrey Symcox. Berkeley: U of California P, 1977.

Spear, Larry. "The Halloween Mask Episode." *Natural History* June 1988: 4–8.

Stael, Mme de. *Considérations sur les principaux événements de la Révolution Française.* 4 vols. London, 1818.

Wordsworth, William. *Selected Poems and Prefaces.* Ed. Jack Stillinger. Boston: Houghton Mifflin, 1965.

# "Who Kills Whores?" "I Do," Says Jack: Race and Gender in Victorian London

## Sander L. Gilman

"I am down on whores and I shan't quit ripping them till I do get buckled," wrote Jack the Ripper to the Central News Agency on 18 September 1888 (Parry 12). The question I raise in this essay reflects not on the reality of Jack the Ripper—real he was, and he never did get buckled—but on the contemporary fantasy of what a Jack the Ripper could have been. To understand the image of Jack, however, it is necessary to understand the image of the prostitute in Victoria's London. It is also necessary to comprehend the anxiety that attended her image in 1888, an anxiety that, like our anxieties a hundred years later, focused on diseases labeled sexual and attempted to locate their boundaries within the body of the Other (Nelkin and Gilman).

Who could truly kill the prostitute but the prostitute herself? Who else could expiate her sins against the male? For the prostitute's life must end in suicide. In Alfred Elmore's image *On the Brink,* exhibited at the Royal Academy in 1865, we see the initial step before the seduction of the female, the beginning of the slide toward prostitution and eventual self-destruction. Alone, outside the gambling salon in Bad Homburg, having lost her money, the potential object of seduction (Everywoman) is tempted by the man to whom she is indebted (Nead, Walkowitz). Women, all women, were seen as potentially able to be seduced, as having a "warm fond heart" in which "a strange and sublime unselfishness, which men too commonly discover only to profit by" exists—or so writes W. R. Greg in the *Westminster Review* of 1850 (456).

The well-dressed woman has come to the spa, has exposed herself to exploitation by the male, and is caught between the light and darkness of her future, a future mirrored in the representation of her face, half lighted by the moon, half cast in shadow. She is at the moment of choice, caught between the lily and the passionflower. According to *The Language of Flowers,* a standard handbook of Victorian culture, the lily signifies purity and sweetness and the passionflower, strong feelings and susceptibility (19, 22). The gambling salon was the wrong locus for the female. As early as Hogarth's *The Lady's Last Stake* (1758–59), the female's seduction might be seen as the result of being in the wrong place. Males can gamble; females cannot. Males can indulge their passions; females cannot. Sexuality is a game for the male; it is not for the female. But gambling here is also a metaphor, though a socially embedded one, for the process by which the seduction of the female takes place. Playing upon the innate biological nature of the female makes the seduction possible, but the metaphor of losing at gambling also points to the model of infection and disease.

Alfred Elmore's picture shared this vocabulary. Gambling is a "fever" (*Times* [London]), the gambling is "infected by the fever of gambling" (*Illustrated London News*), the gambler is thus "feverish" (*Athenaeum*). (Nead 316). Gambling is a disease that infects and makes ill, infiltrating the purity of the female. Seduction thus has a course of illness: it begins with the signs and symptoms of disease, the fever of gambling, the result of the individual's being out of place—much like the colonial explorer expecting to get malaria—and leads inexorably to the next stages of the disease, prostitution and death. The image of the gambler who stands at the moment of choosing between vice and virtue, who is gambling with life itself, is appropriate. Gambling is the sign of the moment before seduction, and thus the male stands in proximity to the female, but not touching her. The sexualized touch is prepared but has not been consummated. Once it is (if it is, and that is the ambiguity of this image), the course is inevitable—at least for the female—for "seduction must, almost as a matter of course, lead to prostitution," as W. M. Sanger observed in 1859 (322).

The appropriate end of the prostitute is suicide, "deserted to a life of misery, wretchedness, and poverty . . . terminated by self-destruction" (Tait 96). This is her penalty for permitting herself to be seduced by immoral men, to be infected, and thus to spread infection to—innocent men? This is the chain of argument that places the seducer and the prostitute beyond the boundary that defines polite sexuality: a sexuality that led Victoria's prime minister William Gladstone, who was fascinated with prostitutes, to attempt their conversion at his own hearthside and to simultaneously solicit sexual contact with them. The seducer and the prostitute are the defining borders of diseased sexuality. The seducer is parallel to the image of Bram Stoker's

*Dracula* (1897), for in the act of seduction he transforms the innocent female into a copy of himself, just as Dracula's victims become vampires. She becomes the prostitute as seductress, infecting other males as he has infected her with the disease of licentiousness (and not incidentally, syphilis). Sexuality, disease, and death are linked in the act of seduction. As a contemporary reformist source noted, in this image "the Deceiver recognizes the Deceived . . . he, the tempter, the devil's agent. . . . Men, seducers, should learn from this picture and fallen women, look at this, and remember 'the wages of sin is death' " (Tait 96). The sign of transmission of the disease of polluted (and polluting) sexuality, the sexualized touch, is as of this moment missing in Elmore's icon of seduction. In Thomas Hood's widely cited poem on the death of the prostitute, "The Bridge of Sighs" (1844), the sexualized touch, the source of disease, becomes the forgiving touch of the dead prostitute:

> Take her up instantly,
> Loving not loathing.
> Touch her not scornfully;
> Think of her mournfully,
> Gently and humanly;
> Not of the stains of her,
> All that remains of her
> Now is pure womanly . . .
>   (Hood 1: 27)

Death seems to purge the dead prostitute of her pollution in a series of images of dead prostitutes in the nineteenth century, from George Frederic Watt's *Found Drowned* (1845–50) through to the ubiquitous death mask of the *Beautiful Dead Woman from the Seine* that decorated many bourgeois parlors in France and Germany during the fin de siècle.[1] The touching of the dead body is not merely a piteous gesture toward the "fallen," it is a permitted touching of the female, a not contagious, not infecting touch, a control over the dead woman's body.

Once the prostitute was dead by her own hand, it was the physician who could touch her. His role was to examine and dissect the body condemned to death by its fall from grace. And that body becomes the object of study, the corpse to be opened. For one of the favorite images of late nineteenth-century medical art is the unequal couple transmogrified into the image of the aged pathologist contemplating the exquisite body of the dead prostitute before he opens it. In the striking image by Enrique Simonet (1890) we are present at the moment when the body has been opened and the pathologist stares at the heart of the whore. What will be found in the body of these drowned women? Will it be the hidden truths of the nature of the woman, what women want, the answer to Freud's question to Marie Bonaparte? Will it be the biological basis of difference, the cell with its degenerate or potentially infectious nature that parallels the image of the female and its potential for destroying the male? Will it be the face of the Medusa, with all its castrating power? Remember that in that age of "syphiliphobia" the "Medusa" masks the infection hidden within the female. In Louis Raemaker's 1916 Belgian poster representing the temptation of the female as the source of the disease, much of the traditional imagery of the seductress can be found (fig. 1). Standing among rows of graves, wearing a black cloak and holding a skull that represents her genitalia, she is the essential femme fatale. But there is a striking fin-de-siècle addition to the image—for here "La Syphilis" is the Medusa. Her tendrils of hair, her staring eyes, present the viewer with the reason for the male's seduction—not his sexuality, but her vampirelike power to control his rationality. The Medusa is the genitalia of the female, threatening, as Sigmund Freud has so well demonstrated, the virility of the male, but also beckoning him to "penetrate" (to use Freud's word) into her mysteries.

What will be found in the body of these drowned women? If we turn to the German expressionist Gottfried Benn's 1912 description of the autopsy of a beautiful drowned girl, we get an ironic, twentieth-century answer to this question:

> The mouth of a girl, who had long lain in the reeds
> looked so gnawed upon.
> When they finally broke open her chest, the esophagus was so full of holes.
> Finally in a bower below the diaphragm
> they found a nest of young rats.
> One of the little sisters was dead.
> The others were living off liver and kidneys,
> drinking the cold blood, and had
> here spent a beautiful youth.
> And death came to them too beautiful and quick
> We threw them all into the water.
> Oh, how their little snouts squeaked!
>     (Benn 1: 11; my translation)

The physician-poet Benn ironically transfers the quality of the aesthetic ascribed to the beautiful dead prostitute to the dead and dying rats. What is found within the woman is the replication of herself: the source of disease, of plague, the harbor rats, nestled within the gut. The birthing of the rats is

Figure 1. A woman with spiderlike hair, wearing a black cloak, stands among rows of graves. She holds a skull in her hands in this powerful illustration of the evils of syphilis in Louis Raemaker's *L'Hécatombe. La Syphilis* (ca. 1916). National Library of Medicine, Bethesda, Maryland.

the act of opening the body, exposing the corruption hidden within. The physician's eye is always cast to examine and find the source of pathology, in the role assigned by society. Here again it is the male physician opening the body of the woman to discover the source of disease, here the plague, hidden within the woman's body.

But in the fantasy of the nineteenth century the physician could not remove the prostitute from the street. Only the whore could kill the whore.

Only the whore, and Jack. Killing and dismembering, searching after the cause of corruption and disease, Jack could kill the source of infection because he too was diseased. The paradigm for the relationship between Jack and the prostitutes can be taken from the popular medical discourse of the period: *Similia similibus curantur,* "like cures like," the motto of C. F. S. Hahnemann, the founder of homeopathic medicine. The scourge of the streets, the carrier of disease, can be eliminated only by one who is equally corrupt and diseased. And that was Jack.

Jack, as he called himself, was evidently responsible for a series of murders that raised the anxiety level throughout London to fever pitch in the cold, damp fall of 1888. The images of the murders in the London *Illustrated Police News* provide an insight into how the murderer was seen and also how the "real" prostitute, not the icon of prostitution or of seduction, was portrayed in mass art. The murders ascribed to Jack the Ripper all took place in the East End of London, an area that had been the scene of heavy Eastern European Jewish immigration. Who, within the fantasy of the thought collective, can open the body? Who besides the physician? No one but Jack, the emblem of human sexual perversion out of all control, out of all bounds. Jack becomes the sign of deviant human sexuality destroying life, the male parallel to the destructive prostitute. He is the representative of that inner force, hardly held under control, that has taken form—the form of Mr. Hyde. Indeed, an extraordinarily popular dramatic version of Robert Louis Stevenson's *Dr. Jekyll and Mr. Hyde* was playing in the West End while Jack (that not-so-hidden Mr. Hyde) terrorized the East End.

The images of the victims of "Jack"—ranging in number from four to twenty depending on which tabulation one follows—were portrayed as young women who had been slashed and mutilated. The Whitechapel murders most probably included Emma Smith (2 April 1888), Martha Tabram (7 August 1888), Mary Ann Nichols (31 August 1888), and Annie Chapman (8 September 1888). Elizabeth Stride and Catherine Eddowes were both murdered on 30 September 1888. But because of the sensibilities of even the readers of the *Illustrated Police News,* the mutilation presented is the mutilation of the face (as in the image of Annie Chapman). The reality, at least the reality that terrified the London of 1888, was that the victims were butchered. Baxter Philips, who undertook the postmortem description of Mary Ann Nichols, described the process: "The body had been completely disembowelled and the entrails flung carelessly in a heap on the table. The breasts had been cut off, hacked for no apparent purpose, and then hung on nails affixed to the walls of the room. Lumps of flesh, cut from the thighs and elsewhere, lay strewn about the room, so that the bones were exposed. As in some of the other cases, certain organs had been extracted, and, as they were missing, had doubtless been carried away" (cited in Parry 14).

The police photographs of the eviscerated prostitutes appeared at the time only within "scientific" sources such as Alexandre Lacassagne's 1889 study of sadism (fig. 2). In the public eye the prostitutes were their faces, the face of the prostitute in death. But the true fascination was with those "certain organs [that] had been extracted" and had "been carried away." The whore's body had not merely been opened; her essence, her sexuality, had been removed. These images are quite in contrast to those of the contemporary "Whitehall" murder, where a decapitated torso was discovered and the body reconstructed with limbs found throughout the city. The mutilated body was understood over the course of further killings to be one of Jack's victims, even though it contrasted with the bodies of the prostitutes he killed. The bodies of Jack's victims were opened and their viscera removed. Such sexual disfigurement, along with the amputation of the breasts of some of the victims, made it clear to both the police and the general public that his actions were sexually motivated. And indeed, most of the theories concerning Jack's identity assumed that he (or a close family member) had been infected with syphilis by a prostitute and was simply (if insanely) taking his revenge. But the vague contours of Jack the "victim" soon gave way to a very specific visual image of Jack.

"Jack" is the caricature of the Eastern Jew (fig. 3). Indeed, the official description was of a man "age 37, rather dark beard and moustache, dark jacket and trousers, black felt hat, spoke with a foreign accent" (Frayling 183). There appeared scrawled on the wall in Goulston Street, near the place where a blood-covered apron was discovered, the cryptic message: "The Juwes are The men That not be Blamed for nothing" (187). The image of the Jews as sexually different, the Other even in the killing of the Other, led to the arrest of John Pizer, "Leather Apron," a Polish-Jewish shoemaker (fig. 4). Pizer was eventually cleared and released, but a high proportion of the 130 men questioned in the Ripper case were Jews.

Sir Robert Anderson, the police official in charge of the case, noted in his memoir:

One did not need to be a Sherlock Holmes to discover that the criminal was a sexual maniac of a virulent type; that he was living in the immediate vicinity of the scenes of the murders; and that, if he was not living absolutely alone, his people knew of his guilt, and refused to give him up to justice. During my absence abroad the Police had made a house-to-house search for him, investigating the case of every man in the district whose circumstances were such that he could go

Figure 2. The police photograph of the mutilated corpse of Emma Smith reproduced in Lacassagne, *L'homme criminel* (1882). National Library of Medicine, Bethesda, Maryland.

and come and get rid of his blood-stains in secret. And the conclusion we came to was that he and his people were low-class Jews, for it is a remarkable fact that people of that class in the East End will not give up one of their number to Gentile justice. . . . I will only add that when the individual whom we suspected was caged in an asylum, the only person who had ever had a good view of the murderer at once identified him, but when he learned the suspect was a fellow-Jew he declined to swear to him. (356–57)

The claim that Jack the Ripper was a "sexual maniac" and a Jew led to repercussions with the East End community. When the body of Catherine Eddowes was found on 30 September outside the International Working Men's Educational Club by a Jew, a pogrom almost occurred in the East End, at least according to the *East London Observer* (15 October 1888; fig. 5). "On Saturday

Figure 3. The image of the Jewish Jack the Ripper from the *Illustrated Police News* (September 1888). Olin Library, Cornell University. Ithaca, New York. Used by permission.

the crowds who assembled in the streets began to assume a very threatening attitude towards the Hebrew population of the District. It was repeatedly asserted that no Englishman could have perpetrated such a horrible crime as that of Hanbury Street, and that it must have been done by a JEW—and forthwith the crowds began to threaten and abuse such of the unfortunate Hebrews as they found in the streets" (Frayling 189). The powerful association between the working class, revolutionaries, and the Jews combines to create the visualization of Jack the Ripper as a Jewish worker, marked by his stigmata of degeneration as a killer of prostitutes. Here Jack had to intervene. In one of his rhyming missives sent in 1889 to Sir Melville MacNaghten, chief of the Criminal Investigation Division at Scotland Yard, he wrote:

> I'm not a butcher, I'm not a Yid
> Nor yet a foreign skipper,
> But I'm your own light-hearted friend,
> Yours truly, Jack the Ripper.
>     (Kelly 14)

When during the 1890s the German playwright Frank Wedckind visualized his Jack the Ripper killing the archwhore Lulu, he represented him as a degenerate working-class figure: "He is a square-built man, elastic in his

Figure 4. The arrest of an Eastern Jew for the Whitechapel murders. *Illustrated Police News* (September 1888). Olin Library, Cornell University. Ithaca, New York. Used by permission.

movements, with a pale face, inflamed eyes, thick arched eyebrows, drooping moustache, sparse beard, matted sidewhiskers and fiery red hands with gnawed finger nails. His eyes are fixed on the ground. He is wearing a dark overcoat and a small round hat" (Wedekind 298). This primitive figure was quite in line with the views shared by the Italian forensic psychiatrist Cesare Lombroso and his French rival, Alexandre Lacassagne, as to the representative image (if not origin) of the criminal, but specifically the sadist. For the Germans, at least for liberals such as Wedekind, Jack was also seen as a member of the lumpenproletariat in reaction to the charge, made in 1894 in the anti-Semitic newspapers in Germany, that Jack was an Eastern European Jew functioning as part of the "international Jewish conspiracy" (Pulzer 6). But in Britain this image evoked a very specific aspect of the proletariat, that of London's East End, the Eastern Jew.

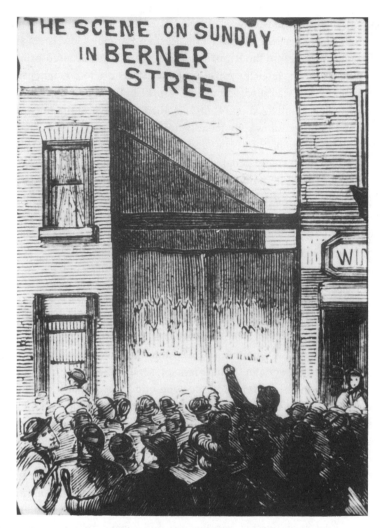

Figure 5. A mob threatens the East End Jewish community in response to the Whitechapel murders. *Illustrated Police News* (September 1888). Olin Library, Cornell University. Ithaca, New York. Used by permission.

But why Eastern European Jews? The charge of ritual murder, the murder of Christian women by Polish Jews, appeared in the *Times* during this period, but this was only a subissue or perhaps a more limited analogy to the events in Whitechapel. Nor can we simply recall the history of British anti-Semitism, from the Norwich pogrom of 1144, caused by the charge of the ritual murder of a child, to the King's Road murders of 1771, which were laid at the feet of the Jews. The "real" parallel to the fantasy about the Jewish Jack the

Ripper as a sexual monster was played out in the courts of London in the accusation of murder lodged against the Eastern European Jew Israel Lipski in 1887, the year before the Ripper murders. Lipski was accused of having murdered a pregnant Jewish woman by pouring nitric acid down her throat. Her exposed body was discovered with Lipski hiding under the bed. This case was widely publicized and found detailed coverage in the press of the day. Lipski's conviction was understood (at least by his supporters) as a sign of the prejudice against "foreign" Jews in London. Lipski was hanged in 1887. His case was widely debated; it was charged that he had been accused because he was an Eastern European Jew. Indeed, the most recent commentator on the case agrees that Lipski was most probably not give a truly fair trial because of his identity as a Jew (Friedland).

The search for Jack the Ripper was the search for an appropriate murderer for the Whitechapel prostitutes. The murderer had to be representative of an image of sexuality that was equally distanced and frightening. Thus the image of Jack the Ripper as the shochet, the ritual butcher, arose at a moment when there was a public campaign by the antivivisectionists in England and Germany against the "brutality" of the ritual slaughter of kosher meat.

This image of the Jewish Jack rested on a long association of the image of the Jew in the West with the image of the mutilated, diseased, different appearance of the genitalia. This mark of sexual difference was closely associated with the initial image of the syphilitic Jack. The Jew remains the representation of the male as outsider, the act of circumcision marking the Jewish male as sexually apart, as anatomically different. (It is important to remember that there is a constant and purposeful confusion throughout the late nineteenth and early twentieth centuries of circumcision with castration.) The prostitute is, as has been shown, the embodiment of the degenerate and diseased female genitalia in the nineteenth century. From the normative perspective of the European middle class, it is natural that the Jew and the prostitute must be in conflict and that the one "opens up" the other, since both are seen as "dangers" to the economy of the state, both fiscal and sexual. This notion of the association of the Jew and the prostitute is also present in the image of "spending" semen (in an illicit manner) that dominates the literature on masturbation in the eighteenth and early nineteenth centuries. For the Jew and the prostitute are seen as negating factors, outsiders whose sexual images represent all the dangers felt to be inherent in human sexuality. And to consciously destroy, indeed touch, the polluting force of the Other, one must oneself be beyond the boundaries of acceptability.

The linkage between Jew and prostitute is much older than the 1880s. This association is related to the image of the black and the monkey (two icons of "deviant" sexuality) in the second plate of Hogarth's *A Harlot's Progress* (fig. 6). Here Moll Hackabout, the harlot, has become the mistress of a wealthy London Jew. The Jew has been cheated by the harlot; her lover is about to leave the scene. But her punishment is forthcoming. She will be dismissed by him and begin her slow slide downward. Tom Brown, Hogarth's contemporary and the author of "A Letter to Madam ——, Kept by a Jew in Covent Garden," which may well have inspired the plate, concludes his letter on the sexuality of the Jew by asking the young woman "to be informed whether Aaron's bells make better music than ours" (Brown 200). It is this fascination with the sexual difference of the Jew, parallel to the sexual difference of the prostitute, that relates them even in death. Each possesses a sexuality different from the norm, a sexuality that is represented in the unique form of their genitalia.

The relationship between the Jew and the prostitute also has a social dimension. For both Jew and prostitute have but one interest, converting sex into money or money into sex. "So then," Brown writes to the lady, " 'tis neither circumcision nor uncircumcision that avails any thing with you, but money, which belongs to all religions" (Brown 200). The major relationship, as Tom Brown and Hogart outline, is a financial one; Jews buy specific types of Christian women, using their financial ability as a means of sexual control. "I would never have imagined you . . . would have ever chosen a gallant out of that religion which clips and diminishes the current coin of love, or could ever be brought to like those people that lived two thousand years on types and figures" (199).

By the end of the nineteenth century this linkage had become a commonplace in all of Christian Europe. In 1892 there reappeared in London an early nineteenth-century (1830s) pornographic "dialogue between a Jew and a Christian, a Whimsical Entertainment, lately performed in Duke's Palace," the *Adventures of Miss Lais Lovecock* (*Bagnio Miscellany* 54–55). This dialogue represents the Jew, and it represents him in a very specific manner. First, the Jew speaks in dialect. By 1888 the British Jewish community had become completely acculturated. With Disraeli's terms as prime minister, as well as with the Prince of Wales (later King Edward VII) attending the wedding of Leopold de Rothschild on 14 January 1881 at a London synagogue, the boundary between the "native" Jews and the "foreign" Jews had to be drawn. This explains the use of dialect, which in 1892 would point toward the Eastern Jew, toward Jack the Ripper, who could not command written English at least about the "Juwes." The text may well have reflected the image of the Jew in the 1830s, but it clearly had a very different set of associations after Jack the Ripper's appearance. The Jew, Isaac, describes

Figure 6. Moll Hackabout as the Jew's mistress, the second plate of William Hogarth's *A Harlot's Progress* (1731). Private collection, Ithaca, New York.

his seduction of his father's Jewish (and therefore, since all Jews are deviants in one way or another, hermaphroditic) maid, who has a "clitoris, which was hard and shaped like a penis," while he seduces the Christian prostitute Polly. She is described by him as having "little feet and ankles, I think of your pretty legs, and den I think of your snowy thighs, and den my fancy glowing hot got to de fountain of bliss, and dere I vill go immediately" (66). She is the object of the Jew's desire, for his women (servant girls or whores) are as sexually marginal as he is himself. But it is only for money that Polly is willing to ring "Aaron's bells," for "nothing under three hundred a year" (62). The prostitute is little more than a Jew herself. Both are on the margins of "polite" society. And as we know from the degeneration of Hogarth's Moll Hackabout following her relationship with the Jewish merchant, such sexuality in women leads to corruption and physical decay. The Jew, with all of his associations with disease, becomes the surrogate for all marginal males, males across the boundary from the (male) observer, males who, like women, can be the source of corruption, if not for the individual, then for the collective.

The association of the venality of the Jew with capital is retained even into the latter half of the twentieth century. In a series of British comic books from the 1980s in which an anthropomorphized phallus plays the central role, the Jew is depicted as masturbating, committing an "unnatural" act (whereas the other phalluses are depicted as having a potential female partner) while reading a financial journal. What is striking in these comics is that all the phalluses are circumcised (Joliffe and Mayle). This is a problem of contemporary culture. In the post–World War II decades circumcision became a commonplace—even among non-Jews—in the United States and (less so, but more prominently than before World War II) Great Britain. How then to differentiate between the Jew and the non-Jew, between the "deviant" and the "normal"? We are faced with a problem analogous to why George Eliot's eponymous character Daniel Deronda did not know he was a Jew. Did he ever look at his penis? Here the hidden is not marked upon the skin, for the skin hides rather than reveals. It is the Jew within that surfaces. Here, in seeing a financial journal as the source of power and therefore of sexual stimulation; in Eliot's novel, with the "natural" sexual attraction between the crypto-Jew Deronda and the beautiful Jewess Mirah Cohen. (Deronda never defines himself as sexually different, for his own body is the baseline that defines for him the sexually "normal." His circumcised penis is not a sign of difference until he understands himself to be a Jew.)

The image of the Jew revealed in his sexuality seems to be an accepted manner of labeling the image of the deviant. Even his phallus does not know for sure until he performs a "perverse" act. Here the icon is a reversal of the traditional image of the phallus as the beast out of control. In this image it is the man, not his phallus, who is bestial (read Jewish). The perversion of the Jew (and thus the "humor" of this depiction of the phallus) lies in his sexualized relationship with capital. This of course echoes the oldest and most basic calumny against the Jew, his avarice, an avarice for the possession of "things," of "money," which signals his inability to understand (and produce) anything of transcendent aesthetic value. The historical background to this is clear. Canon law forbade charging interest, which according to Thomas Aquinas was impossible, since money, not being alive, could not reproduce. Jews, in charging interest, treated money as a sexualized object. The Jew takes money, as does the prostitute, as a substitute for higher values, for love and beauty. And thus the Jew becomes the representative of the deviant genitalia, the genitalia not under the control of the moral, rational conscience.

But the image of the Jew as prostitute is not merely a reflection of the economic parallel between the sexuality of the Jew and that of the prostitute. That relationship also reveals the nature of the sexuality of both Jew and prostitute as diseased, as polluting. Just as the first image of Jack the Ripper was that of the victim of the prostitute, the syphilitic male, so too were the Jews closely identified with sexually transmitted diseases. For the Jew was also closely related to the spread and incidence of syphilis. This charge appeared in various forms, as in the anti-Semitic tractate *England under the Jews* (1901) by Joseph Banister, in which there is a fixation on the spread of "blood and skin diseases" (61). Such views had two readings. Banister's was the more typical. The Jews were the carriers of sexually transmitted diseases and spread them to the rest of the world. This view is to be found in Hitler's discussion of syphilis in *Mein Kampf,* and there he links it to the Jew, the prostitute, and the power of money: "Particularly with regard to syphilis, the attitude of the nation and the state can only be designated as total capitulation. . . . The cause lies, primarily, in our prostitution of love. . . . The Jewification of our spiritual life and mammonization of our mating instinct will sooner or later destroy our entire offspring" (247).

Hitler's views, like those of Banister and the earlier British anti-Semites, also linked Jews with prostitutes. Jews were the archpimps; Jews ran the brothels; Jews infected their prostitutes and caused the weakening of the national fiber. Indeed, according to Hitler, it was the realization of this very "fact" during the first few days of his stay in Vienna in 1907 that converted him to anti-Semitism. The hidden source of the disease of the body politic is the Jew, and his tool is the whore: "If you cut even cautiously into such a tumor, you found, like a maggot in a rotting body, often dazzled by the sudden light—a kike!" (57).

Such a view of the Jew as the syphilitic was not limited to the anti-Semitic fringe of the turn of the century. It was a view that possessed such power that even "Jewish" writers (writers who felt themselves stigmatized by the label of being "Jewish") subscribed to it. One such was Marcel Proust, whose uncomfortable relationship with his mother's Jewish identity haunted his life almost as much as did his gay identity. In Proust's *Remembrance of Things Past,* the series of novels written to recapture the world of the 1880s and 1890s, one of the central characters, Charles Swann, is a Jew who marries a courtesan. This link between Jew and prostitute is mirrored in Proust's manner of representing the sexuality of the Jew. For Proust, being Jewish is analogous to being gay—it is "an incurable disease" (2: 639). But what marks this disease for all to see? For in the *mentalité* of the turn of the century, syphilis in the male must be written on the skin, just as it is hidden within the sexuality of the female. Proust, who in the same volume discusses the signs and symptoms of syphilis with a detailed clinical knowledge, knows precisely what marks the sexuality of the Jew upon his physiognomy (2: 1086). It is seen upon his face as "ethnic eczema" (1: 326). It is a sign of sexual and racial corruption as surely as the composite photographs of the Jew that Francis Galton made at the time reveal the true face of the Jew (Jacobs xl).

This mark upon the face is Hitler's and Banister's sign of the Jew's sexual perversion. It is the infectious nature of that "incurable disease," the sexuality of the Jew, Proust's Jew fixated upon his courtesan. (This is an interesting reversal of one of the subthemes of Zola's *Nana*. There Nana, like Moll Hackabout, is first the mistress of a Jew whom she, quite easily reversing the role of Jack the Ripper, bankrupts and drives to suicide.) The Jew's sexuality, the sexuality of the polluter, is written on his face in the skin disease that announces the difference of the Jew. For Proust, all his Jewish figures (including Swann and Bloch) are in some way diseased, and in every case this image of disease links the racial with the sexual, much as Proust's image of the homosexual links class (or at least the nobility) with homosexuality. ("Homosexuality" is a "scientific" label for a new "disease" coined by Karoly Benkert in 1869 at the very same moment in history when the new "scientific" term for Jew hating, "anti-Semitism," was created by Wilhelm Marr.) The image of the infected and infecting Jew also had a strong political as well as personal dimension for Proust. For the ability to "see" the Jew who was trying to pass as a non-Jew within French society is one of the themes of the novels, a theme that, after the Dreyfus affair, had overt political implications. Seeing the Jew was seeing the enemy within the body politic, seeing the force for destruction. And Proust's "racial" as well as sexual identity was tied to his sense of the importance of class and society in defining the individual. Thus Proust's arch-Jew Swann was visibly marked by him as the heterosexual syphilitic, as what he was not (at least in his fantasy about his own sexual identity).

The second model existing at the close of the nineteenth century that represented the relation between Jews and sexually transmitted disease postulated exactly the opposite—that Jews had a statistically lower rate of syphilitic infection—because they had become immune to it through centuries of exposure. Syphilis was understood at the close of the nineteenth century as an African disease predating Columbus. In the medical literature of the period, reaching across all of European medicine, it was assumed that Jews had a notably lower rate of infection. In a study of the incidence of tertiary lues (the final stage of the syphilitic infection) undertaken in the Crimea between 1904 and 1929, the Jews had the lowest consistent rate of infection (Balaban and Molotschek). In an eighteen-year longitudinal study H. Budel demonstrated the extraordinarily low rate of tertiary lues in Estonia during the prewar period (Budel). All these studies assumed that biological difference as well as the social difference of the Jews was at the root of their seeming "immunity."

Jewish scientists also had to explain the "statistical" fact of their immunity to syphilis. Studying the rate of tertiary lues during World War I, the Jewish physician Max Sichel addressed the general view that the relative lower incidence of infection among Jews resulted from their sexual difference (Sichel). He responded—out of necessity—with a social argument. The Jews, according to Sichel, evidenced lower incidence because of their early marriage and the patriarchal structure of the Jewish family, but also because of their much lower rate of alcoholism. They were therefore, according to the implicit argument, more rarely exposed to the infection of prostitutes, whose attractiveness was always associated with the greater loss of sexual control in the inebriated male. He made the relation between these two "social" diseases into a cause for the higher incidence among other Europeans. The Jews, because they were less likely to drink heavily, were less likely to be exposed to both the debilitating effects of alcohol (which increase the risk for tertiary lues) and the occasion for infection. There is a hidden agenda in these comments. According to Sichel, the prostitute is the source of infection. And the prostitute is the offspring of alcoholic parents, according to one common theory of nineteenth-century psychopathology. If you have no Jewish alcoholics then you have no Jewish prostitutes, and thus the Jews are isolated from any charge of being the "source of pollution," one of the common calumnies lodged against them from the Middle Ages through the nineteenth century.

In 1927 H. Strauss looked at the incidence of syphilitic infection in his hospital in Berlin in order to demonstrate whether the Jews had a lower rate, but also to see (as in the infamous Tuskegee experiments among blacks in the United States [Jones]) whether they had "milder" forms of the disease because of their life-style or background. He found that Jews indeed had a much lower incidence of syphilis (while having an extraordinarily higher rate of hysteria) than the non-Jewish control group. He proposed that the disease might well have a different course in Jews than in non-Jews. The reason given by non-Jewish scientists was the inherited tendency of male Jews to be more "immune." Just as "Jewishness" was an inherited tendency, so too was the nature of a "Jewish sexuality," a sexuality so markedly different that some Jewish male infants were even born circumcised (Gilman)!

Both of these arguments saw the Jew as having a "special" relation to syphilis (through the agency of the prostitute) and carried on the association between the Jew and the prostitute. But this special relation could literally be seen on the Jew. Joseph Banister saw the Jews as bearing the stigmata of skin disease (as a model for discussing sexually transmitted disease): "If the gentle reader desires to know what kind of blood it is that flows in the Chosen People's veins, he cannot do better than take a gentle stroll through Hatton Garden, Maida Vale, Petticoat Lane, or any other London 'nosery.' I do not hesitate to say that in the course of an hour's peregrinations he will see more cases of lupus, trachoma, favus, eczema, and scurvy that he would come across in a week's wanderings in any quarter of the Metropolis" (Banister 61). Banister is fixated on the nose of the Jew, a not so subtle anti-Semitic reference to the circumcised and, thus, diseased, phallus. For the "nose" is the iconic representation of the Jew's phallus throughout the nineteenth century. Indeed, Jewish social scientists, such as the British savant Joseph Jacobs, spend a good deal of their time denying the salience of "nostrility" as a sign of the racial cohesion of the Jews (Jacobs xxxii–xxxiii). It is clear that for Jacobs (as for Wilhelm Fliess in Germany) the nose is the displaced locus of anxiety associated with the marking of the male Jew's body through circumcision, given the debate about the "primitive" nature of circumcision and its reflection on the acculturation of the Western Jew during the late nineteenth century (Sulloway 147–58).

Jews bear their diseased sexuality on their skin. Indeed, they bear the salient stigma of the black skin of the syphilitic. For at least in the Latin tradition, syphilis (like leprosy, another disease understood to be sexually transmitted) was understood to turn one black, the syphilitic rupia. Francisco Lopez de Villalobos, court physician to Charles V, in his long poem on syphilis of 1498, observes that the "color of the skin becomes black" when one has the "Egyptian disease," the plague of boils recounted in the account of the Jews' escape from slavery (Villalobos 159–61). Blackness marks the sufferer from disease, sets him outside the world of purity and cleanliness.

The Jews are black, according to nineteenth-century racial science, because they are "a mongrel race which always retains this mongrel character." So says Houston Stewart Chamberlain, arguing against the "pure" nature of the Jewish race (1: 388–89). Jews had "hybridized" with blacks in Alexandrian exile, and they were exposed to the syphilis that becomes part of their nature. They are, in an ironic review of Chamberlain's work by the father of modern Yiddish scholarship, Nathan Birnbaum, a "bastard" race whose origin was caused by their incestuousness. But the Jews were also seen as black (Birnbaum 2: 201). Adam Gurowski, a Polish noble, "took every light-colored mulatoo for a Jew" when he first arrived in the United States in the 1850s (Gurowski 177). Jews are black because they are different, because their sexuality is different, because their sexual pathology is written upon their skin.

Gurowski's contemporary Karl Marx associates leprosy, Jews, and syphilis in his description of his archrival Ferdinand Lassalle (in 1861): "Lazarus the leper, is the prototype of the Jews and of Lazarus-Lassalle. But in our Lazarus, the leprosy lies in the brain. His illness was originally a badly cured case of syphilis" (Marx 459). Jews = lepers = syphilitics = prostitutes = blacks. This chain of association presents the ultimate rationale for the Jewish Jack the Ripper, for the diseased destroy the diseased, the corrupt the corrupt. They corrupt in their act of touching, of seducing, the pure and innocent, creating new polluters. But they are also able in their sexual frenzy to touch and kill the sexual pariahs, the prostitutes, who like Lulu at the close of Frank Wedekind's play (and Alban Berg's opera) go out to meet them, seeking their own death. Being unclean, being a version of the female genitalia (with his amputated genitalia), the male Jew is read (as Jack's Viennese contemporary Otto Weininger had read him) as really nothing but a type of female. The parish can thus touch and kill the pariah, the same destroy the same. Wedekind's Lulu dies not as a suicide but as the victim of the confrontation between two libidinal forces—the unbridled, degenerate sexuality of the male and the sexual chaos of the sexually emancipated female. But die she does, and Jack leaves the stage, having washed his hands like Pontius Pilate, ready to kill again.

## Notes

1. The image of the dead woman is a basic trope within the art and literature of the nineteenth century; see Bronfen. On the general background of the fascination with and representation of death in the West see Ariès, as well as Praz, McManners, and Dijkstra.

## Works Cited

Anderson, Robert. "The Lighter Side of My Official Life." *Blackwood's Magazine* 187 (1910): 356–67.

Ariès, Philippe. *The Hour of Our Death*. Trans. Helen Weaver. New York: Knopf/ Random House, 1981.

*Bagnio Miscellany Containing the Adventures of Miss Lais Lovecock*. . . . London: Printed for the Bibliopolists, 1892.

Balaban, N., and A. Molotschek. "Progressive Paralyse bei den Bevölkerungen der Krim." *Allgemeine Zeitschrift für Psychiatrie* 94 (1931): 373–83.

Banister, Joseph. *England under the Jews.* 1901. 3rd ed. London: [J. Banister], 1907.

Benn, Gottfried. *Sämtliche Werke.* Stuttgart: Klett-Cotta, 1986.

Birnbaum, Nathan. "Über Houston Stewart Chamberlain." *Ausgewählte Schriften zur jüdischen Frage.* 2 vols. Czernowitz: Birnbaum und Kohut, 1910.

Bronfen, Elisabeth. *Over Her Dead Body: Death, Femininity and the Aesthetic.* New York: Routledge, 1992.

Brown, Tom. *Amusements Serious and Comical and Other Works.* Ed. Arthur L. Hayward. London: Routledge, 1927.

Budel, H. "Beitrag zur vergleichenden Rassenpsychiatrie." *Monatsschrift für Psychiatrie und Neurologie* 37 (1915): 199–204.

Chamberlain, Houston Stewart. *Foundations of the Nineteenth Century.* Trans. John Lees. 2 vols. London: John Lane, 1910.

Dijkstra, Bram. *Idols of Perversity: Fantasies of Feminine Evil in Fin-de-Siècle Culture.* New York: Oxford UP, 1986.

Frayling, Christopher. "The House That Jack Built: Some Stereotypes of the Rapist in the History of Popular Culture." *Rape.* Ed. Sylvana Tomaselli and Roy Porter. Oxford: Blackwell, 1986.

Freud, Sigmund. "Notes on Medusa's Head." 1940. *The Standard Edition of the Complete Psychological Works (SE).* Trans. James Strachey. 24 vols. 1953–74. London: Hogarth, 1986. 18: 273–74.

Friedland, Martin L. *The Trials of Israel Lipski: A True Story of a Victorian Murder in the East End of London.* New York: Beaufort, 1984.

Gilman, Sander L. "The Indelibility of Circumcision." *Koroth* 9 (1991): 806–17.

Greg, W. R. "Prostitution." *Westminster Review* 53 (1850): 456.

Gurowski, Adam G. de. *America and Europe.* New York: Appleton, 1857.

Hitler, Adolph. *Mein Kampf.* Trans. Ralph Manheim. Boston: Houghton Mifflin, 1943.

Hood, Thomas. *The Complete Poetical Works of Thomas Hood.* 4 vols. New York: Putnam, 1869.

Jacobs, Joseph. *Studies in Jewish Statistics, Social, Vital, and Anthropometric.* London: Nutt, 1891.

Joliffe, Gray, and Peter Mayle. *Man's Best Friend.* London: Pan, 1984.

Jones, James H. *Bad Blood: The Tuskegee Syphilis Experiment.* New York: Free Press, 1981.

Kelley, Alexander, and Colin Wilson. *Jack the Ripper: A Bibliography and Review of the Literature.* London: Association of Assistant Librarians, 1973.

Lacassagne, Alexander. *L'homme criminel comparé à l'homme primitif.* Lyons: Association Typographique, 1882.

———. *Vacher l'éventreur et les crimes sadiques.* Lyons: Storck, 1889.

*The Language of Flowers.* London: Milner, 1849.

Lombroso, Cesare, and Guglielmo Ferrero. *La donna deliquente: La prostituta a la donna normale.* Turin: Roux, 1893.

Marx, Karl. *The Letters of Karl Marx*. Ed. and trans. Saul K. Padover. Englewood Cliffs, NJ: Prentice-Hall, 1979.

McManners, John. *Death and the Enlightenment: Changing Attitudes to Death among Christians and Unbelievers in Eighteenth-Century France*. Oxford: Clarendon, 1981.

Nead, Lynda. "Seduction, Prostitution, Suicide: *On the Brink* by Alfred Elmore." *Art History* 5 (1982): 309–22.

Nelkin, Dorothy, and Sander L. Gilman. "Placing the Blame for Devastating Disease." *Social Research* 55 (1988): 361–78.

Parry, Michael, ed. *Jack the Knife: Tales of Jack the Ripper*. London: Mayflower, 1975.

Praz, Mario. *The Romantic Agony*. Trans. Angus Davidson. Cleveland: World, 1956.

Proust, Marcel. *Remembrance of Things Past*. Trans. C. K. Scott Moncrieff and Terence Kilmartin. 3 vols. Harmondsworth, England: Penguin, 1986.

Pulzer, Peter. *The Rise of Political Anti-Semitism in Germany and Austria*. London: Halban, 1988.

Sanger, William M. *The History of Prostitution: Its Extent, Causes, and Effects throughout the World*. New York: Medical Publishing, 1927.

Sichel, Max. "Die Paralyse der Juden in sexuologischer Beleuchtung." *Zeitschrift für Sexualwissenschaft* 7 (1919–20): 986–1104.

Strauss, H. "Erkrankungen durch Alkohol und Syphilis bei den Juden." *Zeitschrift für Demographie und Statistik der Juden* 4 (1927): 33–39.

Sulloway, Frank J. *Freud: Biologist of the Mind*. New York: Basic, 1979.

Tait, William, *Magdalenism: An Inquiry into the Extent, Causes, and Consequences of Prostitution in Edinburgh*. Edinburgh: Rickard, 1840.

Villalobos, Francisco Lopez de. *El somario de la medicina con un tratado sobre las pestiferas bubas*. Ed. María Teresa Herrera. Salamanca: Instituto de Historia de la Medicina Española, 1973.

Walkowitz, Judith R. *Prostitution and Victorian Society: Women, Class, and the State*. Cambridge: Cambridge UP, 1980.

Wedekind, Frank. *Five Tragedies of Sex*. Trans. Frances Fawcett and Stephen Spender. New York: Theatre Arts Books, n.d.

Weininger, Otto. *Geschlecht und Charakter*. Vienna: Braumüller, 1903.

■

# Representing Sati: Continuities and Discontinuities

## *Rajeswari Sunder Rajan*

### I

As "the woman who dies," the sati eludes full representation.[1] The examination of some texts of sati that I undertake in this essay leads to the realization that it is, ironically, through death that the subject-constitutive "reality" of woman's being is created at certain historical junctures. The construction of the Hindu widow's subjectivity in terms of sati that these texts propose is a foreclosure of her existential choices; but to identify the woman as "widow" is already to have defined her proleptically. Around the subject position that is thus cleared for her in terms of death—her own, her husband's—various other positions, dictated by ideology and politics, irresistibly come to range themselves. I trace in this essay the intertwining of death, gender, and the politics of representation as it shapes the subject of sati.

My focus will be on some texts of colonial and contemporary (post-Independence) India that map out the discursive field of sati. They have in common, as I shall try to show, the following features: the identification of sati as a gendered issue; hence the definition of the widow as exclusively the *subject* of sati (conceptualized only as one who chooses to die or is forced

I am grateful to Tejaswini Niranjana, Uma Chakravarty, and Kamala Visweswaran for their attempts to save me from errors, ambiguities, and mistakes of fact and interpretation in this essay. Any that remain are my own responsibility. Grateful thanks also go to Sarah Goodwin and Elisabeth Bronfen for their editorial guidance.

A version of this essay is appearing simultaneously in my book *Real and Imagined Women: Postcolonialism and the Female Subject* (London: Routledge, 1993).

285

to die); and finally, a pronounced ambivalence toward the practice.[2] It is necessary, nevertheless, to mark within this discursive field the gradual but significant *changes* from colonial history to the postcolonial present, especially as they relate to the question of female subjectivity, and to note the *divergences* between British (or, broadly, European) attitudes toward sati and the indigenous, mainly liberal/reformist adoption and adaptation of these.

In the concluding part of the chapter I offer, by way of contrast, an analysis of the classical Tamil epic the *Shilappadikaram*, to point to what seems to me the entirely different ideological investments that are made in indigenous, precolonial representations of sati—so that it is possible to suggest that a major paradigm shift occurred at the point where a specifically colonial discourse on sati began to emerge and then gain ground.[3] The identification of sati as a woman's issue (as a practice that reflected women's status in society), and the consequent focus upon the sati's subjectivity only in terms of her willingness or reluctance to die, may be historicized as an aspect of the colonial and postcolonial discourses of sati. This occurs when we are able to recognize that, by contrast, in precolonial periods and cultures (i.e., in ancient, medieval, or Islamic "India") sati, though always an act of suicide specific to women, subsumed gender within other social categories— of class, community, region, or nation—of which women were treated as representative members. In this construction of the widow's subjectivity, every act of sati is an expression of choice on the part of the woman (but such representations have also, invidiously, informed recent Hindu fundamentalist defenses of sati). More crucially, the woman who does *not* commit sati is equally, if often implicitly, expressing choice—an aspect of "choosing" that nowhere figures in later representations.

Since I have risked an oversimplified contrast in the interest of fore-grounding a thesis, several clarifications and qualifications are in order. In the first place, the "precolonial past" of India is by no means a single, homogeneous period: it comprises several millennia of civilization, within which sati (which some scholars attribute to Dravidian cultures that predate the Aryan invasion of India) has had widely differing manifestations at different times and places. So any single notion of "sati in precolonial India" is only a broad generalization about a conceptual paradigm rather than an indication of invariable or prescriptive ritual.

In the second place, it is not my intention to read the various representations as unmediated reflections of different "realities": such a reading would lead one to the invidious distinction between "authentic" (voluntary) and "inauthentic" (forced) sati that nationalist and contemporary fundamentalist social scientists and religious leaders in India postulate, which corresponds to the distinction between sati in an early "golden age" of Hinduism and sati in "Kaliyuga," or the fallen age of the recent past. Such an idealized history is in danger of validating the concept of sati while condemning only its practice, and thereby reinforcing its ideological valorization. I must therefore repeat that by "representations" I mean not "representations of reality," but autonomous and paradigmatic conceptual structures.

Finally, I do not undertake here a history of sati. Such a history is yet to be written. The dialectical relation between "reality" and its representations, between history (itself a text but not reducible to it) and the "texts" of sati, remains unexplored here. Outside the circuit of ideology-narrative representations that I trace here lies (we cannot escape the reminder) the "reality" of a woman's death, which they both occlude and deploy in different ways. Colonial representations of sati, for instance, acquired force and materiality when they shaped colonial policy—precisely because they were offered as representations *of reality*. Therefore "history" is the always present subtext of my argument, and the readings of the handful of representative texts that I propose here are intended as a contribution to the historical enterprise.

My discussion in the following sections begins with an exposition of three exemplary ideological paradigms that structure the texts of sati in the nineteenth and twentieth centuries; I then offer a historical "placing" of contemporary feminist critiques of the colonial discourse on sati; and I conclude with some tentative observations on the representation of women in precolonial indigenous literatures, focusing on the *Shilappadikaram*.

## II

The abolition of sati in 1829 was the first major legislation of the East India Company's administration in India. That it—like the series of laws that were subsequently enacted on behalf of women—served as the moral pretext for intervention and the major justification for colonial rule itself does not have to be argued further.[4] What is of concern here is how the colonial imagination seized upon and ordered the self-representation of such an administrative procedure: not merely, as Gayatri Spivak has succinctly formulated it, as a case of "white men . . . saving brown women from brown men" ("Can the Subaltern Speak?" 121), but as an actual narrative scenario of *a* white man saving *a* brown woman from a mob of brown men. In other words, it is the trope of *chivalry* that provides the contours of the scenario.

Whether the institution of chivalry in medieval and Renaissance Europe had an actual material basis or was nothing more than a literary invention, historians seem to agree that the ideology of knighthood was profoundly influential in constructing and sustaining actual structures of power based on class (ruler and vassal, as in feudal society), gender (lady and knight, as in the courtly love tradition), or religion (the church and its followers, as in the Crusades against Islamic "infidels"). It created reciprocal bonds of duty and obligation between the two parties that mediated relations of power and dependence. Further, chivalry, even while it formed and authorized the class, gender, and racial/religious superiority of the knight, also provided the young male of an aspiring lower aristocracy the means of upward social mobility at a historically transitional period; in other words, it was both a birthright and a career.[5] How eminently transferable such a concept is to the context of colonization is obvious. Large numbers of British young men, in the administrative, judicial, military, trading, and education services of colonial rule, or in missionary orders, found themselves unexpectedly authorized in the exercise of power. But they also discovered that they had to undergo rites of initiation into it. For the colonizer's racial superiority, however flagrant skin color or the appurtenances of power may have rendered it, had also to be demonstrated by acts of valor and authority.[6] It was this expectation that made intervention in the custom of sati both a test and a legitimation of British rule.[7]

The two texts I invoke here, Jules Verne's adventure tale *Around the World in Eighty Days* (1873) and M. M. Kaye's novel *The Far Pavilions* (1978), reproduce the ideological contours of the trope of chivalry in their representation of British India. Jules Verne's popular story is the account of an eccentric English clubman, Phineas Fogg; and in the portion of the narrative that covers his journey across India, from Bombay on the west coast to Calcutta on the east, Fogg manages to rescue a young princess from sati in the jungles of central India. In conformity with what had by then developed into a stereotype, the widow is young, beautiful, and a princess; the dead husband is old, ugly, and a king; the other villains are a bloodthirsty mob and a cabal of scheming Brahmans; and the rescue itself is an act of chivalry, combining daring adventure with the humanitarian gesture.

Sati, as one can see from the example of this late nineteenth-century French novel, continued to exercise the European imagination long after it was legally abolished by the 1829 act. It could continue to be regarded as one of the "realities" of "India" because the division of the country into "British" India and the princely "native" states meant that sati's legal abolition could be officially enforced only in the former. Hence the necessity for heroics in the 1872 escapade of Fogg and Company. With the growing dominion of British rule (India was taken over by the Crown in 1858), the native states were reduced to mere pockets that were regarded as backward ("medieval") and decadent, in contrast to the provinces of "enlightened" British rule.[8] The sati in *Around the World* is planned by the natives as a consciously transgressive act, a horrible ritual, to be performed in a clearing in the jungle of a native state; and the "heart of darkness" is penetrated by the band of adventurers who then emerge from it into light, the railways, British-administered provinces, and safety, with the rescued Indian princess in tow.[9]

The same demarcation of two worlds is emphasized in *The Far Pavilions,* whose hero, Ashton Pelham-Martyn, is a conflict-ridden product of the two cultures. But these opposed worlds are not only those of "Britain" and "India," but also of "British" India (the North-West Frontier provinces), and "native" India (the kingdoms of Gulkote and Bhithor); and Pelham-Martyn's constant crossings over from one to the other are intended to emphasize the contrast between the two. One is the area of light, the other an area of darkness; the one is represented by the club and the army barracks, the other by labyrinthine palace interiors. Within the first world the hero is able to develop uncomplicated homoerotic relationships, with a British army fellow officer as well as a Pathan "subedar," whereas in the other he is caught up in a frustrated romantic affair with a half-caste Indian princess. His British life is the "open" life of war and heroism, his "native" experiences involve him in intrigue and treachery. And most strikingly, the position of women is marked differently in the two worlds: the English belle, Belinda, is a flirt, while the Indian princesses are forced into marriage and then sati.

*The Far Pavilions* describes two major historical events, the Indian Mutiny of 1857 and the Second Afghan war of 1878, and spans the years between them. The "scene" of sati and the rescue is one of the climaxes of the book, the one that concludes the hero's involvement in native India with marriage to the princess Anjuli, whom he has rescued. The other climax is the storming of the Residency in Kabul, after which he makes his own "separate peace" and wanders off into the sunset in search of the no-man's-land of the "far pavilions." We must not forget that *The Far Pavilions* is a project of the late 1970s postempire, pre-Thatcher Britain, a book that has both marked and in a sense even inaugurated the whole complex cultural phenomenon now labeled "Raj nostalgia." Such a book would not have been complete without a scene of sati; but it would also have been expected to display a self-conscious liberal rectitude about the imperialist mission—which it does.

This is why the clear outlines of the scenario of "rescue" are somewhat blurred. The "rescue" is preceded by a brief history of sati, its origins and practices, provided by Ashton's Indian friend Sarji. With this friend Ashton also engages in a debate about sati, and Sarji's "native" views are allowed space: for the Indian nobleman death is a matter of little consequence, conjugal love is admirable, the women wish to die, faith is not to be mocked—and did not the West have its witch burnings? But the last word is allowed to Ashton: "Well if we have done nothing else, at least we can mark up one thing to our credit—that we put a stop to *that* particular horror" (618).

The rescue itself is in one sense not that: the princess Anjuli whom Ashton sets out to rescue is finally saved not from death but from blinding and incarceration (the rumor of her sati turns out to be false) while the queen, her half-sister Shushila, who actually wishes to die, is in fact not saved but only shot dead by Ashton at Anjuli's insistence so that she may be saved the horror of death by fire. Ashton's heroism is complicated by issues of morality and by considerations of the pragmatic costs of the enterprise. The moral issues include his guilt over the killing of Shushila (which is compared to the mercy killing of his wounded—and much loved—horse Dagobaz): "But then Shushila was not an animal: she was a human being, who had decided of her own free will to face death by fire and thereby achieve holiness: and he, Ash, had taken it upon himself to cheat her of that" (778). The pragmatic costs include his sorrow over the loss of his three loyal Indian friends, Sarji, Manilal, and Govind, who die while escaping.

The analogy with knight-errantry is explicitly drawn but is ironically repudiated immediately after (780). British officialdom, whose assistance Ashton first invokes to prevent the satis, is finally impotent and lacking in political will, so that the friends who finally help him effect the rescue are Indian. In spite of these complexities, the ideological core remains intact. *The Far Pavilions* retains the main structural aspects, and the ideologemes they encode, that we notice in *Around the World in Eighty Days:* the same actors; the discrediting of the woman's conjugal love as a possible motive for the sati; the suggestion of an actual or potential romance between the rescuer and the rescued; the representation of the rescue action as individual enterprise ("adventure") rather than official intervention; the establishment of a disinterested good through the act in a climate of benightedness. Ashton's scruples and his partisanship toward Indians therefore only embellish his knight-errantry, exemplifying both noblesse oblige and chivalric love.[10]

These texts record the progressive consolidation of what has come to be an essentially fixed British attitude to sati. By foregrounding Hindu women as passive and unresisting victims of Hindu patriarchy, as these texts do, it could be established beyond argument that the women were in need of saving.[11] However, the possibility that some widows might have *wished* to die as an act of conjugal love persisted as a doubt and gave rise to other views. This possibility is given some cursory credence in Ashton's self-questioning: "He had interfered in something that was a matter of faith and a very personal thing; and he could not even be sure that Shushila's convictions were wrong, for did not the Christian calendar contain the names of many men and women who had been burned at the stake for their beliefs, and acclaimed as saints and martyrs?" (778) It is no idle question. In the next section I examine how the conceptual paradigm of Christian martyrdom accommodated the unsettling possibility that the widow "chose" her death.

## III

The positive view of sati—with its flip underside—had popular currency, as this mid-nineteenth century jingle advertising Maspero Egyptian cigarettes suggests:

Calm in the early morning
Solace in time of woes,
Peace of the hush of twilight,
Balm ere my eyelids close.
This will Masperos bring me,
Asking naught in return,
With only a Suttee's passion
To do their duty and burn.

The jingle is accompanied by an illustration of a burning cigarette in an ashtray: appearing in the swirls of smoke rising from the cigarette is the shrouded figure of the sati, suggestive simultaneously of a Christian martyr and of a genie from a magic lamp awaiting orders. The commodification of the sati's self-sacrifice effectively eclipses her subjectivity.

Even as the Indian widow's death with her husband was elevated to fit into the more recognizable paradigm of religious martyrdom, it was also, less admiringly, trivialized as a form of feudal—or "native"—subservience, an act of unthinking if not actually deluded loyalty. Therefore the two views of the sati—as a woman forced to die and as a woman who chooses to die—did not necessarily have to collide. [12] The perception that Hindu women were victims was the basis for the establishment of sati as a woman's issue, as I noted earlier; it provoked an implicit comparison of their devalued social position with the freedom and privileges of British women, thus offering further proof of the superiority of British civilization.

But the British women's movement was gaining ground at home even as British rule was being consolidated in the colonies, and its members were denying the superior advantages ascribed to their status in British society. It is in the face of this conflict that the powerful ideology of the family as the "woman's sphere" was assiduously developed on behalf of women (see Sangari). Within this ideological structure the Indian widow as *subject* of sati could be selectively admired as exemplifying chastity and fidelity—

important components of the model of behavior that was being constructed for the Englishwoman at "home." Thus sati, whatever subject position was assigned to the Hindu widow, could be usefully fed into different ideological conjunctures.

These procedures of subjectification are less transparent in the literary text. A complex and suggestive ambivalence toward the sati can be located in the following passage from Charles Dickens's *Dombey and Son* (1848), which serves as my exemplary text in this section.

Susan Nipper, Florence Dombey's personal maid, is seen upbraiding Mr. Dombey for his ill-treatment of Florence; and she describes thus her own courage and determination in confronting the formidable man: "I may not be an Indian widow Sir and I am not and I would not so become but if I once made up my mind to burn myself alive, I'd do it! And I've made up my mind to go on!" (704). In this startling metaphor, Susan's simultaneous disavowal and embrace of the act of sati is characteristically ambivalent: however *like* an Indian widow Susan may be, she "would not . . . become" one; but at the same time the qualities of determination and courage that motivate her are attributed to the Indian widow as well. Susan's allusion suggests that sati could be raised above its cultural and gender specificity to express, in popular usage, any kind of excessive zeal. Susan had earlier sought another analogy to convey her loyalty: "She's the blessedest and dearest angel is Miss Floy . . . the more that I was torn to pieces Sir the more I'd say it though I may not be a Fox's Martyr" (703). This conflation of sati with Christian martyrdom is a familiar cognitive procedure.

But the invocation has other implications in this narrative. For *Dombey and Son* is a profound study of marital discord, and one that is remarkably sympathetic to the wronged wife. Dickens's discomfort about the particular *form* that Edith Dombey's disloyalty toward her husband eventually takes— sexual infidelity—is well known (so much so that he does not permit actual adultery to take place: Edith defends her honor at knifepoint!). The allusion to sati, occurring at the precise juncture in the narrative when she is planning her elopement with Carker, is a brilliant irony. Susan's own blindness to this application of her metaphor—which she has displaced from conjugal love to feudal loyalty—is no less striking.[13] Between the actual English wife of the narrative (who plans to leave a living husband) and the figurative Indian widow, transiently evoked as a trope in its discourse (and who will burn with a dead husband)—between these two female subjects an implicit contest of conjugal loyalty is set up, and cultural relativism (racial otherness) is effectively elided.

Two feminist critics have recently carried further the analysis of the ideological uses to which are put the interracial "contests" between women around the subject of sati. Nancy Paxton has astutely diagnosed how, in Flora Annie Steel's *On the Face of the Waters* (1897), "the sexual politics of colonial life in India" drive the British heroine, Kate Erlton, into emulation of and rivalry with her Hindu maidservant, Tara. Ultimately, "Kate concedes the contest of purity to Tara, accepting her assertion of the absolute cultural differences that separate the English and the Indian woman." After her husband dies Kate marries again; it is Tara who "triumphs" by dying a satilike death in the fires of war while helping Kate to escape.[14]

Steel's novel has a special significance because it is set in 1857, the year of the Indian Mutiny. This was an event in which the British women in India, because of the indignities and danger they publicly suffered at the hands of the native sepoys in the attack, became the objects of British men's protection. Thus they briefly came to occupy the same position as their Indian sisters, the women who committed sati, becoming, like them, both public spectacles and objects of salvation. Steel uses this historical irony to bring about a confrontation of the two women's worlds.

Such confrontations are of course stage-managed by an interested patriarchy. But an emergent feminist individualism could also deploy the "native" woman toward its own ends, as Gayatri Spivak has brilliantly demonstrated through her reading of three women's texts of the nineteenth century. She shows how another kind of struggle between the women of the two cultures may also have been the price paid for an "imperialist project cathected as civil-society-through-social-mission" ("Three Women's Texts" 244). In such a situation the emergence of the feminist individualist in the West cannot be an isolated development but is, instead, achieved through an imperialist project (that of "soul making") in which the "native female" must play a role. Spivak is talking of *Jane Eyre* (1848); and to counter the temptation to "see nothing there but the psychobiography of the militant female subject [Jane Eyre]" (245), she invokes Jean Rhys's *Wide Sargasso Sea* (1966), whose "powerful suggestion" is that "*Jane Eyre* can be read as the orchestration and staging of the self-immolation of Bertha Mason as 'good wife' " (259). *Jane Eyre* must be read in conjunction also with the history of sati in British India for such a reading to carry conviction. Given such a perspective, we might also be able to see how Tara's death in Steel's *On the Face of the Waters* is directly the cost of Kate's escape and of the Englishwoman's eventual "liberation" of consciousness from the excesses of martyrdom.

To sum up: in the colonial encounter the Hindu "good wife" is constructed as patriarchy's feminine ideal; she is offered simultaneously as a model and as a signifier of absolute cultural otherness, both exemplary and inimitable.

She is also, as Spivak points out, both indispensable (the justification for the imperialist project itself) and eminently dispensable (the sacrifice offered to an emergent Western feminist individualism). The colonial ambivalence toward sati was, in any case, productive for the achievement of the diverse goals of imperialism.

## IV

The three Indian texts I identify in the following discussion—Henry Derozio's long poem *The Fakeer of Jungheera* (1826), Rabindranath Tagore's short story "Saved" (1918), and Gautam Ghosh's film (1987) based on Kamal Kumar Majumdar's novel of the same name, *Antarjali jatra* (1965)—are representative of what I shall call briefly, for convenience, the male indigenous reformist/liberal position on women's issues. The abolition of sati, as well as other colonial laws on behalf of women in nineteenth-century India, was considerably aided by the growing spirit of reform among the indigenous male, increasingly Western-educated elite. The reform movements on behalf of women tied in with other issues relating to caste, education, and later nationalism. In the texts listed above, therefore, while sati is undeniably viewed as a "women's issue," its abolition is also located within a matrix of broadly reformist ideals.

Within the constraints of narrative, what is retained in these texts is the paradigm of rescue, shorn no doubt of its trappings of European chivalry, but exploiting several of its other significant structural elements. As in the colonial texts of imperialism described earlier, the dramatis personae are stereotyped, and their triangular relationship persists.

The break with the past that we associate with "modernity" is never a clean one. Among the indigenous reformers, a sentimental affiliation with indigenous "tradition," the early stirrings of nationalism, and an acute recognition of the resistance of social forces to change created a complex inheritance that considerably complicated the ideological stance toward issues relating to women. Thus, although sati could be condemned on both humanitarian and religious grounds, the prescribed alternative for widows, ascetic celibacy, was not so easily opposed. Therefore widow remarriage, long after it was made legally permissible, was a practically nonexistent practice.

It is this conflict of allegiances between "tradition" and "reform" that modifies the narrative paradigm of "rescue" that structures these texts. The crucial feature common to all of them is that, in spite of not submitting to sati, *the woman dies*. The inhibition about representing the rescued widow with an afterlife of romantic/sexual fulfillment with her rescuer is striking. What her death also implies is the impotence of her rescuer, an inability to work out her salvation that accurately reflects the perceived difficulties of social change (as opposed to the ease of official intervention). The failure also reflects an internalization of the notion that the colonized male was not "man enough" to protect his womankind. Ashis Nandy has suggested that the sudden and major changes brought about by colonial rule produced effects of alienation in the Hindu male, and that the strong defense of sati advanced by some members of the indigenous male elite was an attempt to recover its identity by enforcing traditional patriarchal norms. Finally, what these texts also offer is a more complex construction of the subjectivity of the heroine than the polarities of "damsel in distress"/"martyr" (i.e., she was forced to die/she chose to die) scripted by the text of imperialism. Nevertheless these are texts that are historically divergent, and we must plot their interaction with the texts of imperialism differently.

Henry Derozio's *The Fakeer of Jungheera* (1826) runs to a thousand lines, but it has a simple enough plot: the young and beautiful widow Nuleeni is about to be burned with her dead husband, a rich old man whom she was forced to marry. She is rescued from the sati site by her former lover, an outlaw masquerading as a holy man (a *fakeer*), and his band of robbers. They enjoy a brief idyll on his solitary island-rock Jungheera. Meanwhile Nuleeni's distraught father approaches the Muslim ruler, Prince Soorjah, and with his help raises an army to fight the fakeer and avenge his daughter's "dishonor." The lovers are forced to part. The father kills the outlaw in a fierce battle. Nuleeni finds her slain lover on the battlefield and dies of heartbreak in his arms.

Henry Louis Vivian Derozio (1809–31) was the first Indian poet of any note to write in English. He was a precocious East Indian youth (of mixed Portuguese-Indian and English blood) who produced most of his poetry, including the *Fakeer,* before he was twenty. Derozio's role in what came to be called the Young Bengal movement has been recognized by historians to have had a significant impact on the later Bengal "Renaissance," itself a forerunner of nationalist struggles. Among the "superstitions" of religion that Derozio attacked was sati, which was in the 1820s, the decade preceding its abolition, an issue of intense debate and division among the indigenous elite as well as between its members and the colonial administration.

But if we expect *The Fakeer of Jungheera* to be an antisati tract we will be disappointed. There is little or no comment on the cruelty of sati or on the social debasement of women that it reflected. Instead, as the epigraph to the first canto makes clear, it is loveless marriage that Derozio condemns, and romantic love that he extols in its place. Romantic love as the only valid basis for marriage was, of course, a radically Westernized notion, and it is disconcerting to find an argument in its favor in the context of a widow's imminent death. Almost it seems that for Derozio sati would be tolerable if the wife had married the husband for love in the first place. And in fact to die of love is to die of a recognized Western disease. It is *this* death that Derozio devises for his heroine at the end of the poem.

Derozio is constructing a romantic tale, and it is the formal thrust of the genre that determines its message rather than a social critique of women's oppression. The poem is actually a pastiche of several English poetic forms, a medley of inset ballads, songs, and madrigals within a larger narrative made of rhymed couplets.[15] At the same time, Derozio exploits many of the features of self-conscious "exoticism": the set piece iconic sati scene (resembling the scene of religious martyrdom), the elaborate nature descriptions, and the fervent invocations to Vedic gods (Surya). But for all its formal derivativeness, the poem is still significant for our argument when we recognize that Nuleeni, the heroine, is granted a measure of selfhood: she submits to her sati not because she is coerced or deluded but because she is pining for her lost lover. And she is totally daring in expressing her love for a man other than the one she is married to and one who, further, belongs to a class and caste so different from her own (the outlaw is a Muslim, and Derozio makes a passing point about true love breaking caste barriers). The union of the lovers is of course frustrated. Nuleeni's death is sanctioned by the conventions of romantic poetry, and the social status quo is preserved by the cautionary deaths of both the lovers. However heroic the rescuer's death, it defeats the purpose of the rescue.

Rabindranath Tagore's short story "Saved" could not be more different. Whereas Derozio uses large contrasts of love and war, "nature" and "society" virtually to swamp the human characters. Tagore stages a small (five-page) domestic drama and tells the story of a frustrated wife, a jealous husband, and a swami (ascetic monk) to whom the wife turns for religious consolation. The swami begins to see himself in the role of rescuer and finally makes an assignation to meet Gouri and take her away: "I will with god's help rescue his handmaid for the holy service of his feet" (210). Gouri hides his letter in the loops of her hair, "as a halo of deliverance" (211), but it falls into the husband's hands. Gouri finds him struck down in his room, dead of apoplexy, the letter clenched in his fist. Gouri discovers that the swami's real intention was to seduce her: she then kills herself. The story ends: "All were lost in admiration of the wifely loyalty she had shown in her *sati,* a loyalty rare indeed in these degenerate days" (212). It is a laconic ending, the last line packed with a multitude of ironies. The authorial free indirect speech transcribes the nostalgia for and idealization of sati that is characteristic of large sections of orthodox Hindu society at the same time that it highlights the titillating sensationalism the double death provides. Does the irony lie in society's conclusion that Gouri committed sati, when she died perhaps for reasons quite other than conjugal loyalty? Or is there irony in the extent of Gouri's reformation the transformation from her hatred of her husband to the guilt, remorse, and expiation of her death? Is she indeed "saved" by death—from her "savior"?

The notion of rescue is therefore itself framed for ironic examination. Gouri is beset and betrayed by both men, and when finally—trapped—she kills herself it is to be apotheosized as a sati. Her terseness in communication has been marked all through the story ("she was a woman of few words": "his wife treated it [his jealousy] with silent contempt"); and so the reticence about her final motive is appropriate.

Tagore's privatization of the bourgeois family drama, and his psychological subtlety in probing the woman's consciousness, parallels his ironic manipulation of the typical sati narrative. The figure of the "rescuer" as outlaw is here unequivocally reduced to that of would-be seducer; the *sanyasi* or ascetic monk is frequently a socially anomalous and displaced figure, treated either with veneration as a holy man or with suspicion as a charlatan. Gouri herself is given the responsibility for a number of the events of the story, and she acts decisively and even rebelliously at various crises. The jealous husband is treated with a measure of sympathy, as a financially insecure and perhaps sexually impotent failure. Tagore diagnoses this tragedy as the product of a certain "modernity" (characterized by skepticism, some mobility for women, the anomie experienced by the Bengal middle-class male under colonial administration) in conflict with residual orthodoxy (characterized by "faith," purdah for women, and traditional patriarchal authority). The status and meaning of the widow's death serve as the focus of this ironic inquiry.

My third text representing a male liberal/reformist view of sati, like the first two, is marked by a failure to imagine a viable way out for the widow; at the same time, it renders the "rescue" paradigm considerably more complex. *Antarjali jatra* (Death by drowning), directed by Gautam Ghosh, is a recent Bengali film. Set in 1832, immediately after the abolition of sati in Bengal, it narrates the story of Yashobati, a young girl hurriedly married off to a dying old man with her father's promise to the "pundits" and the family that she will commit sati. She is left with her dying husband at the burning ghats on the banks of the river Ganga, with only the *chandal* (the untouchable ghat-keeper, the burner of corpses) for company. The chandal urges her to escape; but she refuses, even though she dreads her death. Instead she tends her dying husband, who seems to revive under her care. The chandal pities her and reviles her fate. They are drawn together and become lovers. One night the river floods, and the old man's bier is swept away. Desperately,

Yashobati swims out in search of her husband, finds the empty bier and clings to it, but is drowned. The sati prophecy appears to have been ironically fulfilled, but through death by drowning rather than fire. The chandal is full of rage and sorrow at her death.

Whereas Ghosh retains the features of the "rescue" paradigm, these are reworked to an almost unrecognizable degree. The characteristics of the chief dramatis personae—Brahmans, dying/dead husband, widow, rescuer—are intensified versions of the stereotypes. Thus the Brahmans, although they are identified as the chief "villains," are also seen close up: Ananta, the chief Brahman and astrologer, is at least partially motivated by the desire to defy the alien edict against an indigenous religious rite; the father of Yashobati, a poor Brahman, is tempted by the prospect of marrying off his daughter without having to provide a dowry; the doctor, an "enlightened" Brahman with some access to modern systems of medicine, does protest on legal and humanitarian grounds, but he is blackmailed into silence; the dying man, a *kulin* Brahman, and his grown sons welcome the glory and prestige of a sati in the family. This differentiated characterization makes it possible for Ghosh to probe the complex social phenomenon of sati. The husband, dying and comatose for most of the film, is a grotesque caricature whose resurrection is a parody of lust for a new and nubile wife.

The heroine too is shown as young and beautiful, but not merely to highlight her vulnerability sentimentally. The fact is an aspect of this film's insistence upon the female *body* as what is at stake in sati. The obsessive male gaze, directed by the husband, the lover, and the filmmaker himself at the female body, is inevitably sexual; but it is equally a reminder that the body will burn. A single episode makes the point. The chandal, prohibited by caste restrictions from touching a living Brahman, rakes Yashobati with his gaze in order to measure her for the pyre: a gaze that is necessarily enacted by the viewer as well, but with no such purpose to legitimize it. Yashobati's subjectivity includes the "objectification" that is cinema's characteristic endowment; but it is also given the more familiar novelistic dimension of "consciousness" through her "choosing" to die. Her acquiescence, however, is made more complex than a matter of faith. At one point she turns on the chandal for his incessant badgering; between him and those who wish her to die, she protests, she is made to feel a mere object. She seeks the realm of her true subjectivity outside the parameters of the question of her death—and her lovemaking with the chandal is one expression of this search.

The most complex rendering, finally, is that of the would-be rescuer, the chandal. His outsider status is not merely a romanticization of individualistic antiestablishment heroics: he is by class, caste, and occupation the most outcast of society's members, and his helplessness to save Yashobati is a function of this social marginality. By allying these two subaltern figures, the chandal and the woman fated to die, Ghosh tries to make the most telling point in his film. Further, the chandal does not intervene from the outside: his habitation is the cremation grounds, he is part of the hierarchical social structure, and he asserts his dharma (social/religious obligation) by refusing to burn a living body. By making him an articulate and fearless spokesman for the oppressed, Ghosh compensates for the speechlessness of the "victim." So we are forced to ask why, given this, as well as the desperation of the two characters, the frank sexuality of their relationship, and the pragmatic possibilities of escape (solitude, a moored boat), a different, happy ending was not envisaged for the film. Finally it seems to be only a grim naturalistic fatalism that forecloses it.

*Antarjali jatra* is a contemporary film, and its relation to its material is mediated by its historical distance from sati in Bengal 150 years ago. This distance makes possible a materialist analysis of sati based on contemporary historical and sociological research.[16] Paradoxically, it also proceeds from an understanding of the contemporary phenomenon of bride burning: the problem of providing dowry for unmarried daughters is so acute that their deaths may even be viewed as a "solution" by their parents. Further, *Antarjali jatra* reveals the attempt of the contemporary Left to explore the possibility of an alliance between women, the working class, and the lower castes based on the similarity of their oppression and the commonality of their oppressors.

Finally, female sexuality and its social control are allowed to appear as dominant rather than recessive aspects of the phenomenon of sati in this narrative. The imperialist text covered over sexuality by discrediting conjugal love and by sublimating chivalric love into disinterested justice or "romance"; or by elevating sati to an act of martyrdom, it represented it as transcending human, and merely sexual, affective bonds. In the indigenous liberal/reform-ist text the issue of female sexuality became a more overt factor in the social dynamics of marriage and widowhood, and consequently of sati. But although in *Antarjali jatra* the woman's body is blatantly foregrounded, the potency and the potential anarchy of her sexuality are not let loose; the metaphoric flood instead ravages the land, while she herself dies. In this sense Ghosh remains captive to his inheritance from the past.[17]

## V

Though I conclude this part of my analysis with a brief consideration of the work on sati in the colonial period by two Indian feminist scholars, Lata Mani and Gayatri Spivak, it is not to offer it as the culmination of a progressive narrative.[18] Rather, I see their work, identified dialectically as *critique*, as being representative of the present historical moment of postcolonial feminism. Their own self-conscious adoption of the stance of the postcolonial woman intellectual whose politics—anti-imperialism and feminism—is overt, makes such a representation possible.

Mani and Spivak operate within the boundaries of the earlier discourse of sati, but with two major breaks. In the first place, they radically interrogate the "rescue" paradigm through fresh historical evidence (Mani), and through semiotic analysis (Spivak). Second, they reconceptualize and centralize the subjectivity of the sati as part of an explicitly feminist project.

In both cases, narrative intervenes significantly to structure their arguments. Though Mani, in fact, explicitly privileges synchronicity (discourse) over diachronicity (narrative), her "legislative history of sati" is nevertheless chronologically traced ("Production" 32–33). It emerges as a powerful counternarrative to the scenario of rescue that was the ideological translation of the colonial pretext for intervention. What Mani's researches restore is the long prehistory of abolition, a period of debate primarily concerning "the feasibility rather than the desirability" of abolition, so that "rather than arguing for the outlawing of *sati* as a cruel or barbarous act . . . officials in favour of abolition were at pains to illustrate that such a move was entirely consonant with the principle of upholding indigenous tradition" ("Production" 32). The settlement of this issue was sought through appeal to Brahman pundits who were to investigate the scriptural authority for sati. During this period (1789–1829) a number of circulars were issued to district officials based on official interpretation of the pundits' *vywasthas* (rulings), and a meticulous surveillance of all satis was undertaken to ensure that they were "legally" performed. In spite of this, the incidence of sati rose. The two were even connected in some analyses: "Government attention had given 'a sort of interest and celebrity to the sacrifice' . . . [The circulars] had a tendency 'to modify, systematise, or legalise the usage' and made it appear as though 'a legal sutte' was . . . better than an illegal one" ("Production" 34). This is a very different scenario from that of "rescue." At the same time, colonial reports on sati incidents assiduously circulated the stereotypes of cruel Brahmans, bloodthirsty mobs, and above all the widow as victim, which found their way into the narratives of rescue.[19]

It is not my intention to offer Mani's reading of the archives as the "correct," "historical" version in opposition to a "fabricated" colonial narrative construction. But neither do I subscribe to an extreme poststructuralist position that reduces history to narrative and makes all truth indeterminate or relative. The truth-value of Mani's reconstruction of the "production of an official discourse" seems to me inestimable. I merely refrain from positing these opposed versions as contests of truth. Instead, I emphasize Mani's historical location and the politics of postcolonial feminism as important constituents shaping the counternarrative that she (re)constructs.

Gayatri Spivak is also obliged to frame a narrative in order to keep the woman as signifier from disappearing into "a violent aporia" between (native patriarchy's) "subject-constitution" and (imperialism's) "object-formation." In responding to indigenous patriarchy's "constructed counter narrative of woman's consciousness" as "woman's desire [to die]," Spivak is led to "tabulate a psychobiographical norm" ("Can the Subaltern Speak?" 123). She concludes with an "example" to "illuminate the social text," the case of a young girl, Bhuvaneswari Devi, who hanged herself (129). In another essay in "reading the archives," Spivak demonstrates that colonial intervention in the decision of the rani of Sirmur to commit sati had little to do with "saving" her: the rani had to continue to rule "because of the commercial/territorial interests of the East India Company" ("Rani of Simur" 263).

Since Mani and Spivak undertake a reconstructive project in history, motivated by a concern to "know" the subject of sati, both are frustrated by the unavailability of records of women's consciousness. "One never encounters the testimony of the women's voice-consciousness" (Spivak, "Can the Subaltern Speak?" 122); "precious little [is] heard from them; . . . one learns so little about them" (Mani, "Contentious Traditions" 152–53). It is, of course, this significant absence that engenders their powerful criticism of the British imperialist construction of the Indian woman as perennial victim (Mani) and of the native patriarchal endowment of her with a "dubious" free will (Spivak). Their historical analysis is clinched when they reveal how such constructions legitimated colonial intervention.

The force of their attacks upon the partial and interested representations of the woman who committed sati has significant implications in the area of female subject production. In Mani the reaction to "the discourses of salvation" is the privileging of what Spivak has called "the woman's unrepresentable willing subjectivity" ("Can the Subaltern Speak?" 122); in Spivak, on the other hand, the hegemonic repression of the woman's consciousness results in her stress upon the *abjectness* of women's subject constitution.[20]

The preoccupation with the sati as colonial female subject, which is a function of Mani's and Spivak's reiterated feminist concern with contemporary Indian women's issues in the postcolonial context, pushes them to further speculations that pounce upon absences in the text of history. For Mani, such partial and systematic subjectification "precludes the possibility of a complex female subjectivity" ("Contentious Traditions" 152); for Spivak, what is of "greater significance" than the debate on sati is that "there was no debate upon this exceptional fate of widows [i.e., celibacy]—either among Hindus or between Hindus and British," with the resultant "profound irony [of] locating the woman's free will in self-immolation" ("Can the Subaltern Speak?" (125–26). The role of the postcolonial woman intellectual is then clearly but variously indicated: there are suggestions that Mani's project would be the *restoration* of "full" subjectivity to the woman through more assiduous historical research. She counters, for instance, the "infantilising" of the Hindu woman by offering statistical proof that "a majority of *satis* were undertaken by women well past childhood" ("Contentious Traditions" 130). Spivak's lack of faith in such positivistic enterprises is well known. Noting that the archives have no records of the eventual fate of the rani of Sirmur (who had announced her intention to commit sati and whom British officials had sought to dissuade), Spivak responds, "I intend to look a little further, of course. . . . [But] to retrieve her as information will be no disciplinary triumph. . . . [T]here is no 'real Rani' to be found" ("Rani of Sirmur" 270–71). Since the subaltern "cannot speak," it is she herself, through an "exorbitation" of her self-assigned role as postcolonial critic, who must undertake to "plot a story, unravel a narrative and give the subaltern a voice in history."[21]

In attempting to locate both the gendering of sati and the subjectification of the woman who dies within a cognitive structure that is historically produced, it has not been my intention merely to subsume feminist critiques of imperialism and native patriarchy within the larger colonial/postcolonial discourse. These critiques advance the terms of the argument considerably and promise an alliance between the project of feminism and the female victim-as-subject that is entirely new and is both theoretically and politically challenging. At the same time it is important not to discredit the epistemological breakthrough achieved by the colonial establishment of sati as a "woman question"—however suspect its politics—that has fed into the contemporary feminist analyses of the issue. An examination of some texts of precolonial India that I will undertake in the next section—which produce a different focus on the issue of self-immolation, and consequently a different subjectivity for the widow—makes retrospectively clear where the "break" may be identified.

## VI

The ancient epics and tales, the *Mahabharata,* the *Ramayana,* and the *Bhagavata Purana,* draw attention to the women who commit sati by celebrating their courage and devotion in panegyric verses. Such women are invariably the wives of warrior-heroes, kings, or *rishis* (sages)—"great men" of one kind or other—and their behavior is therefore intended to serve as a reflection of/on the status of the men on whose behalf they die rather than to be read as a gratuitous act of self-willed heroism. The failure of a woman to commit sati never seems to call for corresponding comment of any kind, whether of censure or surprise; the four wives of King Dasaratha (Rama's father, in the *Ramayana*), for instance, continue to live on after his death as revered dowager queens, leading the celibate life prescribed by the *shastras*. In the *Mahabharatha*, both wives of King Pandu (the father of the Pandavas) wish to commit sati at his death, and they argue about who should exercise the privilege. Finally Madri persuades Kunti, the senior queen, not to die since, because of her great love for her stepchildren as well as her own, she would be the better mother.

The three most famous of the legendary good wives—the eponymous "Sati" herself (the goddess Parvati), Sita (in the *Ramayana*), and Savitri (in the Puranas)—did not actually commit self-immolation as widows.[22] After the death of Savitri's husband Satyavan, she does battle with the god of death, Yama, himself and journeys to the underworld to reclaim her husband; because of her penances she is able to win back her husband's life as a boon from Yama. I do not argue that these women are not, in anything but a literal sense, satis: the word itself means only "good wife," and in all these cases the women must submit to trials of various kinds to establish good wifehood. But Savitri's "death," her journey to the netherworld, is a trial that is at least undertaken to some purpose: she not only reclaims her husband but herself comes back to the living. Although the widow's continuing concern (or obsession) is with the dead husband, her devotion may at least find expression in life rather than death.

The recourse to texts of the Indian past is of course a familiar move; it figured prominently in the debate on sati initiated in colonial India and has been resurrected—within a different political framework—in recent times. I have no wish to reproduce their dubious idealization of the past, or of Hindu women's status in earlier societies.[23] My argument that the identity of the "good wife" (sati in the original sense) is a broader framework for female subjectification than that of the widow who burns (sati according to later usage) is based on the observation that good wifehood has different manifestations, and some of these included the option of life rather than death. The representation of the female subject as good wife in the *Shilappadikaram*, which I examine next, occupies this larger space cleared for the widow who "chooses" life over death.

The *Shilappadikaram* (The ankle bracelet) is one of the three surviving "great poems" written in the third and last epoch of classical Tamil literature. Its author is the prince Ilanko Atikal, and the date attributed to the main body of the work is the second century A.D. The story is summarized in a "preamble" to the book:

> In the ancient town of Puhar, immortal capital of the Chola kings . . . , there lived a rich merchant named Kovalan. He dissipated his great wealth in the pleasure offered him by a dancing girl expert in her art. He had a wife named Kannaki. With her he went to Madurai, the capital of the celebrated Pandya kingdom. In need of funds, he wished to sell her beautiful ankle bracelet, and went into the main bazaar looking for a buyer. There he showed the ankle bracelet to a goldsmith, who said, "Only a queen can wear such jewelry." He suggested that Kovalan wait near his shop, and ran to the palace to inform the king that he had found the thief of the queen's gold bracelet. At that moment Kovalan's hour of destiny had come. The king . . . did not bother to make an investigation, but simply ordered a guard to put the thief to death and bring back the queen's bracelet. The wife of Kovalan found herself abandoned and shed abundant tears. She tore away one of her breasts, adorned by a string of pearls. By the power of her virtue, she burned down the great city of Madurai and called down upon the Pandya king the anger of the gods.[24]

There are two major thematic aspects to this work, as the poet takes pains to point out: the domestic, or love (*aham*), and the political, or war (*puram*) (204). Its drama is also of two kinds, the "human tragedy" and the "mythological play" (144), and the precepts it illustrates deal with both justice and conjugal love (209). Thus Kannaki is at once an *instrument* (of political, as well as divine justice) and an *agent:* she therefore simultaneously asserts her righteousness in burning down the city and expresses sorrow and guilt at her crime; she must inflict punishment upon the king and queen and upon the entire polity, but also upon herself, as she tears out her left breast as a symbolic repudiation of her femininity.

These contradictions are resolved because Kannaki's virtue is conceptualized as a social trait, just as the Pandya King's injustice is a national shame. It is not individual motivation that prompts human action, but social roles. When Kannaki confronts the king it is as the representative of a city, a nation, a class, and her sex, and also as a subject. Kannaki claims she cannot act otherwise than she does because she comes from "Pukar, where these noble women with fragrant braids [whose stories she has narrated] live. If these stories are true, and if I am faithful, I cannot allow your city to survive" (131). Here it is the community that dictates women's behavior; the reverse of this, the invocation of the status or behavior of women to define a community as backward or "advanced," is a later argument, and one that has figured prominently in the debate on sati.

What is especially significant is that Kannaki is faced with a choice as soon as she confronts Kovalan's corpse, between abject, helpless widowhood and death. In an extended, fluently rhetorical passage, she repudiates the ways of widowhood (122). But the vision of Kovalan appears and advises her to stay: "Beloved! Stay there, stay! Remain peacefully in life!" (125). Kannaki takes this as an injunction to avenge his death: "I shall not search for my husband [follow him in death] before he is avenged. I shall meet this inhuman king and ask for his justice against himself" (126). After she has burned down the great city by the power of her curse, she leaves, wanders forlornly for fourteen days, and then dies "naturally," to ascend thereafter to heaven with her husband.

We cannot deny that Kannaki emerges as a complex and tragic figure if she is read from the familiar perspective of Western literary representation of character. But we must also recognize that within a different "worldview," that of the Tamil classical epoch, roles are prescribed for human beings by social expectation and divine arrangement (duty and fate). We see this in the comparison of Kannaki's action with that of another good wife's reaction to her husband's death. Kannaki's reproaches had shamed the king of Madurai so keenly that he died of heartbreak. His queen then, "unable to bear her sorrow . . . died, saying: 'I must follow my king.' " The question is posed: "A virtuous woman lost her life because her husband died. Another wandered in anger through our kingdom . . . [I]n your judgment, which one should we admire?" And the answer is that while both are great, the queen wins her rewards in heaven, but Kannaki has become "a new goddess of Faithfulness" who will be "forever honored" here, in this kingdom (158).[25]

The queen's death is a manifestation of sati, whereas Kannaki's curse is an expression of *shakti,* the powerful, ferocious, feminine cosmic principle. But it is the excess of sati, the ascetic virtue of good wifehood, that is converted into *shakti.*[26] These two generally opposed aspects of femininity in Hindu representations of the goddesses are linked in Kannaki, indicating that the source of feminine power lies in the virtue accumulated as a good wife.[27] And yet to envisage that such virtue can prove excessive—can over-flow the domestic, conjugal relationship into the realms of history and polity—is to give another dimension to "good wifehood." In Kannaki's case "the woman who burns" has more than one meaning.

If we seek a more radical repudiation of the entire syndrome of "good wifehood" of which the act of sati is only an item, we shall find it in the lives and works of the women Bhakta poets of India.[28] These women—

saints, mystics, poets—had to make life choices: their devotion to their god came into conflict with their sexuality and with the life of domesticity, both of which were normally regulated by the institution of marriage. They resolved this conflict either by bypassing marriage altogether or, once married, by opting out of marital commitment.[29] Here too we must be careful not to read their poems as feminist credos. The ideological structure of the man-woman relationship is not itself displaced; the god of these women poets is male, cast as lover, husband, father, or child, frequently indeed the first two, so that a highly eroticized idiom is brought into play (Ramanujan, "Talking to God" 14). Nevertheless, as Madhu Kishwar has pointed out, bhakti did make a "social space" available for women who "outrageously defied what are ordinarily considered the fundamental tenets of *stri dharma* [women's duty]—marriage and motherhood" (6).

The foregoing comparative exercise has not been substantial enough to prove absolute differences between two structures of representation, the one indigenous, the other characterized as colonial/postcolonial or British/European; still less does it seek to establish the superiority of one over the other.[30] The absence of any gendered perspective, and the ultimately deterministic framework of "choice" in precolonial representations of women, prevents any easy sentimentalization of the indigenous cultures. On the other hand, the colonial perception of a *collective* gendered identity for the women who die sharply contradicts a focus of the *individual* female subject, the sati, who is framed for scrutiny.

The identification of differences serves to indicate only the newness of the discursive terrain explored by colonial rulers in response to new ideological pressures. In this discourse death came to define women's behavior not descriptively—as male heroism, martyrdom, or suicide do—but absolutely; the subject of sati came into being as the absent (dead) subject. But of course, beyond the woman's death in life (burning alive) lay life-in-death, the (re)construction of her subjectivity: it is this paradox that I have tried to uncover.

## Notes

1. "Sati" is the self-immolation of a Hindu widow along with the corpse of her husband. The word is used here to refer both to the practice and to the widow who performs it.

2. The texts are for the most part narratives of various kinds—tales, long poems, short stories, novels, epics, and a film. I am interested in the way narrative structures encode ideologemes and, conversely, in the way ideological structures are accommo-

dated within, and expressed through, narrative paradigms. See Jameson 76, 87–88. There is an interesting argument here about the *differences* among the narrative genres in the production of specific ideological constructs, but I have allowed it to remain implicit.

3. Lata Mani ("Production" 32–40, esp. 32) has argued for the emergence of a specifically colonial discourse on sati.

4. Robert Southey's *The Curse of Kehama* (1810), a poem now little read but influential in its own day as the precorsor of the exotic "Eastern tale" made popular by the younger romantics (especially Byron and Moore), represents the clearing of the ground for such intervention, at a time when the East India Company was engaged in large-scale territorialization in India. It narrates the story of Kehama, a despotic Indian prince who represents the debasement of Hindu rule. Two vivid set pieces are provided to illustrate his unfitness to rule: the first, a scene where the victims are two young and beautiful Hindu princesses about to die with an old king, their husband; the second, a court scene where the king curses a peasant to a life of perpetual suffering. Thus a certain "Hinduism," with the spectacular inequities of its class, caste, and gender relations, provided the necessary pretext for the overthrow of "native" rule; and Southey's poem creates the picturesque and narrative version of such cultural and civilizational decay.

5. See, for instance, Boase and Benson.

6. Often such acts involved big-game hunting. The most complex exposition of this "white man's burden" is found in George Orwell's "Shooting an Elephant."

7. My point will be clearer if I make a distinction between colonial self-representation and earlier interventions in the practice of sati in Islamic India. Muslim rulers had regarded sati as suicide and hence illegal according to the *Sharia* (the Muslim code), but they permitted it to Hindu women. The Mughal ruler Akbar took a strong stand against forcibly burning women and passed an ordinance to prevent such deaths. According to contemporary historians, Akbar personally intervened to rescue a Rajput princess, widow of his friend Jai Mall, who refused to die as a sati. But her son Udai Singh forced her onto the pyre; Akbar sent his agents, who saved her when the pile was already lighted and seized Udai Singh. See Thapar 1: 292; Malleson 164–66. The point is that the prohibition of sati did not become a strategic political move, and hence did not feature in the Mughals' self and Other representation of the Islamic and Hindu communities. Sumit Sarkar has commented on the "secularism, rationalism and non-conformity . . . of pre-British Muslim ruled India" (53), within which the issue of sati could be raised.

8. Colonial historians like Edward Thompson could declare that after the abolition of sati in British India, "a practice which had caused the sacrifice of many hundreds of women annually was driven into the Native States." Henry Laurence, the British agent in Rajputana, boasted in 1854 of effective law enforcement even in the princely states, especially those under strong British supervision (Thompson 26, 28–29).

9. In Conrad's novella, in contrast, Kurtz is unredeemable. Not only is he guilty of "unspeakable rites," he also has a native woman.

10. The afterlife of the rescued widow remains vague. However, in both books the heroines have some European blood/education, a great deal of predisposition to adapt to European ways, and sufficient Eastern acquiescence to ensure that the new partnership will work.

11. See Mani, "Production of an Official Discourse," for the establishment of such a view, esp. 32.

12. See Mani, "Contentious Traditions." Mani points out that in annual reports of sati, "women were cast as either pathetic or heroic victims." In the former instance they were seen to be "dominated by Hindu men," in the latter they were considered to be "victimized by religion" (129).

13. Susan makes the terms of her loyalty explicit: "I take no merit for my service of twelve years, for I love her . . . but true and faithful service gives me right to speak I hope" (703).

14. I am grateful to Nancy Paxton for making this paper available to me.

15. *The Fakeer* is closest in plot outline to Walter Scott's ballad "Lochinvar." In both, a dashing outlaw rescues his mistress dramatically in the nick of time. The differences—between death and marriage—are of course significant, but their elision is even more so.

16. Among these, Nandy's book cited above is important.

17. A slightly different version of this analysis of *Antarjali jatra* appears in my "Subject of Sati."

18. In addition to the works already cited, see also Spivak, "Rani of Sirmur."

19. This paragraph summarizes part of Mani's long and intricate argument in "Production of an Official Discourse."

20. These are only the implicit and perhaps merely logical corollaries of their theoretical positions. But they are given significant emphasis precisely through the disavowals they issue (such disavowals must surely be gratuitous given the transparency of their political commitments): "This criticism of the absence of women's subjectivity in colonial accounts is not to argue either that women died voluntarily or that I in any way endorse *sati*. From my perspective, the practice was and remains indefensible" (Mani, "Contentious Traditions" 130); "it should therefore be understood that the example I discuss . . . is in no way a plea for some violent Hindu sisterhood of self-destruction" (Spivak, "Can the Subaltern Speak?" 129).

21. The observation is made by Parry 27–58, esp. 35.

22. According to legend, Sati is so distressed by the exclusion of her husband, the god Shiva, from her father's court that she dies. Shiva dances the *tandava* (the dance of destruction) carrying Sati's corpse on his shoulder. In the *Ramayana* Sita, wife of Rama, has to undergo an ordeal by fire in order to establish her chastity after she is rescued from Ravana, who had abducted her.

23. Romila Thapar comments on the status of women at various periods. Their changing features have to be understood within a specific historical context. For example, in the early Aryan civilization, she argues, "the position of women was on the whole free" (40–41). Sati was only a symbolic act, and the remarriage of widows

was common. But in a later age, from about A.D. 300 to 700, women developed "a distinctly subordinate position" (151). The practice of widow burning appears to have begun at this time. The only women who had "a large measure of freedom" were those "who deliberately chose to opt out of . . . the 'normal' activities of a woman" and became Buddhist nuns, or else actresses, courtesans, or prostitutes (152). Feudalism in the Rajput states (from about A.D. 800 to 1200) led to the glorification of military virtues, so that "women . . . were taught to admire men who fought well" and were themselves expected to commit sati when their husbands died (247). During Muslim rule, from the thirteenth century to the sixteenth, the position of both Hindu and Muslim women of all classes was an inferior one (301–2). Women's seclusion (purdah) was the normal custom. There thus seems to be little ground for celebrating the status of precolonial women—at least without careful qualification.

24. According to the translator's note (207–8), the preamble is considered by the ancient commentators to be not part of the original text but a later addition.

25. The differences between the queen's passive behavior and Kannaki's active response are, of course, functions of their class positions. The *Shilappadikaram* presents a vivid picture of the wealth, power, and aspirations of the rising mercantile class, of which Kovalan and Kannaki are members.

26. See Das 28.

27. Kannaki has been shown to be a "good wife" in the first half of the book; she forgives Kovalan for his desertion of her, makes him a gift of her gold anklet to be sold, and uncomplainingly accepts the hardships of the journey to Madurai and of poverty with him.

28. Bhakti is a religious devotion that signals a different, more personalized and intimate relation between the devotee and his or her god; the members of the cult were often, though not always, women, peasants, artisans, or untouchables. The movement began in the fifth or sixth century A.D. in the Tamil kingdom and continued for well over a thousand years, spreading from region to region throughout the country. I am indebted to a special issue of *Manushi* on women Bhakta poets for information contained in this paragraph; especially to articles by Madhu Kishwar, "Introduction," 3–8; A. K. Ramanujan, "Talking to God in the Mother Tongue," 9–17; and Uma Chakravarty, "The World of the Bhaktin in South Indian Traditions: The Body and Beyond," 18–29.

29. Chakravarty 18–29. The Kannada poet Akka Mahadevi (twelfth century A.D.) writes:

So my lord, white as jasmine, is my husband.
Take these husbands who die, decay,
and feed them
to your kitchen fires!
    (Trans. Ramanujan, *Speaking of Siva*)

And Mira, the Rajput princess-poet (sixteenth century), asserts in a well-known prayer/hymn:

> I will sing of Girdhar [the lord Krishna]
> I will not be a sati.

30. My omission of any texts of Islamic India from this analysis reflects only the constraints of length and the inadequacies of scholarship; it is not intended to exempt this period from colonial prehistory.

Gauri Viswanathan has pointed out that in "the relativized domain of history," where differences are attributed to "the effect of historical change and movement," "concepts like absolute truth have no place"—instead "there is only formation, process, and flux" (97). This of course does not prevent the diagnosis of the political imperatives underlying ideological constructs. In other words, my method offers an explanatory model.

## Works Cited

Benson, Larry D. *Malory's Morte d'Arthur: A Fifteenth-Century Chivalric Romance*. Cambridge: Harvard UP, 1976.

Boase, Roger. *The Origin and Meaning of Courtly Love*. Totowa, NJ: Rowman and Littlefield, 1977.

Chakravarty, Uma. "The World of the Bhaktin in South Indian Traditions: The Body and Beyond." *Manushi* 50–52 (1989): 18–29.

Danielou, Alain, trans. *Shilappadikaram: The Ankle Bracelet*. New York: New Directions, 1967.

Das, Veena. "Shakti versus Sati: A Reading of the Santoshi Ma Cult." *Manushi* 49 (1988): 26–30.

Derozio, Henry Louis Vivian. *Poems*. Intro. F. B. Bradley-Birt. Foreword by R. K. Das Gupta. Delhi: Oxford UP, 1980.

Dickens, Charles. *Dombey and Son*. 1848. Harmondsworth, England: Penguin, 1970.

Jameson, Fredric. *The Political Unconscious*. Ithaca: Cornell UP, 1981.

Kaye, M. M. *The Far Pavilions*. 2 vols. New York: St. Martin's Press, 1978.

Kishwar, Madhu. "Introduction." *Manushi* 50–52 (1989): 3–8.

Malleson, G. B. *The Emperor Akbar and the Rise of the Mughal Empire*. Delhi: Sunita, 1986.

Mani, Lata. "Contentious Traditions: The Debate on *Sati* in Colonial India." *Cultural Critique* 7 (1987): 119–56.

———. "Production of an Official Discourse on *Sati* in Early Nineteenth Century Bengal." *Economic and Political Weekly* 21.7, Review of Women Studies, April 26, 1986: 32–40.

*Manushi* 50–52 (1989). Special issue on women Bhakta poets.

Maspero advertisement. *Bombay Times and Journal of Commerce,* n.d. Rpt. in *Times Magazine* November–December 1988: 13.

Nandy, Ashis. *At the Edge of Psychology*. New Delhi: Oxford UP, 1982.

Orwell, George. "Shooting an Elephant." *"Shooting an Elephant" and Other Essays*. London: Secker and Warburg, 1945.

Parry, Benita. "Problems in Current Theories of Colonial Discourse." *Oxford Literary Review* 9.1–2 (1987): 27–58.

Paxton, Nancy. "Unma(s)king the Colonial Subject: Subjectivity and the Female Body in the Novels of Flora Annie Steel and Anita Desai." Paper prepared for MLA Convention, Dec. 1988.

Ramanujan, A. K. *Speaking of Siva*. Harmondsworth, England: Penguin, 1985.

———. "Talking to God in the Mother Tongue." *Manushi* 50–52 (1989): 9–17.

Sangari, Kumkum. "What Makes a Text Literary?" Paper prepared for Conference on English Studies in India, Miranda House, Delhi University, Apr. 1988.

Sarkar, Sumit. "Rammohan Roy and the Break with the Past." *Rammohan Roy and the Process of Modernization in India*. Ed. V. C. Joshi. New Delhi: Vikas, 1975.

Spivak, Gayatri Chakravorty. "Can the Subaltern Speak? Speculations on Widow-Sacrifice." *Wedge* 7–8 (1985): 120–30. Reprinted in *Selected Subaltern Studies*. Ed. Ranajit Guha. Oxford: Oxford UP, 1988.

———. "The Rani of Sirmur: An Essay in Reading the Archives." *History and Theory* 24.3 (1987): 247–72.

———. "Three Women's Texts and a Critique of Imperialism." *Critical Inquiry* 12.1 (1985): 243–61.

Sunder Rajan, Rajeswari. "The Subject of Sati." *Yale Journal of Criticism* 3.2 (1990): 1–28.

Tagore, Rabindranath. "Saved." *"Mashi" and Other Stories*. Delhi: Macmillan, 1918.

Thapar, Romila. *History of India*. 2 vols. Harmondsworth, England: Penguin, 1966.

Thompson, Edward. *The Reconstruction of India*. Delphi: Kaushal Rakashan, 1985.

Viswanathan, Gauri. *Masks of Conquest: Literary Study and British Rule in India*. New York: Columbia UP, 1989.

# Afterword

# Walter Benjamin and the Crisis of Representation: Multiplicity, Meaning, and Athematic Death

## Ronald Schleifer

> Just as in its most uncompromising representatives modern
> music no longer tolerates any elaboration, any distinction
> between theme and development, but instead every musical
> idea, even every note, stands equally near the center, so too
> Benjamin's philosophy is "athematic." It is dialectics at a
> standstill in another sense as well, in that it allots no tie to
> internal development but instead receives its form from the
> constellation formed by the individual statements. Hence its
> affinity with the aphorism. At the same time, however, the
> theoretical element in Benjamin always requires farther-rang-
> ing linkages of ideas.
>
> —Theodor Adorno, "Introduction to Benjamin's *Schriften*"

In this afterword to *Death and Representation* I will examine the mode of
representation that Walter Benjamin developed in his work in response to
what Georges Bataille describes as "base matter": a description of "intransigent materialism" that is not susceptible to traditional representations but is
"external and foreign to ideal human aspirations" (*Visions* 51). In this collection, Regina Barreca pronounces this occasion and problem in a whole
different register, in the second person, speaking for death itself: "Just in
case you thought there was no distinction between representation and reality,
there is death. Just in case you thought experience and the representation of
experience melted into one another, death provides a structural principle
separating the two. See the difference, death asks, see the way language and

vision differ from the actual, the irrevocable, the real?" More even than Bataille, this collection takes death as its explicit focus, yet its most important contribution to the ongoing debate concerning what the editors call "the relation between death and culture" is its articulations of the relation between language and the irrevocably real, its exploration of the possibilities of death's representation. Such articulations—between discourse and time, representation and reality—are central to the poetics of allegory, fragmentation, materialist temporality, and redemption in Benjamin's work. *Death and Representation* sets forth the problem Benjamin and his contemporaries address, the incongruence between the concept and event of death and the multiplicity of approaches—avoidance, repetition, metonymy, particularized descriptions of historical moments and events—that this incongruence occasions.

The book's chapters are wide-ranging, treating subjects as different as Charles Segal's masterly philological reading of the cultural practices of ancient Greece and Ernst van Alphen's study of postmodern works and the sublime. One of the most striking aspects of this collection is its very range. In part 1, "Reading Death: Sign, Psyche, Text," it offers van Alphen's discussion of graphic representations of death; Garrett Stewart's semiotic reading of its narrative representation; Ellie Ragland's account of Lacan's definition of the death drive; and Elisabeth Bronfen's enactment of the role of repetition in the "representations" of mourning.

Part 2, "Death and Gender," offers studies on the representation of women in relation to death in the Victorian era by Carol Christ, the manipulation of death's power by women in Barreca's "Writing as Voodoo," and women's representations of war and death in World War I by Margaret Higonnet. Sarah Webster Goodwin's essay, with her coeditor's essay in part 1, delimits the modes of representing death—those of elision as well as repetition—that will help me define the larger issue this collection engages. I will turn to this in a moment. The focus on death and gender is important, entailing as it does the crisis of representing women, the crisis of the concepts "woman" and the "feminine." Barreca describes this crisis in terms of the "particular relationship" between women writers and death, a relationship based upon the fact that those writers create "female characters who are unsure of any reality besides death."

If part 2 is tightly focused on particular representations, part 3, "History, Power, Ideology," chooses widely different historical moments to offer what the editors describe as close analyses of "a text or group of texts for historical insights" that seem to sustain themselves only locally, based on the power of their particularized readings. In fact, these analyses present fine insights into the relation between death and representation at particular historical moments—ancient Athens, revolutionary France, late nineteenth-century Europe, the present moment of "subaltern studies" of Indian culture and history—yet as this survey suggests, the very particularity of its studies does not lend itself to what the editors call generalizations of diachronic sweep.

The explicit aim of this book, as I see it, is to present interdisciplinary discussions of the representation of death in art history, literary history, philological anthropology (Is there such a thing?), psychoanalysis, feminism, cultural history, literary criticism, and narratology. Such an aim is amply fulfilled: the essays delimit the volume's *thematic* concern with death and the fascination it holds in different modes of representation—mostly literary, but also representation in art and film, in narrative more generally conceived, and in popular and scholarly treatments of death and violence. The book as a whole presents chapters on a wide variety of topics that, brought together, help define the theme of death as a subject of representation. This is a great strength of this collection: it is contributing to the definition of a new interdisciplinary "field" that calls upon a large number of areas of specialization in a collective effort of disciplinary redefinition.

A key to that redefinition as it is presented in *Death and Representation* is the term "representation" in the book's title, and examining this helps account for the seeming diffusion of focus I have described. What these essays share is their own diversity, the impossibility of offering a totalizing theme or approach beyond the particularities of individual studies and the particularities of "death" itself. Death, as material event, bears a problematic relation to generalization. That is precisely the issue this collection presents in its progressively more local understandings. In one instance, Bronfen's chapter "Risky Resemblances: On Repetition, Mourning, and Representation," the discussions of the "excessive sameness" of repetition, Poe, and refound texts and bodies in Poe and other narratives present a procedure or "method" that precludes conclusion, what Bronfen calls the constellation of "a mode of representation called for by death"—as if marshaling examples of death's irrevocable reality somehow foreclosed conclusion and totalizing representation. Van Alphen's chapter also offers a less pronounced version of the seeming fragmentation of the "parts" of its argument—the treatment of Armando followed by a discussion of the sublime—that Benjamin describes as his own procedure of "method" and representation "as digression," whose "primary characteristic" is "the absence of an uninterrupted purposeful structure" (*Origin* 28). Within the exposition of Van Alphen's chapter, "death" is quickly sidelined, as the primary subject becomes the problematics of representation, the difficulty of historicizing metaphor. Yet the quick elision of death and violence (like that of Garrett Stewart's Greimassian reading of *Villette*, which thematizes "death" as an object or element of semiosis) marks the incongruence between theme and its mode of representation. This incongruence calls for the repeated discussions within individual chapters and across *Death and Representation* as a whole.

If death, as it is presented in this collection, seems to call for both parataxis and elision and to manifest itself in repeated versions of both, then the motive for this mode of representation ("metonymic" representations, or what Benjamin calls the "constellation" of an idea) is suggested by Goodwin's evocation of "the ghost of prostitution" and Regina's Janes's history of beheadings. Goodwin's essay spends a good deal of its energy not addressing the question of death, but avoiding it through "metaphor" and "indirection," as she says. At the end, it seems to plead for death's presence even though it is absent from the discussion of prostitution. In this it helps delimit the problem of representation by marking the difference between historical and semiotic analyses, the "line of demarcation" that Benjamin repeatedly returns to "between physical nature and significance" (*Origin* 166). In tracing the quick moves of social semiotics to make prostitution metaphorical and to express death only "indirectly," in describing the prostitute as "the empty and infinitely mobile sign," the "subject, as well as the object, of her own exchange," it sets forth the ways avoidance and absence inhabit representations of death; it enacts the semiotics of death's "haunting" in powerful local understandings of historical representations of death. Pursuing the opposition between history and semiotics from the vantage point of seeming repetitions rather than haunting disappearances of death from meaning, Janes examines the double sense of repeated fact and semiotic object, *Vorstellung* and *Darstellung*, by examining the history and meaning of guillotine and pike. "Although severed heads always speak," she argues in a mode that complements Goodwin's, "they say different things in different cultures."

The relation between historical event and semiotic understanding defines in large part the problematic relation between death and representation that this book presents and explores. In fact, what emerges from these essays individually and collectively is the multiplicity of the modes of representing death—phenomenally, narratively, semiotically, psychoanalytically—in the unrolling of its repetitions. Rajeswari Sunder Rajan describes such multiplicity in her study of the history and semiotics of sati as the "comparative exercise" of repeated gestures toward death's facticity, repeated deixis. It is precisely this unrolling of examples without possibilities of generalization and coherence once and for all—the fissure between history and semiotics, or Benjamin's "jagged line of demarcation between physical nature and significance," that is marked by death (*Origin* 166)—that the book as a whole presents. The editors are well aware of this in their introduction: they mention that the organizing principle here is that of "clusters" set up to create "resonances" (another version of Goodwin's "hauntings"). Such incongruence contributed to what I have described as the crisis of representation in the early twentieth century (Schleifer, *Rhetoric*). At that time Benjamin attempted, more fully than many of his contemporaries, not simply to react to and describe this crisis, but to devise representational tactics that might offer possibilities, in the face of it, of recovering meaning in history. In the rest of the afterword I will examine Benjamin's attempt to comprehend base matter and intransigent materialism—to answer death's question that Barreca and *Death and Representation* pronounce—by creating a representational mode for the semantic void of material violence and death. This attempt, I believe, presents a tactic and a rhetoric to grasp what Benjamin's contemporaries thought ungraspable. In this examination I hope to present a mode of comprehending one aspect of the relation between death and representation that is implicit in this book.

## I

In his "Introduction to Benjamin's *Schriften*," Theodor Adorno notes that "Benjamin's philosophy provokes the misunderstanding of consuming and defusing it as a series of unconnected aperçus responding to the contingencies of occasion." Nevertheless, Adorno writes, "each insight has its place within an extraordinary unity of philosophical consciousness. But the essence of this unity consists in its moving outward, in finding itself by losing itself in multiplicity" (222). Adorno's description of the difficulty of reading Benjamin—what he later calls, following Benjamin's own terminology, the difficulty of his "constellation of ideas," in which the concrete is "never denigrated . . . to an example of the concept" (223, 224)—encompasses the difficulty of the relation between representation and death, between representation's need to find the general case, the common denominator among disparate phenomena, and the fact that the *power* of death is its indivisible uniqueness, its existence as only what Benjamin describes as a "small, individual moment" that creates its authority ("N" 48; *Illuminations* 94). This is the problem in Benjamin's study of baroque *Trauerspiel* (lamentation plays) that George Steiner describes in his introduction to the English translation (*Origin of German Tragic Drama*): "How can there be a general and generalizing treatment of artistic-literary objects which are, by definition, unique?" (23).

Benjamin's philosophical interest, Adorno says, "is not directed to the ahistorical at all, but rather to what is temporally determined and irreversible. Hence the title *One Way Street*. Benjamin's images are not linked with nature as moments of a self-identical ontology but rather in the name of death, of transience as the supreme category of natural existence, the category toward which Benjamin's thought advances. What is eternal in them is only the transient" ("Introduction" 226). Focus on the temporally irreversible produces the difficulty of representation: as Michel Foucault has argued, representation possesses "the obscure power of making a past impression present once more," so that an impression can "appear as either similar to or dissimilar from a previous one" (*Order* 69). When transience is the supreme category of existence, then the "self-identical ontology" that allows for judgments of similarity and dissimilarity—that allows for representation itself—becomes a problem. Nowhere is this problem more pronounced than in the category or conception of death. For like the isolated ideas in modern music that Adorno describes, the particularity of death as *event* can never be encompassed by its conception; the particular event of death is never simply "an example of the concept."

This situation, for Benjamin, is a touchstone for his understanding of representation, allegory, and meaning. "Socrates," he writes in *The Origin of German Tragic Drama*,

> looks death in the face as a mortal—the best and most virtuous of mortals, one may insist—but he recognizes it as something alien, beyond which, in immortality, he expects to return to himself. Not so the tragic hero; he shrinks before death as before a power that is familiar, personal, and inherent in him. His life, indeed, unfolds from death, which is not its end but its form. For tragic existence acquires its task only because it is intrinsically subject to the limits of both linguistic and physical life which are set within it from its very beginning. (114)

Here Benjamin is describing the paradox that death both is inherent in the life of the tragic hero and is also its limiting Other. Socrates, in this narrative, sees death as fully alien to himself, something he can situate himself "beyond" in an immortal home where he expects to return to himself. For the tragic hero, however, death is familiar, personal, quotidian, yet at the same time a limit to life in both its meaning and its base materiality. It is a concrete event that can never be reduced to an example of the concept of "death." This is the import of Maurice Blanchot's unnerving description in *The Writing of the Disaster* of "the dying which, though unsharable, I have in common with all" (23). It is the import of Georges Bataille's description of death as "in one sense the common inevitable, but in another sense, profound, inaccessible" (*Inner Experience* 71). Benjamin's fascinated contemplation of this situation provokes the power of his discourse. "What Benjamin said and wrote," Adorno says, "sounded as if it came from the depths of mystery. It received its power, however, from its quality of self-evidence" ("Introduction" 221).

This situation, which Benjamin encounters, is a function of death's *materiality,* a "base" materiality, as Bataille says, "not implying an ontology, not implying that matter is the thing-in-itself" (*Visions* 49). "Base matter," Bataille says, "is external and foreign to ideal human aspirations, and it refuses to allow itself to be reduced to the great ontological machines resulting from these aspirations" (51). That is, base matter—and death itself—is not the "opposite" of life in a system of representations in which the same and the opposite play together in a homogeneous system of meaning. Rather, Bataille argues, "matter, in fact, can only be defined as the *nonlogical difference* that represents in relation to the *economy* of the universe what *crime* represents in relation to the law" (129). These phenomena—excessive, unique, powerful events rather than objects of knowledge—he describes as the "heterogeneous." For Bataille—and, as we shall see, for Benjamin as well—the materiality of death disrupts objectivity, representations, and knowledge conceived as science. In this discussion he shares with Benjamin, as his translator has noted, an attempt "to find an alternative to both idealism and traditional materialism (which starts out with material facts but then goes 'beyond' them to construct an abstract, conceptual edifice)" (Stoekl xxv; see also Tiedemann 176). For Bataille traditional materialism is simply a variant of the same "metaphysical scaffolding" as idealism. "Two verbal entities are thus formed," he writes: "an abstract God (or simply the idea), and abstract matter" (*Visions* 45).

The alternative to idealism and abstract materialism fully acknowledges irreversible time and its unique moments; it "exposes," as Benjamin says, "the passing moment in all its nakedness" (*Illuminations* 185). Unlike Bataille, however—or at least more systematically and self-consciously than Bataille—Benjamin attempts to recover such events for comprehension. Bataille, as Foucault argues, attempted "through every detour and repetition of his work" simply "to circumscribe" an *experience* ("Preface" 36) of what might be called the sacred but really cannot be comprehended in a concept or an idea. That is, for Bataille the alternative to idealism and traditional materialism is precisely "ungraspable": "Christianity," he writes, "has made the sacred *substantial,* but the nature of the sacred . . . is perhaps the most ungraspable thing that has been produced between men: the sacred is only a privileged moment of communal unity, a moment of the convulsive communication of what is ordinarily stifled" (*Visions* 242). Christianity has "substantialized" the sacred, Steven Shaviro has argued, glossing Bataille, because "there are no limits to idealization. We can always move self-reflexively to a higher level, take our own limits and presuppositions into account, create a metalanguage" (20). A. J. Greimas, in more technical terms, describes this *linguistic* process as one of "substantifying" relationships, "freezing all intentional dynamism into a conceptual terminology" (see Schleifer, *Rhetoric* 7, 118–19). All three of these descriptions, however, present the ubiquitous power of generalizing representation. *Anything,* as Shaviro argues, can serve representation's "obscure power" to reduce things to markers for other things, to create relationships of example and concept, to establish a hierarchical, synecdochical order of meaning.[1] This is why Bataille is in no way concerned with comprehending death and nonidealistic materiality: "Bataille's writing," Shaviro argues, "neither designates objects, nor signifies ideas, nor manifests a hidden order of reality. Rather it charts the *expérience-limite* (limit-experience), as Blanchot puts it, of a 'détour de tout visible et de tout invisible [turning away from every visible and every invisible]' " (85–86).

Comprehending and recovering unique and unrepeatable moments—what he calls "legibility" and "recognizability" ("N" 50)—are precisely Benjamin's project. In the instance I have already given, where he describes the tragic hero in the *Trauerspiel* book, he seeks to discover in "tragic existence" an alternative to both philosophical idealism and the idealism that inheres in traditional materialism. The power Adorno describes in Benjamin's language, ringing with the "depths of mystery" yet possessing the quality of self-evidence, is a function of his attempt, beyond that of Bataille and Blanchot, not simply to describe and provoke the energy and disruption of death's base materiality, but to harness it to human ends. Benjamin tried to develop an alternative to idealism and to idealized materialism. Unlike Bataille or Blanchot and more explicitly than Derrida, he attempts this alternative by redefining the notion of "idea" against "concept," so that a material idea is imaginable. One such material idea is that of death itself and its representation beyond the limits of both conceptual schema and physical existence.

Benjamin argues in *The Origin of German Tragic Drama* that the idea "belongs to a fundamentally different world from that which it apprehends" (34), a world of what Benjamin calls "nonsensuous similarity" (*Reflections* 334; Buck-Morss translates the same phrase as "non-representational similarity" [90]). Speaking of the "ideas" of the Renaissance or the baroque period, he notes that "as ideas, however, such names perform a service they are not able to perform as concepts: they do not make the similar identical" (*Origin* 41). Making the similar identical is precisely the work of "concepts"; ideas, on the other hand, "exist in irreducible multiplicity" (43). The figures Benjamin uses for such multiplicity are astral and family *constellations*. The idea, Benjamin writes,

> belongs to a fundamentally different world from that which it apprehends. The question of whether it comprehends that which it apprehends, in the way in which the concept genus includes the species, cannot be regarded as a criterion of its existence. That is not the task of the idea. Its significance can be illustrated with an analogy. Ideas are to objects as constellations are to stars. This means, in the first place, that they are neither their concepts nor their laws. They do not contribute to the knowledge of phenomena, and in no way can the latter be criteria with which to judge the existence of ideas. . . . Just as a mother is seen to begin to live in the fullness of her power only when the circle of her children, inspired by the feeling of her proximity, closes around her, so do ideas come to life only when extremes are assembled around them. Ideas . . . remain obscure so long as phenomena do not declare their faith to them and gather round them. It is the function of concepts to group phenomena together, and the division which is brought about within them thanks to the distinguishing power of the intellect is all the more significant in that it brings about two things at a single stroke: the salvation of phenomena and the representation of ideas. (*Origin* 34–35)

This is a difficult passage whose opacity resides in the way Benjamin *analogizes* understanding.[2] For here the analogies—"constellation," "mother"—do not function as *examples* of the principles being explored. Rather, they offer what Benjamin calls elsewhere in the *Trauerspiel* book an "allegorical" understanding, an understanding in which different realms confront one another without reduction of one to the other.[3] As Susan Buck-Morss has noted, "Like atoms, like cells, like solar systems [constellations] each had their own center: without hierarchy, they stood next to each other 'in perfect independence and unimpaired' " (94; the citation is Buck-Morss's translation from *Origin* 37). In these cases, Benjamin unfolds his discussion of ideas without reducing astrology to a debased species of knowledge and without reducing family life to a species of abstract relationship.

Allegory achieves the independence of its elements, Benjamin argues, by marking most deeply "the jagged line of demarcation between physical nature and significance" (*Origin* 166); like the *Trauerspiel* Benjamin is studying, it presents "reality in the form of the ruin" (177). "Where in the symbol," he notes,

> destruction is idealized and the transfigured face of nature is fleetingly revealed in the light of redemption, in allegory the observer is confronted with the *facies hippocratica* of history as a petrified, primordial landscape. Everything about

> history that, from the very beginning, has been untimely, sorrowful, unsuccessful, is expressed in a face—or rather in a death's head. . . . This is the heart of the allegorical way of seeing. . . . The greater the significance, the greater the subjection to death, because death digs most deeply the jagged line of demarcation between physical nature and significance. (166)

In the *allegory* of constellated significance, the "center" of meaning (as in the novel [*Illuminations* 99]) or the "kernel" of thought or the "heart" of an idea does not exist. Rather, like the "slow piling on top of the other of thin, transparent layers . . . of a variety of retellings" in the story (93) or the fullness of a mother's power that Benjamin describes balanced between the independent power of children and parent, the power of *analogous* generations is the result of the nonlogical difference that is intrinsically subject to the ineluctable and irreversible *time* of generations. In these analogies Benjamin creates representations that do not have the "obscure power" of erasing time that Foucault describes. Analogies *mark time:* they underline the very "power of recall" Foucault mentions (*Order* 69) that inhabits—unconsciously, without a mark—the generalizing abstractions of idealism and traditional materialism. Analogies bring together two fundamentally different orders: by marking similitude (with "as" or "like"), they form an intralinguistic deixis. "*Deixis,* or indication," Giorgio Agamben writes, "does not simply demonstrate an unnamed object, but above all the very instance of discourse, its taking place" (25). Agamben argues that this aspect of language can help us comprehend the "unthought" essential relation between language and death; but for Benjamin, I think, matters are less burdened with Heideggerian metaphysics. For him analogical thinking is dialectical: "It is the unique property of dialectical experience," he writes, "to dissipate the appearance of things always being the same" ("N" 63).

This is why the analogy of generations, more than the astrological figure of constellations, combines the mystery and self-evidence that Adorno asserts constitutes Benjamin's power. Thus, in describing the relation between capitalism and nature in "One-Way Street," he offers the analogy of generational relationships. "Who would trust a cane wielder who proclaimed the mastery of children by adults to be the purpose of education?" he asks. "Is not education above all the indispensable ordering of the relationship between generations and therefore mastery, if we are to use this term, of that relationship and not of children?" (*Reflections* 93). In this passage the term "mastery," like the term "power" describing the mother in the *Trauerspiel* book, is a form of quotation that, like the bringing together of different generations in one household or community, underlines the temporal disparity encompassed by allegory.[4] In "One-Way Street" such quotation is particularly clear in the sentence preceding this passage: "The mastery of nature, so the imperialists teach, is the purpose of all technology" (*Reflections* 93).

Death itself, the unique fate of every generation, becomes in allegory's unfolding a figure for a representational mode that avoids, to some degree, the *reductiveness* of representation. But it avoids it only in its base materiality, or what Benjamin calls the "creaturely guilt" associated with "the core notion of fate" (*Origin* 129). Such materiality, guilt, and fate are not only—or not *simply*—the opposite of ideality. In the end, Benjamin argues, allegory "loses everything that was most peculiar to it: the secret, privileged knowledge, the arbitrary rule in the realm of the dead objects, the supposed infinity of a world without hope. All this vanishes with this *one* about-turn, in which the immersion of allegory has to clear away the final phantasmagoria of the objective and, left entirely to its own devices, rediscovers itself, not playfully in the earthly world of things, but seriously under the eyes of heaven" (232). The "turn" Benjamin describes is allegory's turn on itself, accomplished by "displaying" rather than repressing (through the generalization of representation) its own "transitoriness" (232). Geoffrey Hartman says that "allegorizing, though driven by a desire for transcendence, remains skeletal, grimacing, schematic" (90). Yet for Benjamin this mode of sublunary understanding, with its reified, commodified, and substantified semiotics, "turns" and emerges, in its very transitoriness, under the "eyes" of heaven, into something else.

In the same way, death itself is irreducibly complex—as an "event" that exists within a series of events and also as a singular occurrence in what Terry Eagleton calls the "double sense" of "the absence of death": "its erasure, but also its sinister blankness" (35), and what Ellie Ragland describes here as "embedded in flesh, repeated in behavior and myth," but "inaccessible to reflection or contemplation." "The characters of the *Trauerspiel* die," Benjamin writes, "because it is only thus, as corpses, that they can enter into the homeland of allegory" (*Origin* 217). In these instances—not examples, but particular allegorical moments—"death" is *there,* deictically, just in case, as Barreca says, you thought there was no distinction between representation and reality. In the display of allegory, "death" loses its power of representation even while its connection to the world and to meaning is asserted. "Allegory," Benjamin says at the conclusion of the *Trauerspiel* book, "loses everything that was most particular to it" and "goes away empty-handed" (*Origin* 232, 233).

## II

All this, though, seems to have returned us to the incomprehensible materiality of Bataille and Blanchot, what Benjamin describes in *The Origin of German Tragic Drama* as "soulless materiality" in "an empty world" (230, 139). In what ways, he asks, can the idea "redeem" the material world? In what ways can death be represented without empty-handedness, ruination, or the idealizations of traditional metaphysical materialism? How can allegory rediscover itself, "seriously," under the eyes of heaven? The modes of comprehension Benjamin uses in his uncompleted *Arcades Project* to suggest alternatives to idealism and traditional materialism are those of quotation and the image. Of the project itself—left significantly incomplete at his death—Benjamin wrote, "This project must raise the art of quoting without quotation marks to the very highest level" ("N" 45). Elsewhere he had said of the *Trauerspiel* book that it "consists almost entirely of quotations. The drollest mosaic technique one can imagine" (cited in Smith xxxix, n. 111).

The "mosaic technique" of repeated quotation inhabits, as I have already suggested, Benjamin's sense of allegory and analogy. Moreover, it creates a form of radical metonymy, allowing one to present material without abstracting a theme: it creates the possibility of athematic death, in which, as Jacques Derrida has said, "the part is always greater than the whole" (cited in Schleifer, *Rhetoric* 4). In such analogies the figure used, ostensibly as an example, takes on a life of its own because it *has* a life of its own. It takes on this "other life" in the same way that Benjamin argues translation is "only a somewhat provisional way of coming to terms with the foreignness of languages" (*Illuminations* 75), since even the most commonplace words— the German *Brot,* the French *pain,* the English *bread*—lead different lives in their respective languages (see De Man " 'Conclusions' " 87). Translation is an instance of quotation that is at once minute and global, and in it the irreducible differences inherent in all quotation are markedly pronounced. Similarly, the analogical figures in Benjamin—"constellation," "mother," even his figure of "mosaic" (*Origin* 28–29)—cite and translate texts into different contexts to arrest discourse and transform it into what Benjamin calls "irreducible multiplicity" (43).

That is, quotations (including the quotation of translation) are other versions of the analogical figures that function like "monuments in the discontinuous structure of the world of ideas" (*Origin* 33). "With every idea," he writes later in the *Trauerspiel* book, "the moment of expression coincides with a veritable eruption of images, which gives rise to a chaotic mass of metaphors" (173). The analogical figure takes on this life of its own because, as a version of quotation, it is *other* than the progress and "life" of the discourse in which it appears, just as the metonymic "hauntings" of nonlogical death and its "primitive and prelogical silence . . . : nothingness or pure non-sense" (Derrida 130) are different from the "word" or "concept" or "representation" of death (all of which domesticate "death" just as the metaphors and synecdoches of discourse domesticate meaning, reducing it to simple "communication"). Quotation, analogue, and metonymy are different from discourse yet embedded in it. They function like language itself, which, Benjamin says, "is in every case not only communication of the communicable but also, at the same time, a symbol of the noncommunicable" (*Reflections* 331). Like Benjamin's "images" that I will turn to in a moment, and even more like the genuine "hauntings" of the dead and of the past, these figures *arrest* the progress of discourse. "Thinking," he writes in the "Theses on the Philosophy of History" (Thesis 17), "involves not only the flow of thoughts, but their arrest as well" (*Illuminations* 262).[5]

Benjamin's metonymic mosaic technique, in bringing together things in a nonhierarchical dialectic (pursuing different levels of meaning in examining a single object), disrupts progressive causal explanation. It is precisely the "life of its *own*" that resists the reduction of analogue to example and history to (causal) continuity. "The materialist presentation of history goes hand in hand with an immanent critique of the concept of progress" ("N" 67). Historical materialism "blasts the epoch out of the reified 'continuity of history.' But it also blasts open the homogeneity of the epoch" (65). Analogical discourse accomplishes this on the "authority" of quotation. "In the canonic form of the treatise," Benjamin writes, describing the philosophical treatise such as the *Trauerspiel* book,

> the only element of an intention—and it is an educative rather than a didactic intention—is the authoritative quotation. Its method is essentially representation. Method is a digression. Representation as digression—such is the methodological nature of the treatise. The absence of an uninterrupted purposeful structure is its primary characteristic. Tirelessly the process of thinking makes new beginnings, returning in a roundabout way to its original object. This continual pausing for breath is the mode most proper to the process of contemplation. For by pursuing different levels of meaning in its examination of one single object it receives both the incentive to begin again and the justification for its irregular rhythm. . . . The relationship between the minute precision of the work and the proportions of the sculptural or intellectual whole demonstrates that truth-content is only to be grasped through immersion in the most minute details of subject matter. (*Origin* 28–29)

In the analogical discourse of quotation, as in the later Nietzsche (as Adorno points out), truth is not "a timeless *universal,* but rather it is solely the historical which yields the figure of the absolute" (Adorno, "Portrait" 231).

However, Benjamin's focus on quotation rather than phenomena and his emphasis on the temporally situated nature of meaning bring him closer to his contemporary, M. M. Bakhtin, than to Nietzsche. (In his aphorisms he is closer to Nietzsche.) For Bakhtin, "*any true understanding is dialogic in nature.* Understanding is to utterance as one line of a dialogue is to the next" (*Marxism* 102). This is why, in *Marxism and the Philosophy of Language,* he spends so much time examining versions of quotation in discourse: direct discourse, indirect discourse, and free indirect discourse (what the translators call "quasi-direct discourse" [142 and part 3]). The kind of language Benjamin is describing—quotation without quotation marks—is a form of free indirect discourse, and much of Bakhtin's materialist analysis of language and genre attends to what I call the "unfinalized wholes" of discourse, language that conveys meaning (hence is "whole") yet *always* calls for an answer within the historical situation of its utterance. What distinguishes Benjamin from Bakhtin is his emphasis on the sacred within experience and discourse, "the transcendent force of the sacred image and the truth itself" (*Origin* 28–29). Whereas Bakhtin wants to account for meaningful discourse without (necessarily) discovering the sacred within the quotidian, Benjamin attempts to comprehend the sacred in experience—what he calls in the "Theses on the Philosophy of History" "a conception of the present as the 'time of the now' which is shot through with chips of Messianic time" (*Illuminations* 263).

It is for this reason that death is important for Benjamin as a material event in ways that it is not for Bakhtin (or for that matter Nietzsche). Throughout his career—in *The Origin of German Tragic Drama,* in *One-Way Street,* in the essay on Baudelaire, and above all in the essay on Nikolai Leskov—the authority of discourse and experience is realized at moments of death. In his essay on Baudelaire he even notes that "the *durée* from which death has been eliminated has the miserable endlessness of a scroll" (*Illuminations* 185). Quotation breaks up the endlessness of a scroll by recalling and remembering, as do analogies that take on a life of their own, another time and also "the time of the now," the "now of a specific recognizability" ("N" 50). Moreover, quotation of dying words—*citing* the event of death—punctuates discourse and experience with the sacred. "Today," he writes in "The Storyteller," the essay on Leskov,

> people live in rooms that have never been touched by death, dry dwellers of
> eternity, and when their end approaches they are stowed away in sanatoria or

hospitals by their heirs. It is, however, characteristic that not only a man's knowledge or wisdom, but above all his real life—and this is the stuff that stories are made of—first assumes transmissible form at the moment of his death. Just as a sequence of images is set in motion inside a man as his life comes to an end—unfolding the views of himself under which he has encountered himself without being aware of it—suddenly in his expressions and looks the unforgettable emerges and imparts to everything that concerned him that authority which even the poorest wretch in dying possesses for the living around him. This authority is at the very source of the story. (*Illuminations* 94)

The structure of quotation Benjamin is describing carries "the montage principle over into history" by detecting "the crystal of the total event in the analysis of the small, individual moment" ("N" 48). Yet as the absolute disruption of death—as apocalyptic or messianic—such moments are sacred for Benjamin. They combine quotation and an image—here in the expression and look of the dying man—so that *something* can be passed along in history to another generation.

It is just such "transmissibility" that characterizes Bakhtin's dialogics (*Dialogic Imagination* 341). So, too, in Benjamin's reading, "Kafka's real genius was that he tried something entirely new: he sacrificed truth for the sake of clinging to its transmissibility, in haggadic element" (*Illuminations* 143–44). Yet Benjamin (and, in his understanding, Kafka as well) lacks Bakhtin's *cheerfulness* about history and its metonymic repetitions that go on and on. "The concept of progress," Benjamin writes, "should be grounded in the idea of catastrophe. That things 'just keep on going' *is* the catastrophe" ("N" 64). The incongruence of transmissibility and truth, communication and language, the continuity of history and chips of messianic time, makes death itself a constant element or "level" of his discourse and experience, hovering amid each constellated idea he pursues, that creates the necessity to blast open "the homogeneity of the epoch [and saturate] it with *escrasite,* i.e., the present" (65).

Benjamin's use and understanding of quotation is analogous to his idea of a dialectical image that he develops in an attempt to create a mode of representing historical events—and especially death—in his notes for the *Arcades Project.* Together, they create parataxis and elision. "It isn't that the past casts its light on the present or the present casts its light on the past," he writes; "rather, an image is that in which the Then (*das Gewesene*) and the Now (*das Jetzt*) come into a constellation like a flash of lightning. In other words: image is dialectics at a standstill. For while the relation of the present to the past is a purely temporal, continuous one, the relation of the

Then to the Now is dialectical. . . . Only dialectical images are genuine (i.e. not archaic) images; and the place one happens upon them is language" ("N" 49). The vehicle for dialectical images is the paratactic, analogical dialogue of quotations, and the most *authoritative* quotations are those of the dying and the dead: "The community of all the dead is so immense that even he who only reports death is aware of it. *Ad plures ire* was the Latins' expression of dying" (*Reflections* 90). Yet it is a vehicle because it creates unique moments. Later in his notes, he adds that "the dialectical image is a lightning flash. The Then must be held fast as it flashes its lightning image in the Now of recognizability. The rescue that is thus—and only thus—effected, can only take place for that which, in the next moment, is already irretrievably lost" ("N" 64). Here Benjamin is describing Bakhtin's *dialogical* meaning, the interplay of discourses in an ongoing conversation that one joins and leaves.

The difference, though—and this, I think, is crucial for the possibility of *representing* death—is Benjamin's attempt to discover the sacred within death and dying and so see it as more than *another* event within a history of events, to see it as a focal point for the quotation of dialectical images: like the "love," which is after all the fullness of the power of mothers (and, as I know, of fathers as well), the allegorical Other of that power, the Now of (remembered) love flashing in the Then of power. Responding in his notes to a letter from Max Horkheimer in 1937 in which Horkheimer accuses Benjamin of being idealistic in his assertion of "incompleteness . . . , if completeness isn't included in it," since "past injustice has occurred and is done with [and the] murdered are really murdered" ("N" 61), Benjamin replies:

> The corrective to this way of thinking lies in the conviction that history is not only a science but also a form of remembrance. What science has "established" can be modified by remembrance. Remembrance can make the open-ended (happiness) into something concluded and the concluded (suffering) into something open-ended. This is theology; however, in remembrance we have an experience which forbids us from conceiving of history fundamentally a-theologically, despite the fact that we are hardly able to describe it in theological concepts which are immediately theological. (Cited in Wolin 225; also translated in "N" 61; Tiedemann cites both of these letters more extensively [181–82])

Remembrance forbids us to conceive history as atheological, and it forbids us to conceive death as (fully, purely) the athematic excess of Bataille or Blanchot—what Nietzsche calls "the stupid physiological fact" (484)—because remembrance (like "experience" itself throughout Benjamin) is a function of "collective existence as well as private life. It is less the product of facts firmly anchored in memory than of a convergence in memory of accumulated and frequently unconscious data" (*Illuminations* 157). The "eyes of heaven" Benjamin mentioned earlier and the "theology" he mentions here describe the context of generational temporality, of *human* temporality—the fact that the present can change the past, give it a different issue, so that while murder remains murder and each particular death remains its material self, nevertheless its meaning can flash up and be recognized in relation to its own future. These things, in other words, exist also within the context of their future history, the context of "human life" as a species phenomenon, temporal, transitory, comprehensive, so that without losing their intransigent materiality they can be examined, as single objects, on "different levels of meaning" (*Origin* 28).

"*Memory,*" for Benjamin, "creates the chain of tradition which passes a happening on from generation to generation" (*Illuminations* 98), and it is precisely the lack of such tradition that produces the "issueless private character" of "man's inner concerns" in the twentieth century (158) and fills "the idea of death . . . with profound terror" (*Origin* 139).[6] In other words, the form "remembrance" takes is the constellation of a dialectic image from quotations that is a function of human life conceived as communal as well as individual, existing in a mode of time that is not Newtonian universal time, possessing "the miserable endlessness of a scroll" (*Illuminations* 185), but rather "traces" of atmosphere in the same way that "traces of the storyteller cling to the story the way the handprints of the potter cling to the clay vessel" (92). (Such handprints are a form of quotation.) That is, human life realizes itself most fully when it is comprehended as constellated, mothers with children, the dying with their heirs, the dialectics of Then and Now at a standstill. In this Richard Wolin sees "a 'secret agreement' that the present generation has with the preceding generation . . . that serves as the basis for the redemption of the past by the present" (225). Moreover, Benjamin notes that human beings also possess a "general lack of envy" toward the future. "This lack of envy," "indicates that our idea of happiness is deeply colored by the times in which we live our life. We can only conceive of happiness in terms of the air that we have breathed, or among those people with whom we have lived. In other words, the idea of happiness . . . resonates with the idea of redemption. This happiness is founded precisely upon the despair and the foresakenness which were ours. . . . [T]he true conception of historical time is wholly based on the image of redemption" ("N" 71).

In Thesis 2 of the "Theses on the Philosophy of History" Benjamin quotes (without quotation marks and with small changes) this passage from his notebooks. (Here is a final version of analogical quotation in Benjamin's self-citation: it is remarkable how often he repeats and quotes himself throughout his work.) "In other words," he writes, "our image of happiness is indissolubly bound up with the image of redemption. The same applies to our view of the past, which is the concern of history. The past carries with it a temporal index by which it is referred to redemption. There is a secret agreement between past generations and the present one. Our coming was expected on earth" (*Illuminations* 254). The secret agreement is one-way, irreversible, like death itself, contained in the jagged line of death, in its resonating image. This agreement creates the possibility of representing death only when the particular dead are remembered in constellations that do not denigrate past concrete events in concepts and symbols and "representations," but rather expect (or hope) that others will follow us to create significance in a world of seeming barbarous meaninglessness. In "The Storyteller" Benjamin quotes and glosses a passage:

> "A man who dies at the age of thirty-five," said Moritz Heimann once, "is at every point of his life a man who dies at the age of thirty-five." Nothing is more dubious than this sentence—but for the sole reason that the tense is wrong. A man—so says the truth that was meant here—who died at thirty-five will appear to *remembrance* at every point in his life as a man who dies at the age of thirty-five. In other words, the statement that makes no sense for real life becomes indisputable for remembered life. (*Illuminations* 100)

The vehicle for remembered life is quotation, analogy, and image, which make the material representation of death possible. Benjamin offers a final version of these in his essay "A Small History of Photography," in what he calls the photograph's "caption." "The camera is getting smaller and smaller, ever readier to capture the fleeting and secret moments whose images paralyse the associative mechanisms in the beholder. This is where the caption comes in, whereby photography turns life's relationships into literature. . . . Not for nothing have Atget's photographs been likened to those of the scene of a crime. . . . Is it not the task of the photographer—descendant of the augurs and haruspices—to reveal guilt and to point out the guilty in his pictures?" (*One-Way Street* 256).

## III

The mode of representation whose description is scattered throughout Benjamin is realized in *Death and Representation*. The form of representation I am imagining is multiple and dialogic; it does not oppose completeness with incompleteness or idealism with "materialism" as Horkheimer does, but attempts a community of images and quotations that exist, constellated, within a field of nonlogical differences. I shall choose one "image" of this modality to conclude this afterword. In Carol Christ's essay, she cites an important passage from Roland Barthes's *Camera Lucida* that argues, as she says, that "the photograph always carries the sense of death by implying an anterior future": "In front of the photograph of my mother as a child, I tell myself," Barthes writes, "she is going to die: I shudder, like Winnicott's psychotic patient *over a catastrophe which has already occurred*. Whether or not the subject is already dead, every photograph is this catastrophe" (96). Here is an instance of Benjamin's image, a caption for a remembered moment captured in a photograph and indissolubly bound up with the Now: it is the anterior future that the past bequeaths to the present, our ability to remember what happened next so that what Barthes calls "asymbolic Death, outside of religion, outside of ritual, a kind of abrupt dive into literal Death" (92) can be rescued or redeemed in memory, and statements that make no sense for real life become indisputable for remembered life. The Victorians, Christ argues, construct narratives that represent and repress that anterior future.

Barthes, like Benjamin, does the opposite: he transforms narrative to image and repression to shock. "With the Photograph," Barthes writes,

> we enter into *flat Death*. One day, leaving one of my classes, someone said to me with disdain: "You talk about Death very flatly."—As if the horror of Death were not precisely its platitude! The horror is this: nothing to say about the death of one whom I love most, nothing to say about her photograph, which I contemplate without ever being able to get to the heart of it, to transform it. The only "thought" I can have is that at the end of this first death, my own death is inscribed; between the two nothing more than waiting; I have no other resource than this *irony:* to speak of the "nothing to say." (92–93)

But Barthes's response, his "caption," is also narrative. He gets the tenses right and tells a story beginning, like the traditional stories Benjamin describes, with "one day." Still, this story is punctuated by his own experience, his death inscribed in the photograph he sees and the story he tells, like the trace of a handprint. As in *Death and Representation* as a whole, Barthes (and Christ, citing Barthes) offers a particular instance of parataxis and elision, the odd combination of representation (with the repression inscribed within representation) *and* transmission (with the flashing punctuation of time inscribed within transmission). As a whole, this constellation of essays offers material representations of death, the analogic dialectic of history and semiosis.

## Notes

1. I have argued in *Rhetoric and Death,* following Roman Jakobson, that all meaning is synecdochical because in language the whole is always greater than the sum of the parts. (Paul de Man uses this argument to assert the "absolute independence" of the hermeneutic and the poetic, grammar and meaning, and the symbol and what is being symbolized in his discussion of Benjamin [" 'Conclusions' " 89].) The synecdochical order of meaning, however, *needs* to repress, hide, and exclude— such procedures create the hierarchy of meaning—and what is left out is precisely the "nonlogical difference" of metonymy, which both is and is not the opposite of synecdoche. Metonymy, then, is a figure for death insofar as "death" locates or gestures toward base matter and intransigent materialism beyond what Derrida calls in his essay on Bataille the "restricted economy" of meaning (252). It participates in and disrupts the "ubiquity" of meaning in its "nonlogical difference" from synecdoche. (See *Rhetoric and Death* chap. 1.) As such, then, it creates the effects of hauntings, free-floating anxiety, and even Benjamin's "aura" and Bataille's "sacred" alongside quotidian experience.

2. George Steiner has called the whole of the "Epistemo-critical Prologue" to *The Origin of German Tragic Drama* "one of the more impenetrable pieces of prose in German or, for that matter, in any modern language" (13), and the editors of Benjamin's *Gesammelte Schriften* call it "the most esoteric text that Benjamin ever wrote" (cited in Moses 233–34).

3. See my essay "Analogy and Example" for a version of this distinction in quantum physics and structural linguistics contemporaneous with Benjamin's work.

4. See De Man's essay "The Rhetoric of Temporality" for an elaborate unfolding of the temporality of Benjamin's concept of allegory.

5. See Adorno's essay "Progress" for an adumbration of Benjamin's aim in the *Arcades Project* to cancel "the ideal of progress in itself" (47). As Adorno notes, "progress," to be meaningful at all, would be "transformed" precisely into that which arrests the flow of history: progress, he writes, "wants to disrupt the triumph of radical evil, not to triumph in itself" (101).

6. Benjamin uses this last phrase to describe the "element of German paganism and the grim belief in the subjection of man to fate" in the baroque protestantism of the *Trauerspiel.* With these elements, he writes, "something new arose: an empty world" (*Origin* 138–39). Whether his description of the response to this world— "mourning is the state of mind in which feeling revives the empty world in the form of a mask, and derives an enigmatic satisfaction in contemplating it" (139)—is an apt description of his definition of the "image," "dialectics at a standstill," and the "power" of tradition and remembrance I am pursuing here is an open question. If it is, then these things remain "masks" and the mode of representation they promise is enigmatic indeed: if so, the "salvation," "rescue," and "redemption" that punctuate his writing become empty promises. In any case, the openness of the question marks

the profoundly dialectical and momentary nature of his thinking, in which the concrete is never denigrated to an example of a concept.

## Works Cited

Adorno, Theodor. "Introduction to Benjamin's *Schriften*." *Notes to Literature*. Trans. Shierry Weber Nicholsen. 2 vols. New York: Columbia UP, 1992. 2: 220–32.

———. "A Portrait of Walter Benjamin." *Prisms*. Trans. Samuel and Shierry Weber. Cambridge: MIT Press, 1981. 227–42.

———. "Progress." Trans. Eric Krakauer. Smith 84–101.

Agamben, Giorgio. *Language and Death: The Place of Negativity*. Trans. Karen E. Pinkus with Michael Hardt. Minneapolis: U of Minnesota P, 1991.

Bakhtin, M. M. *The Dialogic Imagination*. Trans. Caryl Emerson and Michael Holquist. Austin: U of Texas P, 1981.

[Bakhtin M. M.]/V. N. Vološinov. *Marxism and the Philosophy of Language*. Trans. Ladislav Matejka and I. R. Titunik. Cambridge: Harvard UP, 1986.

Barthes, Roland. *Camera Lucida: Reflections on Photography*. Trans. Richard Howard. New York: Hill and Wang, 1981.

Bataille, Georges. *Inner Experience*. Trans. Leslie Anne Boldt. Albany: State U of New York P, 1988.

———. *Visions of Excess: Selected Writings, 1927–1939*. Trans. Allan Stoekl, with Carl R. Vovitt and Donald M. Leslie, Jr. Minneapolis: U of Minnesota P, 1985.

Benjamin, Walter. *Illuminations*. Trans. Harry Zohn. New York: Schocken, 1969.

———. "N (Re: the Theory of Knowledge, Theory of Progress)." Trans. Leigh Hafrey and Richard Sieburth. Smith 43–83.

———. *"One-Way Street" and Other Writings*. Trans. Edmund Jephcott and Kingley Shorter. London: New Left, 1979.

———. *The Origin of German Tragic Drama*. Trans. John Osborne. London: Verso, 1977.

———. *Reflections: Essays, Aphorisms, Autobiographical Writing*. Trans. Edmund Jephcott. New York: Schocken, 1978.

Blanchot, Maurice. *The Writing of the Disaster*. Trans. Ann. Smock. Lincoln: U of Nebraska P, 1986.

Buck-Morss, Susan. *The Origin of Negative Dialectics: Theodor W. Adorno, Walter Benjamin, and the Frankfurt Institute*. Hassocks, Sussex: Harvester Press, 1977.

De Man, Paul. " 'Conclusions': Walter Benjamin's 'The Task of the Translator.' " *The Resistance to Theory*. Minneapolis: U of Minnesota P, 1986. 73–105.

———. "The Rhetoric of Temporality." *Interpretation: Theory and Practice*. Ed. Charles Singleton. Baltimore: Johns Hopkins UP, 1969. 173–209.

Derrida, Jacques. *Writing and Difference*. Trans. Alan Bass. Chicago: U of Chicago P, 1978.

Eagleton, Terry. *Walter Benjamin; or, Towards a Revolutionary Criticism*. London: New Left, 1981.

Foucault, Michel. *The Order of Things*. New York: Pantheon, 1976.

————. "A Preface to Transgression." *Language, Counter-Memory, Practice: Selected Essays and Interviews*. Trans. Donald F. Bouchard and Sherry Simon. Ithaca: Cornell UP, 1977, 29–52.

Hartman, Geoffrey. *Criticism in the Wilderness: The Study of Literature Today*. New Haven: Yale UP, 1980.

Moses, Stéphane. "Walter Benjamin and Franz Rosenzweig." Smith 228–45.

Nietzsche, Friedrich. *The Will to Power*. Trans. Walter Kaufmann and J. J. Hollingdale. London: Weidenfeld and Nicolson, 1968.

Schleifer, Ronald. "Analogy and Example: Heisenberg, Negation and the Language of Quantum Physics." *Criticism* 33 (1991): 285–307.

————. *Rhetoric and Death: The Language of Modernism and Postmodern Discourse Theory*. Urbana: U of Illinois P, 1990.

Shaviro, Steven. *Passion and Excess: Blanchot, Bataille and Literary Theory*. Tallahassee: Florida State UP, 1990.

Smith, Gary, ed. *Benjamin: Philosophy, Aesthetics, History*. Chicago: U of Chicago P, 1989.

————. "Thinking through Benjamin: An Introductory Essay." Smith vii–xlii.

Steiner, George. "Introduction." Benjamin, *Origin* 7–24.

Stoekl, Alan. "Introduction." Bataille, *Visions* ix–xxv.

Tiedemann, Rolf. "Historical Materialism or Political Messianism? An Interpretation of the Theses 'On the Concept of History.' " Smith 175–209.

Wolin, Richard. "Experience and Materialism in Benjamin's *Passagenwerk*." Smith 210–27.

# Notes on Contributors

*Ernst van Alphen* teaches comparative literature at the University of Leiden, the Netherlands. His most recent book is *Francis Bacon and the Loss of Self* (1992).

*Regina Barreca* is the editor of the recent volume *Sex and Death in Victorian Literature* (1990) and of *Last Laughs: Perspectives on Women and Comedy* (1988); she is the author of *They Used to Call Me Snow White, but I Drifted . . . Women's Strategic Use of Humor* (1991) as well as of numerous essays. Barreca is founder and managing editor of *LIT*. She teaches at the University of Connecticut.

*Elisabeth Bronfen*, professor of English at the University of Zurich, has published *Over Her Dead Body* (1992), *Der Literarische Raum* (1986), and numerous articles.

*Carol Christ*, of the University of California at Berkeley, has published extensively on Victorian literature, including *The Finer Optic: The Aesthetic of Particularity in Victorian Poetry* (1975) and *Victorian and Modern Poetics* (1984); she is currently working on a book on death in Victorian literature.

*Sarah Webster Goodwin* is the author of *Kitsch and Culture: The Dance of Death in Nineteenth-Century Literature and Graphic Arts* (1988) and coeditor of *Feminism, Utopia and Narrative* (1990) and *The Scope of Words* (1991). Her essay here is part of a book in progress on romanticism, kitsch, and domesticity. She teaches at Skidmore College.

*Sander L. Gilman* is the author of numerous books, including *Difference and Pathology: Stereotypes of Sexuality, Race and Madness* (1985), in which he shapes a theory of cultural stereotypes of the Other. He holds a chair in English at Cornell University.

*Margaret R. Higonnet*, professor of English and comparative literature at the University of Connecticut, mourns the murder of her sister, Ethel P. Higonnet, as well as the unnecessary deaths inflicted by war.

*Regina Janes* is professor of English at Skidmore College. She has just completed *Edmund Burke and India: Political Trials* and is most recently the author of *One Hundred Years of Solitude: Modes of Reading* (1991). The article from which the present essay is distilled was awarded the Clifford Prize for 1990–91 by the American Society for Eighteenth-Century Studies.

*Ronald Schleifer,* of the University of Oklahoma, is editor of *Genre* and coeditor of the "Oklahoma Project for Discourse and Theory." He has published extensively on modern literature and literary criticism. His most recent books include *Rhetoric and Death: The Language of Modernism and Postmodern Discourse Theory* (1990), *Criticism and Culture: The Role of Critique in Modern Literary Theory* (with Robert Con Davis, 1991), and *Culture and Cognition: The Boundaries of Literary and Scientific Inquiry* (with Nancy Mergler and Robert Con Davis, 1992).

*Charles Segal,* of Harvard University, has published widely in the classics and comparative literature; he is perhaps best known for several books on Greek tragedy, including *Interpreting Greek Tragedy: Myth, Poetry, Text* (1986). Among his other books are *Orpheus: The Myth of the Poet* (1989) and a recent work on death in Lucretius.

*Garrett Stewart,* James O. Freedman Professor of Letters at the University of Iowa, is most recently the author of *Death Sentences: Styles of Dying in British Fiction* (1984) and *Reading Voices: Literature and the Phonotext* (1990).

*Ellie Ragland* is the author of *Jacques Lacan and the Philosophy of Psychoanalysis* (1986) and of the forthcoming *From Lacan to Freud*. She teaches at the University of Missouri.

*Rajeswari Sunder Rajan* was until recently reader in English at Mother Teresa Women's University, Madras. She is the author of *Real and Imagined Women: Postcolonialism and the Female Subject,* and of a critical work on Dickens. She is also the editor of the recently published *The Lie of the Land: English Literary Studies in India.* Her work has appeared in *Signs,* the *Yale Journal of Criticism,* and *Victorian Literature and Culture.*